TIME LONGA' DAN TWINE

TIME LONGA' DAN TWINE

*Notes on the Culture, History, and People
of the U.S. Virgin Islands*

ARNOLD R. HIGHFIELD

ANTILLES PRESS

2009

Second printing 2019

Set in Adobe Caslon
Layout, design and cover graphics by Paul Hoffmann
Front cover illustration by Joffre George
Printed in the United States of America

ANTILLES PRESS

St. Croix, United States Virgin Islands

www.antillespressvi.com

ISBN 978-0-916611-23-1

TABLE OF CONTENTS

ACKNOWLEDGEMENTS

IT WOULD BE LESS than completely honest of me if I did not note here that Robert Merwin has played a large role in the appearance of this book. On a number of occasions he encouraged me to make available to a wider audience various of the pieces that appeared over the months in *The Crucian Trader* and elsewhere. Likewise my brother Terry Highfield has been a constant source of encouragement, to whom I owe much gratitude. My friends Alfredo E. Figuerdo, Lisa Spery and Shirley Ziegler performed stalwart proofing; I am grateful to each of them. Likewise Jeff Sutton was always available to offer expert technical help. Finally, I wish to thank Paul Hoffmann for his expert assistance with the layout and design.

INTRODUCTION

SOME MONTHS AGO as I was sitting on the beach enjoying an incomparable St. Croix winter day, a friend approached and asked about a certain article that I had written sometime back. Would I mind making a copy and sending it along to him? That must have been the hundredth or so time that I said yes to such an inquiry and then put myself to the task of finding the article, making the copy and going to the post office to send it off. I suppose I am a slow learner for it was only then that it dawned on me that perhaps there might be some merit in publishing the entire lot of those articles and making them available to whomever might be interested. Therein lies the genesis of the present little volume.

The forty-one chapters here presented extend over a period of some thirty years. They were published in a number of different journals and newspapers, and they cover a broad variety of topics, all of them focused more or less on the Virgin Islands. In general, they reflect what has been the principal interest of my research and writing over the long haul, namely the culture, the history and the people of these islands, in particular, of St. Croix. It is inevitable, I suppose, that those subjects and those people who have attracted me most will appear in bold relief in these pages, namely the marvels of language, the indefatigable labors of the Moravian missionaries, the mysterious soul of the African background, the subtleties of culture and the attraction of individuals who dreamed and dared to extend themselves beyond their normal limits.

It is remarkable to me that when I wrote some of these pieces, I considered their content to be current. And now, as I look back over the list, I see that many of them have already become a part of our accepted past. This is a reminder that our present is daily being swallowed into what we call the past as it constantly grows, ever just behind us. At times one is puzzled as to how to know exactly the manner in which that growing mass of memory constitutes a real part of our lives. Each one of us has a long, complex past and together we all have a long, even more complex common past. We are at once a product of that mysterious entity at the very same time that we are attempting to grow out of it. So how do we come to grips with it?

In some ways, the contents of this book represent my own inclination to do just that. Of those who are buried under time, who among them merits being revived and allowed to speak with us once again? Which events, long terminated and by most forgotten, are most worthy of revisiting and with what purposes in mind? Which subtleties of past human behavior, now only faintly recognizable, will still speak in compelling voices to us? The articles and notes here included are my own unintended answers to these vexing questions. And in rendering them, I am under no illusion that they represent anyone or anything other than my own idiosyncratic and individual views of life and the world. Having said as much, I am nevertheless hopeful that some friend, some stranger, someone perhaps as yet unborn will at some time take up these lines and make a connection.

ARNOLD R. HIGHFIELD
La Grande Princesse, St. Croix
September 2009

HISTORY

A view of how the islands appeared to the earliest settlers of the Virgin Islands

CHAPTER 1

BEFORE THE ENTERPRISE
OF THE INDIES

IN THE COMPLEX DRAMA of human events, it is often forgotten that there have been, and are, players in the game of human history who are even more fundamental to things than ourselves. The island beneath our feet is itself a living organism in every sense of the word, albeit presently a besieged one. It has had a history of its own, a life, if you will, beside which our own short, troubled existence fairly well pales by comparison. Our story then begins with the island—*Ayay, Cibuqueira*, Santa Cruz, St. Croix—before it had a name

Many hundreds of thousands of years ago, over scarcely imaginable stretches of time, the island that millions of years later would be given the name St. Croix, literally emerged, like the other Caribbean islands, from the waters of the surrounding seas as a result of the geological forces that were shaping the planet—volcanism and plate tectonics. Once it had broken the surface, simple thermal differentials produced by the alternation of blistering days and cool nights caused the island's rocky mantle to expand and then contract repeatedly and regularly, opening the first fissures in the process, ultimately breaking crusty surfaces down into primitive soils. The passage of seasons too numerous to count brought winds and life-supporting rainfall. That rain flowed through natural waterways and eventually cut beds down to the sea. At their estuaries, lagoons formed and provided a waiting matrix for the life-forms that would with time proliferate there, just as they would flourish on the offshore coral reefs that rose from the sea floor in the shallow inlets ringing the island's shores.

The weathered rocky slopes of the new island were in time colonized by sea- and airborne flora, which established, first, grasslands, then savannah, and finally semi-tropical and, in some places, tropical forests. Later yet came animal life—sea fauna perhaps first, then birds and, at length, representatives of the various phyla. Gradually the island came to teem with life, members of numerous species competing with their fellows for space and for a living in the primordial business of each reproducing its own kind. Between the species, the same cruel but inevitable drama of "eat or be eaten" and the endless cycles of life and death were repeatedly played out, giving, over the ages, a distinct character to every square foot of the land.

For many thousands of centuries, then, the island developed and maintained an existence and character of its own, generated by the rhythms of its life forms in birth, struggle, death and regeneration. Natural destruction was not without its place in all this. With the tropical seasons came regular storms as well as less frequent but infinitely more destructive hurricanes. In an equally devastating manner, the land was shaken at intervals by tremors and earthquakes, forces that often produced great waves, or tsunamis, which ravaged adjacent shore lands. Fire too played its part, first consuming and leveling living flora as well as debris but in the end clearing the land and making way for manifold new life starts and experiments. These natural forces visited the island periodically and dashed and destroyed all in their paths; but in so doing, those same forces strengthened the whole, by eliminating among the parts the old, the infirm and the weak. Those plants and animals that could survive the havoc and then afterwards reproduce were inestimably strengthened by the stern tests. What might now appear, in brief, as mere chaos, when considered against the pitifully short measure of human life and in the context of "civilized" needs, assumed over the long-term the clear contours of regularity, balance and natural harmony.

These same natural forces were at work generally but unevenly throughout the archipelago of the islands of the Caribbean Sea, large and small alike, volcanic and coral, high and low-lying; they created and left in their train a generalized tropical land-, shore- and seascape, a natural theme, along which variations emerged here and there, conferring differences, peculiarities and local particularity. Although each island had a good deal in common with its neighboring islands, each one at the same time maintained a distinct character, in the sense that Aruba, for example, stands in contrast to Antigua and as Jamaica differs from Guadeloupe, St. Croix from Puerto Rico and so on. The result was the creation of the evenly integrated natural tapestry of the whole, woven from the natural strands of the land, the sea, animal life and plant life. And at the same time, the whole was complemented by the splendid variety of the constituent parts. All this required no less than the passage of an inconceivably long time, millions of years in fact, before the first human beings put in their appearance, before the first human eye marveled at its perfection, before the first human tongue ventured names for its parts.

Our island, at first having no name, became *Ayay*, followed by *Cibuqueira*, Santa Cruz and finally St. Croix, and stood in relative isolation in the primordial seas. Eastward across a broad reach of ocean and against the prevailing winds and currents lay the islands today known as the Leeward Islands. To the west and north lay the larger landmass that today we call Puerto Rico. To the northeast of that island extended an undersea plateau or shelf out into the sea, several peaks of which broke the surface of the water, becoming a host of steep-sloped, mountainous islands. These are the splendid isles that today we call the Virgin Islands. The forty-five miles or so of deep, open ocean that separated St. Croix from the Virgin Islands proper exerted, and continue to exert, a greater influence on the respective destinies of the islands than a casual glance at a map might suggest, not only in the affairs of nature but in those of the later arriving humans as well.

But this isolation can be deceiving. In their own peculiar fashion, islands "know" each other. Some contact and "communication" between the Virgins to the north and St. Croix, for example, was effected naturally and inevitably by means of sea and air currents, on which pollen and seeds travel so mysteriously but so surely. And once it had appeared, animal life—migratory birds in the air and turtles under the sea as prime examples—exercised a like influence in the movement of germinal life forms from island to island. In this manner, and in manifold other instances, the mantle of living organisms moved freely from place to place, without, at the same time, ever duplicating an ecosystem.

Here was a perfectly functioning, self-regulating and self-renewing biosphere, shaped and tested by impersonal natural processes over millions of years. It was as flexible in its reactions to the harshest of nature's forces as it was responsive to the minutest of its own life-forms. It may be characterized as "harmonic," in the exact sense of the word, inasmuch as its organic reaction to the random disturbances of natural forces tended to return the system ultimately to equilibrium and balance, but never stasis and entropy, wherein creative and destructive forces were harmonically resolved in an inevitable but natural, continuous evolutionary flow. The modern term that we employ to describe such an environment, though no doubt incorrectly insofar as it speaks to narrowly human concerns and desires, is "paradise." But such it must have been. The question to which we must turn is how would paradise respond to humankind, *Homo sapiens* of various shapes, sizes and proveniences, and perhaps more important, how would humankind respond to paradise?

According to the archaeological record as we now understand it, the first of our human species to set foot in the New World were neither Africans nor Irishmen nor Scandinavians nor Spaniards but Asians. From the vast Asiatic landmass flowed a human migration into the Western Hemisphere, sometime between 12,000 and 18,000 years ago. That vast migration, however, was neither a planned undertaking nor a simple accident but rather an extended, amorphous movement of people in response to the exigencies of ecological pressures, the availability of game, the vagaries of weather and the shifting access to corridors of passage across the ice. Hunting and foraging groups, one after another, followed the movements of game animals from the Asian continent across an area that today we call the Bering Sea (Beringia), which was at that time part landmass, as the sea levels were then lower, and part icepack. On the eastern side, the migrants emerged onto another great landmass that today we call North America, in another recently named area, the New World, or the Western Hemisphere. It is doubtful that they had any awareness, in the geographic or geologic sense of the term, that they had passed from one great continent to another; that, however, has held little significance in comparison to the ultimate importance of the event—the settlement of an entire hemisphere of the earth, many millennia before others of their human species effected a subsequent entry from the opposite direction.

Once in this "new world," their migrations continued, ever to the south and east, occupying new areas with new climates, all the while adapting their cultures and lifeways as they advanced. New ethnicities rapidly evolved as individual groups responded to the daily task of satisfying the essential human needs of food, shelter, security, procreation and communication, developments witnessed by the Inuit of the far north, the Iroquois in the east, the Pueblo in the southwest, and the Olmecs in Central America, to mention only a few of the larger, better known groups. In time, some of these peoples reached South America and some crossed the great Andean Mountain range, descending down into the upper reaches of the Amazon and Orinoco River basins. Eventually, groups of these people fanned out, diversified and filled every available habitat of the continent, including those of the Meso-American and continental littorals that look east and north respectively into the Caribbean Sea and to the islands set in it. Ever at the ready to try a new possibility, some took to the sea—this was perhaps the first sea-crossing during the entire great migration—moving slowly but inevitably out into the Caribbean archipelago, the first one, eastward into the Greater Antilles and later ones, northward through the Lesser Antilles.

In the Caribbean islands, as well as on the mainlands, these migrating peoples settled down and made the inevitable compromises with the land and the sea, evolving new, ever-adapting cultures; some proved scarcely more than adequate to meet the hard dictates of survival, whereas some others variously exceeded that limitation. Considered in the broader perspective, against the universal coordinates of time and place, that selfsame variety which is shown preference everywhere by nature was much in evidence among these folk—the subsistence peoples, such as the Archaic Indians, who everywhere lived quite close to nature; the agricultural groups, such as the Taínos, with their evolving class systems; the more predatory communities, like the Caribs in the eastern Antilles, with their decidedly egalitarian dispositions; and in the distant lands to the west and to the south, the advanced civilizations of the Olmecs, the Aztecs, the Mayans and the Incas, based upon the long-term practice of intensive agriculture and the genesis of complex social and political organization. The diversity of human experience came to be as much in evidence everywhere in the New World as it had ever been in the Old.

By the fifteenth century A.D., the world was ripe with possibility. A number of human societies had already struck advantageous compromises with nature in the most fundamental sense of the term. The agricultural revolution of the Neolithic Age, which provided cereal-based food systems and animal domestication, had long since passed in various regions of the world. In its train came manifold experiments in social and political organization. Chiefdoms, states, kingdoms and empires by turns rose, flourished and declined as in the cases of Egypt, Ghana, Mali and Songhay in Africa; the various dynasties in China; Greece and Rome in Europe; the Persian, Parthian and Sassanid states in Middle East; the welter of polities in Mesopotamia and the Near East; and, not least, the Aztec, Mayan and Inca states in the New World. It is remarkable that for centuries these societies, for all the fullness of their development, knew little of one another and maintained only the vaguest contacts, as they gradually extended their trade, their political power and their awareness of the world.

At the same time, it was inevitable that well-developed states such as these would sooner or later establish greater contact among themselves. In the fifteenth century increasingly, a growing corpus of knowledge of the world and its peoples, along with an impressive technology in the form of maritime advances and trade along the ancient roads and sea lanes, had the effect of shrinking the real distance between once totally isolated human communities. Moreover, these same developments, especially in the domains of knowledge acquisition and the creation of technology, made travel between various of these world states not only feasible but practical as well for the first time.

As early as the fourteenth century A.D., several Mediterranean societies had already made the political and technical advances required to advance from the relatively safe haven of their inland sea and thrust out into the infinitely more challenging but at the same time more promising Atlantic Ocean. No sooner had daring seamen in their caravels and carracks begun to ply those waters with regularity than commenced a struggle for control and domination of sea routes and trade between the war-hardened monarchies of Portugal and Castile. Hanging in the balance were first the Atlantic islands, then the seemingly endless West African coast south to the equator and all the allure and promise of the exotic places and lucrative trade that lay beyond.

Due to its excellent geographic location and to long years of experience on the world seas, Portugal assumed the initial advantage in the struggle and clung to it tenaciously and jealously. Advancing down the West African coast and maintaining control of strategic points there, Portuguese sea power proceeded surely and methodically to retrace the sources of the fabled eastern trade around the African continent and, at length, into the vast Indian Ocean. In a surprisingly short time, they achieved all their goals, realizing their own version of "the enterprise of the Indies." The legendary trade wealth of the East fell into their hands. The struggle for access to the East, it seemed, was over.

The nascent Spanish state, a late medieval composite polity of Aragon and Castile, fused ultimately in the crucible of the *reconquista*, did not languish. Fired by victories over the Muslim states in Andalusia and inspired by the extraordinary energies of Catalan and Genoese merchants and seamen, Spanish monarchs expected their fair share of the world that lay beyond the Pillars of Hercules. Accordingly, adventurers in the service of that nation did not fail to establish a strong presence along that maritime frontier, first in the Canary Islands, where they swiftly introduced a form of Mediterranean plantation economy, based on sugar and slavery, a model that would in time become the transplanted prototype for all the as yet unknown tropical islands that lay over the western horizon. Despite these efforts, as the fifteenth century entered into its last decade, Spanish fortunes on the world sea appeared to be on the wane, what with Portuguese arms and shipping dominating the Guinea coast and the lucrative routes to the east; and at the same time, the Atlantic Ocean appeared to be unsurpassable. Enter the Genoese navigator Christopher Columbus and his "enterprise of the Indies." What was soon to follow was a family reunion of sorts of the scattered human species, in the form, of course, of a collision that would banish forever our splendid isolation.

Petroglyph from near Reef Bay on St. John

CHAPTER 2

IF STONES COULD TALK:
THE PETROGLYPHS OF ST. CROIX

IF YOU ARRIVE EARLY ENOUGH in the morning at the Parque Indìgena de Caguana on the northern slope of the Cordillera Central in Puerto Rico, you will see dew lingering on the grass and a cloud or two hanging about the peaks of the surrounding mountains. Aside from the chatter of birds, all will be tranquil and calm, as it should be, in this special place. Here generations of Taíno Indians came to worship their gods and enact the most sacred rites of their people. It is a special place.

Today Caguana is a slumbering village near the mountain town of Utuado in Puerto Rico. It has been the site's relative isolation from the centers of modern activity that perhaps saved this ancient Amerindian ritual center from the ravages of civilization. One must make a bit of an effort and go out of one's way to get there. But it is worth the effort.

The modest plateau is inset with several rectangular ball courts or ceremonial courts, each one lined with large, inscribed stones. The designs carved into the flat-faced boulders are abstract representations of various chiefs, gods, and spirits. It was among these sacred stones that the Taíno people congregated regularly to appeal to the power of the other world through their rituals, to dance in tireless processions and to chant their Areytos.

Taíno remains of this kind have also been found along a migration path from South America to Cuba, including impressive displays in various of the individual islands along that route. Such a ceremonial center with its stone witnesses once stood on the littoral of Salt River on St. Croix though it has been all but forgotten.

Amerindian presence on St. Croix stretches back some two thousand years before the Common Era. The people who came to be known later as the Taínos—called Arawaks or Island Arawaks by some—settled on the island just before the onset of the Common Era. At some point in time since then, they came to call the place "AyAy."

Their culture on St. Croix in those beginnings was Neolithic, founded on conuco agriculture (planted mounds), the production of varied ceramic wares, refined tool-making traditions and practical marine technology. They lived in modest thatch dwellings in small settlements and farmed the land located on the parameters of their villages. Additionally, they fished the off-lying reefs and the deeper seas beyond for their protein-rich treasures. Such was the material bases for the settlement at Salt River.

Taíno social and political structure was hierarchical, not at all the completely class-free and egalitarian paradise as some modern observers would have it. At the top of the hierarchy stood the chieftain, or *cacique*, with members of the three noble classes (*matunherí, guaoxerí and baharí)* arrayed under him, ruling over the *naborias*, or common class. This system of inherited status and unequal power distribution imposed stability and order on the people in this form of rigid class society.

The cacique effected his task of leading his people by making constant appeals from this world to the powers in the other world, to the gods, the spirits, the ancestors. Whenever the connection with the divine was properly realized, it was assumed, the rain fell, the land yielded its bounty and the community thrived. But if that connection failed for whatever reason, the very existence of the social order appeared threatened, be it by inclement weather, drought, pestilence or warfare. The Taíno concern for the spiritual element in life was therefore paramount.

Since this spiritual and societal function was viewed as the most essential human activity of all, its implementation required the knowledge, experience and creativity of a highly trained priest, or shaman—here often called a *behique*—who was capable of traversing the magical demarcation that separated this world from the other one. That task he undertook for the purpose of influencing and even directing the immense power that resided in the realm beyond.

It was the behique then who acted as an intermediary between the world of people and the world of divine power. He himself was adept in traveling between the two realms. It was more problematic, however, to make that power available to the common people, who, for the most part, remained planted on this side of the sacred divide. In order to overcome that difficulty, the shaman presided over various rituals, all intended to open the sacred door.

One of these rituals was the spiritual procession. It took place along a procession-way, or ceremonial court, which was located in the village and which was vaguely reminiscent in its physical dimensions of an earthen tennis court but lined with large stones on at least two sides.

These place-delineating stones were inscribed with linear figures, often times simple representations of human and animal heads, of spirits, and of deities. One is immediately struck by the simplicity of the designs, especially when a comparison is made with the sophisticated curvilinear forms on their pottery. One might conclude that it was therefore that the stone carvings were an art form that had not fully emerged from its infancy into full maturity.

It was down this ceremonial plaza and before the aligned sacred stones that rows of Taínos passed in procession, arms locked together, as they moved through ritual paces and chanted songs and verses of their ancestors, offering the ceremony up to the divine powers in supplication.

In those moments, the figures on the stones became iconic, magically coaxing the spiritual into the real by means of ritual, thereby enabling the real to participate in the spiritual. In that short arc of time, human flesh came into direct contact with powerful eternal spirits, thereby transforming the former from animal through human states toward the divine. Here we are at the heart of Taíno life and culture. The petroglyphs are their most prominent, surviving material artifact of this transformation.

Whereas the petroglyphs on St. Croix were carved in large stones and set in a ceremonial court, those found on St. John and on Congo Cay were inscribed onto natural stone outcroppings. The St. John carvings are special in that they are engraved on the stone face of an outcropping through which passes a meandering, natural watercourse. Who can doubt that those petroglyphs were carved in honor of the water spirits that resided at that spot, offering as they did the life-sustaining bounty of fresh water?

Indian culture came to an abrupt and catastrophic end with the mid-16th century arrival of first Spaniards and then other Europeans. With the advent and dominance of Christianity, little attention was paid to these works of spiritual art, which were summarily dismissed as heathen and primitive and crude. Soon they were overgrown by the tropical forest and they disappeared from view though not altogether from memory.

In the late 19th century with the appearance of modern anthropology and archaeology, the stones' flickering memories were sparked back to life. Archaeologists Theodoor de Booy, Folmer Andersen and Gudmund Hatt began to excavate, and their findings astounded everyone. How could an island as small as St. Croix have produced so many fine artifacts?

Gudmund Hatt, a Danish scholar with a world-class reputation, led an expedition in 1922–23 to St. Croix that revealed the mysteries of Salt River to the modern world. In those excavations he uncovered a ceremonial court, or ball court (*Batey*), which he proceeded to analyze and interpret. His findings established that Ayay had once been a thriving center of Taíno culture, with considerable settlements and a substantial population.

Given the political status of the island at the time, Hatt judged that it would be better to send the rediscovered petroglyphs back to Denmark. In retrospect, it was probably the correct decision for that time, especially in light of the subsequent "pot-holing" by well intended amateurs and by the general misuse of the Salt River site over the past seventy years or so.

But we have come a long way since 1923. Might the time not be right to evaluate the proper context of the artifacts and bring those special stones and related artifacts back to their original home, along the shores of the Salt River estuary? At the very least, one might question if they have found a suitable resting place so far from their home.

With those stones as a centerpiece, we might reconstruct the former Taíno village at Salt River around a ceremonial court, a ball court, scattered bohios, a beach lined with canoes, and fields inset with conucos stretching off into the forest. Provided they could be securely cared for and properly maintained, the homecoming of the displaced petroglyphs back to St. Croix would afford the inhabitants of our island and the many visitors who come every year the opportunity to understand the people who preceded us here by some two thousand years as well as to demonstrate respect for their tenancy of this island that has all too often been lightly regarded.

Satellite photo of Hurricane Hugo just after it passed over St. Croix,
moving along the coast of Florida

CHAPTER 3

NOTES FROM THE EYE OF A STORM: HURRICANE HUGO, 1989

F ROM THE BEGINNING of known history, hurricanes have ravaged these islands again and again. But every dozen or so years, as in 1642, 1692, 1726, 1772, 1785, 1827, 1867, 1899, 1916 and 1928, an exceptionally severe storm visits its wrath upon us. On the evening of Sunday September 17 and into the morning hours of September 18, 1989, Hurricane Hugo bore down on the island of St. Croix, U.S. Virgin Islands, bringing with it 12 hours of unparalleled havoc and destruction. The following is an account of that event, as extracted from a journal that I kept during the days immediately after the storm.

On the day before the storm, September 16, 1989, I choose to spend that Saturday morning in Christiansted, having coffee and some conversation with two friends and later browsing for some books. As we take our last cup of coffee at the Café Collage around midday, it comes over the news that the approaching storm would pass just to the south of St. Croix during Sunday night. Everyone had been hoping that it would turn sharply to the north somewhere in the Leewards or meander further south before roaring up into the Gulf. Those had been oft-repeated scenarios for the passage of hurricanes in the past. But just to the south! I am dumb struck. As we walk down King Street to our cars, Alfredo wipes heavy perspiration from his brow and remarks that this is true hurricane weather. Calm, hot and muggy. Is the barometer dropping? It seems such a foolish thing to wonder about.

Driving home, I notice several trucks on the roads, loaded with plywood and two-by-fours. Should I give it a try? Panic seizes me! There are still four hours. And then I think of the waiting lines. And I remember how I'd done that for hurricanes David and Frederick in 1979. I am still entertaining the vain hope that the great storm will veer away. And then I think that maybe it will be another David—a lot of water and lower level hurricane winds. We had coped with that well enough the last time in spite of everything. Then I try to remember the effect of the force of those winds but somehow cannot conjure them up.

So, I say to myself forgivingly that it is too late to do anything in any event. I rationalize further that it probably would not do any good anyway, if this storm is as big and powerful as the weather reports have it. Ironically enough, my lackadaisical rationalizations will prove to be absolutely correct. Though I did not know it Saturday morning, there was *nothing* I could have done to blunt the ferocity of what was to come. So I proceed to lay in a few supplies and pick up a few batteries and then return home for an anxious Saturday night.

Sunday morning I arise at about 8:30 a.m. and notice that the calm has passed and that the wind has picked up considerably, now blowing between 20 to 25 mph, kicking up fields of white-caps out at sea to the north. I look to the east with a dull feeling in my head and a sinking sensation in my stomach. The sky has turned to cotton. Dirty cotton. It is coming. It is out there. I feel it in my gut. But is this the big one we have wondered about for so long? Maybe it will still pass. That sequence of thought keeps coming back to me.

In the early afternoon, I drive to our other house at Cotton Valley on the east end of St. Croix to see how Kevin is progressing in securing things there. I arrive around three and begin work to secure the little office I maintain there for writing. The sky is rapidly growing dark in the east. The winds are picking up noticeably. I do all that I can and then try to give Kevin and his girlfriend Lisa some advice. They are clearly excited, perhaps immaturely so. Before I leave, I invite them one last time to come with me to the bigger house in La Grande Princesse. No, they wish to ride it out here. As I walk to the car, the wind is gusting well past 30 mph. The light rain begins to sting my face. As I wave good-bye to them they look like two campers, their courage buoyed by their six dogs.

Driving back to Christiansted along the east end road, I notice changes in the normal nature of things. The guinea grass is stretched out flat under the wind along the roadside. Fields of it dance madly on the open hillsides. Several papaya trees have fallen; their trunks stretch across the road like great snakes. They are always the first to fall, followed by the yuccas. Also some mahogany branches have been snapped and scattered. Litter and debris race across the road in front of my car. Everything is now in motion. I glance at my watch. It is only five o'clock! A voice comes through the growing static and crackling on the car radio: "The storm proper—Hugo—will hit around 9:00 p.m." It seems like such a silly name. This is it, a weak voice inside me squeaks.

Driving up our private road to the house in La Grande Princesse, which overlooks the north shore of St. Croix and the ocean at an elevation of about 300 feet, I am flabbergasted by what I see. Stretching to the dimming horizon to the north, the ocean has been whipped into an angry, turbulent, white froth. The sky is all but black. The sun has abandoned us. On this hilltop the wind has always been significantly stronger than in the flatter areas below. So it is today.

Inside the house there is a good deal of activity. Marjo Norring and her daughter have come to ride it out with us. In our family, there are four of us—Shirley, Chris, Leslie and I. Nervous laughter accompanies our feeble preparations. Feeling guilty, I take up the roll of tape and begin to apply it to the windows. A hollow ceremony. As I do so, I am attacked by a squadron of wasps; I receive three bad stings on my fingers, which remain with me for weeks. The insects seem to know that something evil is afoot. Within a few minutes, I am forced back inside the house by the constantly rising winds. We have done what little that we can.

At about 8:00 p.m. the children barricade themselves with their bedding in the living room downstairs. There is a pajama party air to their squealing. Though on the windward north side of the house, it is the one room farthest away from the direction of the wind. It seems a wise choice for them to hunker down. Moreover, we recall that we spent

Hurricane Frederick in there. I go outside one last time to check the exterior of the house. Rain is now being driven horizontally from the northeast. I would now place the wind velocity at 50 mph, with gusts even higher. In the driveway, I turn my back to the wind some 50 feet to the east of the house and click on my flashlight. Inside the house everyone looks safe and snug. A tropical Currier and Ives. As I pass my beam along the roofline, however, I am horrified to see that the gusts are lifting up edges of the roof. Quickly I think: What will happen if the wind speed doubles to 100 mph? My heart sinks.

Drenched, I hurry back into the house but do not break the news. Everyone is cheerful; there is even a certain sense of camaraderie in the air. Why upset the others now? But outside, the wind is beginning to clutch at the front windows and doors. I can see the glass in the steel-framed windows beginning to bow out under the constantly increasing pressure. Their incessant rattling fills the house. I remember how this happened with David and Frederick but also how things held together in spite of it all. I begin a quick patrol of the interior of the house. As I reach the top of the stairs, I am stopped in my tracks by a tremendous crash, followed by screaming. I turn on my heels and race back downstairs, expecting the worst. The two eight-foot sliding glass doors in the living room have been blown completely out. As the wind came in, it instantly blew out the plywood sheets nailed into the concrete wall on the other side of the room. So much for my one defensive measure. The curtains now stand out horizontally and whip about madly in the wind. The chandelier is banging loudly against the ceiling. Leslie and Chris have sprung up and jumped through a small interior window into the dining room. Their faces are now horror-stricken. The beast is upon us sooner than I expected.

The wind is now shrieking through the house. It drives the furniture across the living room. I grab at one of Shirley's favorite tables and try to pull it from beneath the twisted window frame. I cannot budge it. As I tug at it, the wind snatches it from me and *drives* it further across the room. I am astonished by the brute force with which I am now locked in personal combat. It threatens me in a high pitched whine as it races through the broken frame. In an instant, everything is shattered and broken and wet. In an instant, the intruder has broken through our defenses and is within our perimeter. In an instant it has been transformed from a storm into a living entity, no longer a simple meteorological phenomenon but an evil presence that threatens us and our place in the world.

Witnessing these events, Shirley, Marjo and her daughter are frozen in the kitchen at the other end of the house, their eyes bulging. Then I hear them screaming. Some glass and splinters are beginning to fly through the air, threatening them. I ask them to go upstairs. They are paralyzed. I order them. They pick up a few things and run upstairs quickly, the wind pursuing their every step. The world has changed irrevocably in a span of several minutes. We have taken a giant step backward in time.

Once upstairs, I select the room with the strongest walls against the howling storm outside. That is my study. I herd everyone inside and pull the door shut. There is no margin now for a mistaken judgment. We wait, scarcely breathing. Shortly, we hear something ripping at the roof. Marjo's daughter begins to whimper. "We are trapped! We will die!" She tries to go out into the hall, but I have to force her back into the room. If the doors of the bedrooms in front of us give in, the hallways will become wind tunnels—a certain death trap.

Over the protests of Shirley, I make a quick reconnaissance downstairs. It is quite dark now, for the power was turned off just after six by the authorities to avoid accidents. I edge along the wall and then shine my torch into the invaded room. An invisible beast is in there ripping, tearing, smashing, destroying everything. Foolishly, I think: Maybe we can hold it to this one room. Hold it? I am struck by how silly such an expression now sounds.

I would feel better if I could act. Foolishly, I again dash into the besieged room and grab a chair. Shirley is shouting at me from upstairs. I hear doors banging from every direction. The rainwater blinds me and the flailing curtains whip me in the face. Now I can taste the salt content in the rain. This is not rain! This is the ocean! The first of much glass enters my hands. I tug at the chair and curse at the wind but also at my own stupidity. Finally, I dislodge the damaged piece of furniture and then lug it into the dining room. I look at it. Saved! A minor victory! But what am I going to do with it now?

Glass crashes. Pictures are flying off the walls; windows are breaking; lamps are hurtled against the back wall. I look in again. Oh, God! I've made it angry! The wind has picked up another notch and it is thrashing everything! I am overawed by the force of it and I stand gawking in wonder. But it has invaded my home! I realize in an instant the utter folly of trying to save anything in that room. Take it, bastard! I turn and run.

Back upstairs things seem relatively safe. I delude myself again, thinking maybe it will just *take* the downstairs. Take! What a horrible word! I stoop to avoid glass and scurry across the atrium to our bedroom, which is sealed off by heavy mahogany doors. I pull at the handle but the door does not budge. I put my ear to the crack and hear a howling, whirring sound inside. The hair on my neck tingles. Some powerful thing is in there! In that one moment, I realize that my home of the last 20 years—the home that I built and raised my children in—is under siege. And if the house is threatened, then we are threatened. My God! This is no longer just an inconvenience. It's now an immediate matter of life and death. As the full impact of that reality settles over me, the door slips open in my hand, almost as if my deadly opponent is saying—here, have a look.

Inside my bedroom, a maddening whirling sound is coming from beyond the ceiling. The windows are incredibly bowed out and vibrating fiercely under the wind. They hum madly at varying pitches, seemingly at the breaking point. The curtains are standing straight out. And there is the bed that I awoke in this morning—the bedding ripped back, the pillows thrown off, my nighttime reading flying. I curse the storm for it has invaded my most secret, intimate place. It is now attacking me personally. Just at that point, as my anger is mounting, the door is ripped from my hands by the shifting air pressure and slams shut again.

On my way back across the atrium to the others in my study, I open the front door to relieve a little the mounting pressure inside the house and it flies out of my hand, clanging mightily against the wall. A great river of wind now rushes past me, through the house and out the new opening, knocking me a little off balance and surprising me by its intensity.

Back in my study, everyone is huddled in the corner, visible only by the light of one flashlight. They are listening intently to the radio. The announcer is stating that 40 to 50 mph winds are hitting St. Croix. Idiot! I would like to strangle him. He also notes that some reports of looting are filtering in. Looting? In this kind of weather? I am amazed. Marjo's daughter feels trapped and wants to go back into the hallway. I have to tell her no firmly. She begins to whimper. I see fear in Leslie's eyes. Even Chris is now quiet; his eyes have lost the sparkle of adventure. For once, he has no questions brashly but wears a look of concern.

I shine the light on my watch. It is now 10:00 p.m. and I continue to peer out the door to monitor the havoc being wrought in the rest of the house. Should we stay here? The question nags me. The noise level has risen perceptibly. If we wait another 30 minutes, we probably will not be able to get out. Already small pieces of glass and wood are hurtling through the air like bullets out in the hallways and atrium. What happens if the entire front of the house collapses? Sobering thought. There is a small 12 x 15 guest cottage, located beside the pool and directly behind the main house. It is constructed of concrete block and has a low sturdy roof. It has the additional advantage of being in the lee of both our house and the pool-side pagoda. I decide to reconnoiter it; reluctantly I take a big-eyed Chris with me.

We dash out the front door and enter a confused, agitated sea of turbulence. Immediately we are knocked sideways. We then squat and frog-march to the cottage. I have no means of measuring the velocity of the wind. But I do know that I have lived through hurricanes Frederick,

David and Klaus, all of which packed winds of around 100 mph and I have never experienced anything like this. Everything outside is taking a frightening beating. The cottage, however, is intact, and inside it is dry. It seems to me that this will be safer than our house. I make the decision to move. We scamper back into the house to get the others. They are reluctant to go but go we must. We move quickly in a Conga-line out the same door toward the cottage. After being buffeted by the winds momentarily, we arrive wet and stung and breathless. Having now been directly in the wind for the first time, the others are amazed and shaken. But there is less noise here and they immediately if prematurely feel safer and more secure. It is 10:15 p.m.

I notice that we forgot one of the flashlights and the radio. We really need them. Chris and I go back for them. Before we dash out the door, Chris says: "Can I hold onto you?" He seizes me by the belt. We make a run for it. As we enter the house, we are met by a great roaring. The beast is completely inside now, stomping, bellowing and trashing. It has claimed the *entire* house. I feel that it will all explode now at any second. It sounds as if a great train is bearing down on us. I am mesmerized. "Dad, let's get out of here," Chris pulls at my arm. We make another dash for it. Projectiles are in the wind all about us, coming at us from behind. The trees are howling in their resistance. Blasts of wind come shrieking over the roof like demons. The house moans. The entire world is in motion and we are about to be blown away. I have the sensation that I could fly if I stood up and spread my arms. We scurry inside the cottage. I whisper to Shirley that the house is about to go. She can say nothing.

For the next four hours we are subject to the unbridled ferocity of nature. A pattern is established amidst the chaos. The wind blows steadily for 10 to 15 minutes at a powerful velocity and then suddenly gusts to a new, more ferocious level. It holds there for a while and then gusts again, repeating the pattern over and over. The pitch of the accompanying sound increases at the same time. After two hours of this, it seems that the world will come apart. We are all whispering or praying, "please stop just for a minute so we can get a good grip. Let us get a good grip!" But it does not stop. No one is listening. We are abandoned. The storm bears down on us and gusts again. The girls are on the floor, heads buried in pillows. They are crying softly. Stop, stop! It gusts again and again, never returning to the previous level of intensity, but rather raising it. I have the distinct feeling that there is a great hammer over my head, about to come down on me with deadly force at any instant.

For the moment we feel relatively safe, at least until around 11:00. At that time the wind seizes one of the doors and rips it open, tearing out the latch, leaving only the handle. I grab it and pull it closed again. However, the storm toys with me, jerking me bodily outside every 10 minutes or so. There is a single necktie hanging on a hook on the wall. I double it and tie it around the handle and then wrap it around my hand, pulling back with all my weight. In 15 minutes the door is ripped open again, leaving me with torn strands of the tie in my hand and my shoulder joints aching. I must now hold the door (for the next 4 hours) with both hands through the window. Each time the wind seizes it in this little version of the cat and mouse game, I pull it back, crashing it unavoidably into my knees. I think I have cracked one kneecap.

From all that I can gather from the radio and what I see about me, the storm is due south of us, moving in a west by northwest direction at about 12 mph. If it swings slightly north, the eye will pass directly over us. We will know it if it happens, I console myself. By midnight the winds have increased to perhaps 150 to 170 mph. I think to myself that at least it cannot get any worse than this. But I am wrong so many times during this long night. And so it is once again.

From the confines of the cottage, I can now hear the house breaking up. The beast is inside and rampaging. We hear glass breaking, metal screeching as it is twisted, wood crashing and splintering and great crashes as if objects are being thrown crashing and careening into walls. My home is being destroyed before my eyes and I can do nothing about it. I scream helpless, pitiful obscenities at the rampaging brute and it roars back in its awesome rage. When it gusts the next time, I hear what sounds to be bullets hitting the exterior wall of our refuge. A new element. Evidently, glass, nails, stones and pieces of wood are being hurled at us from the dying house. It presents no immediate danger so long as we remain inside and away from the windows but it is nerve-wracking.

At about 1:00 a.m. the wind shifts direction slightly and gives me momentarily relief from my door-holding duty. I grab the flashlight for a look outside. I can see the nearby trees being driven into a frenzy, twisting this way and that under unbelievable pressures. I cheer them. They are living things, like us, out there fighting. I planted most of them about 20 years ago with my own hands so they are like children. In fact several of them were planted expressly to mark the births of our children. I am enraged when the biggest of the palms is ripped up and thrown into the swimming pool right in front of me. One by one they are violently uprooted. I grieve in silent rage for each of them. One last palm struggles on to the end. I cheer it on. Fight, damn you, fight! The wind roars and whips it from every side. A macabre dance of death is enacted before my eyes. This one tree will make it. It will make it! At that moment, the next great gust comes and I lower my head in fear that a powerful blow is about to fall on me. When I look up again, the tree is in the air, suspended, twirling. Then it disappears. Goddamn you, you're killing my trees, my living trees! Goddamn you! Goddamn you! I am enraged. I strike the wall. I am powerless.

In the weak beam of my flashlight, I can see large objects flying past—eight-foot sections of one inch and a quarter thick sheets of plywood flutter by like postage stamps; two-by-fours zing past like darts; large ceiling beams seem to move more slowly, twirling past like helicopter rotors in slow motion. They crash into the hill behind us. Thud! Thud! The earth seems to shake. Only at that point does it occur to me that this airborne flotsam presents an immediate danger to us. If part of the house roof hits the cottage at 200 mph it will surely crush it and us with it. At the very least, it will destroy our refuge and force us out into the teeth of the wind.

I hear a plopping sound outside the door, as if someone were rubbing along the wood. I shine the light out the crack in the door and there lies our bedroom drapes. It appears to me at this moment as a studied insult, a gesture of arrogance underlining my own pitiful impotence. I can do with you as I will, it says. And the arrogance of it rings in my ears.

It is no longer a question of inconvenience, or minor loss, or loss of a home; it's now a question of our lives. I look around the room. I see in their eyes that they are aware of it also. I also see in those eyes that I am their last hope. They want me to do something! And I am as frightened and helpless as they are! My last bastion, then, before the relentless advance of my enemy will be pretense, only the first of a score of tactical retreats this long night.

It is now 1:30 a.m. Unbelievably, the storm continues to gust and rage, gust and rage. Around us on all sides, there is fierce lightening but, unaccountably, no thunder. For the next 30 minutes it increases in intensity until the darkness is momentarily banished. Consequently, I can clearly see the drama of the awful destruction outside. To my right I notice something moving. It's the pagoda, swaying violently before the onslaught! It is only three feet from us and we are in its lee. If it falls, it might crash into us, knock down the adjoining wall, and bury us! If it falls any other way, we will be exposed to the full blast of the beast. A very bad set of prospects. I gather the women together quickly and align them against the opposite wall, as close to the door as possible. I then try to visualize what would happen if that wall were to collapse. Our roof would dip in the direction of the falling wall and be exposed broadside to the full force of the wind. It would then be driven back upon us, all in a second or two. We would all be crushed! Or at best, trapped.

We have one possible alternative and I study it quickly. We could crawl along the concrete slab alongside the pool to its far end. At that point there is a jumble of broken trees and a blown down fence. If we could make our way over or around that mess, we might be able to make it to a nearby retaining wall there, behind which we could crouch down and wait. We would be safe there at least until the eye passes; at that point we would have to stare back into the direct blast of the wind for another three to four hours.

The pagoda next to us is now swaying so violently that I feel we have no choice. I instruct the others in what to do and then bunch them together at the door. Just as I am ready to lead the way out, several large ceiling beams from the house come flying into our proposed crawl space with a resounding crash. If we had been there, some of us would have died. Then several sheets of galvanized metal fly across my line of sight making a shrieking noise, like razors ripping through the air. Our last alternative has been pushed beyond our reach. We are now truly powerless. We can only stay where we are and hope. I put my arms around them and give my back to the threatened wall. They are all crying quietly. Do what you will, you bastard! This is the end of the line.

We stand there huddled together for what seems an eternity. When we think the velocity can go no higher, it does so, mocking us. Then we hear the sickening sound of disintegration. Here it comes! The pagoda is finally collapsing in the relentless onslaught—wood screeching, concrete popping, nails breaking and then an earthshaking thud! As I peer outside I can see that the structure hit the ground no less than six inches from the cottage and now lies there in a tangled mass of destruction. That was the best luck we have had all night. But our rejoicing is short-lived. Now there is nothing between us and the monster that relentlessly bears down on us.

We can feel the awesome power. The little cottage shutters now in the full exposure. Leslie says: "Daddy, feel the wall!" It vibrates under my hand. I look at my watch. 2:00 a.m. We are lost. Instead of holding steady, it roars at us again and a mighty force hovers over our heads. A deafening roar passes over us and seems to settle over the cottage, like the passing of a mighty train. Around me I hear weeping, louder now. Outside the world is coming apart, Pandemonium. Thrashing all about us, crashing behind us and above all the shrieking of the great beast. I have the distinct impression that someone is outside shooting a machine gun against the side of the cottage. Another few minutes of this and there will be nothing left. But I dare not hope, for the wind will only gust again.

And just at the point where we would have expected another gust accompanied by a new wave of destruction, there is nothing. The wind drops sharply and completely. The lightening stops. The rain all but ceases. Complete calm. I look at my watch. It is 2:15 a.m. This must be the famous eye of the storm. Dead calm. Eerie silence. We are stunned. But thankful.

I decide to attempt a quick reconnoiter. I step outside over the protests of the others and begin to make my way around the pool and toward the house. I am astonished, slapped in the face. There is no other word for it. The world has been rearranged. Everything has been transformed. There are obstacles everywhere. It takes me 10 minutes of picking my way and clambering about in order to cover a distance of 30 feet, little of which I can now recognize in spite of having lived here 20 years. Just as I approach the house, a few blasts of wind come from out of nowhere and rock me. I cannot tell if they are tornadoes but they come with tremendous force, throwing and breaking things around me. It is almost as if the beast has come back to rifle through the remains in order to break whatever might have been left unbroken. I curse it as it rummages invisibly but powerfully all around me.

I cannot get into the house and I know I do not have much time. As I turn to retrace my steps back to the cottage, I hear a distant howling, coming apparently from the south. It is plaintive and haunting. As I am standing there listening, the wind rises suddenly to near its previous force, with a rapidity that is nothing less than startling; only this time it is coming from somewhere to the south of us. Now, thank God, we have the top of the hill between us and the storm's full ferocity. As I shine my beam toward the sky, the rain is being driven horizontally from that quarter. Still, I feel vulnerable. I hurry back to the cottage and secure the door.

The winds continue to blow from 2:30 until about 4:00 a.m. at a high velocity. From 4:00 until 6:00 a.m., they subside gradually. From 4:00

a.m. on we no longer feel threatened at least. The killing edge of the storm has passed us and it moves toward the northwest. There are no winds to match those that were raging around 2:00, when the end of the world appeared eminent. I now notice for the first time the water that has come in under the doors and the leaks in the roof. I am soaked, standing in two inches of water. How little it all seems to matter. I also begin to think rationally, perhaps for the first time in several hours. We will live!

What has happened to the house? My study? My books? My computers? What about the rest of the island? Kevin and Lisa on the east end? Surely, I think, we got the worst of it. Imagine that the storm did this to *us*! Is anyone hurt? Only a few scrapes and bruises. It would make little difference anyway. We are trapped in here. All the roads will be blocked. The hospital will be destroyed. That much I can guess. The safety net that we ordinarily expect is now gone. We are on our own! That realization hits me squarely between the eyes.

By 6:00 a.m., the winds have died down to the point where I can move about safely outside. Rain is falling lightly. The faint light of the new day appears in the eastern sky. I take my first tentative steps outside.

There are no words to describe what I see now in the light of early morning and my reaction to it. Simply, the world that we knew on this spot of earth has been destroyed. Large sections of my house lay scattered over the yard, pool and hillside. Nothing is whole; everything is broken. I can scarcely move, being hemmed in on all sides by destruction and debris. Several times I must take my bearings, for this is not the same place. Slowly the coming morning light reveals to me the full extent of the disaster. No, this cannot be! This is a dream! I cannot stop repeating my pitiful attempt to negate this crushing new reality—no, no, no! My vocabulary is reduced to that one word.

I am struck by an urge to see the rest of the island. Like a cockroach scurrying over the remains of a deserted world, I pick my way around to the front of the house, to the driveway overlooking the north shore of St. Croix. My first glimpse of this once lovely island appalls me. It looks as if the island has been burned. Everything is a charcoal gray color or brown. There is no more color! And now I see why. *Every* leaf on *every* plant has been stripped. It sounds like an exaggeration but it is literally true. The grass is sheared off even with the ground. There are no more weeds! With a closer look I see in amazement that most of the plants and some of the trees have been stripped of their very bark. Hundreds of trees are down. Others are snapped like twigs, some of them numerous times along their massive trunks. Every power pole I can see has been snapped in pieces or blown down. I can hear no sound. No dogs, no roosters, no engines starting. The world, it seems, is not waking up. Nothing but the spine-tingling howl of the trailing winds of the hurricane that rush over the hills, through the now denuded trees, causing them to resonate in a lingering cry of desolation that one usually associates with northern forests in the dead of winter. I stare at this broken place, bewildered.

I turn to face the house. What I see is a broken-toothed, blind-eyed hulk of a thing where I once ate and slept and played with my children. It takes me 30 minutes to find a way in. I must climb over ceiling beams, broken walls, glass, nails, twisted metal—it is all there, only re-arranged. Inside, water is pouring through what was once a roof, as if the place had been bombed, and is splashing down onto the floor. The walls are broken or cracked along the bond beam. Everything has been smashed beyond recognition and left in the oddest postures. There is no way to enter our bedroom; a mass of debris blocks the doorway from floor to ceiling. The bedrooms of Leslie and Chris have simply collapsed. About half of my books (app. 12,000 volumes) have just disappeared into the air; those remaining litter the floors, twisted and soaked. My computers are either smashed or soaked. Personal files have been ripped apart. And personal items, especially photos, are scattered everywhere and ruined. Even our collective past in these precious few photos has not been spared. So it is throughout the house—a trail of destruction and desolation. I look at it all in disbelief. Angry, impotent words lodge in my throat. I cannot go on talking about it.

As I make my way back outside, I pass the others, who are now picking their way into the house, muttering words of disbelief. I cannot stand to hear their words. This is the end of a small world that we had built as a family. This is war. This is the Ardennes Forest. This is Vietnam. This is one of life's very worst dreams come true. It is seven o'clock of a new day and the rain begins to come pouring down on us.

Hurricane Marilyn seen from satellite

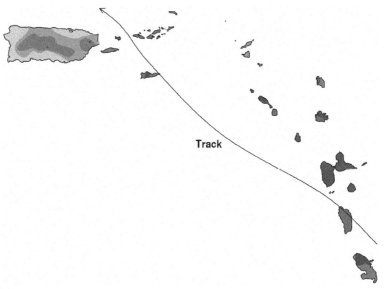

The track of Hurricane Marilyn from its entry into the Caribbean and passage between St. Croix and St. Thomas

CHAPTER 4

NOTES FROM HURRICANE MARILYN, 1995

W E HAVE HAD not much luck with hurricanes of late. Just one week after having received a glancing blow from the very destructive Hurricane Luis, we got a direct hit from Hurricane Marilyn on September 16. By 2:00 p.m. of that day the winds had already reached tropical storm intensity, with a good deal of rain. We were hoping to the end that it would veer away to the north as Hurricane Luis had done, but no such luck. Rather the eye of the storm was destined to pass directly over St. Croix, following much the same path as Hugo had taken in 1989, in spite of Weather Service reports that it was moving north of us, well out at sea.

I am once again given pause to consider the origins of these great storms that rampage about in the Atlantic Ocean. The sea off the coast of West Africa is their nursery. Hot air blows from the Sahara Desert in a westerly direction into the Atlantic and is greeted in the months of July and August with warm sea water, generated by increased sunlight on the sea's surface in the summer months. As the two air masses meet, the warmer land air rises, and as it does so, it begins to rotate in a counter-clockwise direction under the influence of the so-called Coriolis Effect, caused by the rotation of the Earth on moving objects on its surface. At the same time, the rotating air mass continues to move in a westerly direction across the open ocean. In a matter of days, this dynamic low pressure area may strengthen in intensity, due largely to the heat it absorbs from the ocean water in its path. The strengthening is manifest in the phenomenon of increasing wind speed. By the time it reaches the Caribbean islands, it may have hurricane wind speeds between 75 and 100 miles per hour and be laden with rain. With a well defined center, or "eye," and outlying bands rotating in a counter-clockwise direction, it will generally begin to veer to the right, or the north, under the influence of continental air pressure, upper level troughs and, of course, the Coriolis Effect. Such storms do not occur near the Equator because of the absence of this force even though all the other essentials are present. Now fully formed and growing in intensity, such a storm will slam blindly into anything it encounters in its path, bringing unimaginable damage and destruction.

This is exactly what happened on St. Croix on that September day. By about four o'clock in the afternoon, the winds had attained hurricane speeds of well over 80 mph and began gusting up to 100. In addition, the approaching storm brought tremendous amounts of rain—hard, driving rain that stings the face and hands. We had already boarded up the windows and doors of the house and settled into a dry corner downstairs to hope that this time the roof would hold. But we didn't sit idle for long. Water began to pour into the house from every possible crack and crevice. Soon we were doing a bucket brigade to keep the place dry. But as the winds rose, it proved to be a hopeless task. We finally gave up and just sloshed around in it.

At about 5:30, the winds seemed to peak, roaring out of the north and gradually, the northwest. It kept coming over the radio that the winds were just over a hundred miles per hour, but no one among us could believe that. Marilyn was indeed an extremely powerful hurricane, packing winds of well over 125 mph, with gusts that simply took our breath away. When it roared every several minutes or so, we could only hunker down and hope that the next one would not take the roof.

The sounds of destruction were overpowering, first and foremost from the wind itself. Then came the ripping and tearing of rain gutters, telephone and electrical wires and just about everything that wasn't hammered down with eight-inch nails. At 5:45, part of the front balcony broke away and slammed into the house, exploding like a bomb. The flying timbers hit several of the sheets of ¾ inch plywood that covered the windows and doors, breaking through one of them as it did so. With that little finger-hold, the wind began to tear at the adjacent pieces, one by one ripping them loose. As with Hugo, I had the sickening feeling that some malevolent giant was outside toying with us, taking our puny shelter apart one piece at a time. Kevin, Chris and I looked on as another large sheet of plywood was ripped away right in front of us, spun by the incredible velocity of the winds and then slammed through the now open window. We all ducked. Someone moaned, "Oh no! Not again!" The beast was inside our home.

I was certain that we had driven enough nails into the roof and filled in all the cracks. But not so. The wind came bolting into our living room at over 125 miles per hour. I heard once again the familiar drama of Hugo—wood splintering, glass breaking, metal twisting and scraping. My gut twisted, my heart sank. I completely expected the roof to be wrenched off at any moment. As we retreated back downstairs, we were followed by a flood of water racing everywhere, driven by the force of the storm. Everything was now soaked—rugs, furniture, clothing, appliances. I thought to myself that if the storm slows down in its forward momentum while passing over us as Hugo had done and give us a beating like that previous beast did for several hours, then we would be surely lost. Everything will go.

I stood by a wall listening to the winds, feeling them. They were blowing evenly at an incredible speed for five or six minute stretches and then gusting for several minutes at frightening, increased velocities, each time accompanied by a great roar. But I noticed that it was more of a regular pattern, not like Hugo where the wind seemed to mount to dramatic heights with each new gust, drawing on unbelievable reserves of power and attaining velocities approaching 200 miles per hour. This storm was holding steady. It continued in that pattern until about 6:30 p.m. At exactly that time I noticed a very slight but promising shift in the pattern. The gusts began decreasing ever so slightly. That pattern continued for about a half an hour. If it continued in that way, then we would make it through. I knew that the roof could and would withstand these lesser winds.

Abruptly, at 7 p.m., the winds died altogether. An eerie calm settled over everything. The eye of the storm was passing over us. We ventured outside to survey the destruction, which was everywhere. Looking over the hill on which our house was located, we at first saw only total darkness, followed by the dim flicker of a legion of flashlights We heard voices calling out to one another in the darkness that had now descended upon us. The flashlight beams dancing in the sky revealed the heaviest humidity that I have ever experienced. It was if a vast cloud had descended over us. We rejoiced meekly that we had somehow made it through the first half of the storm. We also knew that it would return very shortly. But if my own calculations were correct, then the winds would reappear out of the southwest and we would be protected by the hilltop that loomed behind and over our home.

Forty-five minutes later that was exactly what happened. Without warning the winds roared back from that new direction but passed for the most part over our heads, blowing now back out to sea. We held on tight. But this was a piece of cake compared to the front end of the storm that we had just experienced. The storm's fury remained on us on for two hours and then suddenly it was spent, leaving a howling trail of squalls and battering rains to mark its passage. We were all dog-tired, exhausted, almost tempted to laugh at how ridiculous we all looked, soaked to the skin and wide-eyed.

Probably an hour or so after it passed over us, Marilyn struck St. Thomas head-on with full force. Yet it dealt them an infinitely more damaging blow than it had us for the curious fact that we here had received the full brunt of Hugo only 5 years previously while they more or less escaped it. That event did not make us on St. Croix any wiser but it did eliminate all the shoddy construction and left our island significantly stronger when it was rebuilt. The St. Thomians had been spared that experience in 1989, but they would pay dearly for it on this night. In terms of destruction, Hurricane Marilyn was truly St. Thomas' Hugo, leaving the island completely wrecked.

I remember sitting in water up to my ankles, listening to a call-in radio show on St. Thomas as this latest beast left our shores and churned a path through the sea towards them. It seemed that an air of frivolity prevailed across the water on our sister island. I remember feeling utter sadness when I heard a St. Thomian call in and announce that he had the steaks on the grill and a pitcher full of martinis all mixed up and, in a word, they were ready for the hurricane.

Sailing vessel of the type that carried the first Dutch settlers to St. Croix
in the 1640s

CHAPTER 5

THE NIEUWE ZEELAND THAT NEVER WAS: THE DUTCH ON ST. CROIX, 1643–1645[1]

SPAIN FIRST LAID CLAIM to the island of Ayay (known as Santa Cruz by the Spaniards and, after 1650, as St. Croix by the French and later colonizers) as a direct result of the visit of Columbus there on November 14, 1493. Within several decades of that visit, the Indian habitation of the island came to an end, probably no later than 1515.[2] During the course of the 16th century and into the 17th, Spain, however, made no attempt to settle or develop the island. On the contrary, Spanish interest in all the islands to windward of Puerto Rico waned rapidly after the beginning of the conquest of the great Indian empires on the mainland in the early and mid-16th century. All this is not to say that the Castilian monarchy simply gave up its claims to and defense of the islands of the eastern Caribbean. Puerto Ricans, for example, valued the islands immediately to the east of them for their marine resources, particularly the abundant turtles of Santa Cruz. They also fished regularly in the waters of the Virgin Islands. Equally important, Spanish commercial and military interests were aware that their shipping from Spain, from the Canary Islands, Trinidad, St. Martin and other key points to the east had to pass through the waters of the Virgin Islands, which they called "the passage."[3] For these reasons, to say nothing of Spanish imperial pride, a strong interest was maintained in holding dominion over those islands, especially Santa Cruz, due to its size and its potential attractiveness to other colonizing powers.

As a result of these contradictory impulses in Spanish policy, Santa Cruz—as the island was called by most interested parties at that time—

· 43 ·

remained effectively unsettled and undeveloped throughout the last two-thirds of the 16th century and well into the 1620s.[4] Mariners in search of fresh water, timbers and food made occasional stops there, as did pirates in need of a place to hide or a secluded cove along which to careen a vessel for repairs. But no one had come to stay permanently. One witness to this isolation was a French *flibustier* named Fleury, who, in 1619, stopped at the island briefly, during which time one of his men noted in his journal that "cette île quoique fort belle et grande n'est néanmoins point habitée."[5] Two years later, in 1621, another party of Frenchmen visited the island in order to cut wood for the building of a long-boat; they were soon captured by a small force of men from Puerto Rico in two ships, under the command of a certain Pedro Hernández. The Puerto Rican Governor Juan de Vargas wrote to his King that the Frenchmen were "properly punished" for their intrusion, by which he most probably meant execution.[6] The Spanish reputation for guarding their possessions in the Indies with a zealous cruelty came to be as well known in the Virgin Islands as it was elsewhere in the islands.

That, nevertheless, did not deter the visits of foreign ships. In 1629, Monsieur de Cahusac, Général de L'Armée Navale of France, set sail from St. Christopher on a long voyage to the Western Caribbean, planning to make a stop in Santa Cruz along the way for the purpose of taking on fresh water. He arrived at the island after a day's sail and found three or four "belles rivières" which supplied him with the "très bonne eau" that he had come for. He also noted that even though Santa Cruz had very attractive flat land and good water, it was nonetheless uninhabited.[7] These relatively uneventful episodes are instructive on two counts. First, they explain why anyone would go to Santa Cruz in the 1620s in the first place, namely to cut the island's virgin timbers for maritime uses, as well as to take on fresh water. Second, and perhaps more significant, they reveal that the French were aware of this large fertile island lying just within the Puerto Rican orbit and esteemed it long before they made any serious attempt to plant a settlement there some thirty years later, at mid-century. Nevertheless, Spain was both willing and still able to make anyone who dared to venture into their domains pay dearly for their interloping, and as a direct result, Santa Cruz remained for the time uninhabited. But that would not be the case for long.

Active European interest in and settlement of Santa Cruz began in the early 1630s.[8] Sometime in 1631, a band of English settlers from Barbados landed on the island and established small plantations, with the intention of growing tobacco and subsistence crops.[9] The inspiration behind the settlement was Henry Hawley, the English governor of Barbados (1629–1641), who sent one of his brothers, perhaps William Hawley, who became Santa Cruz's first English governor. The immediate impetus behind the undertaking had most probably been the local factionalism and quarreling resulting from the confusion surrounding the proprietary grant to Barbados, which disrupted the regular planting and led to food shortages.[10] However that may have been, four months after the Hawley-led band of Barbadians had landed on Santa Cruz, the Governor of Puerto Rico, Enrique de Sotomayor, took cognizance of the English interlopers and challenged their presence by dispatching a small force of his men to dislodge them. The Spaniards attacked the English settlement, uprooted its crops and shipped the lot of the intruders off to Puerto Rico as prisoners.[11] Once that task had been accomplished, however, the Spaniards returned forthwith to Puerto Rico, showing no inclination for establishing a settlement of their own on Santa Cruz. This Spanish practice of driving interlopers from Santa Cruz but failing to secure the island with a settlement of their own, or at the very least protecting it with a garrison, was one that was repeated on several other occasions between 1631 and 1650, never failing in the process to attract other bands of would-be Crucians to the apparently neglected, vacant island.

Word of the Spanish attack travelled quickly through the islands. A short time later, in 1632, the first group of Frenchmen arrived to attempt a permanent settlement on Santa Cruz. Receiving intelligence of these events, the vigilant Governor Sotomayor once again sent a small force to the neighboring island, this time one of some forty men. The Spanish soldiers successfully engaged the Frenchmen, killing ten of them, capturing ten, and proceeding to burn their crops and dwellings.[12] The French were not to pose another serious threat to the island until 1650.

The gravest challenge to Spanish control of Santa Cruz during the 1630s occurred in late 1634 or early 1635 with the arrival of a considerable force of Englishmen from Tortuga (Ile de la Tortue), just off the northern coast of Hispaniola. Those Englishmen had been living for a short time on the latter island when they were attacked there in 1634 by a Spanish force of four vessels and several hundred men. The attackers succeeded in routing the English settlement on Tortuga and in killing or capturing a good number of the settlers. Nevertheless, some were able to flee, and those survivors found their way to Santa Cruz shortly after the attack.[13] But, as usual, their presence did not go unnoticed. About one year later, in March of 1636, the new Governor of Puerto Rico, Ixigo de la Mota Sarmiento, mustered twenty soldiers on a single vessel and assaulted the latest group of interlopers to try to settle the island. During the fierce fighting, forty Englishmen were slain and some others were taken captive. Word of this latest Spanish fury was quickly carried to all corners of the Caribbean, and for the next several years, the island remained peacefully vacant and nominally Spanish.[14]

Sometime during the 1630s, Santa Cruz attracted the attention of the Dutch, particularly certain Zeelanders, and this interest was to have both immediate and long-term consequences for the island's fortunes.[15] The United Provinces had gained virtual independence from the Spanish Habsburgs in 1609 in the Twelve Years Truce. Among other things, this led to a reorganization and reorientation of Dutch overseas trade and commerce, an event that was manifest in the formation of the Dutch East India Company (1602) and the Dutch West India Company (1621–1674).[16] In light of the subsequent Dutch activity on Santa Cruz, it is worth noting here that the West India Company was organized into five sections or chambers, namely Amsterdam, The Maas (Meuse),

Zeeland, The Northern Quarter, and Friesland, along with Groningen. Representatives of the five chambers met in a body called the Heren XIX, which acted as a general board of directors of the company. To this body was added one member from the Staten Generaal.

The various chambers of the company were invested with the power to initiate commercial activity in the form of the so-called "Patron Rights." These rights, partly feudal and partly mercantilist, were granted to an individual who proposed to colonize a particular area. In order to obtain this grant and launch the enterprise, the "Patron" had to acquire the necessary capital and the material wherewithal, activities that ordinarily entailed the formation of a small joint-stock company. Having cleared these initial hurdles, the Patron then obtained the services of a commander, whose task it was to select the colonial area, to plant the settlement, and to oversee its effective development and operation. This commission normally carried with it the additional tasks of acquiring and outfitting a vessel, enlisting colonists, planning and leading the voyage, initiating the settlement, establishing its defenses, promoting agriculture and exporting of colonial products back to the United Provinces through the province of Holland. It was particularly important that the commander make certain that the trade of the new colony be directed exclusively back to the mother country. Such were the arrangements that knitted the commercial activities of the West India Company to the interest of the nascent Dutch republic in the early seventeenth century. And for a short but very intense period, the distant island of St. Croix played a small role in these affairs.

In 1635, Jan Snouck, a seaman and man of commerce from Vlissingen (Flushing), which was an important seaport and commercial town in the province of Zeeland, located on the island of Walcheren on the estuary of the Schelde River, obtained permission from the Zeeland Chamber to plant a colony in the West Indies, presumably on one of the smaller islands which had not as yet been taken by any of the other European nations.[17] Armed with this Patron grant, he enlisted the service and financial support of two other merchants of Vlissingen,

Abraham van Pere, Sr. and Pieter van Rhee. Together they obtained a vessel and recruited a certain Pieter van Corselles to act as their commander. Finally, they recruited forty odd settlers from the province and embarked them on their small vessel to the West Indies, under the command of Corselles. Their island of choice was Santa Cruz (Sint Kruis), also known to some Dutch at that time as Nieuwe Zeeland.[18]

For some unknown reason, the little expedition apparently turned away from its intended destination. If, in fact, it arrived in the early part of the year, then the island was most probably still occupied by the previously-mentioned group of Englishmen from Tortuga. On the other hand, it may just as well have arrived after the Spanish attack and veered away to look for a safer haven. In any event, the small Vlissingen expedition called at several other islands before stopping at St. Eustatius. The rolling hills and flat, fertile land of Santa Cruz, however, had made a strong impression on the Zeelanders, which, in time, would lure them back to make two other attempts at planting a settlement there. In 1637 and 1638, the Governor of Puerto Rico wrote to his sovereign in Spain that Santa Cruz was being threatened "by enemies."[19] Although it is not quite clear if the Dutch figured among those enemies, it is certain that some Englishmen on the island of St. Kitts entertained similar plans and were, moreover, disposed to take action.

Sometime in the early 1640s, an English gentleman by the name of William Caverly approached the Earl of Carlisle, holder of the well-known grant to the "Caribby Islands" from King James I, with a proposal to settle numerous islands in the Lesser Antilles; as a result of that meeting, Caverly obtained the governorship of "Sancta Cruse." Shortly thereafter, perhaps in 1640, or early 1641, Caverly departed England in the company of his wife Elisabeth Teresa Rockwood for the distant English colony of St. Christopher. After a difficult voyage, the Caverlys were received warmly in St. Christopher by Governor Thomas Warner, who immediately recognized the Caverly commission from the Earl. Caverly then met a certain Mr. Brainsby, a man of some experience in the islands. In fact, he had already served as the leader of an English group that had occupied Santa Cruz for a brief span at the behest of Governor Warner, perhaps in the late 1630s or even as late as 1640.[20] Recognizing Brainsby's qualifications, Caverly straightaway made him his deputy in charge of settling Santa Cruz. Sometime in 1641, he dispatched Brainsby with a small force of men to take possession of the island that lay some 300 miles due west, an easy voyage of several days duration under normal conditions of prevailing winds and currents. Quietly, Caverly's charges took possession of Santa Cruz with no direct opposition from Puerto Rico and occupied the island in peace for some fourteen months.[21]

In the meantime, Snouck and his little group of Zeelanders on St. Eustatius still eyed Santa Cruz with interest. In 1641, Snouck obtained a written charter from the Zeeland Chamber, giving him rights to "St. Cruis or also Nieuwe Zeelant," no doubt unaware of English intentions and activities centering on the same island.[22] He wasted no time in appointing a certain Louis Capoen to be the commander of this new Patron. A modest Dutch contingent, including both Snouck and Capoen, landed on Santa Cruz in 1642 and discovered that the Caverly settlement was already settled on the island.[23]

The events of the ensuing confrontation have always been somewhat confused and unclear. According to the English account of those events, the Dutch invaded, directly attacked their settlement and took control of the island. In a subsequent petition, Lady Caverly, representing her deceased husband's interests, claimed that "Brainsby & his men were sett upon by certaine Zelanders the chiefe of whom were one called Capoone & another called Snooke who landing in the said Isle pistolled the said deputy Governour Brainsby, hanged 11 of his men and forcibly possessing themselves of the said Isle to the detriment of this Commonwealth deprived your petitioners husband of the lawfull government thereof...."[24] This account was corroborated by DuTertre, who wrote that "a quarrel arose between the English and the Dutch, and the Dutch governor killed Sir Braselet [Brainsby], the English governor, in his house." Otherwise the account of DuTertre seems confused in regard to the chronology and the sequence of events, placing this initial clash in 1645.

The Dutch newcomers then took command of the fort—such as it was and probably located at Salt River—and proceeded to assert their authority over the entire island. Brutal they may have been, but foolish they were not. Since European settlers were always just as difficult to attract to uncleared islands as they were essential in developing them, the new masters of the place permitted some of the Englishmen to remain on the island, provided that they agree to submit to Dutch authority. Learning of these changes, some Frenchmen from the French part of St. Christopher—nearly all of them deserters—likewise were permitted by the Dutchmen to settle there. The numbers of the Frenchmen quickly grew to some 100 to 120 settlers.[25] In a short time, Englishmen and Irishmen, most probably from the English portion of St. Christopher, trickled into the island until their numbers grew to approximately 300 settlers.[26]

But in a short time, both the French and especially the English group grew increasingly dissatisfied with conditions on Santa Cruz, chafing under what they considered to be oppressive treatment on the part of the Dutch. The latter, for example, would not permit English vessels to call at the island. And their governor forced those of other nations to swear an oath of allegiance to the Prince of Orange. For their part, the French had recently come into possession of a fort and were probably beginning to extend their influence over the west end of the island. Perhaps for that reason, the relations between the English and the French were no friendlier than they were with the Dutch.

William Caverly, who had been watching these events unfolding in his erstwhile colony from his vantage point in St. Christopher, died shortly thereafter, leaving his wife and children to contend with the problem of his lost island. Sometime in the first half of 1645, the widow Caverly sailed back to Europe and, armed with the support of the English King and a strong desire to defend her deceased husband's claim, she contacted the English resident representative for the King of England in the Netherlands, a certain Mr. William Boswell, about the matter. Boswell summed up Mrs. Caverly's case in the form of a petition, dated August 26, 1645, and then presented it, along with a letter of his own, of September 2, 1645, to the Committee of Foreign Affairs of the Staten Generaal in the capital. During the month of September, the petition was reviewed by that committee and circulated to the Chamber of Zeeland and the Board of Admiralty of Zeeland. On September 23rd, a report was sent to Mrs. Caverly. Although the exact disposition of the official Dutch response to Mrs. Caverly's claims remains unknown, it is clear that it was not favorable, since the widow was to be found pressing the same claim as late as 1652 in England under the Cromwellian Commonwealth. However, the heart of the matter had long been rendered moot by events that transpired on Santa Cruz seven years previously.

Matters on the troubled island of Santa Cruz came to a head about half-way through the year 1645. A certain Englishman who visited the island in July of that same year wrote to his cousin, the illustrious John Winthrop, Jr. of New England, that "The Dutch and French did grievously (as the English say) oppresse the English, would not suffer any English vessell to com [sic] and trade at the Iland [sic]. Now the land was first the Englishes, whereupon they sett upon the French with a fury, putt them to the worst, and sent them all off the Iland. They sett likewise upon the Dutch, tooke their fort their Governour was kilt with a wound, and so they now have the whoole Iland in possession, and have received a Governor."[27] Again DuTertre confirms the general contours of these events in writing that "they (i.e., the English and the Dutch) clashed and in a furious battle the Dutch governor was so grievously wounded that he died of his wounds in a few days." The unfortunate Dutch governor was none other than Louis Capoen. DuTertre goes on to say that the Dutch appointed another governor, who was, however, soon arrested by the English and condemned to be executed for the murder of Brainsby. It was in this manner that the approximately three-year dominion of the Dutch over Santa Cruz came to an abrupt and humiliating end.

Fearing the worst from the sudden changes of fortune, the French colonists petitioned the English governor for permission to take their leave and withdraw to some nearby French colony. This they were granted. They immediately struck a deal with a certain Thomas Paul, an English sea captain whose vessel happened to be riding at anchor at Santa Cruz as these events transpired. The anxious French promised him several plantations under cassava cultivation in exchange for their passage, along with their equipment and arms, to Guadeloupe. The antipathy of the departing Frenchmen toward the English was such that upon their arrival at Guadeloupe in the month of July, they prevailed upon the governor of that island, Monsieur Houel, to arrest the hapless Captain Paul for the mistreatment which, according to their testimony, they had received at the hands of the Englishmen on Santa Cruz. All too happy to oblige them, the governor imprisoned Captain Paul and sold off his cargo in order to remunerate his newly arrived settlers. He kept Paul's sailing vessel for himself.

According to both Dutch and Spanish testimony, the head of the new English colony was no less a personage than James Ley, the Earl of Marlborough. It is unlikely, however, that Marlborough himself remained on the island for long, for the same visiting Downing noted that the governor of the Santa Cruz settlement was not in fact the Earl of Marlborough but rather a certain Major Reynoulds. Making a trip through the English islands of the West Indies that lasted from February to July of 1645, Downing arrived from St. Christopher in the last month of his visit to "Santa Cruce, where two English vessels were riding which had then brought Major Reynoulds thither to be governor."[28] In all likelihood, Marlborough, no doubt deeply preoccupied with the course of events in the conflict between King and Parliament in England, could not have entertained serious plans of remaining completely out of contact in an island as isolated as Santa Cruz. More than likely, he simply appointed Reynoulds to travel to Santa Cruz in order to act in his stead.

It was now the turn of the Dutch settlers to lodge a complaint.

Across the Atlantic, in the province of Zeeland, a Dutch vessel, *The Nieuwe Walcheren*, made port on September 18, 1645, after a voyage from the West Indies, carrying those same Dutch settlers who had recently been driven from Santa Cruz by English arms. The aggrieved would-be colonists hastened to present their version of the recent events to the company and sought redress in the matter of their losses. Several leaders from the erstwhile settlement—possibly Snouck himself—were on board the returning vessel, and they reported that they had been "overpowered by a force of Englishmen and Irishmen from St. Christopher."[29] This event occurred most probably in May or June of 1645, though the complainants specified no exact date. They stated that the Englishmen "killed Capoone, drove out the French and then appointed an English nobleman called 'Marlberi' as their governor," the latter a well-known English nobleman and royalist, the Earl of Marlborough. As their governor had been slain in the fight with the English, the aggrieved Dutchmen requested the appointment of a new commander for the colony without delay. Evidently, they were optimistic about regaining what they had lost. Finally, they requested that the Staten Generaal boycott for the present time any Dutch trade coming from Santa Cruz, that is to say, any other Dutch merchants who might deal with the English on that island and transport their produce to Europe.

All these actions made it quite clear that the patrons were looking to their government for immediate support and that they had every intention of attempting to recoup their losses, which were considerable if their claim that they had paid "twee tonnen gouds" (two barrels of gold) for the island is to be believed.[30] Clearly, they wanted to reestablish the settlement. On October 5, the Company finally reacted with the appointment of Claes Jochumsen as the new commander for Santa Cruz.[31] But as late as November 23, little else had actually transpired; the Company, officials wrote, were still holding the matter under advisement.[32] The hard reality was, however, that the Patron of "St. Kruis" had been lost for good and that effective Dutch control of the contested island had already come to an end.

For their part, the English were not to enjoy their prize for long. The rapid growth of the colony over the subsequent five years aroused the usual concerns among the Spaniards in Puerto Rico, who, aroused from their passivity, took effective action. A sizable force was dispatched to Santa Cruz on August 10, 1650, and after much loss of life the English were dislodged from their holdings and forced to evacuate the island.

Having received news of the complete defeat of the English on Santa Cruz, some of the Dutch on St. Eustatius reasoned that the Spaniards would follow their customary pattern and withdraw their forces back to Puerto Rico, leaving the island deserted once again. They forthrightly loaded soldiers and a commissioned governor on two vessels which were lying in the roadstead at St. Eustatius and dispatched them to Santa Cruz. Upon arrival there they disembarked just inside the harbor beneath the Spanish fortification, assuming the place to be abandoned. Their assumptions, however, were incorrect, for some sixty Spanish soldiers sallied from the fort and laid into them with a hail of gunfire. That fusillade killed a number of the Dutchmen; others were captured and the few remaining survivors were driven into the forests into hiding. In this manner, the final Dutch attempt to possess Santa Cruz ended in a complete debacle. Had they laid their plans with greater caution and been more circumspect, they might well have at least had some chance of succeeding, for shortly thereafter, in September of 1650, a force of Frenchmen from St. Christopher, under orders from Chevalier de Poincy himself, attacked the same Spanish garrison and defeated it, thereby taking effective control of Santa Cruz, renaming it Ste. Croix and beginning a period of French dominion that would last until 1734. This brought to an end twenty years of desultory jockeying for position among the English, Dutch and French in the quest to take control of an island that, by the legal reasoning of the day, belonged to Spain.

The historical documentation provides little indeed concerning the manner in which the Dutch settlers on St. Croix actually went about developing the island's resources and managing its external commerce. A limited understanding can be had, however, from a variety of indirect means, most prominently the following: the study of several extant maps;[33] a consideration of the island's geography and the general lay of the land; and an analysis of the subsequent settlement patterns of the island, about which a good deal more is known. The inferences drawn from these resources provide the basis for the following general comments.

It would be overly optimistic to expect even the industrious Dutch to have accomplished much in their less than three-year tenure on the island. It is fairly probable that their principal area of settlement lay between the site of present-day Christiansted and the Salt River Basin to the west, that is, the narrow but fertile plain on the north coast of the island, where hills of 300 feet elevation slope down to the sea. Given the nature of the terrain in that part of the island and the presence of dense vegetation—both of which would have rendered transport difficult under the best conditions—the first Dutch plantations must have been situated in that north shore area, hard by the two usable harbors. In addition to the proximity to shipping, the area offered rich soils and a relatively accessible water supply.

Agriculture was the main economic activity in the colony, as it was in the other Dutch colonies in the West Indies at that time. Their principal crop was tobacco, but before extensive plantings could be made, the dense vegetation, consisting of heavy underbrush and large trees, had to be cleared away. Then the virgin earth had to be prepared, a work that proceeded as the unaccustomed Dutch settlers contended with the usual tropical hardships—insects, the tropical sun, periodic torrential rains, seasonal storms and hurricanes, and rather drastic dietary changes. Their labor force consisted of some free farmers, a few bondmen and a limited number of African slaves. The settlement on St. Croix was most probably not exempt from the high mortality rates among European in the fledgling colonies at that time. Moreover, that fact is the most likely cause for the readiness of the Zeelanders to allow foreigners—in this case their foremost rivals, the English, and the French—to live and work alongside them in their new colony. African slaves were highly prized but equally highly-priced, and this explains why the struggling settlers had so few of them in the 1640s.

Commerce was concentrated at the two north side ports—one at the reef-enclosed windward harbor at present Christiansted and the other in the Salt River estuary. Dutch ships from Zeeland and from other Dutch colonies in the West Indies and in North America appeared in the small harbors from time to time, bringing foodstuffs, building materials, and miscellaneous items such as official correspondence, orders, news and mail for the most part.[34] These vessels also provided the only means of transportation, bringing newcomers for the settlement and transit visitors bound for other colonies. As a consequence of these modest agricultural and maritime activities, small settlements apparently formed in the two port areas. Though the building efforts of the Zeeland settlers were modest and limited by any standard, the colonists did manage to construct a church not far from the harbor at later Christiansted.[35] And, of course, they constructed and maintained a fort—Fort Flamand—on the western shore of the Salt River estuary.[36] Beyond these few known structures, very little else has survived to mark the Dutch tenure on Santa Cruz.

The subsequent English colony on St. Croix was short-lived; the English settlers were expelled by a Spanish force from Puerto Rico in 1650. The island was seized later that same summer, in September, by a French force dispatched by Chevalier De Poincy from St. Christopher. French settlers from St. Christopher removed to St. Croix in September of 1650 and planted a permanent settlement, thereby blocking any further Dutch attempts. The island remained a French colony for the next 83 years, until it was effectively abandoned in 1696 and later sold to Denmark in 1733. Nevertheless, the Dutch influence did not end, neither in St. Croix nor in the Virgin Islands. Individual Dutch settlers had made a place for themselves in St. Thomas after the Danes established a permanent settlement there in 1672, on St. Croix under the French during the period 1650 to 1696, and again on St. Croix after the Danes purchased it in 1733. In fact, in all of the islands of the Danish West Indies, including St. John, individual Dutchmen and their families continued to thrive throughout the entire colonial period, making a strong contribution to the growth and development of the three islands in the 17th and 18th centuries. It is indicative of the continuing Dutch presence and influence that the *lingua franca* of the Danish West Indies down to the middle of the 19th century was neither Danish nor English but Dutch Creole. But that is another story. As a nation and as a colonizing power, the Dutch never again posed a serious threat to retake the island of St. Croix once they had lost it in 1645.

NOTES

1. I would like to thank Louisa Balk of the Algemeen Rijksarchief in 's-Gravenhage and R.C. Hol of the Rijksarchief in Zeeland, at Middelburg, both in The Netherlands, and Rosario Parra of the Archivo General de Indias in Seville, Spain for their assistance in procuring the archival documents without which this paper would not have been possible.

2. Arnold R. Highfield, *St. Croix 1493: An Encounter of Two Worlds* (St. Thomas: The Virgin Islands Humanities Council, 1995).

3. The importance of the "pasaje" in Spanish navigation is clearly spelled out by Fray Tomás de la Torre, who observed: "Yendo así un domingo en la tarde fuimos a pasar por un lugar que los marineros llaman el Pasaje y entre unas hermosas islas, una está a la mano izquierda que llaman Santa Cruz y a la derecha están muchas que llaman las Vírgenes; y por medio de ellas pasan los navíos . . ." in his *Diario del Viaje de Salamanca a Ciudad Real, 1544–1545.* Reprinted in José Luis Martinez, *Pasajeros de Indias: Viajes transatlánticos en el siglo XVI* (Madrid: Alianza Editorial, S. A., 1983), p. 257.

4. Richard Hakluyt, *John White's Journal of his voyage to Virginia in 1587, with three ships carrying the second colony to the New World. In Discoveries of the English Nation* v. 7 (New York: Augustus M. Kelley Publishers, 1969), pp. 387 and 406–409.

5. Jean-Pierre Moreau, ed., *Un flibustier français dans la mer des Antilles 1618–1620. Relation d'un voyage infortuné fait aux Indes occidentales par le capitaine Fleury avec une description de quelques îles qu'on y rencontre, recueillie par l'un de ceux de la compagnie qui fit le voyage* (Paris: Seghers, 1990), p. 248.

6. [Juan de Vargas to the King, 19 de abril 1622] *Archivo General de Indias,* 156. (Hereinafter referred to as *AGI.*) There is evidence for similar Spanish attacks in

the Virgin Islands as well. See Aimery Caron and Arnold R. Highfield, eds., *Jean-Baptiste DuTertre on the French in St. Croix and the Virgin Islands: A Translation with Introduction and Notes.* Ocassional Paper No. 4 (St. Thomas: Department of Conservation and Cultural Affairs, Bureau of Libraries, Museums and Archaeological Services, 1978), pp. 8–12.

7. *Archives des Affaires Etrangères, Fonds Amérique,* no. 4, folio 69. Mention is also made of this voyage in DuTertre, *Histoire générale des Antilles* (Paris: Th. Jolly 1667-1671), I, pp. 25–27.

8. It is sometimes written that the earliest European settlement of St. Croix occurred in 1625; however, it would appear that the only evidence for that date comes from Bryan Edwards' *History, Civil and Commercial, of the British Colonies in the West Indies* (London: 1794), v. 1, p. 184, who in the two later editions of his book (i.e., 1795 and 1801) changed the date to 1635 (see p. 183 of those editions). In support of the later date, we have already heard the testimony of Monsieur de Cahusac that the island was uninhabited in 1629. Edward's original error most probably occurred due to a misreading of the settlement of Englishmen from Tortuga in 1635; whatever the case, the incorrect date has been passed along by subsequent writers.

9. For the best existing treatment of this early period of settlement of St. Croix, see Alfredo E. Figueredo, "The Early European Colonization of St. Croix (1621–1642)," *Journal of the Virgin Islands Archaeological Society* 6 (1978): 59–63; this account was also printed in the *St. Croix Avis* (July 7, 1980), p. 9.

10. See Hilary Beckles, *A History of Barbados from Amerindian settlement to nation-state* (Cambridge: Cambridge University Press, 1990), pp. 7–10.

11. For the Spanish attack, see Figueredo (1978).

12. *Ibid.*

13. [John Milton] *Scriptum Dom. Protectoris Reipublicæ Angliæ, Scotiæ, Hiberniæ &c Ex Consensu atque sententia Concilii Sui Editum In quo hujus Reipublicæ Causa contra Hispanos justa esse demonstratur* (London: H. Hills and J. Field, 1655), pp. 541 and 545.

14. Figueredo (1978).

15. For a masterful study of the Dutch in the West Indies, see Cornelius Goslinga, *The Dutch in the Caribbean and on the Wild Coast, 1580–1680* (Assen, 1971). Also W.R. Menkman, *De Nederlanders in het Caraibisch zeegebied, waarin vervat de geschiednis der Nederlandsche Antillen* (Amsterdam, 1942). See also Ypie Attema, *St. Eustatius: A Short history of the island and its monuments* (The Netherlands: De Walberg Pers Zutphen Holland, 1976).

16. For an overview of Dutch overseas commerce and expansion, see C.R. Boxer, *The Dutch Seaborne Empire, 1600–1800* (London: Penguin Books, 1990).

17. "Resolutions of the Zeeland Chamber," *Oude West-Indische Compagnie,* 22, December 27, 1635.

18. Goslinga, pp. 261–62; also Attema, pp. 16–17.

19. "Carta del Gobernador de Puerto Rico, March 27, 1637 and July 20, 1638." *AGI 156.*

20. It is possible that this was "the enemy" threat referred to by the Governor of Puerto Rico in his correspondence to the King in 1637 and 1638. See AGI, 156.

21. Nearly all we know of the English position in these years comes down to us in the form of a petition that Lady Caverly made to the Dutch government in September of 1645 on her husband's behalf, demanding satisfaction for her husband's loss of the island of St. Croix at the hands of Dutchmen. "To the right honorable Committee for forrein affaires The humble petition of Elizabeth Terresa wife of Colonell [sic] William Caverly Esquier Governor of the Island of Sct. Cruse in the behalfe of her said husband, hee being infirme and beyond the Seas." Copie van Inv. no. 6911, *Archief Collectie States General, Algemeen Rijksarchief* ('s-Gravenhage, The Netherlands). Referred to hereinafter as "the Caverly Petition." The petition was filed by the English resident agent, a certain Mr. William Boswell, along with a cover letter addressed to the "Seignrs Les Estats Generaux des Provinces Unies du Païs Bas." It might be noted in passing here that the petition did not meet with a favorable response from the Dutch at that time, for Mrs. Caverly filed the same petition for a second time in April 14, 1652, on this occasion with the English Committee for Foreign Affairs. In this petition she "prays that in the treaty with the States of Holland, her husband's reparation may be comprised in that due to the Commonwealth" (April 14, 1652), *Calendar of State Papers* (1574–1660): 377.

22. "Minutes of the Staten van Zeeland 1626–1650," p. 301. In *Archives Staten van Zeeland,* nos. 3233–3245.

23. The Dutch version of the story is related in a petition from the investors in the St. Croix expedition, namely: Claeijs Cornelissen Braerkert, alderman of the town of Flushing, Pieter Snellen, Pieter Michelssen, Andries Wisse, Sijmon Been, Pieter Baselier, Daniel du Pire, Cornelis Ceuvelaer, Willem Carker, Claeijs Joachimssen, Daniel Snouck, and Jan Blauwmeulen, to the Directors of the West India Company, which was in session at that time in the town of Middelburg. These men were all merchants from the towns of Vere and Middelburg. See "Edele, Weerdige, Wijse seer Voorstenge Heeren de Bewinthebberen der Geoctroijeerde West Indische Comp[agnie] ter vergaderinge van de XIX [Heer]en jegenwoordich tot Middel[burch] in Zeelandt ("Petition to the Honorable, Worthy, Wise very Provident Gentlemen, the Directors of the Chartered West India Company, present in the Assembly of the Heren XIX at Middleburg in Zeeland) *Staten-Generaal* 5758 II (West Indies).

24. The Caverly petition.

25. Jean-Baptiste DuTertre also recounts a version of this episode, in which the Frenchmen are mentioned; see vol. I, pp. 272–73.

26. Carl and Roberta Bridenbaugh, *No Peace Beyond the Line: The English in the Caribbean, 1624–1690* (New York: Oxford University Press, 1972), p. 21.

27. Sir George Downing to John Winthrop, Jr.: To His Cosen [sic] John Winthrop Esquire these New England," *Winthrop Papers* (The Massachusetts Historical Society, 1945), v. 5, 1645–1649, pp. 42–44. For more on Downing and his travels, see John Beresford, *The Godfather of Downing Street, Sir George Downing, 1623–1684; An Essay in Biography* (Boston and New York, 1925) and *Dictionary of National Biography*.

28. Sir George Downing to John Winthrop, Jr."

29. "Edele, Weerdige, Wijse seer Voorstenge Heeren de Bewinthebberen der Geoctroijeerde West Indische Comp[agnie] ter vergaderinge van de XIX [Heer]en jegenwoordich tot Middel[burch] in Zeelandt," *Staten-Generaal* 5758 II (West Indies).

30. *Ibid.*

31. "Resolutions of the Zeeland Chamber," *Oude West-Indische Compagnie*, 26.

32. *Staten-General* 4845, folio 213.

33. See Alfredo E. Figueredo, "St. Croix Mystery Map Solved," *Information* 11:1 (1986): 1–2. The article is accompanied by a reproduction of the map, showing the fort.

34. "Petition of Captain Adriaan Block," Resolutions of the Zeeland Chamber, *Oude West-Indische Compagnie*, 26. The well-travelled Capt. Block was evidently acquainted with St. Croix as one of his ports of call.

35. "The Dutch had built a beautiful church in the form of a cross on a pleasant eminence on this island. If respecting this sacred sign, which was on the belltower, the Spaniards did not destroy this building. Our own Frenchmen owe this house of prayer to the piety and zeal of a company of merchants from the city of Flessingue; they were the first to inhabit this island under the commission from the States General." Charles-César de Rochefort, *Histoire naturelle et morale des Isles de l'Amerique* (Rotterdam, 1658), v. 2, p. 288.

36. First shown on the so-called Spanish "spy map." See Alfredo E. Figueredo, "St. Croix Mystery Map Solved."

The estate of Governor François DuBois in the 1660s, showing his
château and outbuildings

CHAPTER 6

WHEN ST. CROIX WAS
FRENCH, 1650–1734

THIS COMING MARCH, 2008, will mark 91 years that the
Virgin Islands have been under United States rule. But it has
become an all but forgotten fact that a French flag floated over St. Croix
for 84 years, from 1650 until 1734. How did the French come into possession of our island and what lasting affects has that period of domination
exercised over the long term? An answer to these questions requires a
trip back to the tumultuous 17th century and its world of colonial trade
and politics.

Let us first recall that St. Croix, initially called Santa Cruz, remained
under the nominal domination of Spain from the time of Columbus's
visit to the island in 1493 until 1650. During that century and a half,
Spaniards, however, made no real attempt to establish settlements on
the island but rather were content to use its forests for timbers, its waters
for fishing and its beaches for hunting turtles. At the same time, they
maintained their claim to exclusive ownership. Trespassers and interlopers met with stiff punishments.

Such was the state of affairs toward the end of the 1640s. All the
same, Dutch, French and English settlers all made determined attempts
to take control of Santa Cruz. In 1645, as one example, the English
under the command of the Earl of Marlborough set up the first permanent colony on the island. But in 1650, a Spanish force from Puerto
Rico drove them out and once again took control of their Santa Cruz,
leaving a small garrison behind to discourage any return.

Chevalier de Poincy, an ambitious French nobleman in St. Christophe (St. Kitts), had other plans. He had come to the Caribbean some

years earlier with the objective of building his own colonial empire, in the name of France, of course. Gradually he accumulated a number of islands in the eastern Caribbean, just beyond the reach of Spanish power in the Greater Antilles. In time, he grew bolder as Spanish authority weakened both in Europe and in the Caribbean. Santa Cruz appeared like a plum, ripe to be plucked from the tree.

In 1650, De Poincy sent two ships and several hundred armed men to that island to test the Spanish resolve. Within several days, the Spanish garrison surrendered and left the island. Without the loss of life, Santa Cruz fell into French hands and was renamed Ste. Croix, a name the island has borne from that day to this.

That was just the beginning of the story. What followed was a compendium of conflict, struggle and difficult times. A persistent lack of settlers, inadequate supply lines, difficulty in getting products to market, and the constant fear of attack from Spanish Puerto Rico all contributed to the lean times in the decade that followed, as well as to the development of a negative reputation that discouraged real settlement.

Chevalier de Poincy was a member of the medieval crusading order known as the Knights of Malta, an organization that had great prestige in France at that time and intimate connections with the King. In 1653, when De Poincy became embroiled in a dispute with a high-ranking French nobleman, and it appeared that he might lose all of his possessions in the Caribbean in the inevitable legal wrangling, he moved quickly to transfer his possessions to the Order of Malta, where they would be immune from confiscation. It was in this manner that St. Croix, along with some other islands, came into the possession of the Knights from 1653 until 1664

St. Croix's fortunes began a turn for the better in 1659 with the appointment of Monsieur François DuBois, a young French nobleman, as governor. DuBois made the most of his good connections in St. Christophe to initiate the development of his new island. He brought in new settlers, organized the military, improved shipping, and encouraged the cultivation of sugar at the expense of languishing tobacco. His formula worked and the economy of the island began to grow.

As a sugar-producing island of some size, the importance of St. Croix increased in France. In succession, it was organized as a part of the French West India Company (1664) and later as a royal colony (1674). But with the growth of modest wealth came the opportunity for corruption. Chevalier Antoine DuBois, the brother of François DuBois, succeeded his brother as governor and promptly fell into illegal trading with the Danes in St. Thomas, which cost him both his job and his reputation.

Sugar production had other consequences. It required sizable outlays of labor, which French bondage (engagés) could not supply. Consequently, the French plantations turned to Africa. For the first time, the Senegal Company introduced sizable numbers of slaves into St. Croix from the region of Gorée in West Africa. In a short time, the numbers of the Africans rivaled those of the French.

By the 1680s it appeared to most that St. Croix was French for good. However, Louis XIV's foreign entanglements and wars in that decade and in the one that followed soon set most of the rest of Europe against him and his grand designs. Repercussions of these conflicts were felt as far away as St. Croix. In time, the island was threatened by invasions from various of France's national enemies. And to make matters more precarious, the French military was stretched to the point of being unable to provide the island with adequate defenses.

In 1697, St. Croix was abandoned by the island's French inhabitants. Most of the French Crucians were attracted to the newly acquired and much larger island of St. Domingue, present-day Haiti, when France seized half of that island from Spain. Ships were loaded with settlers, slaves, animals and goods, and the small flotilla sailed off to the western Caribbean. St. Croix was abandoned and so it remained until 1733. But it was not deserted. Several hundred, poor English settlers from the Eastern Caribbean and from the British Virgin Islands came to cut wood, fish and exploit the turtle population.

In the early 1730s, vacant St. Croix sparked the interest of Danish planters and entrepreneurs in St. Thomas, always limited in the amount of sugar they could produce by the rugged terrain. A deal was arranged in 1733 and the island was taken into possession of the Danish West India and Guinea Company in 1734. It is of interest to note that it was reclusive English interlopers who formed the basis of the first Crucian population under Denmark, rendering our history closely related to English from the start in spite of its Danish ownership.

Little of real substance from the French period has directly survived. There is of course the name St. Croix and the division of the island into quarters, as well as the former name for Christiansted, that is "Bazzin" (< Le Bassin) and possibly a few other place names (La Vallée, Mon Bijou, Bonne Esperance etc.). In the broader scheme of things, however, it was the French who were responsible for the founding of the town where Christiansted now stands and the construction of some of its earliest structures, the introduction of sugar cultivation on a significant scale, the building of sugar plantation estates, the introduction of labor directly from Africa, the introduction of the Catholic religion, and the first real development of the island as a non-Hispanic colony. From this perspective, the French period in St. Croix was important indeed.

The standard of the Order of Malta that flew over St. Croix
from 1651 to 1664

CHAPTER 7

THE KNIGHTS OF MALTA ON ST. CROIX

T HE THEME OF ST. CROIX UNDER seven flags is a familiar one with local history buffs. One of those flags is the Maltese Cross, marking the presence of the Order of Malta here from 1651 to 1664. This particular flag has spawned fanciful images of medieval knights, all decked out in breastplate and chain mail, jousting in the lists with their fellows and generally struggling manfully with unnamed malfaiteurs for the honor of God, Church and ladies fair. In spite of the lure that this fantasy might hold for mid-winter visitors, nothing, I'm afraid, could be further from the truth. Nevertheless, the entire episode admittedly lends a certain element of interest to our checkered history.

The original name for this group was the Knights of the Order of the Hospital of St. John of Jerusalem, founded in the eleventh century for purposes of supporting the European crusading effort in the Holy Land, as well as providing support to pilgrims and soldiers struggling along the roads that led to Jerusalem, the eternal city. In time the Order became more military in purpose and organization. These ambitious Knights, however, were expelled from Jerusalem by the great Muslim surge in 1187 along with all the other Crusaders.

In the years that followed, the Order was obliged to seek other quarters. First, they settled in the walled city of Acre in the County of Tripoli but shortly thereafter (1291) were forced to move again, this time to the eastern Mediterranean island of Cyprus. In 1309, they relocated again, on this occasion to the island of Rhodes, which they captured by force of arms and where they constructed massive fortifications that stand as their witnesses to this day. There they maintained a strong presence until 1522, at which time they were expelled by a massive force of Turks under the leadership of Suleiman the Magnificent.

The surviving "Knights of Rhodes" drifted about Europe for some seven years until 1529, when Charles V, the King of Spain, granted them in perpetual fiefdom the western Mediterranean islands of Malta and Gozo, along with Tripoli in North Africa. These renewed "Knights of Malta" occupied their new home but had to repulse repeated attacks from the Ottoman Empire and continue to press their long struggle against the Barbary pirates. For several centuries they steadfastly survived war, reformation and revolution throughout Europe. Through all this turmoil they managed to thrive.

But that came to an end in 1798 when the islands were seized by Napoleon Bonaparte, whose star blazed in a meteoric trajectory across Europe and the Mediterranean. Little could withstand his vaunted ego. However, the Order was allowed to remain on Malta, but it lost its ownership of that island. There it remained to the 20th century, much reduced in power and prestige but still in operation, presently as an international humanitarian organization with headquarters in Rome.

The manner in which the Order of Malta and its Knights came into possession of St. Croix constitutes a short but interesting subtext in their long, tangled history, as well as in ours. To clearly understand these events we must first have a glimpse at the history of the French in the West Indies in the early 17th century. Although Frenchmen had been active in the Caribbean since the 16th century, it was not until a certain Chevalier de Poincy appeared in the islands in 1639 that their colonizing effort was given any direction and staying-power. An avid expansionist, he seized island after island as his private possessions, including St. Croix in 1650. Chevalier de Poincy was, as chance had it, a Knight in the Order of Malta as well, but at the beginning he kept his personal interests and possessions clearly apart from those of the Order, at least until it became advantageous to cease doing so.

That arrangement came to an abrupt end in 1651 when a certain powerful French lord, Monsieur de Thoisy, lodged a suit in Paris against

Poincy that threatened to cost him his fortune and his properties in the West Indies. Very shrewdly, however, Poincy ceded his lands to the Order of Malta, knowing that it was exempt from legal action, while at the same time remaining in charge of those possessions under a special arrangement with title granted by the Order. It was in this manner that all of Poincy's West Indian islands fell under the Maltese Cross from 1651 until 1665.

In effect, however, not a great deal changed as a result of the transfer. Poincy remained in absolute control of his islands, including St. Croix, until his death in 1658. The Order did send out several Knights, including Chevalier Charles Huault de Montmagny, receiver of the Priory of France. He was to act as a watchdog for the Order's interests until Poincy died. Chevalier de Montmagny, however, died first, rather unexpectedly in 1657.

St. Croix, in particular, experienced very difficult times under Poincy's control during the early hegemony of the Order. Ships arrived infrequently, tobacco was transported irregularly, indentured labor was hard to come by, slaves were very rare, famine threatened periodically, and settlers occasionally abandoned the island. And then there was the constant threat from Spanish forces in nearby Puerto Rico. Due to St. Croix's location on the periphery of the other French West Indian islands, neither Poincy nor the Order of Malta was much inclined to invest a great deal to remedy such problems. So St. Croix struggled along as best it could.

After Poincy's death in 1658, Commander de Sales, a Knight of Malta and nephew of the illustrious François de Sales, exercised authority over the Order's holdings in the Caribbean. After death had loosened Poincy's tight grip on his possessions, St. Croix, under the Order's looser control, entered its first stage of real development. Plantations were increased in number, population gradually grew, tobacco was successfully cultivated and the first sugar crops began to appear.

In addition, Commander de Sales liberalized trade policies and reappointed an effective François DuBois to the governorship of St. Croix.

He also extended a ten-year contract to the Dominican Order to provide religious and social services among the islands. The economy of St. Croix slowly improved though the Order complained rather bitterly about their obligation to assume the deceased Poincy's considerable debts, which he had apparently not made known to them when he invited them to take over.

In the 1660s, under Louis XIV's economic minister Colbert, France developed a determination to pull its economic resources together under a policy of strict central control called mercantilism. For the West Indian islands, St. Croix included, it was decided to create a mercantilist company and through it purchase all the islands under French dominion. One by one, the royal authority forced proprietors to sell their islands at bargain prices. The Order of Malta was no exception.

But the Order of Malta was reluctant to sell, citing the money it had invested in running the islands, to say nothing of paying off Poincy's considerable debts. In the end, the Crown prevailed, buying all the Order's French West Indian islands for 500,000 *livres tournois*, about half the Order's asking price. The Order quietly absorbed the loss. In December of 1665, a certain Monsieur DuQuéry, landed in St. Croix and took possession of the island for the newly formed French West India Company, and the last of the Knights departed, bringing an inglorious end to nearly a decade and a half of overlordship by the Order of Malta.

The short period of the Order of Malta in St. Croix was a chance occurrence, having resulted completely from the misadventures of one of the Order's members, Chevalier de Poincy. St. Croix, belonging to Poincy at that moment, just happened to find itself swept up in those events. It is for these curious reasons that the flag of Malta once flew over St. Croix and continues to be honored here on flagstaffs to this day.

The port of Galway from which many Irish lads departed for the West Indies

CHAPTER 8

FROM GALWAY AND CORK TO ST. CROIX: THE IRISH MIGRATION TO ST. CROIX

AT A ST. PATRICK'S DAY parade in Christiansted some years back, I overheard some local folks remark in astonishment that there now seemed to be so many Irish people in St. Croix. Though the annual parade and most of its participants are of recent origin, the Irish are certainly not. In fact, Irishmen made up one of the earliest ethnic groups to become established in St. Croix, as early as the 1640s. That immigration continued down to the end of the 19th century, and, as might be expected, such an early presence and its continuation over a rather lengthy period of time has resulted in a significant impact on our local history and culture.

It was during the period when the island was contested by Dutchmen and Englishmen in the early 1640s that the first of the Irish came to St. Croix. But by 1645, the English won their struggle with the Dutch, only to be thrown out in 1650 by soldiers from Spanish Puerto Rico. In that expulsion the Irish lads departed as well, their compatriots not to return for an entire century. But return they did. The question is, why did so many of them keep coming to Caribbean destinations, as well as, of course, to other New World destinations, to the North American colonies and to various Latin American colonies throughout South America and in the Caribbean?

Under the English boot for centuries, the Irish were subject to numerous economic, social, cultural and religious disabilities in their own homeland. In the 18th century, they were systematically forced off their small landholdings by the great landlords in pursuit of greater wealth.

Disenfranchised and impoverished, the members of the lower orders in Ireland fell victim to hunger, malnourishment and, ultimately, to a variety of diseases. And periodically the blight struck, which resulted in famine and massive dying, especially when combined with the other problems at the same time. For many, the only possible response to these circumstances was simple: emigrate or die. Principal ports that facilitated such departures from the western and southern regions of Ireland were Galway and Kinsale in County Cork.

In the Caribbean, as elsewhere, there were few colonies that welcomed the Irish with open arms, at least outside of the Spanish islands, which were Catholic. In the English Caribbean, which was largely Protestant, the issues of religion, language, lifestyle and culture kept the dominant English and the mostly indentured Irish distrustful of one another and generally at odds. Fearing that the Catholic Irish might unite with the Catholic French in the struggle against the English for hegemony in that realm, especially in St. Kitts, the keystone of the Lesser Antilles, Governor Thomas Warner led a small group of Irishmen in 1631 to the rugged, volcanic Montserrat in order to distance them from the temptation of treasonous uprisings.

Add to that scenario the arrival of Irish political prisoners from the struggles in Cromwellian England (c.1649). In a short time, the island became known as a Catholic refuge in the predominately Protestant Eastern Caribbean. After about a century of Anglo-Irish presence and development by way of exploiting the labor of African slaves and indentured Irish laborers, the Montserratian economy produced its share of functioning plantations, moderate wealth and successful planters.

Although it is often thought to be otherwise, the Irish were not culturally monolithic as a group. In fact, they can be broken down into four major ethnic entities, namely the following: 1. the Native Irish; 2. The Old English; 3. The New English; and 4. the Scottish Presbyterians. Members of all four of these groups found their way to the English islands of the Caribbean—especially Antigua, Nevis, Montserrat and St. Kitts—beginning in the first half of the 17th century.

This cultural diversity largely accounted for the relative complexity of Irish social differentiation in the Caribbean, as well as for distinctions between the rich and the poor among them. And by the middle 1650s, the Irish constituted the dominant European population on Montserrat by an advantage of about seven to one.

In the early 1750s, a number of Irishmen established a foothold on St. Croix in the nearby Danish West Indies. This movement was due mainly to the foresight and leadership of a certain Nicholas Tuite, born of Irish background on Montserrat. But before doing so, he made certain arrangements with the Danish government. First, he promised to introduce about a thousand workers, both slave and free alike into the labor-deficient Crucian economy. In response, the Danish government offered citizenship and promised to allow Catholicism a legal position in the island's religious community. In these developments, Tuite and several other well-to-do Montserratians effected a minor-revolution in St. Croix, which had been predominantly Lutheran from the start of Danish settlement, as well as economically stagnant.

Tuite quickly obtained a dozen or so of the island's finest plantations, including Sion Farm, Cornhill and Concordia. His administration skills and energy soon transformed those properties by means of the importation of a large labor force, the use of Irish overseers, the introduction of broad-scale fertilization, the improvement and increase of sugar production and the significant increase of local wealth.

In so doing, Tuite provided a worthy model for other of the island's planters whose fortunes had previously faltered. Within several years, Tuite was making impressive annual profits, which provided the local economy with the lift-off that it so badly needed. Can it be a coincidence that St. Croix's growth as a profitable colony can be dated from the initial investments of the Irish newcomers?

Tuite's efforts to provide for the religious needs of his new workmen also yielded other impressive results, namely the official acceptance in the Danish West Indies of the Catholic faith (1754), the building of churches and chapels, and the introduction and acceptance of priests.

From that point in time, the Catholic religion grew steadily to become in time the single largest denomination on the island.

But far more fundamental and far reaching was the persistent coalescence of the members of the Irish and African components of the Crucian population, as witnessed by the numerous Celtic family names that abounded everywhere—Armstrongs, Biggs, Blakes, Bradys, Brownes Murphys, O'Reillys, and Simmonds, to name only a few— as well as estate and geographic place names—Tipperary, Longford, Castle Burke, Castle Coakley etc. It would be a mistake indeed to underestimate the breadth of the Irish element in our Afro-Celtic population.

Along with the biological mixing came cultural assimilation as well. The most fundamental and important element in any culture is its language. Who amongst us can fail to see the importance of Crucian speech for our island and for its native Crucians? What has been less evident, however, are the similarities and apparent connections between our speech and that of some parts of Ireland. Many, in fact, are the Crucians who have remarked in astonishment on the intuitive similarities of these two forms of speech after even a short visit to the Emerald Isle.

Some of these connections may in fact account for basic distinctions between Crucian speech and the speech of some of the other islands, especially that of St. Thomas and St. John. One example may not suffice to prove the case, but it certainly points in a very clear direction. Crucian places a yod (a "y " sound) in certain words. One example of this trait occurs in the words car ("cyar"), can't ("cyan") and cart ("cyart") and so forth. And indeed this same phonological trait is shared by the speech of certain parts of Ireland (County Cavan as one striking example). But in St. Thomas where there have been far fewer Irish, the use of this sound marks a speaker as unmistakably Crucian. Other such parallel examples might be readily cited.

In the realm of music and dance there remains the suggestion of Irish traces. The term "jig" refers to a particular kind of local dance step and "to jig" refers to spirited dancing. (Compare "an Irish jig") It appears to this writer that at least some of our Crucian jigs are simply Celtic tunes, transformed slightly and set to lively Ghanaian beats.

By the end of the 19th century as sugar declined precipitously and some estates faltered, as the economy tailed off, and as it became increasingly apparent that the island would sooner or later pass from Danish into American hands, the Irish and Scottish immigration diminished markedly. What had begun in the mid-seventeenth century was by the end of the 19th century clearly a thing of the past.

But at the same time, it became equally clear that the Irish impact on the history and culture of St. Croix over that same period of time has been considerable, first, on the biological level by the introduction of a sizable number of Irishmen who from the 1750s well into the 1890s mixed openly and readily with the local population; second, by the introduction of the Catholic church that rapidly rose to prominence; third, in the advance of plantation economy; fourth, a coalescence in matters of language and popular speech; fifth, in the melding of our music and dance traditions; and sixth, in the introduction of other, new cultural traditions, such as in our story-telling repertoire that benefitted from the Jack and the Devil cycle of stories that at one time circulated widely on the island. The exchange has been an impressive one by any measure.

It has been in this way then that the destinies of the people of two distant islands have embraced in an unexpected manner and quite by chance, leaving us much to take delight in as well as much to puzzle over.

Slave coffle moving from the interior toward the Guinea
coast for sale and transit in the Middle Passage
to the West Indies

The slave ship "Fredensborg" picking up a
cargo of captives at Fort Christiansborg
on the Gold Coast (Ghana)

CHAPTER 9

THE DANISH ATLANTIC AND WEST INDIAN SLAVE TRADE

INTRODUCTION

THE DANISH WEST AFRICAN slave trade began around 1660 and ended in 1807. During those 147-odd years of activity, approximately 120,000 enslaved Africans were transported from West Africa to the Danish sugar producing islands in the West Indies. In addition, many thousands were transshipped from the Danish islands to other destinations—such as Cuba, Puerto Rico, St. Domingue and the thirteen colonies in North America. While this trade promoted agricultural productivity and commercial activity among the Danish islands, it intensified conflict and war among the small states along the "Gold Coast," as well as bringing untold suffering to the unfortunate individuals who were unlucky enough to find themselves enmeshed in it. The objective of this paper is to present an overview of the contours of the Danish slave trade, both from Africa and in the West Indies, for the period in question.[1]

MERCANTILISM

The French model of mercantilism became rather widespread in the nascent European states of the seventeenth century. In this system, a strong centralized state directed the development of the economy in such a way that national industry and commerce produced everything its people needed and then exported the surplus, thereby insuring a flow of bullion into the economy. The goal was the establishment of self-sufficiency and ready reserves of bullion. Hence the name bullionism. After the conquest of the New World and the growth of European demand for tropical products, the need for colonies was perceived, along with thousands of slaves from Africa to make those colonies productive. In theory, trade between these three newly established trade points—Europe, Africa and the colonies—was to be completely sealed and exclusivist.[2] That was the theory at least. The case of Denmark's Atlantic slave trade is illustrative of just how compelling such an idea was in theory but how difficult it was to achieve in practice.

Denmark acquired St. Thomas as its first tropical colony in 1672.[3] On this relatively small, mountainous island, there was little fertile, flat land for sugar production. As a result, the demand for slaves in the first several decades of the new colony remained limited. From the beginning, however, the settlers in St. Thomas made the most of the island's excellent protected harbor and its location at the junction of the Greater and Lesser Antilles. In the 1670s, they developed a transshipment trade with the French settlers in St. Croix, buying sugar and tobacco for shipment to Copenhagen and resale there, in exchange for commodities produced in Europe.[4] Early in its history then St. Thomas became not so much a producer but a handler of commodities. In a short time, the merchants of that island developed a similar "handling" or transit trade in slaves.

The Danish West Indies expanded in 1718 with the annexation of unsettled St. John; this new possession, just a few miles distant from St. Thomas, opened a limited area of land for cultivation and thereby stimulated the need for more slaves. Far more significant, however, was the purchase of St. Croix from France (1733–34), an acquisition that offered thousands of virgin acres of forest for cultivation along with the concomitant need for massive numbers of servile labor.[5] Thereafter the African connection grew increasingly important for Danish enterprise in the West Indies.

The Kingdom of Denmark developed an interest in the slave trade in Africa and in the slave-based plantation economy in the West Indies at about the same time—during the reign of Frederik III in the late 1660s. During that time, the kingdom's political structure became more absolutist and centralized while its economy became more mercantilist.[6]

But it was Dutch mercantile interests that provided the stimulus, first to Sweden and then to Denmark, to begin trading along the Gold Coast, an area from which the aggressive Netherlanders had lately driven the Portuguese.[7] After the Danes had declared war on the Swedes in 1657, they managed to wrest the latter's principal African forts and factories from them and soon thereafter launched their small nation into the "Guinea trade."

It would be a mistake to read into these events an *a priori* "grand design." Danish merchants entered both arenas with an eye simply for acquiring a modest share of the trade and profits—gold, ivory and slaves in Africa and sugar, tobacco, dye woods and cotton from the West Indies. In the early 1670s, however, the complementary nature of the two realms of trade was grasped by high-placed Danish merchants and from that time on, under the direction of various joint-stock managerial schemes, the perceived need for African laborers in the Danish West Indies and their regular supply remained the driving force behind the Danish Atlantic slave trade.

The Glückstadt Company, an enterprise founded on Dutch capital, Dutch trade goods and Dutch expertise, dominated the Guinea trade from 1659 to 1674.[8] At that latter date, the leadership of the newly established Danish West India Company quickly positioned itself to take over the trade, broadening the name to "The Danish West India and Guinea Company." This undercapitalized company limped along until 1689, at which time the Guinea trade was granted exclusively to the wealthy entrepreneur N. J. Arff. The latter met with numerous difficulties and much bad luck, a combination that induced him to give up his exclusive in 1697. These first 38 years of the slave trade produced few profitable results for the investors and even fewer slaves for the new colony at St. Thomas.[9]

In 1697, the Danish West India and Guinea Company decided to re-enter the Guinea slave trade. The Danish toe-hold in Guinea at that time consisted of two principal forts on the Gold Coast—Christiansborg and Frederiksborg—along with several lodges, or trading stations.

Through the eighteenth century the Danes added new possessions in the area of the Volta River.[10] From these tenuous possessions, the representatives of the Company, backed by a handful of soldiers, carried on trade with various nations, including people of the Akan grouping, principally the Akwamu and the Akim. From Denmark, company ships brought trade items such as cloth, clothing, hats, spirits, flintlocks, powder and other items which they exchanged for ivory, gold and slaves. These "commodities" they held in the fort until a company ship arrived from Denmark to carry the enslaved Africans to the West Indies and the other items ultimately back to Denmark. However, the Company's African trade was hardly a model of efficiency. In the early eighteenth century, one ship arrived on the average every three years. And even this desultory commerce was frequently disrupted by any one or several of the following: local wars, opposition from local kings, disease, attacks by both pirates and unfriendly European nations, lack of trade items, scarcity of food, unavailability of ships, natural disasters and the like.

After a brief interruption of African activities in the 1730s, the Danish West India and Guinea Company underwent reorganization in 1747 and thereafter continued its operations along the Gold Coast until 1754.[11] At that time the company was dissolved and its possessions reverted to the Crown. Until 1766, the Guinea trade was thrown open to all Danish subjects, provided they did business in registered Danish vessels and carried slaves exclusively to the Danish West Indies. In 1766, an exclusive charter was granted to Henning F. Bargum, who first operated under the name "The Royal Chartered Danish Guinea Company" (*Det Kongeligt oktrojerede danske guineiske Kompagni*) and later "The Bargum Trading Society" *(Det bargumske Handelssocietet)*. This society traded in slaves to the Danish West Indies for nine years and then in 1775 fell upon economic difficulties. The Guinea operation reverted once again to the Crown and was managed through a royal administrative board until 1781.[12]

The boom times that occurred in the period of the American Revolutionary wars and following led to the foundation of yet another slave-trading company, the Baltic-Guinea Company (*Det østersøske-guineiske Kompagni*) in 1781. Under royally imposed mercantilistic sanctions, the company assumed possession of facilities on the Gold Coast and began to ship slaves to the West Indies. Although trade was brisk in the 1780s, this was the last Danish company to do business in Guinea under an official royal grant, for already in the late 1780s the Danish government had begun consideration of the abolition of the slave trade.

In March of 1792, the Danish government promulgated an edict to abolish the Danish African slave trade to go into effect at the end of 1802 (i.e., 1803).[13] Most authorities agree that Danish policy makers were acting in anticipation of a similar move by Britain, an event that was postponed due to the radical turn of events in the French and Haitian revolutions in the early 1790s.[14] The Danish authorities reasoned that open importation of slaves over the following ten-year period, coupled with amelioration of slave conditions, would provide a stable labor force for the planters in the Danish West Indies, based on procreation rather than purchase, into the foreseeable future. And so occurred the compelling irony that shortly after the abolition of the trade had been decided upon, the exportation of "Negroes from Danish Guinea" was thrown open to merchants of all nations with few restrictions, whereupon slaving in the Danish West Indies reached its peak. Eventually, the Danish Atlantic slave trade came to an official end in 1803. But not quite. There continued a transit trade, principally at St. Thomas, until 1807, in which slaves were transshipped from there to the Western Caribbean, primarily to the Spanish colonies. The *de facto* end came in 1807 when the British navy seized the Danish islands for the second time in less than a decade and on that occasion imposed the Imperial British abolition.

THE AFRICAN CONNECTION

The Danish West African slave trade can be considered as both an export and import commercial activity, and in neither case was it a simple matter.[15] The trade began on the Gold Coast when Danish merchants in the forts purchased prisoners from local dealers or from kings and then secured those unfortunates as "commodities" in the forts. In theory, company officials then waited for company ships to arrive and transport the human cargoes to the Danish West India colonies. That wait was at times a prolonged one due to the chronic shortage of company ships. Sometimes the business did work according to plan, sometimes not. On some occasions there were not enough slaves on hand with the result that an arriving slave ship was forced to wait weeks, perhaps even months. Rather than wait, company ships would often sail further east along the coast, completing the cargo as supply at other locations permitted. The point is that the Guinea component of the trade infrequently worked according to a neatly preconceived plan.[16]

Danish slave ships, whether they secured their cargoes at Danish installations or elsewhere, most usually sailed to the Danish West Indies. The port of preference appears to have been Christiansted, especially in the second half of the eighteenth century. But this was not always the case. Several factors weighed heavily in luring Danish ships from time to time to other West India ports, namely the relative demand for slaves, prices and risk factors. Obviously enough, where prices were high and risk limited, Danish slave ships might venture elsewhere.

When Danish ships did not appear at the Danish forts on schedule, the commandants often sold their supply of slaves, either to private interlopers, who continually cruised the coast in search of bargains, or to the ships of other countries. Just as Danish slave ships did not always carry their enslaved cargoes directly to the Danish West Indies, so the various Danish trading companies on the Gold Coast did not always contract all their slaves to Danish vessels.[17] Again, it is clear that the Guinea operation was never an exclusive, closed Danish system, established and operated on strict mercantilistic principles.

The Danish Atlantic slave trade was chronically limited by a lack of operational vessels. Under ordinary circumstances, there might be as many as three to four ships in operation at any one given time. This limited the volume of the Danish trade, especially when compared to more advanced trading nations like England, France and the Netherlands.

The largest of the Danish ships could accommodate 400 to 600 slaves; the smaller ones, up to 100, though these were considered unprofitable.[18] The average for ships in the eighteenth century on strictly statistical grounds was in the vicinity of 200 individuals per ship. A voyage of three to four months duration was typical for the late eighteenth century; most were even longer.[19] Ships leaving Christiansborg sailed eastward along the Guinea coast through the Bay of Biafra to the Portugese islands of São Tomé and Príncipe near the equator. Dropping down several degrees below the equator, they picked up favorable winds and currents that carried them out into the Atlantic on a northwesterly course toward the West Indies. The mid-Atlantic current bore them through the Doldrums in the absence of the usual prevailing winds. The ships normally arrived in the West Indies near the island of Antigua, thereafter laying a course between that island and nearby Montserrat, skirting to the south of Nevis, St. Christopher, St. Eustatius and Saba on a due westerly course to the Danish islands.[20]

During these voyages, the mortality rate among the slaves below deck might range as high as 13%. That rate was also high among members of the crews, especially during the period of waiting before the ships left the African coast.[21] Shortages of food and water and disease both had a direct bearing on this rate. Nor did the Africans submit docilely to the circumstances of their fate for they rebelled whenever an opportunity presented itself. It appears that at least seven such verified shipboard rebellions occurred on Danish ships in the 18th century.[22]

THE DANISH WEST INDIES

The three West Indian islands of St. Thomas, St. John and St. Croix were the *raison d'être* for the Danish slave trade. St. Thomas and St. John were both small, mountainous islands whose arable land was brought under cultivation not long after their initial settlement. Given the limited size of their plantation economies, their combined slave labor requirements for internal purposes remained low throughout the eighteenth century. In 1791, when Denmark decided to put an end to its slave trade, St. Thomas had just 4,214 slaves and St. John 1,845, only a few of whom had to be replaced on an annual basis due to attrition rates.[23] Slaves were required in this initial enterprise as well as for the subsequent crop expansion. Thereafter there remained a reliance on imports to maintain the population (i.e., to offset deaths against births in the native population). However, the merchants of St. Thomas ultimately adapted their island's most significant physical resource—its harbor—into an instrument for making profit on slaves in yet another way, transshipment. As a result, during the eighteenth century, a substantial, but as yet undetermined, number of slaves arrived in St. Thomas where they were sold onto waiting vessels that carried them to any one of several destinations—North America, the Spanish Main or other West Indian islands.[24]

The nearby island of St. John resembled St. Thomas in several ways, in being both relatively small in size and mountainous. It too had an excellent natural harbor, at Coral Bay, though it never became a factor in the development of the island, curiously enough. Just 15 years after its initial colonization by Denmark, there occurred the slave rebellion of 1733–34 that had the effect of retarding further plantation development.[25] For these reasons both St. Thomas and St. John had a limited need for slaves for internal purposes during the greater part of the eighteenth century.

St. Croix, however, was another story. Larger, flatter and endowed with much more arable land, St. Croix rapidly developed a significant sugar-producing, plantation economy, based in large part on the mass importation of labor from Africa. Christiansted became the major point of entry for those slaves, though Frederiksted also witnessed the arrival of slave ships from Africa. In addition, both these ports attracted local West Indian slave-traders.

Although Christiansted had only a modest, windward harbor, protected marginally by a fringing reef and partially by low headlands, it nevertheless became the island's chief port and entry-way for the slave trade. Frederiksted, with its open roadstead and only fair bottoms, assumed a secondary position. When ships from Guinea arrived, they generally dropped anchor in the Christiansted harbor before the fort. The enslaved were then lightered ashore, assembled in groups beneath the walls of the fort and sold to various planters or their representatives.[26] By the time the enslaved African arrived at the plantation, he might well have already been bought and sold as many as three or four times—first, from a local king or prince to an African dealer, then to a merchant at the Danish fort, then to the captain of a slave ship, and finally to a planter in the islands. At each point in the chain of sales, there was a significant "mark-up." And finally, as we shall see below, that fourth transaction might not have been the end of it, for the Danish islands developed a flourishing export trade in the second half of the eighteenth century.

During the course of the eighteenth century, the island of St. Croix both imported and exported slaves. In the period 1734 to 1754 or thereabouts, the emphasis of colonization was laid squarely on clearing back the forests that had overgrown the island since the French departed in 1696, as well as on the developing of plantations from scratch. During this "take-off phase," the economy, being labor intensive, literally devoured its labor force in the accomplishment of the aforementioned tasks.[27] As a result of these labors, by 1755 some 375 plantations had been laid out and 255 actually occupied; the population grew to 1,323 whites and 8,897 slaves.[28] In the period that followed, various colonial wars disrupted trade among the participants and gave neutral countries and their colonies, such as Denmark and the Danish islands, a golden opportunity to supply the steady metropolitan demand for tropical products. This, of course, required more labor and more labor meant more slaves.

In the period for which we have reliable figures (1766–68, 1770–90, 1799–1800 and 1802), some 30,150 slaves were imported into St. Croix, both directly from Africa and from various islands in the West Indies.[29] Of this number, 20,907, or 69%, came directly from Africa, while 8,444, or 28% came from other West Indian islands. Moreover, the overwhelming majority passed through Christiansted (25,600, or 85%), Frederiksted holding a distant second (4,550, or 15%). The Christiansted trade was preponderantly African (19,597 or 77%), while Frederiksted focused on the local West Indian trade (3,162 or 69%). Svend Green-Pedersen has estimated the annual average for St. Croix to have been 700 slaves between 1766 and 1790 and 2,800 slaves per year from 1799 to 1803.

The importation of slaves from other West Indian islands into St. Croix was centered at Frederiksted. Small ships, adapted to an inter-island rather than trans-Atlantic trade, brought a small but steady flow of slaves from the eastern Caribbean.[30] For the period 1766 to 1777, the principal importation of slaves in this inter-island trade came from the following areas: the British Leeward Islands, 1,950; the British Virgin Islands, 331; from the British Windward Islands, including Barbados, 195; the French islands, 138; the Dutch islands, 115; and from the other Danish islands, 298. Sending 1,494 slaves, or 49% of the total for that period, St. Kitts was by far the greatest single exporter of slaves into the Crucian market, followed distantly by Anguilla (344) and Tortola (307). This inter-colonial trade was stimulated by the Danish edict of April 9, 1764, which permitted foreign vessels to take return cargoes of sugar and cotton in payment for slaves. It would appear that these slaves arrived in small consignments of ten or less, not as the dominant feature but rather as a part of a general inter-island trade that moved various commodities and passengers among the islands. Unreported by the customs ledgers, however, are the resultant cultural linkages and affinities that developed between St. Croix and certain of these islands, most prominently St. Kitts and Tortola.

It is possible at this point to sketch a rough statistical profile of the newly-arrived enslaved Africans. Ethnically they came from a broad area of Guinea, known then as the Gold Coast, stretching along the area to the east of Christiansborg into the delta of the Volta River and perhaps as far as a hundred miles or so inland.[31] Early sources, such as Oldendorp and other Moravian writers, indicate that several sub-groupings of the Akan-speaking people were well represented in the Danish colonies. The preference of the traders was clearly for adult males, especially early in the trade when planters thought in terms of replacement by purchase rather than by procreation. Adolescents also appeared among the imports, though in considerably fewer numbers, and children were present in negligible numbers.

Additionally, slaves were exported from St. Croix. It has been estimated that slave exports from St. Croix for the years 1733 to 1803 totaled 23,000.[32] The majority of these exports came from Christiansted. By way of example, incomplete figures for the years between 1766 and 1802 reveal that of a total of 7,576 slaves taken out of St. Croix, some 6,543 or 86%, were shipped from Christiansted, while 1,033, or 14%, were shipped from Frederiksted. It is rather surprising that slaves should have been exported from St. Croix in any significant quantities at a time when sugar was fetching such profits and slave labor was in such great demand. The answer is to be found in the western Caribbean where sugar was enjoying a tremendous resurgence and where the demand for slaves—and thereby their price—was even greater than in the Danish West Indies.[33] The selling of slaves to the Western regions of the Caribbean must have provided a quick and sure means of gaining liquidity.

ST. THOMAS AND THE TRANSIT TRADE

A small size, a strategic geographical location, an excellent natural harbor and an aggressive, multi-national merchant class all predisposed St. Thomas to commerce rather than agriculture. Jørgen Iversen, the first governor of St. Thomas, set the pattern by developing a transit trade with the French on St. Croix. The Brandenburg Company showed that this could be done on a relatively large scale using African slaves as the principal commodity. Governor Lorentz, in the 1690s, suggested that the Danish West India and Guinea Company take over this trade in order to supply the labor needs of St. Thomas as well as to export slaves to nearby islands. The Company was reorganized in 1697 and Lorentz's suggestion was heeded, thereby setting a pattern of trade that would endure through the next century.[34] The Company's re-entry into the trade coincided with the War of Spanish Succession, a period which witnessed a rapid increase in the price of slaves. From that time until 1807, St. Thomas became a principal point for a transit, or transshipment, slave trade.

Svend Green-Pedersen has pointed out that legislation was produced in Denmark in the eighteenth century aimed at providing slave labor for St. Croix and at making St. Thomas a leading slave entrepôt. Chief among these official decrees were the edict of April 22, 1767, that made St. Thomas a free port and the edict of February 2, 1785, that waived duties on incoming and outgoing slaves, thereby directly promoting the transit trade.[35] The immediate benefactors of these events were the merchants of St. Thomas, who argued that this strong stimulus to trade would benefit the entire colonial economy. At the same time there was occurring a tremendous resurgence of sugar production in the Spanish colonies of the Greater Antilles, as well as a concomittant demand for slaves. Likewise the French colony of St. Domingue fell into full stride and consumed large numbers of slaves, at least until the outbreak of the revolution there in 1791. In some instances, merchants from those islands sailed to St. Thomas in their own ships in search of slaves. In other cases, St. Thomas merchants outfitted ships to deliver slaves to those same islands, principally Cuba, Puerto Rico and St. Domingue.[36] Closer to home, the St. Thomas merchants likewise supplied a part of the need of the British Virgin Islands and the other Danish islands.

The supply for this transit trade came from two principal sources: Africa and the West Indies. Of the 26,700 slaves known to have been imported into St. Thomas between 1789 and 1807, the majority came from other West Indian islands, only about a third coming from Africa.[37] Although information on these imports is limited, the picture emerges nevertheless that the Dutch islands, principally St. Eustatius, were the chief suppliers, paralleling the role played by St. Kitts in St. Croix and perhaps reinforcing, at least in part, some evolving cultural distinctions, such as the use of Dutch Creole vis-à-vis English Creole.[38] Slave imports also came in lesser numbers from the English and French islands. In turn, these same islands received some slave exports from St. Thomas, but overwhelmingly their role was that of supplier.

The degree to which the St. Thomas trade had become re-export in nature is illustrated by the fact that only about 6% of all imported slaves were retained for various employments on St. Thomas. This modest figure is supported by the slight growth of the slave population on that island between 1792 and 1803 from 4,279 to 5,969, a growth rate of only 28% over twelve years. Some of these slaves were employed in the limited sugar cultivation of the island; others as domestic slaves and laborers in and around the expansive port, with its businesses and warehouses. Similarly, the slave population of St. John grew from 1,917 to 2,598, or a growth rate of 26%, over the same years. The majority of the slaves imported into St. John were destined for plantation labor.[39]

Both the importation of slaves into the Danish West Indies and exportation of slaves from those islands increased dramatically after 1792, for reasons that have already been signaled. The transit slave trade in St. Thomas peaked in the years just after 1800. In 1803, for example, approximately 3,500 slaves were transshipped through St. Thomas. This trade remained strong until 1807, at which time the invading British forces put an abrupt end to it.[40] Nothing better illustrates the profitability of the transit trade than the Danish government's willingness to allow its continuation until well after 1803, the year designated by law to bring it to an end. The argument in favor of allowing the trade to continue stressed St. Thomas' status as a free port. Moreover, two restrictions were established and agreed to, namely: that the trade was to be carried on in foreign vessels and that all slaves were to be transshipped without exception, none of them to be brought into the Danish islands. Clearly, foreign merchants played a leading role in this trade, as Green-Pedersen has pointed out.[41] However that may be, the transit trade was widely viewed as producing economic benefits for St. Thomas and Danish colonial trade in general, even though it might have been statistically limited. And finally, it is worthy of note that, had it not been for the British intervention, there was no indication that the transit trade would have been terminated by Danish or Danish West Indian authorities before the onset of the political turmoil some years later in the Spanish colonies, thereby interrupting the strong demand from those areas for slaves.

Two final points need be made. It remains to comment briefly on the question of the profitability of the trade. Again it is Svend Green-Pedersen who has done the seminal research on this matter. He has taken the position that the profitability of the trade was marginal at best.[42] This is far too complex a question to take up in any detail in this brief presentation. I will therefore limit myself here to several observations. First, it remains a matter of record that numerous Danish companies and individual entrepreneurs were willing, even eager, to plunge into the trade, year after year. It therefore must have been a general perception, at least, that profits were to be had. Moreover, those perceptions influenced much of the decision-making in economic circles in the Danish Kingdom for the period in question. Second, it became axiomatic by the time of the royal takeover of the islands from the Danish West India and Guinea Company (1754) that colonies in the West Indies required the direct national participation in the slave trade in order for the colonial enterprise to be fully successful. This perception, it would appear, likewise affected much decision-making in the political sphere. And third, whatever might have been the actual profitability of the African transatlantic slave trade, it seems clear that the transit slave trade in St. Thomas after 1792, operated by local merchants and promoted by Danish officials, especially after its official ban in 1803, was by its very nature significantly profitable.

It has been remarked more than once that even though Denmark was the first European state to undertake the abolition of the slave trade, it did so motivated by practical rather than moral considerations, lacking a vocal anti-slavery movement such as The Anti-Slavery Society in Britain and *Les Amis des Noirs* in France. Are the Danes simply to be dismissed as cold-hearted pragmatists? It should be taken into account that Denmark had an official state church since the Reformation, The Lutheran Church, analogous and comparable in its general contours with the Anglican Church in England. What Denmark lacked in the early modern period, however, was true religious dissent, as generated by sects such as the Quakers, Methodists and Baptists in England which zealously took up the anti-slavery crusade. Moravianism was the closest thing Denmark had to an independent pietist movement, but by the second half of the eighteenth century, the Brethren had themselves joined the plantocracy in the colonies as the most expeditious means, according to their then prevailing reasoning, of saving African souls.[43] The question of slavery in Denmark and in its colonies consequently existed in the equivalent of a moral vacuum, resulting, first, in the total lack of a popular debate of the issue and, second, in the development of a predominantly practical, administrative approach to the issue of abolition, due in large measure to Denmark's still absolutist monarchy, functioning in the absence of any parliamentary organs of government.

SUMMARY

The Danish Atlantic and West Indian slave trade flourished from 1672 until 1803, a period of some 131 years. Documentary sources indicate that during the period 1733 to 1802 alone approximately 123,000 plus slaves were brought into the Danish West Indies; thousands more were imported in the early company period. In addition, a vigorous local trade transshipped thousands more to other slave-holding areas in the West Indies, principally the Spanish Indies and St. Domingue. Thus, the Danish slave trade had two distinct aspects, one that was essentially African and import in nature and another that was distinctly West Indian and export in function.

Second, though both St. Thomas and St. Croix imported and exported slaves, it was by and large St. Croix that consumed them as laborers and St. Thomas that transshipped them as commodities. This pattern of development reflects the resources and early history of the two islands.

Third, though it flourished in the age of mercantilism, the trade was never sealed off nor exclusively Danish, that is, neither the African nor the West Indian components of the trade. On the contrary, the trade was significantly international from whatever angle we approach it.

Fourth, although the numbers of slaves brought into the West Indies by the Danish trade were in themselves imposing, they shrink considerably when compared to the total numbers for the African slave trade by all nations across its duration. According to our most recent and best estimates, the Danish trade accounted for less than 2% of the total African trade.[44] Denmark, then, was a relatively small player in the Atlantic slave trade.

To date the bulk of the research on the Danish slave trade has been done by the Danish scholar Svend Green-Pedersen and several of his students at the University of Århus. Almost single-handedly, he has provided us with the rich archival data for the Danish slave trade as well as its interpretation. It should be noted, however, that the time is ripe for a careful re-evaluation of this work. In the first place, his studies have all been undertaken from the perspective of Denmark and not from the islands themselves. Slavery and the slave trade in St. Croix under the Dutch, English and French from approximately 1635 to 1733, nearly a complete century, has simply not been considered at all. Secondly, Green-Pedersen has limited his research and discussion of the Danish trade to the period 1733 until 1807 for the most part, neglecting a close study of early slave trade on St. Thomas and St. John, the activities of the Brandenburgers and the local trade (St. Croix, Tortola etc.) for that earlier period.[45] Lastly, one has the impression from the treatment of the data as well as some of the conclusions drawn in several of his key works that a re-evaluation and perhaps re-interpretation of the material for the period that he did study most closely (i.e., 1733 to 1807) would most certainly be in order.

One final observation. In this paper and in other recent studies, the African slave trade has been considered primarily relative to the colonial enterprise or against the backdrop of developing national states in Europe and their economies. This focus has been conditioned in part by the nature of the documentary sources. It would appear that the time is at hand to approach the voluminous Danish archival sources for this subject with an eye toward elucidating just how this same trade affected Africa and Africans within the Danish sphere of influence.

NOTES

1. This paper is deeply indebted to the work of my friend and colleague, Svend Erik Green-Pedersen whose work over many years among the Danish archival sources produced a body of seminal publications before his untimely death in 1990.

2. This trade has been explored in detail by the Danish scholar Erik Gøbel in several of his works, including "Danish Trade to the West Indies and Guinea 1671–1754," *Scandinavian Economic History Review* v. 26 (1983): 21–49 and his "Volume and Structure of Danish Shipping to the Caribbean and Guinea, 1671–1838," *International Journal of Maritime History* v. 2 (1990): 103–131.

3. Still the best study of the Danish colonies in the early colonial period is Waldemar Westergaard's *The Danish West Indies Under Company Rule (1671–1754), with a Supplementary Chapter, (1755–1917)* (New York: Macmillan Co., 1917).

4. Nicolai Abrahams, "Nogle Bidrag til den dansk-vestindiske Handels Historie i de første Aar (1671–c. 1680)," *Historisk Tidsskrift* ser. 7, v. 4 (1902–04): 283–316.

5. Westergaard, pp. 199–212.

6. For the standard survey of the evolution of the Danish monarchy in this period, see Knud J. V. Jespersen's *Danmarks Historie. Tiden 1648–1730.* Volume three of the series *Danmarks Historie*, 10 v., edited by Aksel E. Christensen et al. (Copenhagen: Gyldendal, 1989). See also Gunnar Olsen's *Den unge Enevælde: 1660–1721*, in *Danmarks Historie*, edited by John Danstrup and Hal Koch (Copenhagen: Politikens Forlag, 1977). Danish trade and mercantilism has been studied in detail by Kristof Glamann; see his "Et kameralistisk programskrift: Uforgribelige tanker om kommerciens tilstand og opkomst," in *Studier i dansk merkantilisme omkring tekster af Otto Thott.* Edited by Kristof Glamann and Erik Oxenbøll (København: Københavns Universitet Institut for Økonomisk Historie, Publikation nr. 20, Akademisk Forlag, 1983), pp. 12–14. The practice of mercantilism relative to the West India islands is treated by Erik Gøbel in his "Der Merkantilismus—unter besonderer Berücksichtigung Flensburgs im 18. Jahrhundert," *Grenzfriedenshefte* 3/4 (1984): 188–204.

7. Georg Nørregaard, *Danish Settlements in West Africa 1658–1850* (Boston, MA: Boston University Press, 1966), pp. 1–20.

8. *Ibid.*, pp. 21–28.

9. Westergaard, pp. 95–104.

10. Nørregaard, pp. 143–157. See also Ole Feldbæk and Ole Justesen's *Danmarks Historie: Kolonierne i Asien og Afrika.* General series editors, Svend Ellehøj and Kristof Glamann (Copenhagen: Politikens Forlag, 1980), pp. 385–401.

11. Westergaard, pp. 213–241.

12. Ole Feldbæk, "The Danish Trading Companies of the Seventeenth and

Eighteenth Centuries," *The Scandinavian Economic History Review* v. 34 (1986): 204–218. For information on the grants and regulations regarding these various companies, see Ole Feldbæk's, *Danske Handelskompagnier 1616–1843: Oktrojer og interne Ledelseregler* (København: Selskabet for Udgivelse af Kilder til Dansk Historie, 1986), pp. 353–486. See also Erik Gøbel's "Danske oversøiske handelskompagnier i 17. og 18. århundrede. En forskningsoversigt," *Fortid og Nutid* 28: 4 (1980): 535–569.

13. C.A. Trier, "Det dansk-vestindiske Negerindførselsforbud af 1792," *Historisk Tidsskrift* s. 7, 5 (1904–05): 405–508. See also Joseph Evans Loftin, *The Abolition of the Danish Atlantic Slave Trade* (Ph.D. dissertation, Louisiana State University and Mechanical College, 1977).

14. The Danish scholar Svend Green-Pedersen has written several seminal studies on the abolition of the Danish slave trade, incuding the following: "Danmarks ophævelse af negerslavehandelen. Omkring tilblivelsen af forordningen af 16. marts 1792," *Arkiv. Tidsskrift for Arkivforskning* 3 (1968): 19–37; "The Economic Considerations behind the Danish Abolition of the Negro Slave Trade," in *The Uncommon Market: Essays in the Economic History of the Atlantic Slave Trade*, edited by Henry A. Gemery and Jan S. Hogendorn. (New York: Academic Press, 1979), pp. 399–418; and "Slave Demography in the Danish West Indies and the Abolition of the Danish Slave Trade," in *The Abolition of the Atlantic Slave Trade: Origins and Effects in Europe, Africa and the Americas*, edited by David Ellis and James Walvin (Madison, WI: University of Wisconsin Press, 1981), pp. 231–255.

15. The Danish West African slave trade has been studied in detail by Svend Erik Green-Pedersen. The most important of his articles are the following: "The Danish Negro Slave Trade, Some New Archival Findings in Particular with Reference to the Danish West Indies," in *De la Traite à L'Esclavage. Tome 1. Actes du Colloque International sur la Traite des Noirs, Nantes, 1985* (Nantes: Centre de Recherche sur l'Histoire du Monde Atlantique et La Société d'Histoire d'Outre-Mer, 1985), pp. 429–452; "The Scope and Structure of the Danish Negro Slave Trade," *Scandinavian Economic History Review* 19 (1971): 149–97; "The History of the Danish Negro Slave Trade 1733–1807: An Interim Survey relating in particular to its Volume, Structure, Profitability and Abolition," *Revue Française d'Histoire d'Outre Mer* 62 (1975): 196–220, this being an English version of his original "Den danske negerslavehandels historie 1733–1807: En foreløbig oversigt med særligt henblik på dens omfang og struktur, dens økonomiske betydning samt dens ophævelse," in *Från medeltid till välfardssamhälle*, Nordiska Historiker-mötet i Uppsala 1974 (Uppsala, 1976): pp. 347–364; and "Colonial Trade under the Danish Flag: A Case Study of the Danish Slave Trade in Cuba 1790–1807," *The Scandinavavian Journal of History* 5:2 (1980): 93–120. My discussion relies heavily on the raw data supplied

by these articles, particularly the statistical materials compiled by Green-Pedersen from sources in the Danish archives.

16. Green-Pedersen, "The Scope and Structure of the Danish Negro Slave Trade," p. 169.

17. *Ibid.*, p. 175.

18. *Ibid.*, pp. 186 ff. Green-Pedersen cites various slave ships and their capacities during the 18th century. Similar statistics are cited by Westergaard for the late 17th and early 18th centuries (Appendix J, pp. 320–326). The largest number of enslaved carried across the Atlantic in one vessel cited by Westergaard was 624, by the vessel *Frederik III* in November of 1698. Most cargoes were much smaller, however. Of 82 arrivals of slave ships carrying some 15,854 enslaved Africans to the Danish West Indies between 1687 and 1754, as cited by Westergaard, the average per vessel was 193.

19. Erik Gøbel, "Dansk Sejlads på Vestindien og Guinea, 1671–1807," *Handels-og Søfartsmuseet på Kronborg Årbog* (1982): 31 ff. For accounts of some of these voyages, see C. G. A. Oldendorp, *Geschichte der Mission der evangelischen Brüder auf den caraibischen Inseln S. Thomas, S. Croix und S. Jan* (Barby: Johann Jakob Bossart, 1777), 2 v. [English edition and translation by Arnold R. Highfield and Vladimir Barac. *C. G. A. Oldendorp's History of the Mission of the Evangelical Brethren on the Caribbean Islands of St. Thomas, St. Croix, and St. John* (Ann Arbor, MI: Karoma Publishers, 1987), p. 216.] Citations in this article are made to the more generally available English edition.

20. Gøbel, "Dansk Sejlads på Vestindien og Guinea, 1671–1807," pp. 14–18.

21. Svend E. Green-Pedersen, "Om Forholdene på Danske Slaveskibe med særlig henblik på dødeligheden 1777–89," *Handels- og Søfartsmuseet på Kronborg Årbog* (1973): 71–87.

22. Shipboard rebellions took place on the following vessels: *Københavns Børs*, 1698; *Fredericus Quartus*, 1709; *Haabets Galley*, 1724; *Patientia*, 1753; *Christiansborg*, 1775; *Kammerherre Schack*, 1783–87; and *Christiansborg*, 1785–87. See Green–Pedersen, "Om Forholdene...," pp. 42–46. The revolt on the *Christiansborg* was descibed in detail in Paul Erdmann Isert's *Reise nach Guinea und den Caribäischen Inseln in Columbien, in Briefen an seine Freunde beschrieben* (Copenhagen: J.S. Morthorst, 1788), pp. 305–320. Oldendorp also gives a lengthy account of one such revolt on a slave ship bound for the Danish West Indies during the middle passage (pp. 218–219).

23. Isaac Dookhan's *A History of the Virgin Islands of the United States* (St. Thomas: Caribbean Universities Press, 1974), p. 69 ff. The best account of the early years of the Danish West Indian colonies remains Westergaard's work. See also J. O. Bro-Jørgensen, *Dansk Vestindien indtil 1755: Kolonisation og Kompagnistyre*. Volume 1 of *Vore Gamle Tropekolonier*, edited by Johannes Brøndsted. Second edition

(Copenhagen: Fremad, 1966) and Ove Hornby's *Kolonierne i Vestindien*. A volume in the series *Danmarks Historie*, edited by Svend Ellehøj and Kristof Glamann (Copenhagen: Politikens Forlag, 1980).

24. See the articles by George F. Tyson and Myron Jackson in *The St. Thomas Harbor: A Historical Perspective*, edited by George F. Tyson (St. Thomas: The St. Thomas Historical Trust, 1991), pp. 9–40.

25. Aimery P. Caron and Arnold R. Highfield, *The French Intervention in the St. John Slave Rebellion 1733–34*. Occasional Paper No. 7 (St. Thomas: Bureau of Libraries, Museums and Archaeological Services, Virgin Islands Department of Conservation and Cultural Affairs, 1981).

26. Oldendorp, pp. 219–220.

27. Unlike St. Thomas, which was well developed in the early 1700s, St. Croix had gone back to wilderness after the French settlement there was abandoned in 1697. This state of affairs is vividly described by Père Labat in his *Nouveau Voyage aux Isles de l'Amérique* (Paris, 1722), v. 5, pp. 47–50. The initial work of developing the island after the Danes took over in 1734 is outlined by Reimert Haagensen in his *Beskrivelse over Eylandet Ste Croix i America i Vest-Indien* (Copenhagen: 1758), pp. 50–66.

28. See the St. Croix Matrikel for 1755, Rigarkivet, Copenhagen, Denmark; for the population figures, see Green-Pedersen, "Slave Demography…," p. 247, Appendix 13.1.

29. The figures that follow in this paragraph are from Green-Pedersen's "The History of the Danish Negro Slave Trade 1733–1807: An Interim Survey relating in particular to its Volume, Structure, Profitability and Abolition," *Revue Française d'Historie d'Outre Mer* 62 (1975): 208–209.

30. Green–Pedersen's "Scope and Structure…," pp. 179–183, tables three through five.

31. See Nørregaard, pp. 84–100; see also Feldbæk and Justesen's *Danmarks Historie: Kolonierne i Asien og Afrika*, pp. 388–396. Note the map of Danish activities on the Gold Coast on p. 385.

32. Green-Pedersen, "The History of the Danish Negro Slave Trade 1733–1807," p. 207.

33. Cuba's turn to sugar in the 18th century, replacing tobacco, coffee and cattle-raising, was quickened by the British occupation of 1762 and the opening of markets in the North American colonies, followed in 1791 by the revolution in St. Domingue that eliminated that colony's sugars from the world market and sent its experienced planters—some 30,000 to Cuba alone—scurrying to other islands. See Louis A. Pérez, Jr., *Cuba: Between Reform and Revolution* (New York: Oxford University Press, 1988), pp. 70–103.

34. Westergaard, pp. 71–120.

35. Green-Pedersen, "Colonial Trade under the Danish Flag," [p. 5].

36. *Ibid.*, [p. 9 ff].

37. *Ibid.*

38. Arnold R. Highfield, "Toward a Language History of the Danish West Indies and the U.S. Virgin Islands," in *The Danish Presence and Legacy in the Virgin Islands*, edited by Svend E. Holsoe and John H. McCollum (Frederiksted, St. Croix: St. Croix Landmarks Society, 1993), pp. 123–139.

39. For the figures for St. John, see Green-Pedersen, "Slave Demography...," p. 247.

40. Very little has been written on the British occupation of the Danish West Indies. For an older account, see Kay Larsen, *Dansk Vestindien 1666–1917* (Copenhagen: C.A. Reitzel, 1928), pp. 163–182.

41. Green-Pedersen, "Colonial Trade," [pp. 9–11].

42. Green-Pedersen, "The History of the Danish Negro Slave Trade 1733–1807," pp. 209–215. On the other hand, Erik Gøbel has argued that the Danish African trade "yielded a tolerable profit between 1698 and 1733" and has presented statistical evidence to back that point of view. See his "Danish Trade to the West Indies and Guinea 1671–1754." *Scandinavian Economic History Review* v. 31 (1983): 37–41.

43. Moreover, the Moravians themselves "sold" their approach to the matter of slavery and religion to the planters and authorities as a means of making "better" slaves of the Africans, as is witnessed by the following passage written by Johann Bossart in the introduction to Oldendorp's history: "Without question it is advantageous to the progress of the missions that the Whites in the islands support the work of the Brethren, if for no other reason than the obvious benefits which they derive from the presence of the true virtues of loyalty, industry, and obedience in those of their slaves who have converted to Christ" (Oldendorp, p. xxxii).

44. According to Phillip Curtin, the Danish trade accounted for only 56,000, or about 1.7%, of the 3,339,400 individuals shipped from Africa by the major European nations in the period 1761 to 1810. Compare with Green-Pedersen, "The History of the Danish Negro Slave Trade 1733–1807," p. 198.

45. It is altogether possible that Green-Pedersen intended eventually to undertake a more general study of the trade in the Danish West Indies. Whatever the case, his research activities were foreshortened by illness and ended by an untimely death in 1990.

REFERENCES

Abrahams, Nicolai. "Nogle Bidrag til den dansk-vestindiske Handels Historie i de første Aar (1671–c. 1680)." *Historisk Tidsskrift* ser. 7, v. 4 (1902–04): 283–316.

Bro-Jørgensen, J. O. *Dansk Vestindien indtil 1755: Kolonisation og Kompagnistyre.* Volume 1 of *Vore Gamle Tropekolonier,* edited by Johannes Brøndsted. 2nd ed. Copenhagen: Fremad, 1966. 301 pp.

Brøndsted, Johannes, ed. *Vore Gamle Tropekolonier.* Copenhagen: Westerman, 1952–53. 2 v. [Second edition, Copenhagen: Fremad, 1966–68. 8 v. Volume one, *Dansk Vestindien indtil 1755: Kolonisation og Kompagnistyre* by J.O. Bro-Jørgensen; volume two, *Dansk Vestindien 1755–1848: Vestindiens Storhedstid* by Jens Vibæk].

Caron, Aimery P. and Arnold R. Highfield. *The French Intervention in the St. John Slave Rebellion 1733–34.* Occasional Paper No. 7. St. Thomas: Bureau of Libraries, Museums and Archaeological Services, Department of Conservation and Cultural Affairs, 1981. 58 pp.

Dookhan, Isaac. *A History of the Virgin Islands of the United States.* St. Thomas: Caribbean Universities Press, 1974. 321 pp.

Feldbæk, Ole. "The Danish Trading Companies of the Seventeenth and Eighteenth Centuries." *The Scandinavian Economic History Review* v. 34 (1986): 204–218.

Feldbæk, Ole. *Danske Handelskompagnier 1616–1843: Oktrojer og interne Ledelseregler* København: Selskabet for Udgivelse af Kilder til Dansk Historie, 1986. 779 pp.

Feldbæk, Ole and Ole Justesen. *Danmarks Historie: Kolonierne i Asien og Afrika.* General series editors, Svend Ellehøj and Kristof Glamann. Copenhagen: Politikens Forlag, 1980. 468 pp.

Glamann, Kristof. "Et kameralistisk programskrift: Uforgribelige tanker om kommerciens tilstand og opkomst." In *Studier i dansk merkantilisme omkring tekster af Otto Thott.* Edited by Kristof Glamann and Erik Oxenbøll. København: Københavns Universitet Institut for Økonomisk Historie, Publikation nr. 20, Akademisk Forlag, 1983. pp. 11–77.

Green-Pedersen, Sv[end] E[rik]. *Nogle statistiske hovedtræk af den danske negerslavehandel.* Copenhagen: MA thesis, University of Copenhagen, 1967. 151 pp.

Green-Pedersen, Svend E[rik]. "Danmarks ophævelse af negerslavehandelen. Omkring tilblivelsen af forordningen af 16. marts 1792." *Arkiv. Tidsskrift for Arkivforskning* 3 (1968): 19–37. ("Denmark's abolition of the slave trade, concentrating on the origin of the Act of March 16, 1792.")

Green-Pedersen, Svend E[rik]. "The Scope and Structure of the Danish Negro Slave Trade." *Scandinavian Economic History Review* 19 (1971): 149–97.

Green-Pedersen, Svend E[rik]. "Om Forholdene på Danske Slaveskibe med særlig henblik på dødeligheden 1777–89." *Handels- og Søfartsmuseet på Kronborg Årbog* (1973), pp. 71–87.

Green-Pedersen, Sv[end] E[rik]. "Slaver og Sukker, eller en redegørelse for et projekt om den danske slavehandels historie 1733–1807." *1066—Tidsskrift for Historisk Forskning* 5:5 (1975–76): 26–31.

Green-Pedersen, Svend E[rik]. "The History of the Danish Negro Slave Trade 1733–1807: An Interim Survey relating in particular to its Volume, Structure, Profitability and Abolition. *Revue Française d'Historie d'Outre Mer* 62 (1975): 196–220. English version of Green-Pedersen's "Den danske negerslavehandels historie 1733–1807" (1974).

Green-Pedersen, Svend E[rik]. "Negro Slavery and Christianity: On Erik Pontoppidan's Preface to L.F. Rømer." *Tilforladelig Efterretning om Kysten Guinea (A true Account of the Coast of Guinea),* 1760. *Transactions of the Historical Society of Ghana* 15: 1 (1976): 85–102. English version of Green-Pedersen's "Teologi og negerslaveri." (1972).

Green-Pedersen, Svend E[rik]. "Den danske negerslavehandels historie 1733–1807: En foreløbig oversigt med særligt henblik på dens omfang og struktur, dens økonomiske betydning samt dens ophævelse." *Från medeltid till välfardssamhälle.* Nordiska Historiker-mötet i Uppsala 1974. Uppsala, 1976. pp. 347–64. An English version appeared as "The History of the Danish Negro Slave Trade 1733–1807: A Interim survey relating in particular to its Volume, Structure, Profitability and Abolition." (*Revue Française d'Histoire d'Outre Mer* 62 [1975]: 196–220).

Green-Pedersen, Svend E[rik]. "The Economic Considerations behind the Danish Abolition of the Negro Slave Trade." In *The Uncommon Market: Essays in the Economic History of the Atlantic Slave Trade,* edited by Henry A. Gemery and Jan S. Hogendorn. New York: Academic Press, 1979. pp. 399–418.

Green-Pedersen, Sv[end] E[rik]. "Colonial Trade under the Danish Flag: A Case Study of the Danish Slave Trade in Cuba 1790–1807." *The Scandinavian Journal of History* 5:2 (1980): 93–120.

Green-Pedersen, Svend E[rik]. "Slave Demography in the Danish West Indies and the Abolition of the Danish Slave Trade." In *The Abolition of the Atlantic Slave Trade: Origins and Effects in Europe, Africa and the Americas,* edited by David Ellis and James Walvin. Madison, WI: University of Wisconsin Press, 1981. pp. 231–55.

Green-Pedersen, Svend E[rik]. "Dansk-vestindisk slavehandel og dens ophævelse: Konklusioner efter udenlandske arkiv- og biblioteksstudier." In *Festskrift til Kristof Glamann.* Odense: Odense Universitetsforlag, 1983. pp. 51–70.

Green-Pedersen, Svend E[rik]. "The Danish Negro Slave Trade, Some New Archival Findings in Particular with Reference to the Danish West Indies." *De la Traite à L'Esclavage. Tome 1. Actes du Colloque International sur la Traite des Noirs, Nantes, 1985.* Nantes: Centre de Recherche sur l'Histoire du Monde Atlantique and La Société d'Histoire d'Outre-Mer, 1985. pp. 429–452.

Green-Pedersen, Svend E[rik]. "Danish Historians and the Emancipation—The Peter von Scholten Myth." Paper presented at the Symposium on Slavery and Emancipation in the Virgin Islands (Oct. 31–Nov. 2, 1987, St. Thomas-St. Croix, University of the Virgin Islands). 11 pp.

Green-Pedersen, Sv[end] E[rik]. "The Danish West Indian Slave Trade and its Abolition." Ms., [n.d.].

Green-Pedersen, Sv[end] E[rik] and P.C. Willemoes Jørgensen. "Dansk Kolonihistorie—Det Globale Perspektiv." In *Dansk Kolonihistorie: Indføring og Studier,* edited by Peter Hoxcer Jensen et al. Århus: Forlaget HISTORIA, 1983. pp. 9–15.

Gøbel, Erik. "Danske oversøiske handelskompagnier i 17. og 18. århundrede. En forskningsoversigt." *Fortid og Nutid* 28: 4 (1980): 533–724.

Gøbel, Erik. "Dansk Sejlads på Vestindien og Guinea, 1671–1807." *Handels- og Søfartsmuseet på Kronborg Årbog* (1982): 5–53.

Gøbel, Erik. "Danish Trade to the West Indies and Guinea 1671–1754." *Scandinavian Economic History Review* 31 (1983): 21–49.

Gøbel, Erik. "Der Merkantilismus—unter besonderer Berücksichtigung Flensburgs im 18. Jahrhundert." *Grenzfriedenshefte* 3/4 (1984): 188–204.

Gøbel, Erik. "Volume and Structure of Danish Shipping to the Caribbean and Guinea, 1671–1838." *International Journal of Maritime History* 2 (1990): 103–131.

Highfield, Arnold R. "Toward a Language History of the Danish West Indies and the U.S. Virgin Islands." In *The Danish Presence and Legacy in the Virgin Islands*, edited by Svend E. Holsoe and John H. McCollum. Frederiksted, St. Croix: St. Croix Landmarks Society, 1993. pp. 123–139.

Hornby, Ove. *Kolonierne i Vestindien.* A volume in the series *Danmarks Historie*, edited by Svend Ellehøj and Kristof Glamann. Copenhagen: Politikens Forlag, 1980. 394 pp.

Isert, Paul Erdmann. *Reise nach Guinea und den Caribäischen Inseln in Columbien, in Briefen an seine Freunde beschrieben.* Copenhagen: J.S. Morthorst, 1788. 376+78 pp.

Jespersen, Knud J. V. *Danmarks Historie. Tiden 1648–1730.* Volume three of the series *Danmarks Historie*, 10 v., edited by Aksel E. Christensen et al. Copenhagen: Gyldendal, 1989. 376 pp.

Labat, Jean-Baptiste. *Nouveau Voyage aux Isles de l'Amérique.* Paris, 1722. 6 v.

Larsen, Kay. *Dansk Vestindien 1666–1917.* Copenhagen: C.A. Reitzel, 1928. 397 pp.

Loftin, Joseph Evans. *The Abolition of the Danish Atlantic Slave Trade.* Ph.D. dissertation, Lousiana State University and Mechanical College, 1977. 320 pp.

Nørregaard, Georg. *Danish Settlements in West Africa 1658–1850.* Boston, MA: Boston University Press, 1966. 31+287 pp. English translation from the original Danish *Guldkysten, de danske establissementer i Guinea* v. 8 af *Vore gamle tropekolonier.* [Second edition, edited by Johannes Brøndsted. Copenhagen: Fremad, 1968. 414 pp.]

Oldendorp, C.G.A. *Geschichte der Mission der evangelischen Brüder auf den caraibischen Inseln S. Thomas, S. Croix und S. Jan.* Barby: Johann Jakob Bossart, 1777. 2 v. (450+663 pp.) [English edition and translation by Arnold R. Highfield and Vladimir Barac. *C. G. A. Oldendorp's History of the Mission of the Evangelical Brethren on the Caribbean Islands of St. Thomas, St. Croix, and St. John.* Ann Arbor, MI: Karoma Publishers, 1987. 35+737 pp.]

Olsen, Gunnar. *Den unge Enevælde: 1660–1721.* In *Danmarks Historie,* edited by John Danstrup and Hal Koch. Copenhagen: Politikens Forlag, 1977. 512 pp.

Perez, Louis A., Jr. *Cuba: Between Reform and Revolution.* New York: Oxford University Press, 1988. pp. 70–103.

Trier, C. A. "Det dansk-vestindiske Negerindførselsforbud af 1792." *Historisk Tidsskrift* ser. 7, v. 5 (1904–05): 405–508.

Tyson, George F., ed. *The St. Thomas Harbor: A Historical Perspective.* Second edition. St. Thomas: The St. Thomas Historical Trust, 1991.

Westergaard, Waldemar [Christian]. *The Danish West Indies Under Company Rule (1671–1754), with a Supplementary Chapter, (1755–1917).* New York: Macmillan Co., 1917. 24+359 pp.

The servant woman Justina tending to the
children of her master in Denmark

CHAPTER 10

TRANSATLANTIC ENCOUNTERS: TRAVELING AFRICAN-CRUCIANS IN THE 18TH CENTURY

PART I

THE ATLANTIC SYSTEM that evolved in the 17th and 18th centuries saw the creation of numerous connections between Africa, North America and the Caribbean. These followed, for the most part, the lines of trade and commerce. People and cultures also proceeded along these same lines. Europeans migrated to both Africa and the New World while Africans were transported from west Africa in considerable numbers to the broad crescent of plantation America that stretched from the southern United States through central American and the Caribbean to northern South America.

In general, the principal currents of migration flowed from east to west across the expanse of the northern and middle Atlantic, predominantly from the so-called Old World to the New. These facts are all but taken for granted. But was there any significant movement in the opposite direction, in particular by African and African-European peoples, and, if so, what might it reveal about Danish participation within the context of the larger Atlantic world that was evolving at that time? This short article will look into this question, focusing on the movement of slaves and free people of color from the Danish West Indies to Africa, Denmark and, to a lesser extent, North America. The existence of detailed records relative to Danish slave-trading in Africa and to colonization and tropical agriculture in the Danish colonies in the West Indies greatly facilitate the investigation of these questions.

The Danish West Indies—the present Virgin Islands of the United

States—was acquired piecemeal by Denmark in the 17th and 18th centuries—St. Thomas in 1672, St. John in 1718 and St. Croix in 1733. Later, in 1917, these same islands, along with a host of smaller, adjacent islets and cays, were sold to the United States. The approximately 140 square mile archipelago has remained a territorial possession of the United States to the present time. However, it is primarily the period between the acquisition of the islands and their sale to the United States that this particular account proposes to investigate.

For two centuries, the islands of St. Croix, St. Thomas and St. John produced sugar, cotton and other tropical crops for export to North America, Denmark and, from the latter, to other European nations. To provide the labor for the development and maintenance of viable tropical agriculture, between 85,000 and 120,000 Africans were introduced into the islands as slaves between 1672 and 1806.

The overwhelming majority of those unfortunates passed their entire lives in servitude in the Danish islands. In a few cases, however, enslaved Africans crossed the Atlantic in reverse direction, and from there some even returned back to their native lands. The several documented cases provide a revealing commentary on the workings on the Danish Atlantic system and the early adumbration of questions of race, color and ethnicity.

In the 1760s, an enslaved African by the name of Christian—his African name was Qvou Orsu—worked on the royal plantation at Estate Princesse on St. Croix. Through a Danish merchant, he related to his masters that he had been improperly enslaved and that he could prove it. Moreover, he made an offer to the effect that if he were returned to the Guinea coast in Africa, he would pay for his freedom by means of providing *two* slaves as his replacement.

Qvou Orsu was well connected, for the Danish authorities agreed to his offer. He was subsequently taken to Denmark, given a per diem while there and provided with military dress by the Crown until he was returned to the Guinea coast, ironically enough, aboard a slave trading vessel of the Royal Guinea Trading Company.

True to his word, Qvou Orsu, upon setting foot on African soil, supplied the same West Indies-bound ship with two fellow Africans to be enslaved in return for his own freedom. In this manner, he regained his liberty, not due to any leniency on the part of his erstwhile masters, but rather because of the Danish need for the good will of the Guinea kings with whom they traded.

A similar case occurred some 30-years later. An African king, one Naimbanna by name, had for some time worked closely with foreign merchants along the Guinea coast. His relationship with the Europeans was such, in fact, that he sent several of his sons to England and France to be educated.

The King was therefore greatly aggrieved when he learned that a Danish slave trader, one Capt. Severin Koch, had in c.1787 kidnapped three members of his family while they were selling provisions aboard a Danish slave ship bound for the Caribbean. Koch filed his bill of lading with the young men and carried them to the Danish islands to be sold as slaves on St. Croix.

Although King Naimbanna protested immediately to English officials, it was nearly a decade before word of the matter reached the proper authorities in Denmark. Through a series of improbable events and chance occurrences, the whereabouts of the three young Africans—Prince Banna, Corpro and Morbour—became known on the island; the Danish Rector of the School Institute on St. Croix, Hans West, and a local slave dealer named Winther played leading, if improbable, roles in bringing the men's plight before the colonial government.

In the end, it was the slave dealer Winther, ironically enough, who suggested to the local administration that the young man be returned to his family in Guinea. Winther then purchased Banna's freedom for that purpose. King Christian VII was also moved by the remarkable story and not only consented to the request for repatriation but also provided Banna with travel expenses and clothing. Sometime in 1798, the prince boarded an American vessel and took passage to Sierra Leone.

Banna's two companions were not so lucky. Corpro had already died of a fever in 1795 and Morbour was sold to a master smith on St. Croix, under whose tutelage he became so skilled a worker that his master would not part with him. His talent and hence his worth as a slave inadvertently sealed his own fate. In the final analysis, it was political power and social status that led to Prince Banna's freedom, certainly not humanitarianism or Danish policy.

A similar occurrence in the 1770s involving the son of a certain King Dunnukabam, a ruler of a state in the Congo, is reported by a Moravian missionary. C. G. A. Oldendorp writes: "He [Dunnukabam] was a friend of the English and had supplied one of their ships, in which he had a share, with slaves. He arranged for his son to travel with those slaves to the English islands of the West Indies in order that he might go to England from there."

But en route, the English ship was captured at sea by a French privateer, and the young prince was taken to be a slave rather than a royal passenger in transit. He was sold on the Danish island of St. Thomas, where the privateer liquidated his prize. Luck, however, was on the young African's side in this instance. Purely by chance, another Moravian missionary who spoke some English heard the young man's story and reported it to the authorities. Interestingly enough, the prince was treated in accordance with his rank and soon sent to Denmark, where he ultimately was put on a ship back to his father's kingdom in the Congo.

These episodes are instructive beyond their interest as colonial anomalies. In the first place, they reveal that the Danish authorities returned certain Africans to Africa, motivated primarily by political and commercial considerations. Above all, they wanted to avoid antagonizing African rulers whose cooperation they needed in order to maintain their forts and lodges along the Gold Coast, as well as to carry on the trade in commodities and slaves. Denmark, moreover, was chary of tarnishing her international reputation, especially at a time when the abolition of the Atlantic slave trade was a much-debated topic in European commercial and intellectual circles. In fact, Denmark herself took no little pride in being the first state in Europe to pass legislation, in 1792, aimed at abolishing its own slave trade, albeit after a lapse of ten years, in 1803. Consequently, even though slavery might still be viewed by many as an economic necessity, Danes, in general, were loathe to be regarded as a nation of heartless slave dealers.

Finally, it is to be kept in focus that each of these cases, as interesting as they individually are, were resolved almost wholly by chance. They are in no way illustrative of a general government awareness of the problem of slavery or of the existence of a policy of reform. Nor did the returning Africans apparently derive any moral lessons from their brush with fate; the coastal kingdoms of Guinea and the Congo continued to do a brisk business in the trade, in fact long after slavery had been abolished in the Caribbean. Qvou Orsu's seemingly indifferent behavior to the lot of his fellow human beings was no more offensive in his country than Severin Koch's was in his.

In the 18th and early 19th centuries, Africans, though by no means common in Denmark, were present there, as a result of the same trade in humans that carried millions across the Atlantic to the New World. Consequently, Africans were not unknown in the streets of Copenhagen in the early colonial period. In 1825, for example, Noi Dowunnah, a leader along the Guinea coast, sent his son, Frederik Dowunnah, to Denmark where he remained until 1827, for the express purpose of obtaining a military education.

It was not only the sons of African royalty who popped up in Denmark but common folk as well. Henning Frederik Bargum, director of the Royal Guinea Company in the 1770s and slave dealer, brought five Africans with him back to Denmark on his return from a slave-trading voyage, by way of the Danish islands. It is possible that he intended to sell them or, at the very least, retain them in his own service. These particular Africans remained in Denmark after Bargum's African schemes collapsed, raising, most likely for the first time, the thorny question of the rights of Africans to humane consideration and instruction in the Christian faith.

Christian Protten is perhaps the most interesting of the Africans to travel to Denmark, because his life and travels are so well documented. The son of a Danish soldier and an African woman of the Guinea coast, Protten was chosen, as a so-called "Mulatto," to travel to Denmark in order to get an education and then return to teach the Gospel, Moravian style, to those Africans whose languages and cultures were known to him. Protten made several trips between Europe and Africa and became conversant in Danish and German language and culture. Though things did not turn out exactly as his Moravian mentors had planned, Protten did set up a school for the education and Christianization of other persons of mixed descent like himself.

While in Europe, he met a "Mulatto" woman from the island of St. Thomas in 1742, Rebekka Freundlich by name, married her and returned with his wife and their child to his native land. Rebekka Freundlich's story is an interesting one in itself and has been touched upon in a previous article in this column.

Many of these episodes, and in particular the Protten episode, reveal the nature of several points of contact between Europeans and Africans during the slave trading period, which had the potential for interaction between Europe and Africa. The presence of Protten and the other Africans in Denmark reveal just how real that potential was.

For several decades, there existed a narrow but rapidly closing window of opportunity which might have permitted Danes and other Europeans to deal with and view Africa and Africans directly and not through the distorting lenses of the West Indian experience, built as it was on slavery and, eventually, racism. Such a relationship, as the surgeon and traveler Poul Erdmann Isert argued, would have utilized African resources, climate and labor to supply the European markets with the goods they demanded without the imposition of slavery. Moreover, it might have brought the two continents into contact on relatively equitable terms. Most certainly, Isert was convinced that such a relationship would have avoided the tragedy of Caribbean plantation slavery and forced migration.

It would appear, however, that the kinds of personal episodes described above in the 18th and early 19th centuries were neither numerous nor intense enough to transform the relationship based on the slave trade and slavery that had already begun to harden in the early 18th century.

PART II

SLAVES AND FREE BLACKS IN DENMARK

For the majority of the Europeans arriving in the Americas, the attractions of opportunity, land and relative freedom from traditional restrictions in the Old World diminished the desire for return. Particular constraints existed on Africans, however, who, for the most part, had no choice other than to endure the burden of slavery and concomitant limited movement.

Though it has been suggested that the Danish slave system was less rigid and brutal than those of other European nations in the Caribbean, the Danish colonial regime most certainly imposed harsh slave laws in order to intimidate the slave population and to extract the greatest possible amount of labor from a scarce, expensive resource. All areas of the slaves' lives were controlled and regulated, but that was particularly the case regarding personal movement, not only within the colony itself but especially so beyond its confines. While some slaves managed to escape their condition by becoming maritime maroons, the inescapable fact is that the overwhelming majority was tightly bound to their place of labor on the islands' plantations.

Until the mid-18th century, slaves escaped from the Danish West Indies in large numbers to downwind, down-current destinations—Vieques, Culebra and Puerto Rico, in particular. That avenue of flight, however, was closed in 1767 when Governor von Prock's administration concluded an agreement with the Governor of Puerto Rico, whereby all runaways, Danish and Spanish alike, were to be returned to their owners. After 1767, escape by that western route then diminished.

At the same time, passage to islands to the east proved virtually impossible due to contrary winds and ocean currents. But simple marronage was not the only way that slaves might move beyond the shores of the islands. Some slaves and ex-slaves were able to make their way by other means to Europe and, to a lesser extent, North America during the 18th and 19th centuries. This section focuses on that movement, but first a word or two is needed on the Danish colonial system.

The small Kingdom of Denmark entered the competitive world of 17th century colonialism in 1671, with the establishment of the Danish West India and Guinea Company. Modeled primarily on the Dutch overseas experience, the plan was a simple one in theory: carry manufactured goods to West Africa, barter them for ivory, gold and slaves; transport the slaves to the Caribbean colonies for sale to the planters who were engaged in tropical agriculture; and, finally, return with cargoes of sugar, cotton, dye woods and the like for sale in Denmark and northern Europe. The unit of value in this trade, the sine qua non, was the individual slave, whether *bozal* (born in Africa) or creole (born in the West Indies). Regardless of his origin, the individual male field slave was termed, significantly enough, a "piece of the Indies."

It should come as little surprise that the unit of value throughout the Caribbean would soon manifest itself far beyond the fields of sugar cane cultivation. In c.1688, the directors of the Danish West India and Guinea Company in Copenhagen wrote to its officials in St. Thomas that they should send "a couple of attractive, young Negro boys" back to Denmark, as well as "some parrots, flamingoes, turtle doves and other exotic creatures." In a short time, the exotic and the expensive had become fashionable. In Copenhagen, nobles, ranking court officials, merchants, and absentee plantation owners, whenever wealth and position allowed it, obtained black servants and occasionally displayed them prominently as markers of wealth and status. The trade in humans in Africa and the West Indies was not without immediate social consequences, then, in Scandinavia.

Precedents for these displays were not lacking in other slave-trading countries in Europe. The Prussian court, which traditionally exerted strong cultural and political influences on the Danish monarchy, secured a regular supply of Blacks in the late 17th century by means of a treaty with the Dutch. Such Blacks figured prominently in noble and court circles as witnessed by their appearance in at least nine extant Prussian court portraits from the period.

In fact, Blacks had been present in portraiture all across Europe from the late Renaissance to the early 19th century. The portrait of the adventurous Prince Rupert of the Palatinate, attended by a young black servant, was a contemporary model for this type of representation, vaguely mindful of Sir Francis Drake a century earlier. Early in the 18th century the first Blacks made their appearances in Danish paintings, shortly after Denmark's establishment of colonies in Africa and the West Indies.

Several portraits from the 18th century signal the Danish participation in this fashion and the concomitant presence of people of color in high circles. It is in the style of the times that Lorens Lønberg's portrait of Heinrich Carl Schimmelmann shows the great industrial magnate and West Indian plantation owner seated before a portrait of the Danish Queen, with a bust of the King gazing over his shoulder and a young black boy peering in from the background. Similarly, a painting of Baron Joseph von Baudissin as a young boy shows the "Kammermohr" Christoph Tafeldecker gazing attentively at his young master through a doorway, neither completely in or out of the painting's focus, symbolic of the prevailing ambivalence in regard to race and ethnicity.

Even the otherwise pietistic Moravian missionaries were not immune to this trendy posturing. No less a figure than the founder of the Moravian Mission in the Danish islands, the indefatigably pious Friedrich Martin, was painted with a young black boy looking gratefully over his shoulder. These paintings and others of their kind convey the unmistakable link between colonial wealth and social power, as witnessed in all instances by the master at center stage and the black servant on the margins or in the background.

But there were real people behind the margin-inhabiting figures in the portraits. They served the rich, lived in the presence of their masters, served at the royal court and managed to survive in Copenhagen's inhospitable climate. One such early example was Goo, a young girl, possibly of direct African origin, who served from 1695 to 1696 in the Royal Court, before being accused of stealing and then sent to the children's detention house.

Royalty took the lead in obtaining Blacks. By the early 1730s, King Christian VII (1699–1740) was served by a young Black, Moranti by name, and his Queen similarly had a black female attendant. In addition, it was not uncommon that influential court noblemen would retain black servants, usually from the West Indies, where they had traveled and lived. One such example was Anton Ulrich who was born in St. Thomas but taken to Denmark as a personal valet in c.1730 by his master, a well known nobleman. Present at the coronation of King Christian VII in 1732, Ulrich no doubt attracted much attention at the court, both as a black West Indian and as a speaker of the exotic Negerhollands, or Dutch Creole. During the festivities, he met Count Nicholas von Zinzendorf, one of the leading noble figures in Europe of his day and also founder and leader of 18th century Moravian Pietism.

Zinzendorf was so moved by Ulrich's account of his life as a slave in the Danish islands that he arranged to have him visit the nascent Moravian settlement developing on his ancestral lands at Herrnhut. Ulrich's meeting with the Brethren there, especially Brothers Dober and Nitschmann, sparked in them a passionate response, thereby kindling the Moravian world missionary movement in the early 1730s, beginning in the Danish West Indies.

Some of the Blacks who found their way to Denmark did so in the company of plantation owners and their families. Well-to-do planters and colonial merchants in the Danish West Indies made occasional visits to Denmark for a variety of reasons—to place children in schools, to restore failing health, to make commercial connections or simply to visit European relatives. Some of these men returned there to live out their lives after having made—or lost—their fortunes in the islands. In nearly all such instances, they took black servants along with them—nursemaids, cooks, washerwomen, valets, personal attendants and so on.

It was, at least in part, their presence, at once prominent and exotic, that helped inspire the popular belief that returning Creoles were uniformly wealthy.

For the white Creole of the islands who was undertaking a new life in a European country where he had not grown up, the possession of black servants and attendants was not simply a matter of status or style, as it was for court nobles and great merchants of the home country. Indeed, the Creole had most likely been nursed and raised by a slave woman, from whom he imbibed his native language, not Danish, but Dutch Creole or English Creole, along with his first milk. His food was creole, rich in ground provisions, fish, salted pork, salted fish, corn meal, cassava bread and West Indian peppers; many of these items were available in Denmark, requiring only the expert hands of a West Indian cook for its proper confection. The well known DeWindt family, as one example, was never without cassava bread on the table in Denmark, St. Croix planter Reimert Haagensen tells us. This was possible because Caribbean commodities were supplied to Denmark by means of the regular shipping across the Atlantic.

In numerous ways, the Creole's lifestyle differed considerably from that of his European kin. Many of his most personal relationships, not least the sexual ones, had always been with black women and women of color—slave and free alike. In fact, it was not uncommon that such unions produced offspring, paternity being recognized in some instances and denied in others. In a word, it is often overlooked, or simply avoided, that black West Indians and their culture constituted an essential part of the white Creole's life and lifestyle, whether it be in the islands or in distant Denmark.

Consequently, the presence of black West Indians in Creole families in Denmark in the 18th and first half of the 19th centuries is to be expected rather than regarded as a curiosity. One such home-bound Creole was the Creole Johan Lorentz Carstens (1705–1747), who after having made his fortune as a planter and company official in St. Thomas, traveled to Denmark in 1739, where he spent the remainder of his life as a merchant, specializing in the Caribbean trade, especially slaves. Carstens sailed from St. Thomas to Amsterdam and from there made his way overland with his family and four servants. He purchased several respectable properties near Copenhagen and lived there until his death in 1747, served by his small retinue of slaves.

So intimately was Carstens' and his family's life entwined with their slaves and servants that when he departed from St. Thomas for the last time, he placed an experienced, trusted slave, Domingo Gesu (Mingo), in charge of his plantation operations there. The correspondence between the two men reveals an exceptionally close relationship. When Carstens died at a relatively young age in 1747, it was this same Domingo Gesu who journeyed to Copenhagen to report on Carstens two estates on St. Thomas and to attend to his master's extensive business affairs. It is not a little ironic that men such as Carstens, whose lives and fortunes were built upon slavery, became intimately and inextricably tied to the people whom they so badly used. This particular scenario is representative of those instances in which Blacks made their way to Denmark because of their close ties to Creole families.

Later in the century, the powerful Schimmelmann family was directly responsible for the introduction of a number of slaves into Denmark. Heinrich Carl Schimmelmann, commercial magnate and family patriarch in Denmark in the mid-18th century, purchased slaves in Guinea for his Caribbean estates—Princesse, La Grange, Carolina and Thomas—and undertook the production of sugar. The family enterprise shipped the raw muscovado to Copenhagen and refined it in their factories for widespread sale in northern Europe. In a short time, the Schimmelmann holdings became the largest and wealthiest in the Danish islands, as well as the base for one of the wealthiest families in all of Denmark.

From early in his career as an industrialist, the elder Schimmelmann believed that addressing social problems could be profitable for both business and for the state. He believed, for example, that orphans and the children of the poor could be put to mutually beneficial uses in his factories. After he acquired plantations in the West Indies, he applied that same thinking to his young slaves; it was not long before he brought slaves to Denmark to teach them trades in order that they might better serve him eventually in the Caribbean.

In 1765, Schimmelmann brought small groups of slaves to his estate at Ahrensberg in Denmark where he had them instructed in the various trades and, interestingly enough, in medicine. His idea was to send them back to the West Indies and put them to work in positions normally filled by hard-to-find and harder-to-retain white laborers. In his first attempt at this, he brought seven slaves from St. Croix—among them Apollo, Jantji, Carolus, Adam, Thomas and Johannes—who were to become millers, smiths, masons and the like. And in addition to importing slaves for his own uses and industrial experiments, Schimmelmann occasionally provided slaves for nobles and for wealthy merchants, who required black servants as symbols of their status and prestige. So it turned out that, over several decades of the 18th century, the Schimmelmann enterprise became the single greatest source of black immigration into Denmark.

But these were not the only means by which Blacks traveled to Denmark. In 1767, when the vessel "Fredensborg" departed the islands for Denmark, three black men were on board—one translator and two slaves. It was not uncommon at that time for such men to leave the islands, legally or clandestinely, as crewmen aboard vessels of the various nations whose ships made port there. In this instance, fate was unkind to these three travelers, for the Fredensborg sank off the coast of Norway in 1768 in a great storm. We are aware of their existence, ironically enough, only by the very disaster that claimed their lives.

What became of the West Indians who were brought by the Carstens, Schimmelmanns and others to Denmark? Some died, unable to acclimate to the harsh weather and to the northern illnesses. Some returned to the Danish West Indies with their masters; others were sent back. A few were sold into neighboring countries, such as Sweden. And a few remained in Europe and adapted to life there as fully as possible;

and some, in fact, had families and spent their entire lives there, their descendants becoming, in time, fully Danish in every respect.

One such example from this last category was the so-called Kammermohr Christoph Tafeldecker, who belonged to the Baron Carl Ludwig von Baudissin. The Baron wanted a slave who would serve as a show-piece in his household. Although Christoph had been purchased with the idea that he might learn to play the violin, it turned out that he was a poor musician and was consequently demoted to table service (i.e., Tafeldecker). While in Baudissin's service, however, Christoph fathered a child with one of the local Danish chambermaids, causing something of a scandal. Not one to be easily discouraged, he subsequently had two more children with another Danish servant. And interestingly enough, by Danish convention, mixed children were considered free.

But it is altogether likely that it was the potential for race-mixing that bothered Danes most, however little it was to affect the complexion of the local population in the long run. Christoph's own experience and that of his descendants, for example, were clear examples of how people of African background might blend into the population. His first daughter, a so-called "mulatto" by European standards, remained in Denmark, married, presumably a Dane, and raised a family. In this manner Christoph's offspring quickly blended into the general population as was the case with other Blacks in his situation.

Though many of the slaves who were brought to Denmark at times expressed the sentiment that treatment was less harsh for them in the northern land than it had been on the plantations of the West Indies, some of them nevertheless ran away from their masters. Where might they have taken refuge in such a small, ethnically homogeneous Nordic country and what might they have done to survive? Apparently, some runaways became day labors and a few went into the maritime trades. For the most part, however, the records are simply mute to the extent that the runaway succeeded in his objective. But there were several cases that, because of their importance, have left traces in the historical sands.

One Crucian slave, in particular, fled the house of his mistress, a certain Henriette von Schimmelmann, and sought refuge in the Royal naval force. While she was trying to get him back, Hans Jonathan joined the navy and took part in the famous Battle of Copenhagen in 1801 at the onset of the Napoleonic Wars in Europe. Moreover, there is some indication that Jonathan afterwards served on other vessels and eventually made his way to Iceland where he became a merchant, established a family and spent the rest of his life. Apparently some of his descendants are living in Iceland to this day, fully aware of their West Indian connection.

PART III
THE LEGAL POSITION OF SLAVES IN DENMARK

Throughout the 18th century, it had been generally accepted that slaves might be taken to Denmark and retained there for no longer than one year. However, that convention was usually winked at by the wealthier planters—men of affluence and influence whom the government did not wish to offend. Was it the examples of men like Christoph Tafeldecker and Hans Jonathan—having learnt the Danish language, absorbed the culture and engendered families, in the context of something resembling normal lives—that set off alarm bells in the small, ethnically homogeneous country?

The matter came to a head in 1802 when Jonathan's adventures ended in a court case that led to a ruling on the status of West Indian slaves who had been introduced into the Kingdom of Denmark from the West Indies. Did they retain their slave status once they set foot on Danish soil? Or did owners maintain their property rights intact in the home country? Could the slaves be sent back to the West Indies as slaves?

The renowned Danish jurist A.S. Ørsted ruled in the case and has left several publications in support of his view. The case was decided in favor of the owners and the sanctity of property rights; Denmark was not able to take the step that England had taken in the ruling of Chief Justice Mansfield in 1772 that effectively liberated all the slaves in England.

MORAVIAN MISSIONARIES

The intercontinental nature of the Moravian missionary initiative provided slaves with potential for greater personal movement. In the first place, the Brethren strongly encouraged marriage among slaves. After passing into the mission congregation through the highly structured choir system, black Brethren who were respected, trusted and, in general, married might become so-called "national helpers," whose task it was to provide a reliable model for others in the congregation.

In pursuit of this "first fruits" emulation theology, the local missionaries would send the most promising of their black members to Moravian centers in North America or Europe to live among the European Brethren in order to form a better idea of the Moravian lifestyle, which they then were expected to communicate to their fellow slaves in the islands on their return. The Moravian records make mention of the formation of such Christian marital pairs traveling to Bethlehem in the colony of Pennsylvania and then returning home to spread the word. Other black Moravians went to congregations in The Netherlands, Denmark and in German lands.

Rebekka Freundlich, already referred to above in connection with Christian Protten, made such a journey to Herrnhut in 1742 in the company of her German husband, Matthäus Freundlich. Their interracial union was remarkable in itself, setting something of a precedent for the time. Matthäus Freundlich, however, died shortly after reaching Europe and Rebekka found herself alone in a distant land. It was in these circumstances that she was introduced by the Brethren to the Danish-African Protten, also in Europe at the time; they soon married, had a child and went to Africa in order to begin Protten's work among people of mixed race along the coast.

The Moravian movement was centered first in Germany, shifting focus later to The Netherlands and England. Although it did not amount to a great deal in Lutheran-dominated Denmark, the Danish Moravians opened a mission station at Christiansfeld in present-day Denmark, in 1773 and over the years attracted a few souls from the islands.

It is not presently known exactly how many slaves or ex-slaves visited Christiansfeld, in the manner of the Pennsylvania exchanges or otherwise, but there are a few suggestions. Marie Catherine and Christian Gottfried Thomassen, the children of Governor Thomas de Malleville (1739–1798) and Johanne Tønnis, a mulatto woman, were sent there to learn the faith of their parents. But on the whole, the Danish West Indian presence in the Danish Moravian movement was most probably slight.

How many souls from the Danish West Indian population found their way to Denmark at that time? Certainly they were never numerous. The Danish historian Per Nielsen has estimated that there were not more than 150 such Danish West Indians of color in the entire Danish Kingdom for that period.

POST EMANCIPATION, 1848–1917

No more slaves traveled in Denmark after the Emancipation of 1848, and therefore the number of Blacks in the home country apparently declined. But they did not disappear altogether. Some returning Danish families continued the practice of taking their maids, nurses and other domestic servants along with them back to Denmark The portrait of the lovely Danish West Indian maid Justina leading her two charges on a walk through the Frederiksberg gardens in Copenhagen is a striking reminder that some West Indians remained bound by the tradition of personal service. Some freemen were sent to Denmark for education in the trades. And a few were simply displayed as curiosities in the expositions that were at the time popular in Copenhagen.

One such individual was Victor Cornelius (1898–1985), a native of Frederiksted, who, along with another young Crucian boy, was sent to Copenhagen in 1905 to appear in a "colonial exposition" in Tivoli Garden. Though this kind of display must have been personally demeaning, Cornelius remained in Denmark, received a thorough education, worked for many years as an educator, married a Danish woman, raised a family and, in time, became something of a Danish national institution. Likewise, Sister Emma Francis of Frederiksted spent a good deal of time in Europe with her religious order but eventually returned to her homeland. These two cases, however, were exceptions and not the rule.

Prisoners who had been convicted of serious crimes in the islands were sent to Denmark for imprisonment, at least until the time of the sale in 1917. The rate of incarceration amounted to no more than a trickle but attained a rather high profile due to the case of Queen Mary (Mary Thomas), who played a leading role in the Labor Revolt (Fireburn) of 1878. Several years later, her son, Hezekiah Smith, convicted of murdering his girlfriend, was likewise imprisoned in Copenhagen. When he was finally released as an old man, he was deported to Brazil where he apparently lived the remainder of his life.

In general, black Danish West Indians were not attracted to any great extent to Denmark in the period after Emancipation by anything other than personal and family ties. This may be attributed to cultural as well as geographical considerations, to say nothing of the harsh weather. By the end of the 19th century, island people were looking more to other parts of the Caribbean and to North America than to anywhere else as a migratory destination. After all, their language was English, or English Creole; American commercial vessels called regularly at American ports; and the islands' most significant trade partner by then was the United States. There were ample opportunities for travel along these trade axes and free Danish West Indians made the most of them.

On the other hand, black West Indians had been only very superficially influenced by Danish cultural elements in spite of the 200 plus years of colonialism. Very few islanders spoke Danish naturally or fluently. And in the 19th century in the post-Emancipation period, few, if indeed any, black islanders attended academic schools or universities in Denmark. None apparently entered the professions. Nor was the way open to them to migrate readily as apprentices and ordinary workers. Finally, there was no significant native population of people of color to offer them welcome and extend the promise of some hope for success.

As a result, only a limited number of immigrants arrived in Denmark from the Caribbean, the majority going, especially in the last decade of the 19th century, to the mainland United States.

Although Africans, slaves, so-called mulattos and free Blacks were present in Denmark in the 18th and 19th centuries, their numbers were always limited. The failure of the black population to attain a critical mass in the capital of the Lilliputian colonial empire meant that the Danish national conscience was never broadly exposed to the harsh reality of slavery as it had been practiced in the Danish colonies. While black West Indians were able to pique the conscience of the Moravian leaders in the early 1730s and thereby help launch a world missionary effort, their presence was not large enough by 1800 that they might confront Danes with the personal, moral and legal ugliness of slavery as was practiced in their own backyard.

In this regard, the contrast with England and France is revealing. Danish jurists took up the question of slavery on Danish soil about thirty years after England had done so in the famous Mansfield ruling in the Somerset case of 1772. That ruling drove the first stake into the heart of the institution of slavery as a legal entity, as practiced in the country's colonies, by effectively nullifying slavery on English soil. From the pronouncement of that first anti-slavery principle, English law proceeded inevitably, if not smoothly, through the abolition of the slave trade, amelioration of slave conditions, and, ultimately, emancipation, all by 1834.

Such was not the case in Denmark where the slave population was so sparse as to be all but negligible in the nation's collective conscience, and this had significant consequences. Something approaching outrage at the sight of slaves walking among free men was never generated. This may have been in part due to the absence of those Pietistic sects—Baptists, Quakers and Methodists—who were elsewhere strong, vocal opponents of slavery on moral and religious grounds. Consequently, when the Danish jurist Ørsted ruled in favor of the precedence of property rights over human rights in 1802, the matter was not challenged.

It is altogether plausible, as a result, that Denmark's failure to strike down slavery on Danish soil in 1802 extended the life of the institution in the colonies. After all, it was Great Britain, not Denmark, that eradicated the last vestiges of the Danish Atlantic slave trade when that nation seized the Danish islands in 1807. In addition, the much debated amelioration policies that followed the end of the Danish slave trade were weak and uneven, left for the most part to the whims of individual plantation owners. And beyond that, slavery endured another 41 years until such time (1848) as the slaves were able to force their masters' hand in an open rebellion.

A preliminary review of the subject, such as this present one, suggests that there existed subtle but important connections between the existence of only a minuscule black population, slave and free alike, in Denmark during the entire colonial period on the one hand and the slow, gradual decline of slavery in the Danish Caribbean colonies on the other.

A British slaver out of the port of Liverpool of the
same type as the *General Abercrombie*

CHAPTER 11

THE WRECK OF THE SLAVE SHIP
GENERAL ABERCROMBIE

LITERALLY HUNDREDS of shipwrecks are strewn along the ocean floor surrounding the Virgin Islands. None of them, however, has a story more compelling than that of the British slaver the *General Abercrombie* that today lies broken on the reef that encircles Buck Island, just off St. Croix's north coast. The *General Abercrombie* was a Liverpool slaver, owned by the wealthy Tobin firm. The city of Liverpool was the most active British slaving center of the 18th century. The vessel was 250 tons burden and mounted 16 guns, having the sleek look of a privateer. Though she was said to look "swan-like" in the water, she nevertheless beat to wind very nicely.

On August 21, 1802, she slipped anchor in the River Mersey and set sail for the Congo in quest of slaves, who were to be transported across the Atlantic and sold in the British islands of the West Indies to serve as plantation laborers. Under the command of one Captain Booth, the vessel was laden with trade goods. On board was a young surgeon, one Jerrard John Howard, whose diary, letters and other papers provide a vivid narrative of the entire voyage. By the end of September, the *General Abercrombie* had passed Tenerife and was headed for the coast of West Africa. Coasting along the long littoral of West Africa, the ship passed the island of Bulama off the coast of present Guinea-Bissau and then traded with various tribes for ivory, spices and fresh provisions along that stretch. But its destination was further to the south. For several weeks the vessel fought contrary winds, but on October 25, it made the mouth of the mighty River Congo.

The current of the river was at that time of year far too strong to allow the vessel to sail upstream. And the natives who lived along the river estuary and who beckoned the crew to come ashore were notorious for kidnapping sailors and demanding ransoms. For that reason Captain Booth sent longboats up-river in search of trade and slaves. By the end of November, the ship was still taking on African captives that were offered by local kings and traders. These were acquired in barter for the goods carried in the "General Abercrombie's" hold, namely cutlery from Birmingham, assorted wares from Tunbridge and Manchester, civilian and military cast-off apparel, demi-johns of Spanish brandy, and both rolled and leaf tobacco. Finally, by the end of December, 1802, after spending two months at anchor in the estuary of the Congo, the vessel had taken on some 300 captives in exchange for its tawdry trade goods. An anxious crew set sail across the Atlantic for the island of Trinidad, where they arrived in early February 1803.

There Captain Booth received his orders to sail on to St. Kitts in order to dispose of his human cargo. The Kittitian planters, however, were not impressed by the prices and did not make any purchases. On February 28, 1803, the *General Abercrombie* raised anchor and made sail for St. Croix where the company's agent would be contacted for further instructions and a possible place of sale. Tragedy, however, awaited them near the Danish island.

At 11 am on March 1, the hills of the east end of St. Croix came into view on the western horizon. Captain Booth turned the navigation of the vessel over to a Danish sailor who happened to be on board and who claimed that he would be able to steer to the entrance of the Christiansted harbor where they would pick up the harbor pilot. As they approached St. Croix, the Danish seaman decided to steer the ship to the north of Buck Island and its extensive reef system. But his judgment was off by several hundred feet. As Captain Booth and his surgeon Howard stood at the bow of the deck surveying the approach, the vessel struck the reef about a mile and quarter to the north of Buck island and then drove firmly aground. It immediately began to take on water and list markedly. Panic ensued, particularly among the several hundred Africans below deck.

In the ensuing chaos, the ship's crew manned the pumps and began to throw things overboard to lighten the load, in hopes of floating the ship off the reef but to little avail. The disaster had already been witnessed from shore, and a small boat arrived to assist. Booth sent his second mate to Christiansted with that boat to explain things to the authorities and to ask advice from his company agent.

By 10 p.m., the hold of the vessel had taken on some 10 feet of water and was listing badly. The futile pumping was abandoned, and the frenzied Africans were moved from below to the upper deck. In the darkness of night, it was decided to dispatch 90 of the captives in two longboats to the town of Christiansted, for monetary rather than humanitarian reasons, of course. The crew and the remaining Africans spent a dreadful night on the *General Abercrombie* as it broke up, with the sea rushing across the decks

Just before day-break the next morning, the crew began removing to Buck Island the remaining 134 Africans and the remaining trade goods from the sinking vessel. By midday the job was completed as the hulk of the *General Abercrombie* continued to break up and sink on the reef. A hungry, fearful group of survivors spent that night on Buck Island before a schooner was dispatched from Christiansted harbor to pick them all up the next day.

But the story does not quite end there. The captive Africans were most likely bivouacked near the fort in Christiansted in temporary quarters. A crude hospital was set up for them when fever broke out in their ranks, killing several among them. In the meantime the local authorities decided that the cargo could not be sold on St. Croix, not from a British ship and, moreover, entered into judicial proceedings concerning the salvage of the wrecked vessel.

Two months passed as these tedious events played out. Finally, on April 2, 1803, it was decided to transfer the Africans to the nearby British colony at Tortola where they were to be disposed of. It must be said that the captives luck remained bad throughout these events. Not least, the element of time was ironically cruel to them inasmuch as just four and a half years later Britain would abolish the slave trade itself. Their destiny, however, was to labor as slaves in a strange land until Emancipation finally came in 1834.

The ill-fate of the *General Abercrombie* provides a graphic reminder of the greed and cruelty brought upon us by the slave trade, slavery and everything associated with it in another age. Today the slave ship's remaining timbers lie rotting on the ocean floor near Buck Island.

A view of the wharf at Christiansted in the early 19th century

CHAPTER 12

CHRISTIANSTED: OUR TARNISHED JEWEL OF A TOWN

THE TOWN OF CHRISTIANSTED is a good deal older than most think. It is reasonably certain that the town can boast more or less continuous settlement all the way back to c.1630 when the English, Dutch and French all contested the location. This makes the town older than most cities and towns on the American mainland. But in truth, it was the site of human habitation long before the coming of Europeans and Africans inasmuch as the presence of Indian middens in various parts of the town point to a Pre-Columbian occupation that may date back to the first or second century of the common era. And that would make it older than most settlements in Europe.

But antiquity aside, Christiansted is a delightful town, to be enjoyed, cherished and protected. Its rectilinear Danish street layout manages to fit in snugly along the broad curve of its harbor while at the same time striking a harmonious balance with the hills that slope down from the interior. Along the resulting streets have been constructed an interesting mélange of government structures, churches, warehouses, business establishments and private dwellings. The covered arcades bestow on it an architectural touch that makes the town unique in the Caribbean, sheltering inhabitants from the sun and rain as they proceed about their business.

What's in a name? The settlement received its first known name from the French who seized the island from Spain in 1650. They called the harbor "Le Bassin" and the small settlement alongside it "Le Bourg," or the village. When the Danes purchased the island from France in 1733, they officially renamed the settlement Christiansted, "Christian's place," after their reigning King.

The majority of the new settlers were English and not Danish. They showed a marked preference for the Spanish name "Santa Cruz" for their new island home, as well as the French "Bassin" for their town. The original French meaning was soon lost and the name was understood by many to mean "Baas End," or "Boss End," that is, the main town. A similar indifference to the Danish place name "Frederiksted" for the island's second town led to the interesting Anglicism of "West End." In that manner the new Danish island got off to a decidedly English start.

Originally, it was the French who laid the foundations for our town in the period 1650 to 1696. They constructed a fort (Fort St. Jean), a church, a weigh station and scale, several modest warehouses and a few dwellings, all laid out without any apparent order or survey. Roads connected the town with the east end and with Salt River to the west. Then the French departed in 1696 almost as quickly as they arrived, leaving the town to return partly to bush.

The town's fortunes revived, however, when Denmark purchased the island from France in 1733 and began settlement in 1734–35. Frederik Moth, the first Governor of the island (1734–36), laid out a town plan on the site of Le Bassin, and it was named Christiansted, in honor of the then reigning king, Christian VI (1730–46). Moth imposed a NE-SW grid structure plan of development. Thereafter the town grew rapidly in proportion to the island's growth as a sugar- and cotton-producing colony. Both imports and exports passed through the town's harbor, which acted as an intermediary between the island's interior plantations and the greater world beyond.

Defense was the first order of business in that distant 18th-century world of colonial warfare, privateers and pirates. A fort named Christiansvaern was straightaway constructed, along with a battery on a point at the entrance of the harbor (Fort Louisa Augusta) and another gun emplacement on Protestant Key. Their guns were all trained on the narrow entrance in the reef, through which ships passed into Christiansted harbor.

In quick succession there followed the construction of a church, a warehouse for the Danish West India and Guinea Company, a scale-house and customs house. The main streets ran east to west and connected the harbor area to the country side—Strand, Company, King, and Queen streets, all intersected by cross streets. And along these streets soon sprang up other warehouses, churches, commercial buildings, town houses of the wealthiest planters, and private residences, with the occasional rum shop and cook shop mixed in.

Markets were the lifeblood of the town, as produce from the country flowed in to sustain the town dwellers—fruit, vegetables, herbs, teas, chickens, eggs and firewood. A fish market developed alongside the fort and a town market arose at midtown, later supplemented by the Sunday Market further to the west. In addition, vendors of various products walked the streets of town with trays balanced on their heads as they hawked their wares.

The sections of Christiansted soon developed, each displaying its own unique characteristics. The harbor, for example, connected the island with the world beyond. Ships regularly arrived from Europe, Africa and North America, bringing goods for sale and picking up cargoes as export. During the day, the wharf area sprang to life with the sights and sounds of the sea and dockside. Wares were laid out on the wharf and sailors were set to tend to them for sale both to merchants and to private buyers. In this connection, American Hill became a favorite spot where sea captains sometimes lodged, as that location gave them a fine view of their ships at anchor, their seamen at work, and their wares laid out for sale.

As the Free Black and Free Colored populations grew over time, more space in town was required to house them. Such was provided along the banks of a gut that ran down from the hills into the harbor, soon to be named Free Gut. There they built their homes, raised their families and kept their chickens and goats. It remains a part of Christiansted to this day but unrecognized by many.

The Danes called the part of the harbor just to the east of the fort,

Galge Bugt, or Gallows Bay, a place where executions and other severe punishments were carried out. In time, a small community sprang up near the bayside there, one that was oriented toward the sea and fishing. It is today that part of our town that remains strongly Crucian. On the other side of town there appeared another small community called Water Gut. It was built on the less hospitable, marshy land near the bayside, where the town's largest gut entered into the sea.

By early 1815 Christiansted reached a considerable level of development and prosperity with some 600 structures and a population of 5,427, of which 1,764 were Free Colored and 2,608 were slaves. It became the capital of the Danish West Indies in 1755 and retained that title until 1871, by which time sugar production had fallen into deep decline. At that point, the more maritime-oriented St. Thomas stepped back into the limelight, a position that it has held down to this day.

During the latter half of the 19th century, the town became quiet, its growth stifled by economic hard times, especially after the Fireburn of 1878. By 1911, the population had declined from a high in 1835 of 5,806 to some 4,562 souls. Illegitimacy rates were high, infant mortality rates were untenable and living conditions had become generally marginal at best, due in large measure to Danish disillusionment with and ultimately disengagement from the islands.

The sale to the United States in 1917 brought about change, though slowly at first, founded on the mistaken idea that the sugar industry could be revitalized. After World War Two a growth spurt founded on tourism and light assemblage industry led to a modest expansion of the town, though generally away from Christiansted, toward the west. At one time the western limits to the town had stood at Bassin Triangle. But during this latest growth period, the town expanded through Western suburb, Richmond, Orange Grove, Golden Rock and all the way to Princess, in the creation of new businesses and dwellings.

The reason behind this outward expansion was manifold and complex, beginning with the simple proposition that the town was too small. The invasion of the auto and the need for parking played a major role.

New kinds of businesses requiring greater space and the availability of land for construction certainly played their parts as well. Not least, the expansion of governmental bureaucracy and administration demanded more square footage than the town could readily supply.

Finally, with the growth of relative prosperity, many former Crucian residents of the town constructed dwellings in the country areas, leaving vacancies in the town that have since been filled by newcomers, in particular Hispanics, mainly Dominicanos. More recently, with the increase of population on the island's east end, there has been a growth to be witnessed in the Gallows Bay area and adjacent to the Ball Park, producing the beginnings of an "Eastern Suburb."

Though Lady Fortune has often smiled on Christiansted, she has also doled out her fair share of frowns. Such occurred in the 1970s. Since that time, the town has experienced its portion of difficulties and hardships. The prolonged economic downturn produced demographic changes. The Fountain Valley murders put a large dent in the tourist economy, which hit both of our towns extremely hard. Hurricanes severely damaged our infrastructure more recently, and before we knew it, we were facing urban blight, with the attendant drug and crime problems. Without a strong tourism base to rely on, Christiansted, in particular, has suffered noticeably. While the construction of the boardwalk several years ago has led to a modest revival along the waterfront, the rest of the town has remained stagnant.

A considerable number of buildings and their businesses that were destroyed in 1989 by Hurricane Hugo have not reopened. Nor have some of them been repaired. It is a depressing sight at present to pass along our main streets in town and see so many closed buildings where thriving businesses once operated, with little prospect for transformation in the immediate future.

The days of a quiet walk down to the wharf to sit under the Taman tree and listen to a band concert in the evening or just be lulled into peace and quiet by the lap of the sea against the waterfront dock have decidedly passed, for the blight of drugs and crime and prostitution has taken its toll. It will be necessary to take stock of these hard realities if we are ever to get beyond them.

Christiansted will not go away anytime soon. New generations will surely fall under the town's charms just as those have done in the past as well as many here in the present. And fortunately there are those among us who do not accept this state of affairs as inevitable and final. Christiansted can again enjoy its place in the sun if we are willing to recognize it for the jewel that it is and take the measures necessary to restore and sustain it. But the clock is ticking.

Portrait of Ernst Schimmelmann (1747–1831), Danish Finance
Minister who initiated the Abolition Ordinance in 1792

CHAPTER 13

ERNST SCHIMMELMANN AND THE CURIOUS DEMISE OF THE DANISH ATLANTIC SLAVE TRADE

T HE NATION OF DENMARK can rightly lay claim to being the first European country to abolish its participation in the Atlantic slave trade. The Danish activity in that commerce had been in existence since 1671 or thereabouts. The ordinance for the trade's abolition was passed in 1792, but it came into effect only on January 1, 1803. A parallel transshipment slave trade principally from St. Thomas to the Western Caribbean continued for another four years, coming to an end when the Danish West Indian islands were invaded and taken into possession by Great Britain in 1807. It is doubtful that the abolition would have occurred when it did without the active involvement of Ernst Schimmelmann.

Schimmelmann (1747–1831) was an influential merchant, planter, industrialist and politician who came from a wealthy, influential German family. His father Heinrich Carl Schimmelmann (1724–1782) before him had been a powerful industrialist in Germany, who migrated to Denmark at the invitation of the Danish King. He prospered in his new country as a result of the establishment of industries and the development of plantations in the Danish West Indies. Not the least of his profits came from trading in slaves. When he died in 1782, he was the richest man in Denmark. He left the mantel of family leadership to his son Ernst.

Ernst quickly rose to the fore in commerce and then took on political responsibilities, due in large part to his network of contacts and influence that stretched widely across northern Europe. Like various other men of his class and means, he was also greatly interested in the leading intellectual currents of his time. From the French Enlightenment came his humanitarian values and from Germanic Pietism, his strong belief in the redeeming force of religious faith. In Denmark, the various reform movements promoted by the Danish reformers A.P. Bernstorff and Christian Ditlev Reventlow attracted his attention and support. These three powerful 18th century intellectual, spiritual and political currents exerted a strong influence on Schimmelmann's personal life and political actions, not least relative to slaves and slavery.

These influences on his thinking were balanced at the same time by a sober practicality, because Schimmelmann was nothing if not a shrewd businessman and a clever politician. He knew full well that Great Britain was on a direct course toward abolishing the West African slave trade and eventually slavery itself. If that were to occur, Denmark would be in no position to resist the power and decisions of the powerful British nation, especially its naval forces, as indeed ensuing events would amply illustrate. Such being the case, the Danish Caribbean colonies would be completely vulnerable to events far beyond Danish control in the long term view of things.

It is important to recall that Schimmelmann never lost sight of the central fact that Danish property in the West Indian colonies and the wealth which they produced were in no way insignificant to the Danish economy. Moreover, the welfare of those tropical colonies and their contribution to the Danish economy depended, in the broad view of things, upon the availability of slave labor. And slave labor, as it existed at that time, depended solely on the slave trade in West Africa. Now if Britain were to insist on the enforcement of its own abolition of the Atlantic slave trade on other nations, as indeed she was expected to do in the not-too-distant future, the affects of such a policy would be ruinous for the Danish colonies, as well as thereby having an adverse effect on the economy of Denmark itself. Under such ominous circumstances the best possible course of action for the small kingdom of Denmark,

Schimmelmann reasoned, might indeed be a bold move to abolish its own slave trade peremptorily and, to the extent that it might be possible, on its own terms.

A proposal to abolish the trading in West African slaves was certainly in line with the prevailing mood of reform in high government circles in Copenhagen at that time. In 1788, serfdom (*stavnbond*) was abolished in Denmark. And Ernst Schimmelmann was not lacking in the imagination and the perspicacity to attempt to move in a similar manner regarding slavery. The hard reality remained, however, that it was widely believed that the island colonies would simply wither and die without slave labor. Schimmelmann believed that the problem could be obviated by moving to abolish the trade immediately while with the same stroke leaving a ten-year period of opportunity in which additional new slaves could be legally brought into the Danish colonies in great numbers. After that period of time, slave populations would be large enough to sustain themselves, at least if living conditions and protections could be effectively instituted and maintained. Slavery would continue in existence, it was thought, even though the trade itself might have ended.

The essential corollary to this reasoning was that the massive importation of labor would have to be conditioned by two other factors at the same time in order for the program to have the desired effect. First, an attempt should be made to achieve an approximate gender balance because male slaves had traditionally outnumbered female slaves in the colonies. If the numbers of the latter could be augmented, then it would be feasible to think that slave populations in the Danish West Indies might become self-propagating and stable in the near future, thereby eliminating the need for further imports from Africa. And second, it would be simultaneously necessary to make living conditions for the slaves better (i.e., amelioration) in order to lower death rates below prevailing birth rates thereby stabilizing and hopefully, in the long run, augmenting the creole slave population. If this formula could be made to work, then the slave trade would necessarily become superfluous and

the small Kingdom of Denmark would have solved several problems
with one decisive stroke, both for the "Fatherland" and for its colonies;
and no less, the small kingdom would, at the same time, have provided
what would ostensibly appear as a rather bold example from such a
small country for the rest of Europe and the world to marvel at. Clearly,
this was the kind of solution that appealed to the Schimmelmann entrepreneurial genius.

To put this plan in motion Schimmelmann established the Slave
Trade Commission in the summer of 1791, which, after six months' work,
submitted a report containing an array of practical suggestions for the
implementation of the principal ideas outlined directly above. The central suggestions of that report were incorporated into The Ordinance of
March 16, 1792, for the abolition of the Danish slave trade. According
to the ordinance, the slave trade would be effectively ended at the onset
of 1803. During the intervening ten-year period, however, the all-out
importation of slaves into the islands, especially in female slaves, was to
be encouraged by various means. To the same end of augmenting the
slave population, the exportation or removal of slaves from the colonies
by any means was strongly discouraged. In support of these goals, the
taxing power of the realm was to be employed as a means of imposing
the necessary sanctions, both positive and negative. The intent of the
ordinance was clear—the creation of a large population base of slaves
in which the ratio of males to females would be roughly equaliized,
combined with an official policy of general amelioration of working and
living conditions among the slaves; this would result, it was believed,
in a stable and self-propagating slave work force to serve the islands'
sugar-based, labor needs well into the future, long after the ordinance
to abolish the trade itself had been put into effect.

As a result of these measures, the numbers of slaves in the Danish
West Indies did in fact reach new peaks in the ten-year period following
the Ordinance of 1792. In 1791, there had been 21,549 slaves on the island
of St. Croix (4,214 on St. Thomas and 1,845 on St. John by comparison);
by 1802, that figure had risen to 27,006 (5,737 on St. Thomas and 2,492 on

St. John), an increase of about 25 %, resulting in the largest slave population ever attained on the island. By the time the ten-year period of open slave trading drew to an end, it had become so much a part of the lucrative commerce of the islands that the Danish government encountered obstacles in the enforcement of its own ordinance of abolition. St. Croix had continued to consume slaves at an ever-increasing rate to supply its plantations, and St. Thomas continued to process them through its expansive port, that is to say, transshipped them to other islands, most notably to the Spanish islands of the western Caribbean, where sugar production was enjoying a profitable resurgence. Indeed the trade in human cargoes continued to flourish in this manner well after 1803—the date decreed to bring it to an end—until 1807, when Great Britain seized the Danish islands in an act of war in the struggle with Napoleon and imposed its own abolition on the trade. It was in this curious manner that Denmark finally abandoned the trade in African slaves.

The crucial element in Ernst Schimmelmann's grand design was amelioration, that is, the systematic improvement of the material living conditions of the slaves on West Indian plantations. From his perspective the undertaking had both humanitarian and practical dimensions. On the first count, he appears to have been genuinely concerned about raising the standard of living conditions among the enslaved. At the same time, such a policy would have the long-term effect of lowering death rates and thereby enabling slave communities to become self-propagating and demographically self-sustaining. Schimmelmann put such policies into effect on his own estates on the three Danish islands, perhaps in the hope that some of his peers would attempt to imitate his efforts. During the 1780s and 1790s, he made an effort to systematically improve conditions for the slaves on his plantations in the Danish West Indies—"La Grange" and "Princess" on St. Croix, "Thomas" on St. Thomas, and "Carolina" on St. John. Beginning in the late 1780s, Schimmelmann had already undertaken a study of slave life and conditions in order to set in motion certain changes. He drew up long lists of instructions to be followed and reported on by his plantation managers in the West Indies. In 1788, he received a full report from Johan Christian Schmidt, which was published in Denmark under the title *Blandede Anmærkninger samlede paa og over St. Croix i Amerika* (Varied Remarks Collected on and about St. Croix in America). In 1796, he dispatched another observer-manager to St. Croix, one Charles Boudens, Vicomte de Vanderbourg, who had landed in Denmark quite by chance, in full flight from the excesses of the French Revolution. Vanderbourg responded to Schimmelmann's instructions and questions in 1798 point-by-point in a rather large manuscript entitled *Rapport sur l'état présent des Nègres et sur les moyens de l'améliorer* (Report on the Present State of the Negroes and on the Means to Improve It). Although Schimmelmann did in fact institute some of Vanderbourg's suggestions for reform on his West Indian plantations, few, if any, of the planters followed his lead in undertaking such changes on their estates.

If the effects of Schimmelmann's personal amelioration policies were to be judged solely in terms of the success or failure of broad demographic objectives in the Danish West Indies, then those policies were a failure. The goals of amelioration were neither achieved on the Schimmelmann estates nor was the pursuit of those goals imitated to any great extent by the owners and managers of other estates. Nor did Denmark ever developed systematic, official policies of amelioration—that is, policies such as slave registration, restrictions on punishments, consideration for female slaves, especially when they were pregnant, improvement in housing, clothing and food measures, and the appointment of magistrates to look after slaves' well being—as occurred within the British system. Measures such as these were not incorporated into the regulations of the Danish islands until the 1830s, during the governorship of Peter von Scholten and then, only sparingly.

The truth of the matter is that after the abolition of the trade the total number of slaves declined not only in the Danish islands in general but on Schimmelmann's plantations as well. It might be argued that the vigorous continuation of the Atlantic slave trade until 1803, providing thousands of new slaves for Crucian estates, ironically militated against any adoption and effective observance of amelioration practices when they were most needed, thereby compounding the original problem. On the other hand, a Danish apologist might equally argue that the takeover of the islands by Great Britain in the period 1807 to 1814 simply removed the matter from Danish hands.

In the final analysis, Denmark's abolition ordinance of 1792 resulted in a number of several interesting consequences. First, it was the first positive step in the direction of the ultimate destruction of the institution. Moreover, it allowed Denmark the honor of being known as an intrepid innovator in that process. Second, it set the spotlight on Ernst Schimmelmann and highlighted his statesmanship, as well as pointing to the ambiguity of the man and his policies. Third, it revealed an irony in that here was a divided attitude on the commerce, for some it was repugnant and for others it was profitable. And fourth it proved to be, more than anything else, a political maneuver in that it aimed at furthering Danish interests through difficult days in European politics, cloaked in the garb of morality while being in reality above all else a matter of simple practicality. However that may be, it now appears in retrospect that in the wake of the ordinance at the turn of the 19th century the demise of the West Indian slave system in the Danish islands was increasingly regarded as inevitable in the long run and moreover that there was very little that anyone could do about it.

Workers on a Crucian sugar plantation in the period after Emancipation

CHAPTER 14

CONDITIONS OF THE WORKING CLASS IN ST. CROIX, 1848–1878

INTRODUCTION

A FEW WORDS ON Emancipation will be necessary in order to arrive at a clear understanding of the conditions of the working class which that upheaval created. Why did slavery come to an end in the Danish West Indies? And what were its conditions during the last years of its existence? Answers to these questions go far in explaining the plight of the so-called freemen in the three or four decades after Emancipation. Fortunately, a good deal has been said on this topic in previous lectures.

Not enough attention, however, has been paid to the influence of revolutionary events in Europe in 1847–48 on events in the Danish West Indies in the same period, and perhaps a few words at least should be said by way of introduction. The capitals of Europe were, in the final years of the 1840s, ablaze with revolutionary activity. It had been the French Revolution of 1789 which had first loosed the new political philosophy on the continent, a philosophy which soon came to be known as liberalism, one that stressed the basic rights of man to life, liberty, property and the pursuit of happiness. Although the reactionary leaders of Europe tried to stifle the new political program in the years following the revolution and the subsequent Napoleonic period, they ultimately failed. It might be said that for a half century nearly all of Europe was caught up in the contradiction of attempting to restore the old order politically while striving to move ahead economically.

Such a return to the past was not to be, since the bourgeoisie—the dynamic class, economically speaking—was in many areas denied access to full political participation, and ultimately to dominance, which its members so greatly desired. Consequently, revolutionary activity broke out like brushfires, first in the 1820s, later in 1830 and finally in 1848. And though the revolutionaries often fell short of their avowed goals in 1848, that year nevertheless became symbolic, marking as it did, the final victory of liberalism and the emergence of the bourgeoisie, opening the doors wide for the first great advance of modern capitalism.[1]

As strange as it may sound, these events had a great impact on developments in the West Indies in general and in the Danish West Indies in particular in the period around 1848. These same events in revolutionary Europe were also widely followed with great interest by free and enslaved alike in the Danish West Indies, as Governor von Scholten himself pointed out:

"About the same time, or shortly thereafter, it came to the attention of the slaves in our islands that the Danish Constitution had been changed, but, of course, they did not know anything about the importance and consequences of this change so far as the Danish West Indies were concerned. But anybody who has lived in our colonies will understand that the slaves in our islands generally would believe that, just as the change in the French constitution had brought emancipation to their brothers in the French colonies, a change in the Danish constitution would result in theirs. As a matter of fact, many slaves were so sure of their emancipation that they believed the proclamation to be arbitrarily delayed."[2]

For von Scholten, at least, there could be little doubt concerning the direct relationship between the outbreak of revolutionary fervor in Europe and the push for emancipation on the part of the slaves. He wrote: "The fact that the slaves knew about the revolution in France in February and in Denmark in March had severe consequences for the whole situation in the Danish islands."[3]

But not only did the influences from Europe have an impact on the growing movement for Emancipation in the 1840s but, equally important, the new philosophy would influence the coming events in the crucial period 1848–78. Let us not forget that the revolutions under discussion were, in the main, bourgeois revolutions. The genius behind the movement was liberal thought and liberal philosophic ideas which insisted not only on the rights of man (i.e., life, liberty, happiness) but, perhaps most important of all, the right to property. From here it is only a short step to the other key ideas in liberalism, namely the economic axioms which insisted on the free market and its almost mystical qualities, as well as free trade and the free labor force.

What all this meant in practical terms for the common man from Glasgow to Christiansted was a new twist to the old game of one group's dominance of another. Just as the middle class had once been squarely under the boot of Europe's ruling aristocratic class for many centuries, so now that erstwhile "oppressed" class would arise, renewed and reinvigorated, as the modern bourgeoisie and would in its turn exploit to the fullest the presently defenseless laboring classes at its disposal. The newly emerging freemen of the Danish West Indies had the misfortune to gain their freedom in the maelstrom of these changing times. Our purpose in the present lecture is to examine the plight of the working class in the Danish West Indies, primarily St. Croix, against the backdrop of the events outlined cursorily above.

During the second half of 1848 in the period immediately after Emancipation, there ensued a great deal of confusion because freedom meant different things for different people, all depending on one's particular perspective. To the erstwhile slaves, of course, it meant self-determination, personal fulfillment, the pot of gold at the end of the elusive rainbow, the light at the end of the long tunnel. But most of all, they felt that they would now receive a wage for their labor, as other free men did, and that this newly won economic power would improve their lot. And it must have been entertained in the minds of the many that political rights and social improvements would likewise be forthcoming. Their disillusionment was, however, to be complete and not long in coming.

On the other hand, the members of the plantocracy envisioned the loss of servile labor which they had always owned outright, to do with as they saw fit. Liberal economic theory might argue that it was simply bad business to own a man outright, to have to be responsible for his health, his upkeep, his housing, his clothing and in the end to lose one's capital investment in death itself; but it remained a fact that slavery had worked in the Danish West Indies in the promotion of their interests for nearly two centuries. The planters, therefore, had grave doubts that any new system based upon the free labor of ex-slaves would work.

Government and business worked closely together at that time, each promoting the other's interest. When business was good, revenues flowed into the government's coffers. And when it was bad—well, no one likes to think about that. As a result of this intimate relationship, it was in the best interests of the latter two groups to make certain that a supply of inexpensive, docile labor continued to be available. To put it another way—to make free labor, cheap labor.

It must be remembered that in the final analysis 1848 was not a successful revolution which shifted political and economic control from one class or group to another, but rather an effective revolt which forced the ruling powers to reconsider, paradoxically enough, their own archaic economic organization, to conform with the trend of the times, and finally, to alter the means of dominating the real producers in society. In that complex process, the social fabric of the Danish West Indies changed only slightly; economic changes would follow at some distance and political ones only in the distant future.

This is to take nothing away from the brave men and women, like Buddhoe and others, who fought for their freedom. They, in their time, however, like we in ours, were often pitted against forces and circumstances against which they could not prevail. I have remarked in another place that the instruments of oppression are generally forged much more rapidly than are the means of the isolated individual to resist them.[4] To a large extent, that too is the central theme of tonight's lecture.

THE LABOR ACT OF 1849

The Labor Act of January 1849 was the response of the establishment to Emancipation in July of 1848.[5] From the rulers' point of view the attempts of the newly-freed to better their situation in life by moving about freely might result in economic chaos in which production on the plantations would fall off disastrously. Their response was twofold: first, the Labor Act, the purpose of which was to organize free labor for the maximum benefit of the plantocracy, and second, to provide in the long-run for a source of foreign labor to supplement the dwindling local force.

As the fullest expression of the will of the dominant class in society, the Labor Act of 1849 with certain minor subsequent modifications was to have the predominant influence on the lives of free Crucians in the period 1848–78, resulting as it did in new patterns of labor and subsistence, in emigration and immigration, in the genesis of a multicultural and multilingual society and, ultimately, in the eruption of discontent in 1878, the Great Fireburn.

The new free labor population was by no means completely monolithic.[6] First, the former slaves became for the most part "estate laborers." A good deal will be said about these workers in just a moment. There were also laborers or "porters" who generally made higher wages than their counterparts in the country, performing day-labor. This group owed its origins in general to the pre-Emancipation practice of hiring out skilled slaves in town for a fee which the owner pocketed. Since these porters worked for better wages after Emancipation and since they enjoyed greater freedom as well, their status was envied by the estate laborers and tended to draw the latter into the towns and away from the estates which still carried the oppressive odor of slavery.[7] Obviously enough, the towns could only absorb so many laborers of this kind; thereafter their movement became a problem resulting in overcrowding, unemployment and all the other vices which result from idleness in an urban setting.

There is yet another group which merits our consideration here, or perhaps we should say two groups: the free Coloreds and the free Blacks.

The first of these groups owed its origins as a group to the considerable social and sexual mixing of Europeans and Africans long before Emancipation. European fathers of "mulatto" children often gave freedom—free paper or Fribrev—to their offspring and to those children's mothers. By 1800, this was a sizeable group which for the most part chose to imitate the ways of the dominant Europeans, however little successful they may have been in reality.[8]

The free Blacks made up another group which had its roots deep in Danish West Indian history. They generally won their freedom through the process known as manumission, thoroughly described by Oldendorp as early as the 1770s; after being manumitted, they then supported themselves as free laborers and craftsmen long before Emancipation.[9]

It remains one of the important areas of study in Virgin Islands history to trace the development of these two groups through Emancipation and into the turbulent period presently under consideration, for it is certainly here, in my humble opinion, that we will, in all likelihood, trace the origins of that crucial nexus of social relationships and attitudes created by the intersection of class and color in mid-nineteenth Danish West Indian society.

CONDITIONS OF THE WORKING CLASS

Let us now return our attention to the post-Emancipation estate laborers whom we mentioned earlier. Again these were the ex-slaves and they made up the bulk of the population. They constituted, moreover, the productive element in society in that they provided the labor for all phases of the agricultural process as well as for related mechanical or industrial processes in the making of sugar. Without them, the owners of the estates could not produce sugar, cotton and profits. Every effort was therefore made to "lock" the laborer into his position.

A number of measures toward this end were consequently put into effect, some directly in the Labor Act of 1849.[10] They were all aimed at keeping the individual laborer on the same estate, doing the same work he had always done. A brief review of these measures would be instructive. First and foremost, there was the yearly contract system which came to be universally hated among the workers. Contracts were signed on October 1 of each year.[11] The laborer was required to work for the entire subsequent year under the terms of that contract. If he wished to change jobs, that is, change estates, he had to register his intention to do so officially in the month of August with the estate manager. If he did not do so, he was required to sign on for another year.

This system seemed to some relatively fair in the beginning in that it insured workers of a job for the entire year, come what may. As time passed, however, numerous inequities became apparent. In the first place, little regard was shown for individual rights, since a man signed a contract as the head in a household and not as an individual. His wife or mate and all their children between the ages of five and fifteen, as well as any other dependents or elderly relatives, were bound by the same contract.[12] In the second place, the freedom to change jobs was more theoretical than real insofar as various means were developed to keep workers on the same estate. To move about in search of a better job, for instance, required the issuance of a passport.[13] Obviously, these were at best difficult and at worst impossible to obtain.

If a worker attempted to visit another estate without permission, he ran the risk of being arrested on charges of vagrancy.[14] Patrols of armed militiamen moved along the island roads and through the towns, systematically checking papers. When one was arrested for not having the proper passport, he was taken to the nearest fort, locked up and then subsequently returned to his estate—a demonstration of public authority hardly calculated to enhance the hard-won freedom of the estate workers. It was equally difficult to escape into one of the towns to look for a job or attempt to practice a trade, though many, in fact, tried to do so. To discourage this, the police-master was empowered to put any idle individual to work. Moreover, purchased licenses were required in order to carry on business or practice one of the trades.[15] Once again the purpose of these measures, like the others, was clearly intended to keep the worker on the estate.

What then was life like for workers on the estates? Laborers were, first of all, classified as first, second and third class workers, earning 15, 10 and 5 cents per day respectively.[16] This system of labor organization, by the way, was a direct carry-over from pre-emancipation days when slaves were classified by gangs—first, second and third. That meant that a first class laborer would earn approximately 75 cents per week, three dollars per month or 36 dollars per year. Even though money was worth a good deal more then than now, these wages were still pitifully meager, all the more so when one considers that about 25 cents or one-third of the total weekly salary, was deducted by the estate to pay for store provisions—for the most part cornmeal and salt-fish, which were doled out each week. It would have been, without a doubt, a rare and resourceful worker indeed who could have saved enough to leave the estate and establish himself elsewhere.

Estate workers labored from sun-up to sun-down five days a week, with time off for lunch and a rest period during the hot hours of the day. Most hands prepared fields for cultivation—manured, planted, hoed, reaped and ratooned them. Others worked in the mills where the cane was ground, and others in the factory where sugar, molasses and rum were produced. In general, it might be said that the work was strenuous at the peak of the harvest season and monotonous during the rest of the year, and throughout not a little reminiscent of the days of slavery.

Workers were also required to produce part of their own food on their own time. The Labor Act of 1849 stipulated that each household head be allotted a piece of land 30 by 30 feet, called "Negro ground," on which to produce ground provisions—tania, yams, dasheen, corn and the like.[17] These garden crops supplemented the cornmeal and salt-fish, which were purchased from the estate. The enterprising individual might, in addition, carry some of his produce to the town markets on weekends in order to earn a few extra cents. It might be remarked here in passing that although these markets were not at all overly remunerative for the individual vendor, they did provide *in toto* for the energy and nourishment needs of the towns and their relatively sizeable populations.[18]

The estate worker returned from his day of labor to a small dwelling supposedly provided by the estate, but as often as not, built by the laborer himself of simple wood structure with wattle walls around an earthen floor, covered with a thatch type roof. A wooden board door and a window provided entry and ventilation. These units were generally small in size, intended as they were principally for sleeping, not at all unlike the typical peasant dwelling one encounters in the Haitian countryside today. I have been told in fact that a few of these still existed on St. Croix as late as the 1930s.

Most of the family and social activities enjoyed by the laborers took place in front of the small dwelling so that life tended to be communal and open. Everyone knew everyone else's business right down to what they were having for dinner since cooking also was done in the same place on a coal-pot over a charcoal fire.

Some twenty to thirty of these dwellings, taken collectively, constituted the "village" of the estate. It was within these confines on the various estates throughout the island that the traditions of the distant African past, as well as the more recent innovations of the local creole culture (i.e., creole language, folklore, folk medicine, folk literature, etc.) were nourished and kept alive during the long difficult fifty years after Emancipation. What has survived of local culture to this day, in fact, we owe to those tenacious souls. And their heritage is considerable given the restricted circumstances of their lives.

But life was not as totally grim and devoid of purpose as some have a tendency to read it in the historical record from our materialistic perspective in the present. There was the ever present hope of escape, perhaps to one of the towns, perhaps even further away; and there was also the possibility of making things better through those human resources which are available to us all even in the most difficult times. In the first of these categories, one has to be tremendously impressed by the dedication of the individual estate workers to effect the possible betterment of their children's lot in life. Often they sought out relatives or friends in town to act as guardians for their offspring. With education, it was thought, their prospects for the future would be infinitely better than remaining on the estate. Here again, the government opposed this practice of finding guardians in town.

Education was available to all children up to the age of ten in any one of eight government-operated schools on St. Croix, usually administered by the Moravians.[19] Estate youngsters were taught English, sums (arithmetic) and Bible history for the most part. It is not altogether clear, however, exactly what the education would lead to, beyond being able to read the Bible for Sunday church services. Accounts by contemporary educators like the following drew the sincerity of the government program into question:

"Unfortunately the law requires that at the age of ten years children must be discharged from the school, whether they can read or not. Just the years in which children begin to learn with developed intellect are here lost to them. Hence the people here are much more ignorant than in the English islands. This is apparent even in the expression on their faces."[20]

One can only surmise that the government was far more interested in providing strong bodies for agriculture than sound minds for education.

But despite the oppressive conditions of their lives, the Crucian laborers did not surrender to despair. In the evenings, for example, large groups of young people and children would gather around the elderly to hear stories, like those of the Anansi cycle, many of which went all the way back to the African past.[21] On other occasions religious groups visited the various estates for services; these were generally viewed as a welcome relief from the tedium of the estate, and these meetings were consequently well-attended. On more festive occasions still, there was dancing and music, sometimes even cariso singing, the only true native Crucian music that has survived from early times.[22] Dancing, especially the more African varieties, was traditionally discouraged by the establishment, and it is probably for this reason that a more socially acceptable Afro-European dance like the Quadrille has survived whereas the more purely African Bamboula has not. It has been exactly that kind of social selection with its inherent European bias that exerted then and has continued to exert such a strong influence on the evolution of Crucian culture in the years since 1848.

The same processes were at work in the area of language. Dutch Creole had of course been the predominant language among the slaves in the Danish West Indies through the 18th century.[23] Early in the 19th century, perhaps in part due to the English occupation during the Napoleonic wars, Dutch Creole was increasingly displaced in St. Croix by English Creole. And even though that form of speech was at that time quite distinct from British or American English, it is nevertheless clear that the latter two were exerting a tremendous influence on Crucian as is witnessed in the following remarks by a visiting missionary:

"Creole English is in common use among the Negroes but with white men they always try to speak pure English. One of the helpers offered up a prayer at one of the meetings in which the good language was no less striking than the earnest tone and spirit."[24]

In summary then, it is no exaggeration to say that, try as they might to better their condition, the Crucian laboring class in this period was both oppressed and depressed. Considering their severely restricted mobility, low pay, lack of organization, their lack of educational opportunities and perhaps even the loss of the optimism and direction which had existed in late 1848, it is not surprising that their fortunes and prospects for the future had fallen low indeed. Time and again we read in official church correspondence of the "low state of morality" of the Freedmen.[25] A dire picture is painted of their reluctance to attend church, of slovenliness, of low moral standards, of a higher illegitimacy rate, and of a continuing refusal of people to marry in the Christian manner. And in turn this pessimistic portrait of Crucian morals was employed by not a few in the dominant class to justify the low economic and social status of the worker. Yet in the final analysis, it is no doubt just the reverse, namely that deprivation, especially economic deprivation, more than anything else invalidated the dire lamentations of the various missionaries, with the consequence that the Crucians ultimately found themselves caught up in a vicious circle, where, to borrow from Hegel, the actual became the real or the rational.

Finally, it is not a little ironic to hear members of the island's white European population continually carping about the degenerate morals of the erstwhile slaves since it was within the matrix of 200 years of European-controlled slavery that many of those so-called "morals" had been developed. Their moral outcry, therefore, can never be more than an unconvincing footnote in the history of these islands.

The Crucian response to this post-Emancipation situation was manifold. I have remarked earlier on the attempt to escape into the towns even though this route was fraught with numerous difficulties. A far more ambitious and sometimes dangerous solution was to leave the island altogether. But where to go? Crucian slaves had been escaping to Puerto Rico[26] as early as the mid-18th century with the long-term result that there evolved a small expatriate Crucian community there. Others fled to Santo Domingo and Cuba to work as free agricultural laborers. Still others found their way later to Central America to work in the digging of the Panama Canal. And finally, some began to go to the eastern coast of the United States, particularly New York, though we are not at all certain how early that migration pattern began. What is certain is that by the 1890s there was a small community of Danish West Indians in New York,[27] to be greatly amplified by another wave of immigrants in the 1920s.

If one response of the Crucian working population to oppressive working conditions was emigration, the official response of the establishment to a growing shortage of workers was immigration. It must be admitted once again, however, that this latter practice was nothing new. In the pre-Emancipation days, it was possible to purchase slaves from other islands in an inter-island slave trade. And often planters from other islands brought considerable numbers of slaves with them when they moved to St. Croix. As late as the 1840s, free laborers from the emancipated British islands—Barbados, Antigua, St. Kitts—were brought to St. Croix to supplement the slave labor force.

Recent research in this area has added much to our knowledge of labor and immigration in the period 1848-78.[28] It has become clear, for example, that the Crucian labor force did decline by 25% by 1853. The government attempted to stem that trend by a vigorous enforcement of the Labor Act of 1849. It subsequently turned to an aggressive immigration policy. As early as 1851, limited numbers of workers were brought in from the Madeira Islands. Later in that same decade after an attempt to bring in free labor from Africa failed, workers were brought in from Barbados. In 1860 a tax was levied on each acre of sugar land to be paid into an immigrant labor fund. This resulted in more workers being brought to the island from Barbados in the 1860s as well as considerable numbers of Indians from Calcutta (365). The continued trend throughout the 1860s was a general growth of both native emigration and off-island immigration with the former for the most part out-stripping the latter.[29]

Those who today celebrate the *M'ban ya* syndrome a little too vociferously would do well to recall that not only did many of the original Crucians emigrate to other areas of the hemisphere as "aliens" but also that many of those who came here as immigrant workers from "down island" in the 1860s and 70s are no doubt to be numbered among their progenitors. Be that as it may, the trend, though beginning to decline, continued into the 1870s, when economic conditions took a sharp turn for the worse.

THE DECLINE OF THE 1870S

Despite vigorous attempts of the government and the plantocracy to maintain levels of production and despite the continuation of the harsh labor laws, the agriculture of the Danish islands fell upon disastrous times in the 1870s and, as usual, it was the man at the bottom of the structure who paid most dearly. The signs of the decline—we would certainly call it a depression today—are to be seen most clearly in the decrease of sugar production. By the mid-1870s average yearly production declined by 19% of what it had been in the more productive 1860s.

Discounting 1872 which produced an unexpected, and not repeated, bumper crop, yearly production fell by a little over 33% in the 1870s, and in the worst year, 1874, production was off 68%, an economic disaster by any standard.[30]

These gloomy figures are matched by a concomitant decline in the amount of land which was cultivated in St. Croix. In 1850, for example, 20,195 acres were under cultivation. Each decade until 1880 that amount decreased by about 8% until the figure reached 15,664 acres in 1880, a decrease of 22.4% overall from 1850. Again the most startling change occurred in the disastrous 1870s during which time 9.3% of the currently in-use land went out of cultivation by the end of the decade.[31]

Finally, a similar trend is evident in the demography of the island. Country district population declined from 15,500 in 1850 to approximately 10,000 in 1880, a startling loss of over 35% in 30 years. The decline had been gradual in the 1850s (5.8%) and 1860s (4.8%), but in the 1870s there was tremendous acceleration of the decline (27.5%). Town population by contrast grew from 8,300 in 1850 to 9,000 in 1870, a growth rate of 8.4%. Even after the disastrous events of the late 1870s, town populations in St. Croix could still boast of a modest net growth since 1850 of 1.2%, astonishing indeed when contrasted with what had been occurring at the same time in the country districts.[32]

The figures show, then, that the productivity, population and land cultivation remained relatively stable in the 1850s and 1860s but in the 1870s all three fell into sharp declines. What caused these drastic changes and what effect did it all have on the laboring classes? First of all, a prolonged drought struck the Danish islands in the early 1870s and with little interruption endured until nearly the end of the decade, causing a great reduction in sugar cane production. A Moravian visitor gave this view of the islands in December of 1877 just ten months before the Fireburn:

"Externally, St. Croix is in a deplorable position. This once flourishing island has for the last seven years been visited by a succession of dry seasons. Of three streams which formerly flowed between Friedensfeld and Friedensberg, there is no trace. I was much struck by the miserable appearance of the sugarcane fields, when compared with those in other islands."[33]

He goes on to say that "should this state of things continue for some years, the future of St. Croix will be very dark, as the sugar estates will be ruined."[34] Although he had no way of knowing it, his words would prove to be prophetic.

These highly unfavorable weather conditions had the effect of forcing out of business the smaller, less competitive estates which had been struggling along on government loans. And it appears that the development of the new central factory (1874) would have, in the long run, worked in favor of consolidation of larger estates rather than the small independent operator.

Finally, we must not lose sight of the relationship of the economy of the Danish West Indies to the larger outside world. Sugar was by that time being produced from beets in large quantities in many parts of the world.[35] Therefore, West Indian sugars were no longer as important as they once had been in supplying the Western European markets. Moreover, as the supply of refined sugar greatly increased, its price on the world market dropped, creating a squeeze for the small producers.

But even more crucial yet for the disastrous 1870s was the onset of one of the first of the great depressions which the recent capitalistic powers were to undergo.[36] The one in question began in 1873 and endured until the late 1880s, some say well into the 1890s. At its peak, tens of thousands were out of work in the industrial countries and production fell off markedly. Fringe areas like the Danish West Indies felt the inevitable effects. The sum total of this worldwide catastrophe affected not only the plantation owners but the workers as well who with smaller wages because of the decline in local sugar production had increasingly fewer resources to acquire those essential commodities which had become scarcer and more expensive at the same time.

The advent of liberalism, mentioned at the beginning of this presentation, not only sanctioned free labor but the free market as well. If the plantation owners were free to exploit as best they could the free labor of the Danish West Indies, they in their turn were subject to the force of the "market-place" in open and free competition in the primitive spirit of 19th century capitalism. The failure of the smaller capitalistic entrepreneurs in the Danish West Indies in the world market place can be attributed more to their own conservative nature, to their inability to adopt the rapidly changing nature of the world conditions and ultimately to forces by and large beyond their control rather than the lack of an adequate labor force, as is sometimes suggested.

To sum up, conditions of workers after a period of relative stability in the 1850s and 1860s worsened precipitously in the 1870s. By early 1878 it appeared to many as if the bottom were about to fall out. Not only did the lot of the average laborer leave much to be desired by any standard, but moreover, and perhaps more important in the long run, he was severely restricted by an alliance of the estate and the government which attempted to prevent him from doing anything significant to improve his deteriorating lot. All workers were proud of the fact that they had earned their freedom, however belatedly, in 1848; now nearly 30 years later, many felt that numerous oppressive measures with which free labor had been saddled, were making that hard-won freedom something of a sham. Emotions consequently were running high. Nerves were taut and a persistent tension pervaded the air. The unremitting drought in turn did nothing to relieve the situation. And since the future offered little promise of any real change, the laborers finally began to despair. It is against this backdrop that the Great Fireburn of 1878 must be considered.

NOTES

1. For a masterly account of these years see: E. J. Hobsbawn, *The Age of Revolution 1789–1848* (New York: New American Library, 1962), 416 pp., and *The Age of Capital 1848–75* (New York: Charles Scribner's Sons, 1975), 345 pp.

2. Peter von Scholten, "Letter of December 22, 1849, to Liebenberg, Counsel for the Defense, concerning the Negro Rebellion in St. Croix on July 3, 1848," in *Emancipation in the Danish West Indies: Eye Witness Accounts II*, Eva Lawaetz, trans. (St. Thomas: Bureau of Libraries and Museums, n.d.), pp. 8–9.

3. *Ibid.*, p. 9.

4. Arnold R. Highfield, "On the Abortive Rebellion of 1759," (*St. Croix Avis*, January 8, 1979), p. 9.

5. The Labor Act of 1849 is printed *in toto* in: John P. Knox, *A Historical Account of St. Thomas, W. I.* (New York: Charles Scribner, 1852), Appendix 8, pp. 248–55.

6. For a good general discussion of the laboring population in the post-Emancipation period, see: James W. Green, *Social Networks in St. Croix, United States Virgin Island* (Doctoral Dissertation: University of Washington, 1972), 378 pp.

7. *Ibid.*, p. 58.

8. For the best discussion of this group, see: N. A. T. Hall, "The 1816 Freedom Petition in the Danish Virgin Islands: Its Background and Consequences," a paper presented at the Eleventh Annual Conference of the Association of Caribbean Historians at Curaçao April 5–11, 1979, 38 pp.

9. C. G. A. Oldendorp, *Geschichte der Mission der evangelischen Bruder auf den carabischen Inseln S. Thomas, S. Croix und S. Jan.* (Barby: Johann Jakob Bossarty, 1777), Book 4, Section 6, p. 402.

10. See Knox, pp. 248–55.

11. *Ibid.*, p. 248.

12. *Ibid.*

13. *Ibid.*, p. 249.

14. Green, pp. 36–38.

15. *Ibid.*, p. 38.

16. Knox, p. 252.

17. *Ibid.*, p. 251.

18. Address by N. A. T. Hall at Florence Williams Public Library, Christiansted, St. Croix, December 11, 1977.

19. The Moravians began to bring education to the slaves of the Danish West Indies early in the 18th century. See: Patricia Shaubah Murphy, *The Moravian Mission to the African Slaves of the Danish West Indies 1732-1828* (St. Thomas: Caribbean Research Institute, 1969), 23 pp., and Eva Lawaetz, *Black Education in the Danish*

West Indies from 1732 to 1853: The Pioneering Effort of the Moravian Brethren, (St. Croix: St. Croix Friends of Denmark Society, 1980), 90 pp.

20. Periodical Accounts Relating to the Mission of the Church of the United Brethren Established Among the Heathen, vol XXX, 1877, p. 303.

21. For modern renditions of these stories, see: Lezmore L. Emanuel Broo Nansi (Washington, DC: General Learning Corporation, 1973–74), and The Bull and the Golden Calabash and other Anansi Stories (St. Thomas: by the author, 1977). Also see: Elsie Clews Parsons, Folklore of the Antilles, French and English, published by the American Folklore Society (New York: G. E. Stechert and Company, 1933–43), Volume II, pp. 411–69.

22. For a broad general treatment of Virgin Islands musicology see: Margot Leithe, The Musical Culture of the United States and British Virgin Islands. Doctoral Dissertation in progress; University of Cologne, Germany.

23. For an early account of this Creole, see Oldendorp, Book 4, Section 10, pp. 437–44.

24. Periodical Accounts Relating to the Moravian Church. . . . Vol. XXX, 1877, p. 310.

25. Ibid., pp. 303–10. The entire account of the visitation from which this quote is taken carries the tone of decline within the church and a distinct lagging in morals within the community.

26. Oldendorp, Book 4, Section 6, pp. 396–97.

27. Personal interview with Mr. Charles Reubel, New York, September, 1975. Mr. Reubel was a resident of New York from early in the century, subsequently becoming the editor of The Civic, a newspaper for Virgin Islanders in the city. He was extremely knowledgeable about the V.I. community there.

28. The work of a young Danish scholar, Peter Hoxcer Jensen has added much to our knowledge of this period. See: Peter Hoxcer Jensen, Indforsel af Fri Arbejdskraft til St. Croix 1849–76 med særligt Henblik pa immigrations—og Arbejdslovgivningen, (MA thesis: University of Aarhus, 1978), 128 pp. For a sound treatment of the question of labor conditions, see his Plantagearbejdernes Vilkar i Dansk Vestindian Fra slave-emancipation til Oernes Salg, Prize state essay (Aarhus, Denmark: October, 1979), 228 pp.

29. For a concise treatment of the immigration question, see: Jensen, Plantagearbejdernes Vilkar . . . pp. 117–42.

30. Ibid., p. 19.

31. Ibid., p. 13.

32. Ibid., p. 45.

33. Periodical Accounts Relating to the Moravian Church. . . . Vol. XXX, 1877, p. 303.

34. Ibid.

35. Noel Deerr, *The History of Sugar*, 2 vols. (London: Chapman and Hall Ltd., 1950), 636 pp.

36. Hobsbawn, *The Age of Capital*, p. 46.

Seal of Les Amis des Noirs, a French abolition
society from the late 18th century

CHAPTER 15
REPARATIONS FOR
VIRGIN ISLANDERS?

PART ONE

A REPARATIONS movement emerged in the Virgin Islands in the early years of this new millennium, patterned no doubt on an earlier movement that sprang up among African-Americans in the Unites States several decades previously. In that stateside movement, Blacks set out to obtain recompense for the economic and moral injustices imposed on their ancestors during several centuries of slavery. The failed promise of 40 acres and a mule, followed by the failure of Reconstruction, the imposition of harsh Jim Crow laws and systematic racism constituted an inauspicious start as free men for a long-oppressed people.

But what of the reparations question in the Virgin Islands? What was the nature of the offence and who exactly caused it? More importantly, who benefitted from it? From 1672 until 1807 Danes carried on a slave trade with African nations in that part of West Africa then called Guinea. After that trade was abolished by Danish law in 1807, slavery itself continued in existence in the Danish islands until 1848. The Danish colonies therefore profited from the enslaved Africans' labor for a period of 176 years. These are some of the questions for which answers are presently being sought by Shelley Moorhead, founder and leader of ACRRA, the African-Caribbean Reparations and Resettlement Alliance.

During that period of time, between 100,000 and 125,000 persons were ensnared in the African trade. In addition to that number there were also the Creole slaves, or those born in the islands over that same period of time, as well as those imported from other Caribbean islands. Although it would be an extremely difficult task to arrive at an exact figure for the entire number of enslaved individuals for the Danish West Indies from 1671 until 1848, the figure 250,000 might be put forward as a conservative estimate. If the trade was demand-driven, that is, founded on the need for sugar plantation laborers, then it was ultimately the planters in the islands who provided the cause for it all in their demand for an inexhaustible, docile labor force.

Merchants and slave traders in Denmark provided the capital for the trade and presumably made profits from it. African kings along the Guinea coast supplied the product, for which they were paid, largely in trade goods. Trading companies and ship captains carried the human cargoes to Caribbean markets and thereby made profits, though in many cases they were the very same individuals as the Danish merchants and traders.

The resultant slave system produced sugar, molasses, rum, cotton and other tropical products, from which the Danish Government derived income in the form of taxes of several kinds. And finally, certain secondary producers of foodstuffs, cloth etc. provided the slave owners with clothing and material sustenance for the slaves. Each of these exploiters made profits and in so doing benefitted from the entire operation. No one has yet tackled the problem of calculating the actual monetary amount of this exploitation. Certainly it would run into the hundreds of millions of dollars in today's currency, figuring a rough interest rate into the total.

Some proponents of reparations argue that the debt of the former slave owners extends even beyond the date of Emancipation, indeed even as far as the present time. The idea behind this approach might be termed the "deficiency theory," insofar as slavery itself was followed by a period, 1848 down until 1917, when the former slaves were offered no real remediation for their previous condition but were once again exploited by an unfair wage-labor system imposed by a post-slavery plantation demands. This system was, moreover, sanctioned and imposed by a legal system that maintained the status quo in favor of the dominant order in society. According to this view, the freed slaves began their new lives under the burden of a deficit, which has slowed their advancement in most areas of their lives down to the present day. So it is that slavery becomes the great determiner in this view, accounting for nearly every deficiency suffered today by the inheritors of this tradition—negative self-images, family disruption, poor educational achievement, societal marginalization, lack of business acumen and participation, social conflict, and even crime and social violence. All of these faults and more can, in this interpretation, be traced backed to causal roots deep in the slave past.

But perhaps the most serious of all the damages inflicted by slavery and its aftermath has been what might be termed the wound of race. Slave-owners and traders ultimately used racism—the ideology of racial inferiority—as a justification for their nefarious activities and the profits accrued from them. This had a lasting, negative influence that has extended far beyond simple support of an economic endeavor and into the realm of the moral. Indeed, it placed an enormous burden on its victims as well as on their descendants that caused them to question their own worth and abilities as human beings, thereby creating a syndrome of self-doubt, as well as suspicion and trepidation relative to the world around them. This aspect of personal and social damage, proponents argue, is all but impossible to understand by anyone who has not lived within the experience of slavery and its consequences.

Since Denmark was the cause and originator of this system, as the argument goes, then it is Denmark who should be obliged to recognize this obligation and make amends for it. Such a response would take three forms: acknowledgement of responsibility, apology for the wrongdoing, and payment of reparations of one kind or another to the victims. In return, Virgin Islanders who have suffered from slavery would welcome the recognition, accept the apology and make a positive, constructive use of the reparations, whatever form they might take. In theory, the reparations, though they would most likely never completely expunge the magnitude of the original offence, could nevertheless be applied in such a manner as to make the future much better for the victims from this point onward.

What form might these reparations take? Ideally, one might envision a direct payment to individuals whose ancestors were those who were enslaved. But establishing just who these descendents are some seven generations after the fact would be an extremely difficult undertaking. The problem is similar when considering just what might constitute a just amount of payment. If it could be established, for example, that there were 50,000 persons in the Virgin Islands who were eligible and that $20,000 per person might constitute a reasonable sum of restitution, then the resulting payment would come to one billion dollars, or about .5 % of Denmark's annual GNP (2007). On the other hand, the restitution might be made on the societal or governmental level, from Denmark to the Virgin Islands, taking the form of perhaps a developmental undertaking of some kind, or training programs, internship programs, educational programs, a learning center or the like. The calculation of the value of such a plan would depend directly on the nature and the extent of the various programs.

The form or the amount of the reparations notwithstanding, there is little doubt in the eyes of the proponents of reparations concerning the veracity of their claims in their moral, economic, social and political dimensions. Certainly, such a settlement would by its very nature demand compromise. And assuredly not everyone would emerge from the process completely satisfied. Equally important, it is certain that the debate would occupy many of the months and even years that lie before us. It is an issue that merits a considered, just debate.

PART TWO

In the article of March 28, 2008, we looked at the question of reparations for slavery in the Virgin Islands and the arguments in favor of it. The present article will have a look at the objections to this view, to be followed in June by a third and final article that will suggest some measures for compromise. The idea here is to give a fair, balanced view of the issues so as to serve as a basis for the debate.

No one can deny the past reality of slavery in our islands nor the impact it had on the lives of many. Were it possible to directly repay those unfortunates who suffered it, few would oppose such a solution. But is it possible to fairly address this problem some 150 years after the fact? Is it possible to identify with any certainty those who bear the blame for this travesty? Equally important, can the suffering of those who lived five or six generations ago be justly identified in those who live here today?

Opponents of reparations point out, in the first place, that reparations to address past injustices have been historically used only sparingly and with highly mixed results. Yes, Germany paid reparations for its aggression in World War One, but ultimately those measures failed miserably and in fact created in large part the conditions for World War Two. Some European Jews have been compensated for losses in the Holocaust but only partially. And the Japanese Americans who were interned in World War Two were paid for their internment with modest sums, though it is viewed by many as mere tokenism. So reparations have only been moderately successful, even where they were possible. And no one, it appears, emerged from the process satisfied.

Innumerable other equally valid but unaddressed claims—American Indians in most parts of the New World, the Irish in their own country, and millions of the enslaved throughout the modern world, have not even been approached. The result is that where reparations have been paid the results have been mixed and where they have not, such a payment seems quite unlikely to ever occur due to the complexities involved in sorting out the issues. Not least of these issues in all cases has been the matter of the passage of time.

In our case the question comes down to this: should Denmark be expected to pay reparations today to the descendants of individuals who were enslaved in the colonial era over 150 years ago? That seemingly simple proposition becomes quite complex on closer examination. Opponents point out that the Denmark of today is not the same entity as existed in colonial times. From 1671 until 1755, for example, the Danish West Indies and the slave trade were under the control of a private trading company, The Danish West India and Guinea Company, an extremely small fraction of the Danish population at that time. From 1755 to 1848, the islands fell under the direct rule of the Danish monarchy, which operated under the principles of absolutism, leaving no place for popular opinion or popular protest or intervention. That monarchy was not replaced by popular sovereignty until the very end of the slavery period, just before Emancipation in 1848. Any attempt to blame the Danish people then must be viewed through this lens.

Although the monarchy did own and run several of the larger plantations in the Danish islands, the vast majority of the plantations were owned by an extremely small number of private individuals. Moreover, the greater number of those few owners were not Danes but English, Scots, Irish, French, Dutch, German and of other backgrounds. Should Danish citizens today be held responsible for the actions of a few hundred individuals in distant colonies, most of whom were not even Danes?

Indeed, Denmark is presently made up of people who overwhelmingly never lived in the West Indies and who never owned slaves. Nor did their ancestors own slaves. And in addition, the Danish population itself has changed over the years, embracing newcomers, namely Germans, Poles, Croats, Turks and other Middle Easterners, people who were not even present in Denmark at the time in question. Should their tax payments be used for a historical misadventure in which they or their ancestors had absolutely no part?

Those same critics would also ask the following question: how can it be determined just how many individuals in the Virgin Islands today descend directly from slaves in the period before 1848? At present, the Virgin Islands is a strikingly diverse society, consisting of Hispanics from every part of the Caribbean and its littoral, Eastern Caribbean people from every island, extending all the way to Trinidadians to Jamaicans, not to mention North Americans, including African Americans. Should Denmark be expected to pay for the grievances of those immigrant folk, some of whose ancestors were never enslaved or, at most, enslaved in other islands under other jurisdictions?

In addition, it is a well known fact that immigrants from the Eastern Caribbean in particular mixed with Virgin Islanders after Emancipation from the mid-19th century onward, leading one to pose yet another vexing question: exactly how many Virgin Islanders can trace all eight of their great-grandparents to the Virgin Islands in the slavery period? In all probability, very few indeed. Should Denmark then be asked to pay resident Virgin Islanders for the indignities of slavery suffered by individuals whose ancestors ultimately hail either wholly or in part from other islands?

Opponents of reparations also ask if the same standards of moral responsibility that apply to Denmark also apply to certain African states—Ghana, Nigeria, Ivory Coast, Guinea, Dahomey, Togo, Senegal, etc., whose former leaders sold fellow Africans to both European and Arab slave-traders, some of whom found their way to the Danish islands? Or are they to be given a pass, perhaps due to their African background and/or race? Opponents argue, in fact, that reparation demands are often based primarily on race and not on proof of direct injury. To support this view, they point to the existence of numerous Free Blacks and Free Colored individuals from the inception of the Danish colonies whose lot was quite distinct from that of field slaves. Some of these free individuals even owned plantations—small to be sure—and slaves who worked their estates as well. Are their descendants to be included in the reparations along with direct descendants of slaves? And if so, on what basis if not simply race?

These same opponents also ask if the admission of guilt by the Danish government at this late point in time might not open the gates for a flood of individual legal claims? And if the Danish government were to pay reparations on such a basis, who is to say that everyone would be satisfied with his individual lot and consequently not initiate suits based on individual damages? Such a scenario of conflicting claims might well result in a residue of bitterness that would leave us worse off than before we started.

Oddly enough, resentment might be the end result where reconciliation had been intended. For their part, the Danes might well resent the payment of funds 150 years after the fact, to people whose individual claims to such payments they might consider questionable and perhaps exorbitant. And on the other hand, Virgin Islanders might regard any such payment as woefully inadequate tokenism. Just such a scenario would leave both parties feeling wronged and could simply prolong and even intensify the mutual dissatisfaction.

Can all faults and dissatisfactions in the present-day Virgin Islands, opponents ask, be blamed on the slave-holding past as is sometimes claimed? Crime, violence, low self-esteem, family disruption and illegitimacy are often cited in this regard. Opponents of reparations argue that Virgin Islands people have in fact benefitted from their lives in the islands since emancipation in some important ways.

Comparing Ghana (formerly the Gold Coast and ancestral home of many Virgin Islanders) to the former Danish West Indies makes this point. For one thing, slavery was not abolished there until 1874 and, at that, it was mandated by the British. Remnants of slavery remain today in the form of *trokosi*, temple slavery inflicted on young girls, as well as in forced child labor in many parts of that country.

From this same critical perspective, other comparisons with Ghana are equally revealing. Though Ghana is about 125 times larger in land size than the Virgin Islands with 215 times greater population, Ghana's GDP is only about 20 times larger than that of the Virgin Islands. And on a per capita basis, the GDP of the Virgin Islands outstrips that of Ghana by an astounding ratio of approximately 14 to one! Life expectancy in the VI presently stands at 79 years, while in Ghana it is 59; infant mortality is a respectable 7.2 per thousand in the Virgin Islands, while in Ghana, 52 per thousand. Figures of this kind could be extended across the board showing similar disparities in favor of the Virgin Islands and its people.

This comparison is not intended to demean or cast aspersion on Ghana but only to demonstrate that a certain material progress has been undeniably made in the Virgin Islands over time. Does this not stand as proof, opponents of reparations ask, that some very real material benefits have accrued to Virgin Islanders in spite of the evil of the original slavery experience? Have we not political dominion in our own land, economic freedom, complete and open access to education and the freedom to go where we will?

In the final analysis, critics claim, freedom, equality, individual well being and self-esteem, in any event, cannot be donated, bequeathed or bestowed. These are qualities that must be first imagined, then created and finally assumed as an act of free will. To be truly free means seizing responsibility for one's own actions and forging one's own destiny regardless of what may have gone before. To seek blame against another party for all the evils that beset any comity, past, present and future, is unrealistic and to embrace that belief will simply postpone the opportunity of assuming one's place in the world as a proud, free people. To act otherwise, opponents claim, would be a step backward into victimhood.

So it is that such opponents of reparations maintain that the time is right to put the grievances of the past behind us, to be grateful for such progress as we have undeniably made over the past century and a half, and to look to the future with confidence but without recrimination.

PART THREE

In the previous two articles we have been taking a brief look at the pros and cons of the question of reparations for slavery and for its post-Emancipation effects in the Virgin Islands. Those articles demonstrated that both sides of that debate can make and have made compelling arguments. Here we will consider a third possibility, a third way that might provide an alternative, focused on the goal of moral harmony and not simply on the hard logic of economics and legality.

Harmony in societal relations might rightly be viewed as the greatest good to which humanity can aspire. Wherever it is present, serious conflicts can be managed, war can be averted, and peace and prosperity come within reach of the human hand. Due, however, to our natural disposition for seeking advantageous gain, to our inclination for the unequal distribution of material resources, and, not least, to the chance location of various groups on our planet relative to scarce resources, harmony has always been an elusive grail.

From this harsh reality there is little hope for escape from this centuries-old cycle, unless we opt consciously for another approach, one based on giving something rather than withholding everything and on accepting the possible rather than demanding the improbable, all considered within the realm of the rational, the moral and the possible. Such an approach stresses the moral over the narrowly economic path, with a goal of attaining harmony rather than ending in a standoff that insists narrowly on attaining victory and avoiding defeat.

In the first place, a system of reparations in which remuneration would be paid from a government to various individuals or groups of individuals will more than likely become mired in self-interest and legal complexity. If, however, reciprocity were to proceed from government to government, society to society, community to community and institution to institution, then the greater part of the initial difficulties and objections would rapidly diminish and the previously narrow path would begin to open a bit, as a result of the principle of sharing as a group instead of receiving as individuals.

But how might that be attained? What if the Danish government were to establish an agency or commission to nurture and facilitate, in conjunction with the Virgin Islands government, a broad agreement to investigate our past relationships, good and bad? To accomplish that goal such an agency might first promote travel, study, cultural exchange, the development of common interests, and institutional contacts between the two countries and their peoples. There might be an ambassador of sorts in both countries to address these initial undertakings and some of the others mentioned below. In this manner the governments would lead but not manage, suggest but not enforce, arbitrate but not coerce. This idea, in any event, would aim to stimulate the flow of people and ideas in an ambience of cooperation and harmony, with mutual self-interest as the sole point of our participation.

A natural place for such a relationship to be initiated would be among non-governmental institutions of the two partners—our respective schools, universities, archives, libraries, and professional organizations. Teachers, professors and students, as one example, could exchange places for a semester or for a year with Danish counterparts. Questions would be posed, answers offered. In a short time, the record of the past would be available for all to see and from which to draw studied conclusions.

As a response to that grand adventure, the excellent Danish universities might well agree to set aside several tuition-free slots each year in their universities, their medical schools and nurse training programs for the well qualified among our young people. What gift could be more valuable and lasting for us than a single, well-trained doctor or nurse or teacher, insofar as their work would touch the lives of thousands of others in the course of their lifetimes? And what could be more rewarding for Denmark than to provide this gift to a people whose past needs, medical, educational and otherwise, were often left untended?

Such interchanges would of course require training in language and cultural understanding, a need that could be supplied by a Danish program with Danish instructors at the University of the Virgin Islands. And in return, our university might offer a similar program in English and our own Caribbean history and culture, both at UVI for visitors, and perhaps even in Denmark for Danish students. The point here is that once the pump has been primed by the acceptance of a starting point and a set of mutually agreed upon objectives, it would then continue to provide sweet, fresh water.

This institutional beginning might readily be transferred to our respective societies and communities. The types and kinds of exchanges are limited only by the imagination. They would lead, it would be hoped, to social interaction and individual, face-to-face contacts, on that level where meaning and intention take on a human face. Individuals might enter into these activities as often or as seldom as they would like. Or they might even decline to participate altogether. Such an approach stresses the freedom to take part, when, where and however one might desire. And at the same time it avoids the bureaucratic nightmare of insisting on complete equity enforced by external authority.

In the final analysis it is far easier to mend fences than repair hearts. But the latter too can be attempted under certain circumstances. Our own Carib Indians, as one example among others, sometimes entered into the bonds of brotherhood with total strangers, often for life. Why not at least open that door to Virgin Islanders and Danes? How utterly original if a Danish family in Aarhus could join hands in what's called artificial kinship with a family in Fredriksted! Or a family on St. Thomas or St. John might adopt a Danish family in Aalborg. In complete freedom they could one and all explore and pursue the relationship to the extent that they might desire. Some might object that it could never be done; it would never work. Perhaps, but it has not been tried in such circumstances as ours. And what a mighty example it would provide to others in this hopelessly conflicted world!

To help achieve these and other ends, Centers for Cultural Exchange, or some such, might be established both here and in Denmark, each containing small libraries, research facilities, lecture halls, classrooms, small performance theatres, meeting facilities and the like, each operated by a mixed staff of Virgin Islanders and Danes, giving young people, in particular, the opportunity to meet and exchange ideas and lifestyles among themselves. Not the least of its objectives would be an investigation of their mutually shared past, stressing history, culture, the arts and even economic development. It is altogether possible, that, if properly managed, such centers could be made to be self-supporting and perhaps profitable.

Now it might be argued that such activities would reorient The Virgin Islands and Virgin Islanders away from their present and future relationship with the United States and in favor of their past with Denmark. To that I offer this response: what would it be worth for a people to have the opportunity to explore for a time their labyrinthine past in order to set past wrongs right, to expunge ancient bitterness, to temper present anxiety and mistrust by understanding, and to have another chance to look at their erstwhile adversaries and at themselves, hopefully this time in a context of equality and humanity?

It might be further asked—what motive would Denmark have to enter into the lion's share of the cost of such programs? In reflecting on this question, it is hoped that Danes might thoughtfully consider their country's past motives and its past spending of far greater sums in pursuit of far less noble goals. Their recompense would lie in replacing the resultant, long-lingering bitterness for which their ancestors were largely responsible, with a project of moral justice and harmony of their own present design and making, under no obligation to do so other than their own sense of fairness.

Could measures such as these truly result in a resolution of the questions raised by reparations? Maybe so, maybe not. What is certain is that success would depend on the desire of both parties to sincerely experience the will toward transformation of our stubborn human predicament. Moreover, both parties would have to stress the importance, not merely of the material benefits in the transaction but also of the emergence of clearly discernible good intentions that accompany such an ambitious undertaking. We can never change the past, but we have the will to modify our reaction to it.

So in the final analysis it might just come down to this: "So, my brother, by means of these good intentions and actions, I ask your forgiveness for what you have suffered." To which the response might just be: "I accept your words, your intentions, and actions, my brother. Now let us proceed forward together." But we will certainly never hear these words exchanged unless we are willing to give our better nature a try.

Street scene in Frederiksted in 1910, shortly before the sale of the Islands
to the United States

CHAPTER 16
MYTHS AND REALITIES IN VIRGIN ISLANDS HISTORY

IT HAS BECOME A TRUISM among many Virgin Islanders, especially among older ones, that the years before the transfer of the islands to the United States in 1917 could be viewed as "the good old days." Various writers have published articles and books, replete with illustrations, lending weight to this notion. In these images are depicted the passage of donkey carts along quiet country roads amidst fields of waving cane on their tranquil way to predictably somnolent destinations. Picturesque towns doze under a benevolent tropical sun. Stout women balance impossible burdens atop their heads before a picturesque marketplace as carefree island folk make their way in and about the arched arcades, all under the paternal, watchful eyes of Danish gendarmes. It is all the very picture of peace, order and tranquility. It is in this manner that yesterday's hard realities have been cleanly transformed into today's nostalgia and myth.

In truth, it is altogether possible that those former times under Danish rule did indeed at one point appear better to black Virgin Islanders than they actually had been, especially in the years immediately after the U.S. Navy dropped anchor in 1917. At that time, the Navy, due in part to the exigencies of WW I, was developing its well-known "battleship mentality." And, of course, the crews of those vessels had their fair share of uneducated, poor white southerners. The unhappy results of that 14-year stay are well documented.

But what about those "good old days" under the Danes? Were they real or illusory, fact or fiction? How well do the now-enshrined myths of Danish times stand up to critical evaluation? And what import would such an evaluation have on the writing and study of history and culture in these islands? Before attempting to address these questions, a brief survey of the Danish colonial enterprise would appear to be in order, especially as it unfolded in the Danish West Indies.

The Danes embarked on their version of colonial empire in the mid-17th century—their own heroic age. That venture was given shape and coherence by the appearance of royal absolutism within the Danish monarchy in the mid-seventeenth century and in the institutionalization of a Danish version of classic French mercantilism, with a pronounced Dutch influence. It took readily and immediately to the world seas as a consequence of an ancient maritime tradition dating back to Viking times. By the onset of the 18th century, Danish royal officials, merchants and seamen had forged a global micro-network of colonies and trade relations that included dominion over Norway, Iceland, Greenland and the rugged Faroe Islands, all lying along the North Atlantic rim of Europe. In the distant Indian Ocean, they added the extraterritorial city of Tranquebar on the eastern coast of the Indian subcontinent along with the Nicobar Islands, an archipelago strung like exotic emeralds north of Sumatra across the Bay of Bengal. In West Africa, they established a string of forts, lodges and trading stations along the Gold Coast (present Ghana) between Accra and the mouth of the Volta River to the east. From that coast they exported tropical produce, ivory, and gold to Denmark and human beings as slaves to their sugar-producing colonies in the West Indies. Of the latter there were three—St. Thomas (1672), St. John (1718) and finally St. Croix (1733). Together those islands constituted the Danish West Indies, which Denmark retained for well over two centuries, until 1917.

Since that time, numerous popular and scholarly writings have appeared in an attempt to evaluate the Danish experience in the West Indies. From this literature, and in part, as a result of it, there has arisen a set of assumptions which have been, for the most part, uncritically accepted. It would appear that there has indeed grown up a myth of

Danish colonialism in the Danish West Indies, the principal elements of which are the following:

- that slavery as practiced by the Danes was somehow milder, more humane than was elsewhere the case;
- that the Danes were generally color-blind and that they were therefore able to create a colonial society that was relatively free of the racial prejudices and animosities that dogged other Caribbean lands in post-Emancipation and post-colonial times;
- that certain initiatives such as the Ordinance of 1792 abolishing the slave trade illustrate that the Denmark was in the vanguard of the anti-slavery movement in Europe and in the West Indies and thereby provided a humanitarian example for the rest of Europe and the world to follow;
- that certain high-minded individuals, in particular Peter von Scholten, effected social justice and eventually Emancipation in the Danish West Indies by means of heroic, liberal leadership;
- that the Emancipation of 1848 proceeded ultimately from humanitarian sentiments;
- that in the period after Emancipation, from 1848 until 1917, there developed a free Danish West Indian peasantry, which enjoyed the benefits of a benign, paternalistic Danish overlordship and that the islands generated a culture that was an amalgam of all the best that the Danish nation had to offer;
- and finally, that the Danes sold the islands to the United States reluctantly in the face of wartime pressures but left behind a population that longed tearfully for the "good old days" under Danish rule after the islands had had a taste of things under a harsher American rule.

Like all myths, these propositions have in them certain elements of truth that renders it difficult to easily separate the dross from the pure metal. However, a critical examination of the most salient facts relating to the Danish colonial enterprise in those islands and the myths associated with it suggests that there may indeed be precious little to justify an overlong celebration of "the good old days under the Danes," along with other myths now embedded in our history. The time is long overdue to examine these ideas in a critical manner. What I propose here is a cursory examination of several of these myths in the light of what we presently know of Virgin Islands history from Virgin Islands perspectives.

For two hundred years, a nexus of economic relationships bound together the national economy of early modern Denmark, the human resources of the Gold Coast and the land and natural resources of several Caribbean islands. Danish vessels carried products from their nascent industrial economy—cloth, utensils, bulk foodstuffs, building materials etc.—to Africa in exchange for human cargoes whom they transported to the West Indies. On the other side of the Atlantic, plantations in the Danish islands grew sugar, tobacco, cotton, pock-woods and some indigo; these tropical products the Danes produced unabashedly by means of servile labor, first in the persons of their own indentured servants who sprang from the most impoverished sectors of Danish society and, shortly thereafter, from the toil of enslaved Africans. The forced labor of those unfortunates contributed in no mean way to the growth of the modern Danish state, to its national economy in the 17th and 18th centuries and to the aggrandizement of individual fortunes.

When indentured labor in Denmark dried up, the Danes redoubled their efforts at acquiring enslaved Africans from the Gold Coast and elsewhere in the vast region of West Africa then known as Guinea. From 1672 to 1807, Danish slave ships transported no fewer than 120,000 Africans to the New World in bondage, approximately one percent of the total of the entire Atlantic slave trade. What is not well known is that slave dealers in the Danish West Indies participated in a local, West Indian slave trade, one in which they exported many thousands more from the Danish islands, principally from St. Thomas to the larger islands of the western Caribbean, namely Cuba, St. Domingue, Puerto Rico and Santo Domingo, in the second half of the 18th century when the Spanish islands in particular were experiencing a belated surge of cane cultivation and sugar production. The early modern Danish economy was therefore established in part on these slave-based colonial enterprises, in which St. Croix and St. John generally consumed slaves and St. Thomas exported them.

In their slave trading activities and in their system of slavery, the Danes were neither ostensibly better nor particularly worse than other Caribbean slave masters of that age. Anyone, however, who still clings to the quaint notion that Danish masters somehow made slavery more humane, even palatable, a sort of half-way station whose principal aim was the transformation of erstwhile "primitive" Africans into "civilized," Christian Dano-West Indians, would do well to consult the early documentary sources, especially those of the Danish planters and writers such as J. L. Carstens, Reimert Haagensen, Johan Christian Schmidt and others. These men have left candid accounts of Danish slavery which show conclusively that if slavery were no worse than the peculiar institution elsewhere in the New World, it was certainly no better.

However, not a few Danes have been able to overlook the failings of their countrymen of that age by clothing them in the national myth that has it that their country was, after all, the first European state to formally abolish the Atlantic slave trade. Denmark did, in fact, issue an ordinance in 1792 abolishing the slave trade. But that ordinance was written in such a way that its principal provision was not to enter into effect until 1803. It is seldom stressed that during that ten-year interval planters in the Danish West Indies, given the example of no less a figure than Ernst Schimmelmann in a policy paradoxically known as amelioration, were urged to find the means to accommodate slaves to their lot in the West Indies and thereby enable them to biologically reproduce and maintain their own numbers, thereby relieving the planters of the expense and trouble of continually importing new slaves from Africa. Similarly, scant mention is ever made of the fact that during that same intervening ten-year period—1792 to 1802—Danish slave dealers imported more slaves into their colonies—over 30,000 in all—than at any other comparable period in the history of their slaving activities.

When the moment finally arrived in 1803 for Denmark to enforce its own abolition edict, Danish merchants, planters and some government officials found themselves a good deal less than eager to do so. The considerable numbers of human beings whom they had imported between 1792 and that time, they argued, were not adequate to the agricultural and manufacturing tasks required by the existing plantations. Nor had the planters in the meantime made the necessary reforms to lower death rates and raise birth rates in their slave communities in order that the slave population might hold its own demographically and even grow. In short, the policy of amelioration, such as it was, had been a failure.

While the entire matter was being debated, the lucrative transit, or local, slave trade in St. Thomas continued unabated, funneling thousands of African captives through that island's excellent harbor facilities to points west until 1807. It was only after the Danish islands had been seized by Great Britain in 1807—by then the arch-foe of the trade—that the final remnant of the Danish trade came to a quick and inglorious end. It was by that sudden shift of political fortunes during the Napoleonic Wars that the last of the slavers in the Danish islands abandoned their trade, not as the result of a Danish humanitarian effort as we are often left to believe, but by rather by British invasion and occupation, followed by the inevitable imposition of that nation's policy of abolition.

When other nations were beginning to institute policies of amelioration for their slave populations in the expectation of eventual emancipation, Denmark held back, citing economic hard times within the monarchy. With slave population declining and no workable amelioration policies in effect, the lot of the average slave in the Danish West Indies actually worsened. And later, when Great Britain passed the Emancipation Act in 1833, the Danish islands looked on apprehensively but did nothing. Emancipation in the British islands was made possible by the government's willingness to pay the owners compensation for the loss of their "property." No such offer to the planters was forthcoming from the Danish government. Instead there was the creation of yet another very durable myth. Governor-general Peter von Scholten came to prominence with a plan that would extricate Denmark from that impasse, that is, the plan would emancipate Danish slaves, but not at government or planter expense. According to his design, it was not the government that would pay the erstwhile owners for the loss of their "property" (compensation) but rather the slaves themselves who would do so through a policy known as manumission from money earned by their own labors.

Von Scholten attempted to set in motion several plans that would allow slaves to work in their free time and thereby pay their masters for their own freedom over an extended period of time, but this policy of manumission and gradualism had a relatively minor impact on the overall slave population of the Danish West Indies. When King Christian VIII finally got around to proclaiming an edict on July 28th of 1847, based on the so-called "free womb principle," it was another case of too little too late, to say nothing of being too wrong. From 1803 to 1847, the slave population of the Danish West Indies overall had already declined from 36,000 to 21,000, a decrease of some 40 percent. On St. Croix the rate of decline after 1840 had become so pronounced that the slave population might well have died off altogether by the late 1850s, all things remaining equal.

Not being disposed to see their new-born children become free while they would be obliged to wait another 12 years for their freedom or extinction, whichever came first, the enslaved took matters into their own hands in early July of 1848 and forced the granting of their own freedom by Danish authorities in the person of the Governor-general. Notwithstanding the governor-general's liberal attitudes toward and relations with certain individuals among the enslaved and free colored population of St. Croix, the fact remains that his emancipation proclamation had been forced upon him by the Emancipation Revolt, led by General Buddhoe. But as the events that followed played themselves out, it was not the slave community or its leadership that emerged as the heroic element in Danish West Indian history but rather von Scholten. With time he became an almost mythic figure, whose continually evolving legend has played no small role in salving the Danish national conscience in the entire emancipation episode. The simple truth is that the Danish role in Emancipation was nothing if not ignoble.

The story does not get better in the years that followed in spite of the ample opportunities that the Danes had to right past wrongs. Rather than extending economic opportunities to match the face-value political reality of Emancipation, a series of acts between 1848 and 1853 attempted to limit participation in the political process by severely restricting the franchise and to convert erstwhile slaves essentially into quasi estate serfs in spite of the glaring fact that Denmark had abolished serfdom (Ståvnsband) within its own boundaries in 1788. With the sugar industry and the plantations in full decline, Denmark held its ramshackle colonies together for the next several decades by placating the remnant of the old plantocracy on the labor question and by binding the serf-like laborers to the estates by means of inequitable labor contracts, by restrictive vagrancy laws that made it nearly impossible to cast about for alternative employment, and by a passport (read "passbook") system that was designed to limit movement and emigration. In effect, the passage from slavery to freedom in the Danish Islands took a detour through another half century of serf-like conditions on the country estates. By the 1870s, perhaps no country in the Caribbean had neglected the political participation and economic progress of its working population to the extent as had Denmark. Nowhere was free labor more depressed.

The Fireburn of 1878 was the response of the black laboring community to these shameless conditions—principally to the Labor Ordinance of 1849 and the Vagrancy Law of 1853—to which they had for three decades been subjected. Though the destructive effects of that revolt did result in the some slight changes, it did not spur Denmark to bring real progress to the colonies beyond some tepid, general measures toward reforming the economy at the turn of the century. No discernible attempt was made to improve the working or living conditions of the people by the planters or by the Danish authorities. Wages remained abysmally low. Benefits were non-existent. Education was minimal. Disease, including leprosy, was rampant, resulting in high mortality rates. By the end of the century general conditions in the islands had become nothing short of an embarrassment for those Danes who cared enough to inform themselves on matters there.

And over it all hovered the unwritten color and race code which maintained a social structure articulated along caste and color lines. The fact that individual Danes might transgress the generally accepted race and color norms sexually became the cause for the generation of yet another conscience-sparing myth—that of the liberal Dane in the midst of a non-European population in the tropics. It made for a particularly appealing contrast with the harsher system which then prevailed in the United States. But it was the appearance of the St. Croix Labor Union under the leadership of D. Hamilton Jackson and others in early 1916, not Danish liberality, that forced the Crucian planters to deal with the sons and daughters of the ex-slaves as a free people for the first time. Curiously enough, after 200 years of running a colony based upon racial exploitation and the concomitant racial distinctions, the government and the planters had the temerity to characterize the leaders of the labor union movement of promoting "racial agitation, etc." to achieve their ends. The whole business was sadly redolent, though characteristic, of the missed opportunities of 1792, 1803, 1848 and 1878.

The Danish colonial adventure in the West Indies ended in 1917 with the government of Denmark accepting the then enormous sum of 25 million dollars in gold for the underdeveloped and neglected islands of the Danish West Indies. In one final affront, Denmark took the money and did not look back, allowing the new colonial owner to define the erstwhile Danish subjects as citizens *in* the United States but not citizens *of* the United States. In the total absence of Danish concern and protest of this calculated affront, full U.S. citizenship was therefore *not* granted to Virgin Islanders until 1927. The Danish performance—or lack of performance—during the endgame of its colonial adventure provided an inconsiderate but consistent finale to a long, insensitive association, one whose resonances and reverberations are still being felt in the Virgin Islands to this day.

While it is true that the Danes were clearly not rabid, apartheid-practicing racists, their system of bondage and exploitation has nevertheless left traumatic marks from which the Virgin Islands and its people suffer to the present. But on the other side of the Atlantic, so complete has been Denmark's general acceptance of its own colonial mythology of "the good old days," seconded by a certain national penchant for self-congratulation, that most Danes never seem to have given any thought at all to the moral dimension of their long history in the Caribbean. The tenacity of myth has hampered reflection or discourse on that topic so effectively and so completely that the disturbing echoes of our shared past seem to have troubled the repose of few.

Myth is a creature that is always deeply rooted in the past, sometimes closely associated with, if not identical to, the history of a people. One need only glance at the histories of Egypt, Greece and Rome to see this association in practice. And history has its roots in documentation, records and other resources. It is the control and selective use of such records that have to a great extent made possible the imposition of an externally-generated myth-making process on the Virgin Islands past. Those conditions have also determined the course of Virgin Islands historiography. The result has been a long, deep shadow under which we all live, without a truly conscious awareness of it.

The disposition of archives, the availability of documentation, and the cultural perspectives of recent scholarship have all exerted a powerful influence on the development of Virgin Islands historiography. In the first place, the lion's share of the records has been and remains in Denmark. While it can be argued that those records have enjoyed better physical protection and preservation over the past seventy-odd years in the facilities available in that country than would have been the case in our islands, the point needs to be made nevertheless that Virgin Islanders themselves have a strong claim to those same records as part of their own intellectual and cultural patrimony. By any measure, it was the labor of their ancestors that generated the substance of the records and the necessity for maintaining them in the first place. And while the Danish claim on those records has been largely staked on an economic utility, Virgin Islanders' claim may be said to be moral and cultural and therefore equally compelling. In 1996, the discussion centering on those records should not in any event focus on who has the stronger claim to those records, but they should rather focus on the development of common strategies as to how the resources can be shared justly and equitably. And yet we continue to meet with resistance in the discussion of this topic, to say nothing of the actual sharing of the records.

I have heard at least a thousand times that the colonial records stored in Denmark are in Danish and in manuscript form to boot. This assertion is usually proffered as a means to put an immediate end to all further discussion of the troublesome matter, the language of Kirkegaard and Pontopidden being incomprehensible, it is assumed, to anyone other than native-born Danes. Let me make a brief reply to that oft-heard refrain here. If anything, that admission serves to set in high-relief another considerable failure of the Danish tenure in the islands. Very little formal schooling was ever available to the children of the former slaves. Instruction in the Danish language was certainly neglected, in favor of Dutch Creole and English. Danish West Indian history and the Danish language have consequently produced no equivalent to Derek Walcott, V. S. Naipaul, George Lamming, Aimé Césaire, or Jacques Roumain. To my knowledge, no one from the Danish Caribbean colonies ever attended an institution of higher learning in Denmark during the colonial period. And it is largely for that reason that those same islands similarly never produced in the field of history any equivalent of a C. L. R. James or an Eric Williams. Deprived of an opportunity to learn the language, to enter into the metropolitan culture and to gain access to the historical records stored in Denmark, the people of the Virgin Islands have been in effect denied access to the opportunity to analyze and critique Danish historical interpretations and to create fully-formed interpretations of their own.

Perhaps the time has come to right a very old and enduring wrong.

Certain Danish and Dano-American scholars, however, were not denied that access to the historical records. With Waldemar Westergaard, Hermann Lawaetz, J. O. Bro-Jørgensen and other writers and particularly with the appearance of the four volume work *Vore Gamle Tropekolonier*, began the historiography, not of the Virgin Islands, but of the Danish West Indies. That distinction is indeed an important one. It is not my intent to disparage the work of those scholars. On the contrary, they laid the foundation stones for the discipline of local history. Two comments, however, are in order. First, those scholars approached the subject, naturally enough, from a purely Danish perspective. Their slant has been for the most part historical, stressing interpretations focused on economics, politics and Danish colonialism. Such a national bias is to be expected. While more recent scholars such as Ove Hornby, Svend Green-Pedersen, Erik Gøbel, Poul Olsen, Karen Fog Olwig, Peter Hoxcer Jensen and others have been successful in achieving a broader scope in their work, there nevertheless has been lacking an interpretation of the cultural, the social, and the anthropological aspects of the subject. What has been lacking in these works is an approach grounded in more broadly-based studies, made possible, first, by a thorough access to the extant documentation and second, from perspectives, namely African-Caribbean and Virgin Islands-centered for the most part, which have not been appreciated until now, even though we stand at the threshold of a new century and a new millennium.

And that leads naturally to the second point. This imbalance exists because Virgin Islanders have been subject to a de facto denial of access to the use of their own historical documentation. This has resulted in part due to our distance from the archival repositories in Europe and in part due to the absence of educational opportunities that would have enabled potential Virgin Islands scholars to work readily with the language and overcome other technical difficulties. The historical writing of J. Antonio Jarvis, gifted as he might have been, suffers from having been based overwhelmingly on English sources, therefore underscoring the central point of my claim. The same may be said concerning the work of other scholars and writers, including William Boyer, Waldemar Hill, Gordon Lewis, Erik Lawaetz, Isaac Dookhan himself and, most recently, Harold Willocks. The late Jamaican historian, Neville Hall is the exception to this general rule, and his scholarly works in Danish West Indian history, based on Danish archival materials, highlights the urgency of this point in a striking manner. If the Danish writers referred to above may be said to have the substance but lack something in the spirit of and feel for their subject, the very reverse may be said of those writers working on our side of the Atlantic. Clearly the time has come to give Virgin Islanders their chance to write their own history, using all the available resources.

If what I have said here today contains even a grain of truth, how might it be received and what might be done in response to these claims? Denial and dismissal are distinct possibilities. They have both occurred in the past. Perhaps a retreat into business as usual. On the other hand, might not some sort of reparations program be in order, perhaps with the calculation of interest. And I use that term here in the most general sense. The Danish foreign aid program is, after all, most impressive, particularly for a country of Denmark's size. But to my knowledge not a krone has ever gone to the Virgin Islands after the Danes departed. Personally, I do not believe that a monetary "handout" is in order; nor do I think that the people of the Virgin Islands are particularly looking in that direction. What is at stake here falls within the domain of morality and not economics in the strict sense. In my opinion, the Danes owe a considerable moral debt to the people of the Virgin Islands. But, to my knowledge, they have never even considered the matter. On the contrary, they have never looked back on their colonial past with an eye for how it affected the colonized. They scarcely took the time to say good-bye, let alone offer any formal apologies for the many unaddressed wrongs that spread out behind them in their wake. May I be bold enough to suggest that a simple apology from one people to another would be a good place to begin? A hard critical look at our shared history, followed by an admission of responsibility for certain past actions would be as appropriate as it would be appreciated. After all, Virgin Islanders seem to have found a way to esteem Denmark and her people in spite of the historical record. But perhaps most important of all, modern Danes could send a powerful message on behalf of their ancestors to the ancestors of the people of the Virgin Islands by returning the foundation stones of the two peoples' mutually shared past, by creating the opportunity for Virgin islanders to have their own access to their own past, in the writing their own histories and perhaps even in beginning the process of unraveling their own mythologies. I ask here tonight that the matter be considered in the context of the following three related suggestions:

- Establishment of a program of training for Virgin Islanders in the scholarly methods required to develop access to their historical resources, such as the study of the Danish language, the transcription of handwritten archival documents, a grounding in Danish library and archival methods, and research and study of Danish national history and Danish colonial history, to mention only the more prominent. These goals could be achieved by the creation of scholarships, fellowships, exchanges, regular travel and interaction, cooperation between respective High Schools and Universities, regular training institutes and seminars, the exploration of Internet and other connectivities, and the like. The University of the Virgin Islands has already taken the first halting steps in that direction and should be encouraged to continue apace.
- A program for copying the documentation in Danish archives etc. in their entirety without any further delay, insofar as these represent the historical, cultural and intellectual patrimony of Virgin Islands people. Surely, Danish scholars would be willing to share that which they have already used and that which they rightfully own in common with others.
- The creation of connections and the support of organizations, associations, publications, journals and the like, whereby the work of

Virgin Islanders and Danes might be circulated and discussed in order to nurture a transatlantic dialog on their mutually shared past.

Danish historians have already had opportunities to write their histories of their country's deeds in the Danish West Indies, based on a rich documentation. Some have done an admirable job, some less so. But in the process they also wrote the histories of people whom their nation used badly. A case can and should be made for the rights of those people who have in the course of events been slighted and who lived and died without a voice and without advocacy of any kind. Their descendants should now have the opportunity to write their own histories, however brilliant or however dismal those efforts might turn out to be. We cannot guarantee success in such undertakings but we can and we should guarantee the opportunity to try.

Those of you gathered here this evening have it within your power to speak out for those who never had the opportunity to speak for themselves, to create the conditions whereby those who were grievously wronged in the past and those seeking a voice at the present time might have fair access to a long overdue hearing before their fellows.

I am constantly aware of what a young Virgin Islands scholar might think of us some time in the distant future, say the year 2050, when she comes across our names in some dusty file. Did they do all they could when it was possible and relevant to do it? Or did they let the opportunity pass? Among the many things we historians, teachers and other scholars do, there is room on our agendas and there is time on our calendars to use our craft to provide a hearing for silenced ancestors, to put our skills, our resources and imaginations at the disposal of our not so fortunate fellows of today, and to act as advocates for the limitless potential of the yet unborn. Of all craft workers, we historians live and work intimately with the reality of time's fleeting, ravaging nature. Let us therefore begin now.

View of the Moravian Mission station Friedensthal at Christiansted

CHAPTER 17

PATTERNS OF ACCOMMODATION AND RESISTANCE: THE MORAVIAN WITNESS TO SLAVERY IN THE DANISH WEST INDIES

IN SPITE OF THE FACT that the Moravian missionaries to the Danish West Indies of the 18th and 19th centuries have left voluminous documentation of various kinds relative to their work among the enslaved African population in those islands, their efforts have not attracted a great deal of critical scholarly attention.[1] What has been written to date has generally focused rather narrowly on the tremendous successes registered by a few missionaries in Christianizing large numbers of non-believing non-Europeans. The present paper proposes to explore the ambivalent experience of African-Caribbean peoples within the context of the Moravian missionary effort in the Danish West Indian islands during the eighteenth century. More specifically, it will investigate the manner in which the former responded to the Moravian missionary endeavor, through the modes of both accommodation and resistance.

The modern Moravian church—known variously as the Moravian Brethren, the Brethren, the Evangelical Brethren, the United Brethren (Unitas Fratrum), the Herrnhutters, and the Hussites—has its roots in the fertile soil of early 18th century Pietism, the religious renewal sometimes termed the "second Reformation." Ultimately, of course, those roots extend far back into the equally fertile ground of 15th century Czech particularism and nationalism, which produced confrontation with and resistance to Roman Catholic domination. In the several centuries following the death of John Hus, the leader of the movement, this community was persecuted, its followers often being forced to go underground or take flight. It was in this manner that remnants of its long oppressed "hidden seed" appeared in Germany in the 1720s and became re-inspired and rekindled by the intense religiosity engendered by the Pietist movement, which at that time was exerting a broad, powerful influence on religious life in Protestant Europe.[2] In a curious turn of fate, these same refugees would soon find themselves once again on the move, this time as missionaries, administering to enslaved Africans in the West Indies.

Not a decade had passed since their arrival in Germany when, under the spiritual leadership of that energetic visionary, Count Nicholas Ludwig von Zinzendorf, the members of the tiny sect embarked upon their well-known peregrinations that signaled the beginning of the modern Protestant missionary movement.[3] The role of the St. Thomian slave Anton in these events and the response to his condition by the Moravians Nitschmann and Dober in launching the missionary initiative in the Danish West Indies in 1732 have been widely commented upon, especially in the literature of the Moravian movement. From that point in time, some 256 years ago, until the present, the Moravian Church has been a significant force in the development of the Danish West Indies and, subsequently, the Virgin Islands of the United States. In addition, the Moravian movement spread to other Caribbean areas, including Surinam (1735), Jamaica (1754), Antigua (1756), Barbados (1765), St. Kitts (1775), and Tobago (1826).[4]

The Moravian presence in the Danish West Indies in the eighteenth century was significant in several regards. First, the Moravian missionaries were present from quite early in the islands' colonization, arriving just sixty years after the settlement of St. Thomas (1672), fourteen years after the settlement of St. John (1718), and at the very beginning of the Danish settlement of St. Croix in 1734. In the case of the last island, they were, in fact, among the very first European settlers to set foot there after the Danish purchase from France in 1733. As a consequence of their early arrival and their intense activity in the initial colonizing effort, the first Moravian missionaries played a significant role in the lives of many of the more than 120,000 Africans who were subsequently brought to the Danish West Indies as a result of the Danish slave trade in the period 1733–1806. It might even be argued that slavery in the Danish West Indies—and especially in St. Croix—cannot be completely understood or evaluated without taking into account the presence and activities of the Moravians.

A certain ambivalence colors the commentaries of those who have attempted to evaluate the Moravian presence over the years in their work evangelizing among slave populations. Some observers have not failed to note that the Brethren exerted an ameliorative influence on the "peculiar institution" as it existed in these islands. Referring to a report of the work of the Moravians, Bryan Edwards notes that "their conduct in this business displays such sound judgment, breathes such a spirit of genuine christianity, and has been attended with such eminent success, as to entitle its brethren and missionaries to the most favorable reception from every man whom the accidents of fortune have invested with power over the poor Africans."[5] Others, less sanguine regarding the ultimate consequences of that missionary endeavor, have pointed out that the Brethren, whatever their ultimate intentions, did in fact own both slaves and plantations, and, moreover, that they did participate fully in the economic, political, and social life of the slave society.[6] In between these two extremes, C. G. A. Oldendorp, the Moravian inspector who was sent to the islands in 1767–68 to evaluate the progress of the mission over its first thirty-odd years and who produced and published in 1777 a massive history of those events, has himself given ample testimony to the abilities of his confrères in the matter of acculturating the so-called "heathen Africans" and in rendering them more amenable to the yoke of servitude.[7] It was into this position that the Moravians most often retreated in justifying their work in the slave colonies; the validity of that position was ultimately accepted by the planters and colonial authorities within whose domains the missionaries labored.

Although a detailed analysis of the Moravian missionary program and an evaluation of its ultimate influence in the Danish West Indies throughout the colonial period extends far beyond the scope of this study, it would be nevertheless useful to examine, cursorily at least, the explicit intentions of the Moravian missionary enterprise in order to understand more clearly the African responses to it. In matters of theology, the Moravians focused sharply on man's natural depravity and his concomitant disposition to sin; to remedy this condition, they turned to the redeeming properties of divine grace made universally available to mankind by means of the physical and spiritual sacrifice of Jesus Christ. In order to attain salvation, one need only become aware of the availability of grace provided by Christ's sacrifice and then accept it freely. In so doing, one exercised the power of free choice in an act of faith rather than attempting intellectual analysis of one's condition through an act of reason. In this respect, the Moravians clearly revealed their Pietistic origins, embodied in their aversion to "reason," a faculty otherwise dear to the programs of their learned contemporaries in the Age of Enlightenment. From this position, it followed that the task of the missionary was altogether simple, at least in theory. His was merely to make the non-believer (i.e., "the heathen") aware of the aforementioned state of affairs; acceptance, conversion, and salvation should necessarily follow.[8] Reason played no part in it; rather it was a matter of the heart, of blind acceptance based on faith.

For the Moravians, their work among the enslaved Africans of the Danish West Indies, as well as among other so-called "heathen people," provided an opportunity to test the efficacy of this formulation. For them, the object of their attention was not the innocent child of nature, the "noble savage" so dear to the *philosophes* of the Enlightenment. Rather, those whom they desired to convert were viewed as God-deprived people, corrupted by nature and mired in sin. If such people could be brought to attain salvation, then clearly that end would be achieved through a thoroughgoing faith, untainted by reason. Such an accomplishment would represent a clear vindication of this central Moravian theological proposition.

This theologically-driven missionary impulse was the *force motrice* behind the concomitant global Moravian movement as well as for the mass of documentation generated by their activities in the Danish West Indies, found in various Moravian archives today. The project on which the missionaries embarked would periodically require scrutiny and evaluation. Hence they maintained detailed records. Church-books, journals, diaries, registers of all kinds—but especially those relative to baptisms—correspondence, and reports were all dutifully inscribed, maintained and preserved.[9] And, of course, the mission stations were regularly inspected by Moravian visitants, or inspectors, whose job it was to supervise the progress of the individual stations and to report to the mother congregation in Europe on that progress. As a result of their obsessive disposition to test the success and hence validity of their endeavor, they have left a considerable collection of detailed information about not only their own activities but also those of their charges—the members of the African-Caribbean community of the Danish West Indies.

The use of these records to obtain information on the African-Caribbean community presents obvious problems. They are all written from the Moravian perspective, in support of the validity of the aforementioned Moravian "project," and they therefore present substantial difficulties in attempting any critical reconstruction of African-Caribbean life. Nevertheless, they do yield, however grudgingly and obliquely, insights into the African responses to the Moravian presence and evangelical program.

Slave responses to the Moravian project of mass Christianization fell naturally into two general modes of behavior: accommodation and resistance. In the former, the slaves participated, or accommodated themselves to, the Moravian plan. Not surprisingly, this willing participation earned the reward of certain positive benefits, both material and non-material. Slaves who accepted this mode of relating to the Moravians were scrutinized in great detail. As a result, the great majority of the missionary documentation was generated relative to these individuals, depicting them in a generally positive light, ideally as Africans cloaked in the garb of early eighteenth century Pietism. However, the other mode of behavior—resistance in its many forms, whether it be against the colonial settlement in general, individual planters or estates, or, less frequently, against the Moravians themselves—produced condemnation and a negative characterization in the documentation, the "unaccommodating" slave being decried variously as a dangerous rebel, a stubborn maroon, or a recalcitrant heathen "bussal." Herein, ironically enough, the Moravians produced written documentation, in spite of their real intentions of simple condemnation and eradication of offending behaviors, to the non-European perspective of the African-Caribbean experience.

Accommodation has already been characterized as the general acceptance by the enslaved of the overall Moravian program, an acceptance that would lead theoretically to eventual Christianization of his person and salvation of his soul. In order to arrive at this goal, the missionaries created a rather complex developmental process patterned on their own choir system, which segregated the Moravian community by age, gender and marital status and focussed the individual members' complete attention on spiritual concerns.[10] Transposed to the West Indies this system served to guide individual slaves from the status of prospective candidate through various intermediary stages to that of communicant and, ultimately, full-fledged participant in the Moravian congregation.

The Moravian missionaries who undertook this task in the Danish West Indies in the eighteenth century were, for the most part, Germans of all age groups, both male and female. Their professed goal was to serve the mission in two capacities. First, each of the Brethren had to be able to earn his own living through the active practice of some trade or craft—carpentry, masonry, tailoring, mill building, or the like—in order to support himself, along with his family, and to contribute to the material maintenance and growth of the mission. And, second, he had to make a spiritual contribution to the missionary endeavor—preaching, teaching, supervising, exhorting etc.—in order that the mission might pursue and fulfill its fundamental charge. Men held the primary roles in the mission while their wives engaged in general domestic duties in addition to working among the female slaves. In their European and North American congregations, such as the one at Bethlehem, Pennsylvania, the Moravians insisted on marriage and beyond that, a rather strict gender segregation, a practice that they also made every attempt to establish in the black congregations of the West Indies. Moravian males worked exclusively with the male slaves, Moravian women with the female slaves. Additionally, others specialized in working with children. Since the unmarried state was considered potentially dangerous by the Moravians, widows and widowers alike, regardless of age, were persistently nudged into remarriage. Pervasive sexual segregation and the strict hierarchy imposed by the system of instruction (i.e., the classes) were clearly aimed at denying the opportunity for sexual temptation between missionary and catechumen, and it appears to have been generally effective, with a few exceptions.[11] At the same time, much attention was given to encouraging marriage among the slaves.

The mission itself was under the leadership of one man who bore the title of "missionarius," or missionary and who held the important power of approving and administering baptism. The Europeans who worked under him were called "mission assistants." But in spite of this hierarchical arrangement, decision-making reverted at times to a communal approach, that is, a consensus of the mission elders, when not entirely given over to the age-old Moravian custom of the casting of lots.[12] All things considered, the Moravian mission in the Danish West Indies functioned in a relatively communal and open manner.

Mission stations were established first in St. Thomas (New Herrnhut and Niesky), then in St. Croix (Friedensthal, Friedensberg, and, finally, Friedensfeld), and in St. John (Emmaus and Bethany). Initially, the principal thrust of the Moravian effort was concentrated on St. Thomas. That effort, however, appears to have been redirected to St. Croix in the second half of the eighteenth century when that island entered a strong developmental phrase, with capital and slaves being concentrated there.[13] St. John was developed much more gradually than the other two islands due to its fewer plantations and its limited population, both of which resulted from the island's rugged terrain. Once on firm footing, the mission centers continued to grow and thrive in all of the three islands through the 18th and into the 19th century.

In the earliest period, proselytizing was the most important task of the mission assistants. Through the villages, along the roads, and on the plantations, theirs was the task of spreading the message of the Gospels. The slaves' response to these curious German-speaking white men ranged from initial bewilderment to frequent annoyance. Whenever the helpers identified a suitably responsive individual, they convened a meeting of a small group of assistants to formulate a strategy. They then proceeded to approach the targeted individual singly or in a small group, exhorting him persistently to convert. Friedrich Martin, the noted Moravian missionary and educator, was in particular known for the tenacity of his methods, as well as for his success ratio in these matters.[14] In the second half of the century, when the Moravians had achieved enormous success in making converts, this early approach was modified, with the slaves themselves applying to the mission to have their names placed on a list of applicants.

In the next step of the process, the slave became a catechumen. Each catechumen was assigned to a class of instruction, of which there were essentially three: the men's, the women's, and the children's—the last of these also being segregated by gender. Each class was assigned to a European mission assistant (called "Baas" by the catechumens), who acted as its leader, teacher, supervisor, counselor, advocate and spiritual guide. The principal function of the class was to teach the slaves the rudiments of the faith and to introduce them to the ambiance and influence of congregational life. Their social behavior and their work on their particular plantations were also closely monitored. Whenever an individual's performance did not measure up to the standards set by the congregation, he or she was called before the mission assistant who headed his class and was given an admonition, followed by counseling.

Recalcitrants were "excluded," to use the Moravian term. In the final analysis, the goal of the class system was to reshape the behavior and the person of the individual slave and to teach him the essentials of the Moravian belief system.

At the end of his apprenticeship in his particular class, each catechumen was given a verbal examination by the missionary, who then pronounced on his readiness for baptism. It should be stressed that these classes—patterned on the choir systems of the congregations in Europe and North America—were the very heart of the Moravian system.[15] And insofar as they were essentially instruments of education and training where both acculturation and enculturation took place, it is not surprising that quite early in their development of a Moravian pedagogy, the Brethren recognized the importance of the primary language of the slaves, Dutch Creole, and the need to create a religious literature in that language. Consequently, nowhere in the Caribbean at that time did any other Creole language receive the degree of attention and implementation as was provided by the Moravians for Dutch Creole in the Danish West Indies.[16]

Candidates for baptism were elevated to an important new status. They had frequent meetings with the mission workers and their behavior was carefully scrutinized. On an appointed day—second only in importance to first communion—a group of candidates, arrayed in white linen garb, received the sacrament of baptism in a group. The significance that the slaves themselves invested in these festive days and the importance that they attached to the newly-acquired baptized status contributed in no small way to the growing Moravian success.

The newly-baptized at that point had yet another hurdle before them—first communion. To prepare for this infrequent event, each individual, according to gender, was placed in a new class, that of the baptized. Here the process of instruction by a mission helper continued, though on a more advanced level. The close scrutiny continued as well. Any hint of improper behavior, drunkenness, coarse language, fornication, unruliness, or any general disposition to "heathen practices"—that is,

African music, dance, or religion (termed witchcraft)—was met on the first occurrence with a stern admonition, followed by inevitable "exclusion" upon repetition. Everyone was made aware that, once excluded, re-admittance into the congregation would be difficult to achieve. If the candidates succeeded in avoiding these pitfalls, the baptized were again examined by the missionary himself, who determined their fitness for participation in the Eucharist ceremony. Since this sacrament was celebrated sparingly by the Moravians, it came to be viewed by the congregation as a major event and was received with great anticipation by the soon-to-be-initiated and by the slave community in general. This studied hierarchical progression of annual events—registration, catechism, baptism and communion—all of which were accompanied by the regular bestowal of earned status, along with its accompanying aura of prestige following a long period of waiting, worked effectively for the Moravian missions in advancing their principal goals and in attracting ever-growing numbers of applicants.[17]

The new communicants were immediately regrouped into new classes. They had become by that time full-fledged members of the Moravian congregation. As such, they attended church services at the mission churches regularly and on special days. Meetings of various kinds, including prayer meetings, prayer vigils, and mutual support meetings, were held regularly on the plantations, whenever, of course, the permission of the owner or overseer could be obtained. Meetings were also convened whenever a mission assistant or the missionary happened to be traveling through that part of the colonies or visiting a particular area of the island. Under normal circumstances, attendance on the part of the enslaved population at these events was consistently enthusiastic.

With the passing of time and with the accumulation of service to the mission, as well as with the development of a spiritual disposition commensurate with the expectations of the missionary leadership, a communicant might aspire to several additional positions within the congregation hierarchy that recognized merit and bestowed prestige. First, he might become a so-called "national helper," whose job it was to perform the role of mission assistant in the absence of the European "Baas," especially on plantations located at some distance from the nearest mission station. Like their European counterparts, these national helpers served as the leaders of various instructional classes, reporting the progress of their work, as well as that of their charges directly to a European assistant or to the Missionary himself. Since national helpers were often conversant in various of the West African cultures and languages still in obvious practice among the enslaved population, and especially among the bussals, they were particularly useful in advancing the mission's work. Certain of these national helpers, such as John Jacob Kruse (1753–1834), came to be greatly valued for their services as teachers of reading and other matters.[18] And, obviously enough, the helpers provided the Moravian leadership with an eye into the heart of the communities of the enslaved on the various plantations scattered throughout the three islands.

A trusted communicant and helper might aspire to become an "Elder" after long years of meritorious service to the mission, although not many attained that rank. Elders and Eldresses held great prestige in their congregations and often received privileges and recognition from both the religious and secular communities. They were known primarily as good spiritual models for the rest of the community and, in some instances, as effective preachers. Several such preachers were able to sway black and white audiences alike by means of sermons based on knowledge of the Bible and by their eloquence in the Creole. They often traveled freely, both intra-island and inter-island and even on occasion internationally, some venturing to North America, some even to Europe.[19]

The Moravian Brethren were eminently successful in their work of converting the enslaved peoples of the Danish West Indies. After a rather difficult beginning in the 1730s and early 1740s, their work progressed remarkably through the second half of the 18th century. By 1768, a total of 143 European mission helpers and missionaries had toiled in the Danish West Indies since 1732, baptizing 4,560 Blacks, the majority of them slaves. In that same year, the congregation numbered some 2,616 baptized Blacks, with another 636 candidates for baptism—impressive progress for a missionary enterprise that had begun with such limited resources just 36 years previously.[20] But the advances which were made over the next 35 years were even more striking. By 1794, there were 9,345 black Moravians in the Danish West Indies.[21] In 1801, that figure climbed to 10,276, and by 1815 it had reached a total of approximately 15,000.[22] The significance of these figures comes into sharp focus when it is noted that the total number of plantation slaves in the entire Danish West Indies in 1805 came to 27,837.[23] In effect, the mission had enrolled about 54 percent of all the plantation slaves in the Danish West Indies within approximately seventy years of the onset of their missionary enterprise. These numbers become all the more instructive when it is noted that at any given period, the mission stations were never served by more than thirty to thirty-five European missionaries. Clearly, those in the African-Caribbean community had been powerfully drawn to the Moravian program; it is equally clear that individual Blacks themselves were by necessity playing significant roles in the development and success of the missionary effort.

The success of the Moravian enterprise and the powerful attraction it exercised on the black population can be understood in terms of the advantages that full, active membership in the congregation offered the prospective member. In the first place, the new convert received a Christian identity in a strange and hostile land where attempts to maintain an African identity occasioned rather severe penalties and where the status of a slave rested at the very bottom of the social scale—powerless and defenseless in most institutionalized social transactions. The assumption of identity and personhood, from the perspective of the European community, occurred at baptism when the slave was relieved of his African name and was given a Christian or European one. Matamba, for example, became Thomas, Makulu became Anton, Jamba became Maria Magdalena, and so forth. In this symbolic act, the enslaved African became a Christian slave, theoretically liberated in matters of the soul, if not in those of the flesh. As limited a benefit as this new Christian identity may have been, especially in light of the accompanying trauma of acculturation, there is abundant evidence in the documentation to show that the conversion provided slaves not only with a new personal identity, but as well with a moral dimension, from the European point of reference at least. From these followed the benefit of Moravian advocacy in matters both spiritual and legal. This degree of security, however meager, in a world governed by slave codes at best and idiosyncratic individual whim at worst, held a powerful attraction for not a few members of the slave community.

The slave system in the Danish West Indies imposed rather strict limitations of movement on the individual slave. For most, the plantation became the center of a sharply restricted universe. Against this much-hated and often-tested limitation, the Moravians offered the possibility of a certain limited measure of mobility. In normal times, black Moravians enjoyed a modicum of intra-island movement, being allowed to travel in groups to and from the mission stations for church services, funerals, and the like. Although limited to the few, inter-island travel was enjoyed by various of the skilled men in the congregations, such as masons and mill-builders who belonged to the Moravians, and by prominent national helpers and preachers. Finally, some—like the married couple Andreas and Maria along with several others—traveled to the Moravian settlement at Bethlehem, Pennsylvania in North America expressly in order to live in the community of the Brethren there and to obtain a broader understanding of Moravian ways. Afterwards they were to return with that knowledge to their own people in the Danish West Indies. Still others, such as Rebekka Freundlich, Anna Maria, Charles Henry, Hans Jonathan, and others, made voyages to Europe expressly to visit Herrnhut and other Moravian settlements and often to live for periods of time there.[24] Although such experiences were for the most part limited to the few, their impact, through word of mouth and through the reading of letters from distant lands aloud in church, must have been strong indeed.

Literacy was another privilege eagerly sought by the enslaved.

Although expressly denied to them by the Danish government and by island custom in the early days of the colony, literacy in the Creole language of the Blacks was viewed by the Moravians as a powerful tool in the realization of their own evangelization and overall missionary program. The following quote illustrates the rather limited purposes to which the Moravians intentionally directed their literacy program:

"The diligence of some, who have an opportunity to learn the Creole language, with a view better to understand the preaching of the Gospel is truly edifying. Some also have taken great pains to learn to read the Bible, and attend the instruction of the children in that view. But our aim is not so much to teach them to read and sing hymns, as to make them attentive to the truths contained in the Scriptures and Hymns, that they may experience their power in their hearts, and that those, who have gifts to be assistants in the Mission, may be prepared for that office, by the teaching of the Holy Spirit himself."[25]

Perhaps it was the relative linguistic closeness felt by the German Moravians (some of them were, in fact, Plattdeutsch speakers) with Dutch Creole—which they generally viewed as corrupted Dutch—, especially when contrasted to the more linguistically distant Danish, French, and English of the other Whites of the colony, that induced the missionaries to undertake the task of first learning the Creole in order to speak it and then creating a written version of their spoken model for religious instruction and proselytizing. As early as 1736, Bishop August Gottlieb Spangenberg himself was one of the first Moravians to use the language in preaching. Johann Böhner adopted a similar practice several years later, using an adapted form of Dutch. These experiments pro-voked such positive resonance in the black audiences that the mission assistants in their turn were encouraged to follow Böhner's example.

The Dutch Creole language of the Danish islands had originated in the earliest years of the colony on St. Thomas as the direct result of the social and linguistic contact between the newly arriving Africans from the Guinea coast and the majority group of white colonists on the island, who were principally Dutch speaking.[26] In time, the resultant Dutch Creole language became the *lingua franca* of the colony, being spoken by Blacks and Whites alike. When St. John was colonized in 1718, those same planters and their slaves settled the island, taking the Dutch Creole language along with them. When St. Croix was purchased in 1733 and settled in the following year, a similar scenario ensued, with the exception that a fairly sizable contingent of yeomen English colonists and their slaves was already ensconced on the island. Others arrived from nearby English-speaking islands such as Anguilla and Tortola. The result of that encounter was widespread bilingualism. Nevertheless, the movement of considerable numbers of planters, their property and their enslaved, Dutch Creole-speaking labor force dictated that the Creole would be a linguistic force to be reckoned with in the new colony.

The Moravians responded to these circumstances and embarked on their language program with both haste and energy, producing primers, catechisms, psalm books, readers and eventually even a translation of the New Testament.[27] In 1761, the first of the Moravian materials in Dutch Creole appeared in print in the form of a hymnal and prayer book, entitled *Liturgie, de formulieren van doopp en avondmeal en sommige liederen*, revised in 1765 as *Gebeden en Liederen* and again in 1774, as *Psalm-Boek*. Around 1770, a reader appeared, *Taalproeven*, followed in 1785 by a synopsis of Christian teachings, under the title, *Die Hoofd-Inhoud van die Leering van Jesus Christus voor die Negermeente van die Broerkerk*. But the real achievement was the translation and publication in Dutch Creole of the New Testament. To this task the Moravian missionary Johan Böhner had dedicated over forty years of his life in the islands, producing a manuscript of both the Old and New Testaments. Although this work did not find its way into print, it was used as a foundation by another Moravian, Thomas de Malleville, who published *Die Nieuwe Testament na Creol Taal* in 1802.

Equally productive in the area of translation and publication, were the Danish Lutheran missionaries, who were obviously inspired and motivated by the example of Böhner and the Moravians. By 1770, they had published Luther's Small Catechism, An A-B-C Book and a hymnal in Dutch Creole. But the real achievement came in the work of a white St. Thomian Creole by the name of J.M. Magens, who, in 1770, published the first grammar of the Dutch Creole language (*Grammatik over det Creolske Sprog som bruges paa de tvende Danske Eilande, St. Croix, St. Thomas og St. Jan i Amerika, sammenskrevet og opsat af en paa St. Thomas indfød Mand*), followed in 1781 by a translation of the New Testament, *Die Nywe Testament vans ons Heer Jesus Christus ka set over in die Creolske Sprog en ka giev die Ligt tot dienst van Deen Mission in Amerika*, with a second edition in 1816. Minor publications with a religious orientation continued to appear in the Creole until the 1830s, when the black population of the Danish islands turned increasingly to English.

During the seventy years following the initial appearance of religious literature in Dutch Creole, an impressive array of such printed publications appeared, laying the foundation for a highly focussed but limited educational system and, as one consequence, a relatively high degree of literacy among black Moravians. The latter not only read the Bible and other religious works in their own language, but they also corresponded in it with Brethren abroad.[28] In addition, some of them acquired fluency and literacy in several European languages as well.[29] This offer of literacy in an otherwise oppressive, generally illiterate slave society was universally prized and sought after by those within its reach. It should be stressed, however, that the thrust of the Moravian language program was altogether mission-oriented, with little or no concern for the culture whence it came. In fact, the language in its written form was calqued predominantly on the speech of European Creole-speakers and was regarded as an instrument to transform that culture, by christianizing it from an essentially northern European perspective.

Most of the black Moravians led relatively quiet lives, moving regularly between the poles of mission church and plantation. Some distinguished themselves and thereby became models for others to emulate and follow. Certainly, the Moravian congregation itself benefited immeasurably by the achievements and exemplary lives of certain of its individual enslaved members. Domingo Gesu, or simply "Mingo" as he was more generally known, was perhaps the outstanding "national helper" for the early Moravian period. Though he remained a slave throughout his life, he nevertheless became a leader of the black community, a plantation manager in the service of the Carstens family and an entrepreneur of some note, who contributed consistently to the mission both materially and spiritually from the 1730s until his death in 1758. When the missionary Johann Böhner fell on hard times, unable to find remunerative work, it was Mingo who made him a loan, provided him with lodging and ultimately taught him the craft of mill-building, the trade with which Böhner subsequently supported his own missionary effort. When the slave woman Maria Magdalena fell terminally ill and was put out to die by her Free Black mistress, it was Mingo who provided her with shelter and comfort until she passed. For such acts of exemplary charity and Christian love he became well known. When he died in 1758, the unheard of number of 1,500 people, Blacks and Whites alike, followed his remains to the Moravian burial grounds.[30]

If Mingo was unquestionably the outstanding black Moravian figure in the Danish West Indies in the first half of the eighteenth century, then Cornelius, the mason, dominated the second half.[31] Expert mason and builder, gifted linguist and inspiring preacher, he acquired both his freedom and that of his family through industry and perseverance. As an elder in the congregation, he went on to become the beloved father figure of his people until his death in 1801. The list of those who took full advantage of the Moravian opportunity can be extended to include Nathanael, Abraham, Jakob Cruse, Petrus, and Rebekka Freundlich, to name but a few. Quite simply, the Moravian missions provided the opportunity for various gifted individuals to emerge from the general anonymity of a West Indian slave society in the eighteenth century. Moreover, the emergence of certain individuals rendered the movement all the more attractive to the masses and to prospective new members, thereby contributing in a manner that would be difficult to quantify for the mission's success.

In summary, then, numerous Blacks availed themselves of the opportunities provided by the Moravian missionary enterprise. Foremost among those advantages were, a means of achieving individual status, freedom of movement, literacy, an agency of advocacy within the European community, access to the same religion as that of the ruling class and, issuing from the latter, the recognition of their moral status.

The successes of the few should not blind us to the plight of the many, those who led common, uneventful lives under the yoke fashioned for them by a slave society. And just as some succeeded rather admirably within the confines of the system and others found the means simply to endure it, yet others chose to resist in one manner or another. Although the compilers of the Moravian documents intended to record the successes of their program and give precedence to those individuals who accommodated themselves most readily to that program, they nevertheless gave inevitable recognition not only to those who resisted the overall society that had enslaved them but also, to a much more limited degree, to those who attempted to evangelize them as well

The resistance of the enslaved population of the Danish West Indies to their condition of servitude in the most general sense has been widely studied. The literature lists no less than 13 recorded revolts or mutinies on ships in the middle passage from the Danish forts along the Gold Coast to the West Indies.[32] One of the more successful of all the revolts in the Americas was the Amina-led uprising on St. John in 1733–1734.[33] In addition, there were also disturbances and attempted revolts on St. Croix at various times, most notably, 1746 and 1759. And finally, there was the Emancipation revolt of 1848 on St. Croix that led directly to the liberation of all the enslaved population in the Danish West Indies. Before that time, marronage, both petit and grand, was widely practiced as a less extreme but effective means of resistance.[34]

In spite of all their success in converting enslaved Africans into Christians, the Moravians nevertheless also met with considerable opposition and resistance, a good deal of which they dutifully and characteristically recorded. The explanation for this apparently contradictory behavior lay in the Moravian obsession with thoroughness and detail in their record-keeping. Consider, for example, their practice of requiring Moravian believers to compose a *Lebenslauf*, that is, a detailed biographical inventory of one's life and "sins."[35] In general, the need of the individual to recognize the presence of sin and evil within himself was a cornerstone of Moravian belief. One's shortcomings in this life were to be faced and painstakingly examined as the obstacle which blocked the path to salvation; therefore, those impediments had to be first accepted as a part of one's sinful nature and then denounced. Consequently, the Moravian documentation literally teems with "case studies" of "sinners," the moral prescription for which stresses the universally redemptive powers of God's grace through the savior's suffering and blood as made freely available to sinners through the church. In the recording of a good deal of this "sinning," the Moravian scribes were in many cases compiling with the same strokes of the pen a record of the African resistance to their own missionary program and, in perhaps even more instances, to the authority of the other colonial authorities—the plantation and the state.

The Moravians were particularly perplexed by what might be termed "cultural resistance," that is to say, the stubborn adherence on the part of some slaves to certain African modes of behavior in circumstances where a European or Christian alternative had been offered as a replacement. African music, dance, religion, and language were the practices of this kind which appear most frequently in the Moravian records. The following observation by the ubiquitous Oldendorp merits citation in full as an example of a Moravian commentary on activities of this kind.

> When I ascribe to them an aptitude for dancing, that is not to say that they are able to perform very artistic dances. Their dancing consists of jumping about, shaking their shoulders, and moving their arms, wherein the great suppleness and strength of their bodies are displayed to good advantage. Even more monotonous is the instrumental music to which they dance. A skin stretched over a small barrel or a calabash, or if need be, even a pot serves as a drum and

animates their dances, though it does not sound much better than someone pounding on a board. They accompany the sounds of the drumming with singing. And when the dance has ended, the spectators show their appreciation with wild laughter and jubilation. They are great enthusiasts of these festivities, and it is not too much for them to spend their Sunday at it, after having exerted themselves the whole week long with hard work. However, this practice has declined considerably in the Danish islands and is for the most part observed only by the Free Negroes. They find great pleasure in their instrumental music; quite early the children make a kind of fiddle for themselves, constructed by stretching several horse hairs over a shingle and then stroking them with a bow or plucking them with their fingers. They also love to sing and take pleasure in singing the songs of their fatherland while working.[36]

While this observation was intended to serve as a descriptive and instructive means to a corrective end, Oldendorp's account—like those of the other missionaries—supplies abundant testimony concerning the very behavior that the movement was intent upon eradicating. Other writers, especially mission assistants, generally condemned such activities in harsher, more negative terms, thereby recording a good deal less descriptive information than did Oldendorp. But even their criticism often sheds revealing light on activities that signal resistance. We learn, for example, that the venerated Cornelius remained a participant in African dances even after he had been "awakened."[37] The same was said of a fair number of other members of the congregation, many of whom were "rescued" while in the midst of such activities by the relentless, ever-vigilant Friedrich Martin. But neither Martin nor his fellow missionaries could stem this impulse in the enslaved population, for nearly a century later another Moravian diarist writes:

"A custom has long prevailed in this district [Frederiksted] which is much to be lamented. On New Year's Day, as well as during the preceding night, the negroes are permitted to indulge in all manner of worldly and noisy amusements. They parade through all the streets of the town of Christianstadt, with songs, and dances, and beating of drums; and wherever they find a house open, they force their way into it, demanding of the owner either wine or rum, or else a piece of money."[38]

It can be inferred from scattered evidence of this kind that the persistent return to African music and dancing on the part of the slaves continued to pose a thorny problem for the Moravians, a supposition well supported by evidence regarding the persistence of gumbee and bamboula[39] from other sources as well.

Any attempt to analyze the slaves' use of language as a mode of resistance would by necessity extend far beyond the limits of this study. One important point begs to be made, however. There is evidence to suggest that the use of African languages in the Danish West Indies endured longer than has been generally believed. Oldendorp's documentation reveals that at least twenty-odd African languages were brought to the Danish West Indies and spoken there to one degree or another during the second half of the eighteenth century. Moreover, there is reason to believe that some of these languages may have been spoken until well into the following century. For instance, the case of the condemned Mandingo slave Lancaster in 1811 illustrates not only that Mandingo speech was his first language but also that other speakers of that tongue, in this case from the ranks of the Moravian national helpers, were readily available to communicate with him.[40] Similar evidence is provided later in the century by the correspondence of Brother A. H. Ziock, who reported that he baptized 44 "heathens" in 1853, some of whom were "old Africans."[41] It is difficult to believe that individuals such as these and others like them did not retain active use of their native African tongues and thereby maintain to a limited degree at least some part of their African means of communication and culture, regardless of how inhospitable the prevailing atmosphere for their general use might have been.

The Moravian documents give a fragmented picture of the African-Caribbean religious experience in the Danish West Indies, while at the same time including rather extensive accounts of religious practices in Africa as related by enslaved Africans themselves. The latter contain information on polytheism, animism, shamanism, ophiolatry and the use of fetishes. Inadvertently, however, some accounts were recorded that did not convey the "expected" image of African religion. Rather striking in its candor, for example, is Oldendorp's portrait of the Papaa free woman, Marotta, who lived her life in the Danish West Indies first as a slave and then later as a Free Black in St. Thomas, worshipping a single African god, believing in a trinity, and looking forward to her personal salvation through a savior. She met the itinerant Spangenberg and impressed him, as he himself explained, because "she could not understand why the Whites showed such little respect before God and seemed only to be paying him compliments." She concluded that until someone showed her better, she would continue following her African practices.[42]

Other accounts relate to the scattered practice of obeah (referred to generally by the Moravians as "witchcraft") and are for the most part strongly condemnatory and not descriptive. They do establish clearly, however, that such practices continued on the plantations, marginally at least, until well into the nineteenth century.[43]

There are passing references to a Muslim element among the slave population. One such was the case of the slave named Benjamin who had been a Mandingo and a Muslim in Guinea before his enslavement at the age of twenty. He was then transported to the Danish West Indies where he attempted for some years to continue instructing his fellow believers in the ways of Islam, just as his father, a "Mohammedan teacher," had done in Guinea. This interesting story comes to light only because Benjamin was ultimately baptized by the Moravians in 1779, and the missionaries obviously wished to make capital of the occasion.[44] This lone example raises the possibility, however, that there may well have been others of like religious persuasion whose refusal to accept Moravian instruction and baptism earned them the fate of non-recognition and, hence, anonymity.

It was by no means not all of the enslaved population that responded to the Moravian evangelization enthusiastically. Some responded with direct, often violent, overt resistance to the Moravians. Arson was one such device. When the missionary Georg Ohneberg took up residence at Estate Princesse on St. Croix, in July of 1751, the Moravian dwellings were repeatedly burned. Oldendorp concludes that "no other explanation for these wicked actions could be found than the unhappiness of the heathen Negroes over the conversion of their countrymen; their intention was none other than to destroy through fire all the buildings constructed for that purpose." Incidents of incendiarism continued through that summer with devastating effects, and as late as 1753, the resisting Blacks again burned the missionary's dwelling, along with ten "Negro houses." They repeated the act again in 1754. Similar incidents also occurred in the west end of the island.[45] These acts of resistance contradict the widely accepted belief that the enslaved Africans universally accepted Moravianism and Christianization.

The poisoning of Whites as an act of revenge remained a much feared and little discussed mode of black resistance throughout the slavery period. Although no evidence exists that such means were employed against missionaries, their privileged position within the slave community often provided a revealing glimpse of such offenses from their perspective as witnesses. We learn, for example, that the only son of a woman named Ketura, who was both a slave and a devout Moravian, was executed in 1801 for being an accomplice in an attempt to poison an overseer. In recording the incident, the motive of the diarist was to give witness to the consolation offered to the grieving mother by Jesus Christ; inadvertently, however, he provided a brief but revealing image of an individual act of resistance.[46] Incidents of this kind were sometimes cited in the mission diaries, even when they affected congregation members only tangentially.

Suicide proved yet another extreme means by which the enslaved might resist their condition. Newly-arrived Africans, Oldendorp relates, were more likely than others to resort to this measure, either by jumping overboard while on the slave ship during the Middle Passage or by other means soon after their arrival. In the Danish West Indies, numbers of these so-called "Bussals," both men and women, took their own lives, generally by self-starvation, sometimes by hanging. Oldendorp notes that shortly after his arrival on St. Croix in 1767, two newly-arrived African women hanged themselves in protest over their unacceptable circumstances. Shortly afterward, in St. Thomas, he learned of a woman who ate earth and stones until she perished.

Those Africans who had previously held high political or social station in their native lands generally found slavery particularly galling and sometimes resorted to drastic measures. "I am a prince," said one enslaved African to his owner, who prevailed upon him to do slave labor. "For the time being, I am in your power, but nothing will ever persuade me to serve you. I would rather end my life by voluntary death." The man then proceeded to take his own life by starvation. This same means of resistance was undertaken by a certain African woman who told her mistress: "I was much greater in Guinea than you are here. I had many more slaves in my service than you have. Now you expect me to be your slave? I would much rather die of starvation."[47]

Grand marronage and revolt were the two most dramatic means of slave resistance. The latter, or at least the threat of the latter, received short shrift from the Moravians, being mentioned in a general sense in the context of curfews and curtailment of religious services. Marronage, on the other hand, was a constant irritation for the missionaries in that it often meant the loss of the investment of many hours of instruction and training in an instant. As a result, the records contain numerous accounts of this behavior, along with the consequences. Oldendorp himself devotes a chapter to this subject and cites various examples of maritime marronage throughout his text.[48] One of the more interesting episodes concerns incursions made by Maroons from Tortola into St. Thomas. It seems that groups of Maroons from Tortola—both men and women—traveled to St. Thomas from time to time in 1801 and took refuge in the woods near Niesky, raiding the fields, stealing poultry, and even forcing entry into the mission house yard to steal. This particular incident was reported by a Moravian diarist, who was eager to boast about the ready disposition of the mission slaves and other Moravian-trained Blacks to defend the mission and to help capture some of the offenders and drive off the others.[49] Here rather strikingly, two aspects of slave behavior have been inadvertently written into a single historical document, from, of course, the missionary perspective.

The Moravian testimony, through voluminous extant documentation generated by their missionary endeavors, provides an informative and graphic description of slave life in the Danish West Indies in the 17th and 18th centuries. An examination of those records has shown that the Moravian missionary movement offered enslaved Africans certain limited options, which enabled them to enhance their personal security and development. Moreover, the same records open access to an understanding of the manner in which the slaves responded to the offer. A significant number of them accommodated themselves to their new circumstances and accepted the opportunities offered by the Moravian program of Christianization, even though it entailed inevitable deracination and acculturation. In spite of the latter and because of the harshness of the prevailing slave system, the advantages derived from acceptance and cooperation were considerable for those individuals who opted to become a part of the system. Equally significant were the contributions made by the enslaved in all areas of the new life after accommodation—missionary work, preaching, building, the practice of the trades, and the like. It is natural that the missionaries focussed the mass of their documentation on those who chose "accommodation." It was, after all, the purpose behind their work.

On the other hand, some of the enslaved chose to resist the slave system along with the missionary program that functioned within it through retention of cultural practices, arson, marronage, revolt, suicide and other means. Even though the Moravian documentation of their resistance is less abundant as well as distorted by an inevitable Christian, European-centered perspective, that documentation has nevertheless provided a valuable though inadvertent testimony concerning that part of the African community that chose resistance rather than accommodation to enslavement and Christianity.

NOTES

1. Two scholarly, though older, studies of the Moravians in the Danish West Indies are August Karl Ludwig von Dewitz's *Dänisch-Westindien: Hundert und fünfzig Jahre der Brüdermission in St. Thomas, St. Croix und St. Jan*. Part I: "Die erste Streiterzeit in des Grafen von Zinzendorf Tagen: Von 1732 bis 1760" (Niesky: Missions-Direktion der Brüdermission, 1882), 374 pp. and H. Lawaetz's *Brødremenighedens Mission i Dansk-Vestindien 1769–1848: Bidrag til en Charakteristik af Brødrekirken og dens Gerning og af den Farvede Races Stilling til Kristendommen* (Copenhagen: Otto B. Wroblewski, 1902), 256 pp. A short overview of the entire period in English is provided by G. Oliver Maynard in his *A History of the Moravian Church, Eastern West Indies Province* (s.n.: s.l., 1968), pp. 4–28. For accounts of Moravian education, see Patricia Shaubah Murphy's *The Moravian Mission to the Danish West Indies from 1732–1828* (St. Thomas: Caribbean Research Institute, 1968), 23 pp. and Eva Lawaetz's *Black Education in the Danish West Indies from 1732 to 1853* (St. Croix: St. Croix Friends of Denmark Society, 1980), 90 pp. A study dedicated exclusively to the missionary aspect of the Moravians in the West Indies in general is Oliver W. Furley's "Moravian Missionaries and Slaves in the West Indies," *Caribbean Studies* 5:2 (July 1965): 3–16.

2. The basic general account of the Moravians in this period is still David Cranz's *Alte und Neue Brüder-Historie oder kurz gefasste Geschichte der Evangelischen Brüder-Unität in den ältern Zeiten und insonderheit in dem gegenwärtigen Jahrhundert* (Barby: Christian Friedrich Laux, 1772), 923 pp. (Reprinted Hildesheim and New York: Georg Olms Verlag, 1973). See also J. Taylor Hamilton and Kenneth G. Hamilton's *History of the Moravian Church: The Renewed Unitas Fratrem, 1722–1957* (Bethlehem, PA: The Interprovincial Board of Christian Education, Moravian Church of America, 1967), 723 pp.

3. The life of the influential Zinzendorf and the early history of the Moravian missionary movement is presented in August Gottlieb Spangenberg's *Leben des Herrn Nicolaus Ludwig Grafen und Herrn von Zinzendorf und Pottendorf* (Barby: Bruder Gemeine, 1772–1775), 8 parts in 4 volumes. An excellent recent account is Lorenz Bergmann's *Grev Zinzendorf* (København: P. Haase og Søns Forlag), 2 v. The standard account in English is John R. Weinlick's *Count Zinzendorf* (New York/Nashville: Abingdon Press, 1956), 240 pp.

4. See G. Oliver Maynard, *The Moravian Church Among the Churches: Pioneer in the Oecumenical Task* (Barbados: The Moravian Church, Eastern West Indies Province, Caribbean Graphic Production Ltd., 1982).

5. Bryan Edwards, *The History, Civil and Commercial, of the British Colonies in the West Indies*, v. 1 (Dublin: Luke White, 1793), p. 431.

6. Victor Schoelcher, "Colonies Danoises: Saint-Thomas et Sainte-Croix," *Colonies Étrangères et Haiti*, v. 2 (Paris:1843), pp. 6, 20–25.

7. See C.G.A. Oldendorp's *Geschichte der Mission der evangelischen Brüder auf den caraibischen Inseln S. Thomas, S. Croix und S. Jan* (Barby: Johann Jakob Bossart, 1777), 14+1068+46 pp. Several years later there appeared a Danish translation by Olding Johan Jacob Moser of this popular work under the title *Fuldstændig Udtog af C.G.A. Oldendorps Missions-Historie om de evangeliske Brødres Mission paa de caraibiske Øer St. Thomas, St. Crux og St. Jan. Kort Beskrivelse over Vestindien, især de Danske caraibiske Øer St. Crux, St. Thomas og St. Jan. // Historisk Beretning om de hedenske Neger-Slavers Omvendelse paa de Danske Øer i Vestindien* (Copenhagen: Christian Buchs Forlag, 1784), 4+212+184 pp. This was followed in 1786 by a Swedish edition, namely *C.G.A. Oldendorps Historiska Beskrifning Öfwer Ewangeliske Brödernas Missions-Arbete På Caraibiske Öarne St. Thomas, St. Croix och St. Jan.* (Stockholm: P.A. Brodin on commission, 1786–88), 2 v. The more available, recent English translation is cited throughout this paper, namely: *A Caribbean Mission: History of the Mission of the Evangelical Brethren on the Caribbean Islands of St. Thomas, St. Croix, and St. John.* Translated from the German by Arnold R. Highfield and Vladimir Barac (Ann Arbor: Karoma Publishers, 1987), 35+737 pp.

8. Spangenberg emerged as the leading Moravian missionary theologian of the period. Two of his important contributions to the missionary methodology are *Unterricht für die Brüder und Schwestern welche unter den Heiden am Evangelio dienen* (Barby: Brüdergemeinen, 1784), 80 pp. and *Von der Arbeit der evangelischen Brüder unter den Heiden* (Barby: C.F. Laux, 1782), 182 pp. Both of these works draw on Spangenberg's personal experiences in the Danish West Indies.

9. For the most part, the records relevant to the missions in the Danish West Indies are presently located at the site of the original congregation in Herrnhut, Germany, as well as in The Moravian Archives at Bethlehem, Pennsylvania. See Vernon H. Nelson, [Catalogs of the West Indies Materials at the Unity Archives in Herrnhut, Germany] (Bethlehem, PA: Typescript, 1969), [60] pp. For materials at Bethlehem and, to a lesser extent, in the U.S. Virgin Islands, see Arnold R. Highfield, *The Historical Records of the Moravian Churches of the United States Virgin Islands in the Moravian Archives at Bethlehem, Pennsylvania.* Number Four, Bibliographic Series of the Society of Virgin Islands Historians (Christiansted, St. Croix, U.S. Virgin Islands, 1990), 32 pp.

10. A detailed account of the development of the choir system in Bethlehem, Pennsylvania, under the influence of Count Zinzendorf, is provided in Gillian Lindt Gollin's *Moravians in Two Worlds: A Study of Changing Communities* (New York and London: Columbia University Press, 1967), pp. 67–89.

11. These provisions may have been in part racially motivated. It should be noted,

however, that the Moravians enforced equally stringent measures in their settlements elsewhere, among other Europeans. Zinzendorf, for example, prohibited marriages between Moravians at Bethlehem and "other people" living in Pennsylvania, noting: "In particular I positively forbid the intermarriage of members of our Single Sisters' choir with natives of Pennsylvania. Any sister who takes such a step must be left to her own devices. These are two different kinds of people, that is for certain." See Gollin, pp. 111–112. One of the few publicly acknowledged exceptions in the Danish islands was the marriage of the German Moravian Matthäus Freundlich and an ex-slave woman, Rebekka. Theirs appears to have been what Zinzendorf termed a *streiter Ehe*, that is, a "militant marriage" in which husband and wife participated equally in their religious or missionary work. See Arnold R. Highfield, "Rebekka Freundlich: A Moravian Life," *Conference Proceedings of the Society of Virgin Islands Historians.* Edited by Robert V. Vaughn (St. Croix: The Society, 1992), pp. 51–61. See also Oldendorp, pp. 338–339 ff.

12. An interesting account of the nature and evolution of the Moravian practice of casting lots is given in Gollin, pp. 50–63.

13. The white population of St. Croix grew from 174 in 1742 to 1,323 in 1755; for the same period the slave population increased dramatically from 1,906 to 8,897. During approximately the same period, the white population on St. Thomas declined from 324 in 1725 to 228 in 1754 and the slave population from 4,490 to 3,481 in the same period. Svend E. Green-Pedersen, "The Scope and Structure of the Danish Negro Slave Trade," *Scandinavian Econonmic History Review* 19 (1971): 150 and 157. By 1805, some 79% of the all the Danish islands' 27,837 plantation slaves resided on St. Croix. See Neville A. T. Hall, *Slave Society in the Danish West Indies: St. Thomas, St. John and St. Croix* (Jamaica: The University of the West Indies Press, 1992), p. 85. Hall's work is the most comprehensive treatment of slavery in the Danish West Indies.

14. For a short account of Martin's life and missionary activity in the Danish islands, see E. Grunewald's *Friedrich Martin der Treue Zeuge* Kleine Traktate aus der Brüdermission No. 22 (Herrnhut: Missions-Expedition, [n.d.]), 16 pp.

15. These classes represented an attempt by the Moravians to adapt their choir system to the special conditions that they encountered in the Danish West Indies, especially the restrictions imposed on individuals within the system of slavery. See Gollin, pp. 68–89.

16. For a general introduction to the Dutch Creole within the missionary context as well as the religious literature produced by the Moravians, see Jens Larsen's *Virgin Islands Story* (Philadelphia: Fortress Press, 1950), pp. 102–128.

17. Statistical summaries of the growth in the number of baptisms etc. are provided by Oldendorp. For example, for the period 1732 to 1757, some 1,732 individuals

were baptized in all the Danish islands (1,152 on St. Thomas; 466 on St. Croix; and 109 on St. John). Oldendorp, pp. 530–531.

18. *Periodical Accounts* 14 (1836): 147–148.

19. The visits by some of the black Moravians to Copenhagen are noted in Christian Degn's *Die Schimmelmanns im Atlantischen Dreieckshandel: Gewinn und Gewissen* (Neumunster: Karl Wachholtz, 1974), pp. 379–381; also see Poul Olsen's "Disse vilde Karle: Negre i Danmark indtil 1849" in *Fremmede i Danmark: 400 års fremmedpolitik*. Edited by Bent Blüdnikow (Odense: Odense Universitetsforlag, 1987), pp. 103–117, which examines the presence of Blacks in Denmark up to 1849.

20. Oldendorp, pp. 625–626.

21. "Various Accounts," *Periodical Accounts Relating to the Missions of the Church of the United Brethren Established Among the Heathen* 1 (1790–96): 315.

22. "Extract of the Diaries of the Brethren's Missions in the Danish Islands St. Thomas, St. Croix and St. Jan, of the Year 1801," *Periodical Accounts* 3 (1802): 161–181. This demographic breakdown by island (i. e., listing the numbers of Moravian "adherents") illustrates the shift of focus in the missionary work from St. Thomas and St. John to St. Croix that had occurred since the early years of the mission. (St. Thomas—2,333; St. Croix—6,653; and St. John—1,290).

23. Hall, p. 85.

24. There is a narrative account of Charles Henry's various trips to and sojourns at Copenhagen in Degn, pp. 379–381.

25. "Extract . . . ," *Periodical Accounts* 3 (1802): 175.

26. For a general overview of the origins, history and grammar of Dutch Creole, see Anne Graves, "The Present State of the Dutch Creole of the Virgin Islands" (Doctoral dissertation, University of Michigan, 1977). See also Dirk Christian Hesseling, *Het Negerhollands der deense Antillen: Bijdrage tot de geschiedenis der nederlands taal in Amerika*. Utgiven vanwege Maatschappij der Nederlandse Letterkunde te Leiden (Leiden: A.W. Sijthoff, 1905), 290 pp. and J.P.B. de Josselin de Jong, "Het Negerhollandsch van St. Thomas en St. Jan," *Koninglijke Nederlandsche van Wetenschappen, Afdeeling Letterkunde* 57, s. A (1924): 55–71.

27. The publications in the following passage are examined in some detail by Larsen, pp. 112–128 and Graves, pp. 12–35.

28. There is evidence that some of these letters were written quite early. See "To rørende Breve," *Dansk Missionblad* 71 (1904): 443–445, which discusses two letters written from Moravian slaves in the Danish islands to the King and Queen of Denmark around 1739. For other evidence of early writing in the Creole by slaves, see "Enige Brieffe der in St. Thomas zu Jesum Christum bekehrten Negers an die Mährische Bruder-Gemeine in Europa, in Cariolisher Sprache geschrieben, und in Deutsche übersetzt," *Budische Sammlung* (1745): [n.p.]. The Moravian Archives

in Bethlehem, Pennsylvania also contain a sampling of early letters from slaves of the Moravian faith in the Danish islands. See Moravian Archives, Bethlehem, Pennsylvania, [Letters from Natives in the West Indies from 1752 to 1765], 36 manuscript pages.

29. By most accounts, Cornelius, while still enslaved, knew five languages— Creole, Dutch, Danish, German, and English. Multilingualism was apparently common among the slaves of the Danish islands. See *The Life of Cornelius: A Negro Assistant in the Moravian Church at St. Thomas* (Antigua: printed by Loving and Hill, 1820), 12 pp. Also see E. Lawaetz, *Black Education*, pp. 46–47 and scattered references in Oldendorp.

30. Domingo Gesu, or Mingo, is referred to on numerous occasions in Oldendorp's History, including a short biography at his death on October 22, 1758. For the latter, see Oldendorp, pp. 546–547.

31. *The Life of Cornelius: A Negro Assistant in the Moravian Church at St. Thomas.*

32. Svend E. Green-Pedersen, "Om Forholdene på Danske Slaveskibe med særlig henblik på dødeligheden 1777–89," *Handels-og Søfartsmuseet på Kronberg Årbog* (1973): 42–46.

33. Aimery P. Caron and Arnold R. Highfield, *The French Intervention in the St. John Slave Rebellion 1733–34.* Occasional Papers No. 7 (St. Thomas: Bureau of Libraries, Museums and Archaeological Services, Department of Conservation and Cultural Affairs, 1981), 58 pp.

34. Neville A.T. Hall, "Maritime Maroons: Grand Marronage from the Danish West Indies." *The William and Mary Quarterly* 3rd ser., 42:4 (1985): 476–498 and Polly Pope, "Maroon Settlement on St. Croix," *Negro History Bulletin* 35: 7 (Nov. 1972): 153–154.

35. As examples of this kind of confessional writing, see Oldendorp's *Lebenslauf* as it appears, appended to the English translation of his History, (pp. 633–640); see also "Of the Life of Br. Erdman Hohe, Missionary in the Danish West Indies, who departed this life at Herrnhut, March 30th, 1835," *Periodical Accounts* 15 (1839): 1–6.

36. *Ibid.*, p. 249. The dance that Oldendorp describes so awkwardly here is probably the bamboula. It would be another seventy odd years before this dance received an enthusiastic description by a European writer. See V. Schoelcher's "Saint-Thomas et Sainte-Croix," dans *Annuaire des Voyages et de la Geographie pour l'année 1844* (Paris: Guillaumin, 1844), p. 181.

37. "Life of Cornelius, A Negro-Assistant in the Brethren's Mission in St. Thomas, as related in the Diary of New Herrnhut," *Periodical Accounts* 3 (1802): 182–183.

38. "Report of the Mission in St. Croix for 1834," *Periodical Accounts* 14 (1836):147.

39. George Tyson, *Jumpin' Up* (St. Croix: manuscript, forthcoming).

40. "Account of the Imprisonment and Execution of a Negroe Criminal, in the Island of St. Croix, West Indies, who was visited by the Missionaries of the Church of the Brethren, while under sentence of death, by desire of the Judge," *Periodical Accounts* 6 (1814): 421.

41. See A.H. Ziock, [Letter from A.H. Ziock], *Moravian Church Miscellany* 4:9 (Sept. 1853): 314.

42. Oldendorp, pp. 312–313.

43. Neither the Danish authorities nor the Moravians gave this subject a great deal of attention in print. The literature is confined largely to short snippets, such as are found in *Observations Upon the State of Negro Slavery in the Island of Santa Cruz, the Principal of the Danish West India Colonies; with Miscellaneous Remarks upon Subjects Relating to the West India Question, and a Notice of Santa Cruz* (London: Simpkin and Marshall, 1829), pp. 40–43. For a popular account, see A. Paludan-Müller's "Obeah paa St. Croix," *Samfundet Fællesorgan for dansk Haandværk og Industri* 25:12 (1901): [4 pp.].

44. See John Holmes' *Historical Sketches of the Missions of the United Brethren for Propagating the Gospel Among the Heathen from their Commencement to the Year 1817* (London: The Author, 1827), p. 316.

45. Oldendorp, p. 503.

46. "Extract . . . ," *Periodical Accounts* 3 (1802): 179. Incidents of this kind were not rare. Overseers and managers were sometimes poisoned by slaves for refusing to honor promises to purchase the freedom of their children by slave women. See "Peter von Scholten's Letter of December 22, 1849, to Liebenberg, Counsel for the Defense, concerning the Negro Rebellion in St. Croix on July 3, 1848," in *Emancipation in the Danish West Indies: Eyewitness Accounts II* (St. Croix; Bureau of Libraries and Museums), pp. 12–13.

47. Oldendorp, p. 220.

48. *Ibid.*, p. 589.

49. "Extract . . . ," *Periodical Accounts* 3 (1801): 174–175.

Count Nicholas Ludvig von Zinzendorf (1700–1760), the Moravian leader who
was in large part responsible for founding of the Moravian missionary effort

CHAPTER 18

THE MORAVIAN MISSION
TO ST. CROIX

O N A BRIGHT Sunday morning, on the way into Christiansted
along the western end of King Street, you can hear the sound of
singing coming from Friedensthal Moravian Church. Alongside the
church on the same gentle rise overlooking the street sits the ancient
Moravian manse, long since out of use. This complex of buildings traces
its origins to the first Moravian Mission to the island in 1734, and as
such represents the outcome of one of the very first Protestant missionary movements in the New World.

Who were these Moravians and why did they decide to come to St.
Croix in the Danish West Indies so many years ago? The denomination was the result of two powerful forces in Europe that arose well in
advance of the 18th century. The first of these was the Unitas Fratrum
Church which emerged in the mid-15th century. And the second was
the renewal of the Pietist movement within the Lutheran and Moravian Churches in the 17th century, an attempt to regenerate the intense
piety of the original Protestant Reformation.

These two strong religious currents flowed together in eastern Germany, in a small settlement called Herrnhut, near the village of Eber-
storff, on the lands of a powerful contemporary nobleman, Count Ludwig von Zinzendorf. The latter, an extremely religious man, welcomed
refugees from Moravia and Bohemia onto his lands and allowed them
to established a religious community, The Moravian Church, that has
persisted to this day.

How they found their way to the Danish Caribbean islands is another
fascinating story. While Count Zinzendorf was attending the corona-

tion ceremonies of King Christian VI in Copenhagen, Denmark, in 1731, he met Anton, a slave from the Danish island of St. Thomas, who was in Copenhagen at that time in the service of his master. The two men talked, and Anton expressed a strong desire to become a Christian but regretted that he was blocked from doing so by his slave status.

Moved by Anton's story, Zinzendorf made arrangements to take him to the Moravian settlement of Herrnhut where the visitor gave witness to the miserable conditions of the entire slave community on St. Thomas. The Moravian Brethren, and especially David Nitschmann and Leonard Dober, were so moved by meeting Anton that the two of them left Herrnhut for St. Thomas, where in December of 1732 they arrived and initiated the first Moravian Mission and perhaps the first true Protestant mission anywhere in the world.

Purchased by the Danes from France in 1733, St. Croix received the second mission in 1734, when a small group of Moravians set up a mission station near the present Friedensthal. Their goals were quite simple—they wished to give witness to their theology, in which God's free flowing Grace had long since been made available to all of humankind by the sacrifice of Jesus Christ. Their objective was not an easy one, and they were willing to make their own extreme sacrifices to realize it.

The mission station at Friedensthal was the center of the proselytizing effort on St. Croix, headed by an official Missionary. In addition, gathered around the Missionary was a number of Mission Helpers, men and their wives, largely from Herrnhut, who ministered to the enslaved population. Though they tended to die off rather quickly in the tropical climate, the volunteers were not discouraged and continued to arrive from Europe.

In the beginning, they attracted a great deal of attention as presumed troublemakers among the slaves. Consequently, they were opposed on all sides, at least initially. But slowly they gained acceptance to the degree that they accepted slavery as a regrettable norm within the island society. Total freedom and equality were necessarily reserved for the next world, not this one. Such was the price they paid relative to their own ideals for being allowed to preach and teach in the Danish islands.

All the same, the enslaved flocked to the mission of these strange newcomers because of certain advantages granted to them. Most of all, they were allowed to become Christians, to attend religious services, sometimes to travel for that purpose, to move up the hierarchy of the Mission congregation, and, in general, to engage in a number of activities that would have been otherwise denied them. In short, the Mission provided an escape from the monotony and inhumanity of slave life, as well as the opportunity to attain some hope for the future.

In addition, the Moravians provided access to a meaningful religious structure. A convert began at the bottom of that structure as a catechumen. In time that first step led in succession to baptism, confirmation, the title of "Christian" and advancement through the well known "Choir System." Eventually, one might become a "National Helper" and even an Elder in the Church. Motivation and the possibility of achievement served this system and its adherents well.

Moreover, effective leadership by the Brethren and eager participation by the enslaved were the two elements that militated in favor of success of the undertaking. Jakob Böhner, as one example of the former, began the enormous undertaking of a translation of Christian literature into Dutch Creole, the language of the enslaved. But it was Friedrich Martin who provided the heart and soul of the movement, leading his congregation against overwhelming odds in establishing schools, laying the foundations for churches and, in general, providing uncompromising encouragement when things were darkest.

These voices found echoes in the enslaved community. Nathanael rose through the ranks to become a revered Elder and a remarkable preacher. And Brother Cornelius by his death in 1804 was loved and respected by the entire Moravian community as a master mason, builder, teacher, preacher and friend. One is, in fact, rather amazed by the scope of the contributions of these and other members of the enslaved community to the growth and management of the Moravian congregation on St. Croix.

By the second half of the 18th century, the Mission system had borne remarkable results. By the end of the year 1768 the incredible number of 4,711 individuals had been baptized in the three Danish islands by a mere handful of Moravians. And by the early 1800s, that number had more than doubled. The impact of Moravianism was therefore profound and enduring.

Although the Moravian brethren carried out missionary work in other Caribbean Islands, their initial and most intense efforts occurred in the Danish West Indies. Consequently, if one is in search of the causal elements that clearly mark the culture of our islands as unique, this is one significant place to start that search.

Sugar mill and chimney at Estate Whim on St. Croix

CHAPTER 19

SUGAR MILLS OF ST. CROIX

T
HOUGH SUGAR-MAKING has long since disappeared from St. Croix, sugar mills still dot the Crucian landscape. It requires more than a little imagination to visualize that these modest-looking structures were once the engines that drove the local economy. But today many of them are completely abandoned, overgrown and dilapidated.

The need for grinding capacity first appeared in the second half of the 17th century. At that time, sugarcane slowly replaced tobacco as the export crop of preference. Tobacco had been available in Europe for several decades and an overabundant supply led to a steep decline in prices. In the 1650s the appearance of sugar on the market created something of a sensation, causing demand and prices to rise sharply.

That combination of factors led to a revolution across the Caribbean, St. Croix included. The rush to cane cultivation necessitated larger land holdings, a larger labor force, and a suitable infrastructure. The first of these resulted in our plantation or estate system; the second, in African slavery; and the third, in grinding capacity, factories for sugar cooking, warehouses for storage, and distilleries for rum production.

Several schemes were first tried to grind the sugarcane water from the harvested stalks. In an early method, laborers pushed large rollers over cane stalks on a hard, flat surface. This proved largely inefficient and wasteful. Where streams existed, water mills were sometimes constructed. Smaller, drier islands, however, were for the most part excluded from this alternative. More reliable were the animal mills that employed horses or oxen walking in a circle tethered to the roller-mill which was located at the center of their circular path. This proved to be a reliable though slow method.

· 241 ·

Toward the end of that same century, the more resourceful among the planters began to construct windmills on their estates. This project required skilled masonry workers, a large supply of workable stone and coral, cast-iron rollers imported from abroad, and, of course, a sizable investment on the part of the owner. Slowly, toward the mid-18th century, these conical-shaped mills began to appear across the St. Croix landscape.

Over the years some have remarked that these structures should be reduced to rubble since they stood as memorials to the age of slavery. All of the mills were in fact built by slaves and not a few of them under the command of master masons who were slaves themselves, men such as the noted Moravian Cornelius. As such they stand as reminders of what determined people can achieve even under extremely difficult circumstances.

First, a slightly elevated location favorably disposed to the wind was selected. A foundation was constructed from locally quarried stone and from coral taken by workers from the off-lying reefs, using a mortar made from burnt lime, sand and molasses. The design focused on a broad frontal entrance and at least two side windows, all of them open to the weather. As the circular walls proceeded upward, they narrowed, forming an inverted cone-shape. It was topped off by a wooden canopy that supported the four rotating blades and their canvas sails.

The heart of the structure was the cast-iron upright rollers seated firmly on the ground floor of the mill. They were three in number. The largest was located in the center of the three and was called the king roller. It was flanked on both sides by two other rollers, all connected by gears. On top of the king roller sat a gear mechanism connected by a drive shaft to a similar gear just behind the turning rotor at the top of the mill. The energy produced in this arrangement turned the king roller and directly its two companions, creating a crude but effective crushing device in the small spaces between the rollers.

These mills were put into heavy use when the sugarcane was harvested. Slaves delivered cut cane in bundles by cart and on donkey-back to the front of the mill where it was fed by the millman into the rollers. A worker received the crushed stalks behind the rollers and then fed them back through to the front for a second time. The pressed cane juice was collected in a pan below the rollers and fed by a pipe to the cookhouse, or factory, where the fresh liquid was cooked into unrefined brown sugar and molasses.

Though romantic-looking today, the mills offered little other than hard work during harvest time or "crop." On the larger estates they might be in operation around the clock for several weeks until the last of the cane had been cut and processed. During this marathon, work-induced fatigue might cause a worker to have his hand and arm jerked between the rollers along with a cane stalk. Since there was no means to quickly stop the mill or put it "in neutral," the only recourse was to hack off the man's trapped limb with a machete or see him die.

In the first half of the 19th century, many estates adapted their operations to steam power. This switch from wind to steam power generated by fire, required a more robust layout of metal equipment. In addition, numerous smokestacks or stone chimneys had to be built in order to cool the ascending embers lest they fall directly into adjacent fields causing fires. So once again the sugar industry changed the landscape of St. Croix.

The end of the 19th century saw the precipitous decline of sugar on St. Croix and with it the inevitable demise of the mills. During the course of the 20th century, a few continued to be used in various agricultural jobs on the estates. And a few were converted into private dwellings or extensions to dwellings. Some have been damaged by storms and floods. Some have been scavenged for their stones as building materials. But most have simply fallen victim to neglect and the quiet ravages of nature, leaving them inhabited by a few birds and overgrown with trees and bush, slowing causing them to crack and literally fall apart.

What to make of this situation? Preservation and restoration of the excellent variety practiced by Landmarks Society at Whim is one possible response. But how and by whom would such work be carried out? Moreover, perhaps not everyone would agree that their tax dollars should go to refurbish reminders of the era of slavery.

Maybe there is a middle ground. A networked museum/park system might prove attractive for a number of reasons. We might begin by restoring six or so of these mills in various parts of the island and then dedicate each one to a different aspect of our island and culture—one, say for birdlife, and other for plants and botany. Another might be given to Indian culture and a fourth to some aspect of local history. The list could be easily extended. Each one surrounded by a modest park with trees, plants and picnic benches, this trail of refurbished and "retooled" mills, might prove irresistible to the many tourists who visit our island, to say nothing of our own residents. And at the same time, it might just provide some return, say in the areas of cultural-historical tourism and employment.

In the final analysis, however, we will have to decide just how much the mills as conveyors of history, the environment, nature and education really mean to us, how badly we want to keep them, and how much we are willing to sacrifice for their continued existence and use.

The 18th century sugar estate at Constitution Hill, St. Croix

CHAPTER 20

THE ESTATES OF ST. CROIX

W HEN IT COMES TO giving or receiving directions, I think
I have finally been transformed into a Crucian. And it's about
time. A tourist recently approached me and inquired how he might
get to route 553 or some such. I was dumbfounded. I had no idea. I
stood there babbling. It appears that I have grown accustomed to far
less quantitative methods, preferring, when meting out directions, to
deal in estate names, something like the following music to my ears:
"Well, you go 'long North Shore Road., through Princess, past St. John
and Concordia. Turn west at the gas station by Glynn. Head west past
Upper Love til you smell hog plum. Make a right at the Kapok tree. You
pass three cattle gates and then you butt up with a margah, fungi dog
sleeping under a Taman tree. Make a sharp left. But careful not to mash
up de dog tail. Den you dere." So doan tell me nuttin bout no route 52
heading into 64 and then turning onto 551. It's too late for me. I ain able
wid dat. No, give me the good ole days, because to know St. Croix is to
experience its fascinating geography and revel in its diverse history in
the form of its estate names. So let's have a go at it.

Our two towns, Christiansted and Frederiksted both bear Danish
names, but it is interesting that over the years many have preferred
Bazin or Bassin, which is French in origin (<Le Bassin), for the former
and Westend, or simply West, which is British, for the latter. The two
major settlements were connected by a Centerline Road, now Queen
Mary Highway, that passed through King's Hill, which was a kind of
stopover for travelers between the two ends of the island in the days of
horse and cart travel.

In time, a few other very small villages appeared—La Valle, Grove

Place, Gallows Bay etc.—but they were small indeed. This scarcity of modest settlements is largely due to the nature of the island's economic and social organization around plantations, or estates, through most of our history. Workers were required to be close to their work, in fact, at their work. Each estate therefore had its own restrictive rules and economic order, and, as a result, villages appeared on the estates themselves rather than spread independently over the country-side. In the end, everything was centered on the estates.

It is in the island's estate names, rather than among settlements, that we encounter a veritable profusion of nomenclature, located within their particular quarters that, on first glance, makes very little sense. At the very beginning of our history, first the French and then the Danes divided St. Croix into quarters. As might be expected, the French enjoyed an advantage in giving out names over the less imaginative Danes. The French quarters were six in all: Fond de Monery, Mestre de Camp, Rivière Salée, Pointe de Sable, Nord, and Sud, whereas the Danes came up with nine, namely: King's, Queen's, Prince's, Westend, Northside A, Northside B, Company, Eastend A, and Eastend B quarters.

In 1734–35, the Danish West India and Guinea Company ordered a cadastral survey that divided the island into several hundred estates, measured from a "center line" that ran the east-west length of the island. Over the next twenty years these newly marked off estates were sold to investors of several nationalities—Englishmen, Danes, Dutchmen, and Frenchmen, for the most part. Those entrepreneurial beginnings account for a modest flurry of multilingual names. But just as most of the early settlers of St. Thomas came from the Dutch Windward islands, so it was that most of the settlers of St. Croix came from the English Leeward islands, in particular St. Kitts. That fact in itself explains a good deal about what follows.

The number of estates has varied over the years as the island developed. Presently, the number stands at some 271 estates give or take a few, depending on which map one consults. Here I must thank my friend and colleague George Tyson for his recent "estate count." Though that number of estates does not appear on current maps, we can nevertheless arrive at some interesting ideas relative to names and naming.

Danish estate names number some eleven or so (Fredensborg, Hafensigt, Bulow's Minde, Plessen, Høgensborg, Sorgenfri etc.) or about four percent. Not a surprising figure when one considers the very limited population and capital resources of Denmark at that time, especially in comparison with those of the English and her overwhelming marine resources. French names number only a few more at 13 or about 4.7 percent, whereas there are 3 Spanish, and 2 German, the latter coming from Moravian Missionary sources.

English names number 191, or approximately 71 percent. It should be borne in mind that while English linguistically, some of these names are ethnically Irish, Northern Irish or Scottish in inspiration (Fareham, Carleton, Caledonia and Tipperary). Nevertheless, St. Croix was English to the bone in terms of estate nomenclature. Moreover, it should be noted that some of the estates carry no name at all today.

Of equal interest is the meaning that the original owners placed on their properties, both on a conscious and subconscious level. Those lacking in imagination or perhaps those who were nostalgia-stricken, simply opted for a name that reflected their European origins: Richmond, Longford, Granard, and Windsor. Far more revealing, however, are names that relate local geography to the business at hand—growing sugar cane and producing raw sugar. A surprising number of estates have the word "hill'" in their names: Dolby Hill, Lowry Hill, Recovery Hill, Herman Hill etc. These reflect the obvious desire to connect the estate name with a prime, elevated location for a windmill situated to catch strong breezes. By the same token, a raised site for a dwelling above the hurly-burly of daily work on the estate, with fresh air and a view of things was at a premium. It might well also have had an effect when it came time to put the estate on the market for sale, making the real estate more attractive. Similarly, there were several estates with the words "mount" (Mount Victory) and "mountain" (Blue Mountain) in their names, which again shows predilection for the high ground. The words "hole" (Bugby Hole, altogether unattractive) and "valley" (Cotton Valley) appear from time to time but in significantly fewer numbers.

Terrestrial water designations, on the other hand, were apparently also attractive, for they occur in the following forms: pond, (Great Pond); spring, (The Springs); gut (Spring Gut); and river (Salt River), as might be expected on an island that was often threatened by drought. Roads were not all that good at that time and so a location near the sea with a landing place for loading and unloading vessels was desirable. Consequently, the word "bay" appears in 11 estate names, (Hill's Bay, Cane Bay, Teague Bay), again perhaps a subtle advertisement for the desirability of locations near the sea and easy transportation.

For some, however, geography had to take a back seat, considerations of the spirit being more important. Some estates, for example, have religious names, both Biblical, as in the examples of Jerusalem, Canaan, Elijah's Retreat and Lebanon, and Roman Catholic as in: St. John, St. Peter, St. Georges and the like.

Some of the names are altogether pedestrian, indicating that the place was a farm (Peter's Farm), a garden (Spring Garden), or just simply a big (La Grande Princesse) or small (Little Princess) plantation. Big estates were ordinarily the result of an amalgamation of several regular size estates into one large one (Princesse, La Grange and Bethlehem).

It is interesting that the names of some estates reflect the varied expectations of the original owners and name-bestowers. In some instances there dwelled in their hearts the symbols of great wealth as in: Ruby, Diamond, Pearl, Golden Rock and Betsy's Jewel. In other instances, an optimistic name was given, perhaps to insure good karma as in: Morning Star, Paradise, Mary's Fancy, William's Delight, Judith's Fancy, Profit, and Anna's Hope. It is to be noted that most names in this category have a female designation as well.

But others were not so hopeful and the name-givers were obviously trying to ward off their worst fears, as in the following examples: Stoney Ground, Humbug, Retreat, Barrenspot, Slob, and Hard Labor. Finally, it appears that some were simply attempting to get through the day and off to bed for a good night's sleep: Work and Rest, Catherine's Rest and Rust-op-Twist (Dutch for "rest after exertion").

And then there remain a few curiosities. On an island openly devoted to slavery and racial exploitation, we have only Negro Bay and White Lady to show for it. Some things, no doubt, were considered better left unsaid. But perhaps there is a lighter side to all this nomenclature business. Evidently, not all of the early estate owners were dour, nose-to-the-grindstone, old fogey plantation types, giving us these many years later the opportunity to provide a lucky but lost visitor with a set of directions perhaps not unlike the following: first you get to Punch, make contact with Lower Love, and in no time at all you'll find yourself in Sweet Bottom. That beats the daylights out of uninspiring route numbers any day.

Statue of Robert Cofresí, well known
pirate who operated in the waters off
Puerto Rico in the early 19th century

CHAPTER 21
ST. CROIX AND PUERTO RICO: A LONG-TERM CONNECTION

WHEN WE THINK of the relationship between St. Croix and Puerto Rico in these times, it is generally in terms of people coming from the latter island to our own island as immigrants. While that has certainly been the case over the past 80 years or so, it is not the complete story over the long haul. In truth, the links between the two islands have been much more reciprocal and of a much longer duration than is generally believed.

This long-term relationship has been no mere coincidence. Indeed, it owes its existence not to the political but to the physical geography of our region and to that we must turn for a deeper understanding. St. Croix has always been a natural part of those islands that form a crescent around the western curve of the Vieques Sound. In addition, the westerly direction of the prevailing winds and ocean currents in this part of the Caribbean makes Vieques and eastern Puerto Rico the natural destination for anyone leaving St. Croix by sea. And that is an extremely significant fact.

This relationship exerted an influence far back in prehistoric times, several millennia, in fact, before the advent of the Common Era. Taino culture and civilization thrived in the greater Antilles, and not least on the island of Boriquen, our present-day Puerto Rico. Neighboring Ayay, our present-day St. Croix, lay just 70 some miles to the east of that large island; it was, in effect, a satellite of Boriquen society and culture. The presence of numerous artifacts found on St. Croix in recent times gives a clear indication that travel, trade and cultural interchange were all carried on readily and regularly between these two neighboring islands.

But at the same time, it is clear that the focus and direction of the greater part of the traffic was from St. Croix to Puerto Rico as populations are attracted from the periphery to the center where innovation and wealth thrive. This relationship is underscored by the participation of Indians from Ayay in the great uprising that occurred in Puerto Rico in 1511.

By the middle years of the 1500s, Spain reduced the Indian population of Boriquen to inconsequence. Attempts to Christianize the Indians of Ayay, newly named Santa Cruz, and at the same time to enslave them, resulted in their flight from their home island. For her part, Spain was content to keep the island in that status, empty and isolated, making forays into its waters to exploit its rich marine life and onto its beaches to take turtles from its shores. There was never any real interest in setting up a Spanish colony here beyond the occasional garrison. Santa Cruz was therefore an abandoned colony of a colony and remained so for well over a century. It is in that curious manner that the flag of the Spanish Hapsburgs cast its meager shadow over Santa Cruz.

But things did not remain peaceful for long. In the 1630s, the Dutch, French and English all attempted to settle Spanish Santa Cruz. In response, armed flotillas from Puerto Rico made their way frequently to Santa Cruz but only to rid their possession of would-be settlers. So it was during this period that the relationship between the two islands remained something of a stand-off, a period of lull in the coming and going of people of several nations.

In 1650, after Santa Cruz was seized from Spain by a French force from St. Christopher and renamed Ste. Croix, the relationship between the two islands shifted noticeably and maintained a new vector of migration for the next century or so. The transition from a tobacco to a sugar-based economy produced a society that was initially top-heavy with bond laborers and eventually with slaves, all of them highly discontented with the severity of their work and living conditions. Not surprisingly, numbers of them attempted to escape. And again, they moved before the prevailing easterly winds and currents, to Puerto Rico.

Those slaves who managed to cross the open stretch of sea from St. Croix found a refuge in Spanish Puerto Rico. A declaration of fealty to the Spanish king and a conversion to the Catholic faith earned the erstwhile slaves new status as free men within a short period. Word of this possibility spread rapidly and presented a great incentive to others who were enslaved. Their subsequent escape by sea proved to be more than an annoyance for St. Croix's new sugar planters. Moreover, it continued to occur from the French into the Danish period after 1734. So for the better part of a century the flow of migration favored a St. Croix to Puerto Rico direction.

As St. Croix developed in the 1740s and 1750s, more enslaved Africans were imported to fill the growing labor needs. And many of them escaped to Puerto Rico. Reimert Haagensen, a planter on St. Croix at that time, writes: "The latter [Puerto Rico] is an island belonging to the King of Spain, located some eight to nine miles to the west of St. Croix. This island has brought many people to tears, for they and their entire families were ruined, when, in a single night, 20 to 25 of their slaves, indeed sometimes more, deserted to that place. It was in that way that the heirs of Bondwyn lost everything, when all their slaves ran away to that island in the course of a single night; the plantation had to be sold because of that."

Other slaves took the opportunity to steal ships and make their escape by sail. The same Haagensen writes of another incident: "Other men have suffered the same unpleasant fate when several slaves attacked the sailors on the ships anchored on the south side of the island and forced them to weigh anchor and sail to Porto Rico, in addition to the other harm that those same slaves did to the sailors on board. Yes, such events occur often. A man's slaves run away to Porto Rico for the slightest reason. There are few citizens of the island who, in this regard, have not been tarred with the same brush. They can be said to have a fortune walking around among the Spaniards, only it does not earn them any interest!"

So pressing the problem became in the mid-18th century that the Danish Governor von Pröck negotiated an agreement in 1767 with his counterpart in Puerto Rico that provided for the return of such run-aways. But not before a considerable number of slaves found their way to freedom in the west. In spite of the legislation, the enslaved showed themselves willing to take the numerous risks in the voyage to freedom in the years that followed right up to Emancipation. And so it was that Crucians made their way to Puerto Rico in large numbers many years before the tide of migration turned in the other direction.

But turn it did. In the latter part of the 19th century the Puerto Rican economy deteriorated badly under Spanish mismanagement and indif-ference. The Puerto Rican people entered a long period of emigration that has remained a feature of the demography of that island to this day. When Puerto Rico was seized by the United States as a result of the Spanish American War in 1898, new opportunities would soon present themselves, when, in 1917, the erstwhile Danish West Indies became the Virgin Islands of the United States as the result of American purchase. In 1920, the bottom fell out of the sugar market and Vieques produc-ers were particularly hard hit. Over the next 20 years, one by one the island's sugar estates and their factories—called "centrals" such as Santa Maria, Puerto Real, Arkadia and, finally, Playa Grande—all closed. Unemployment immediately surged. In the meantime, a change in the application of U.S. immigration law made it more difficult for plant-ers in St. Croix to procure labor from traditional Eastern Caribbean sources. Those planters therefore turned to Vieques, whose inhabitants were by then American citizens. What had been a trickle in the mid-1920s became a steady flow of immigration in the 1930s as the Great Depression deepened.

In the final analysis, economic hardship in Vieques and Culebra, the closing of the centrals in Vieques and the changes effected in U.S. Immigration laws in 1927 all conspired to induce Puerto Ricans to migrate to the Virgin Islands in significant numbers. Initially the Viequenses came to work as cane cutters on struggling Crucian estates and as ranch hands on cattle farms. In time, they worked their way into positions of property ownership, small business operation and the lower echelons of the governmental bureaucracy. But advancement and acceptance were slow and not without obstacles, the results of which are still apparent today.

A strong impetus for continued emigration from Vieques came with the onset of World War II, when the U.S. Navy obtained 26,000 of the available 33,000 acres of land on the island and in the process removed thousands of Viequenses abruptly from the land. Many of the dispossessed found their way to St. Croix, where conditions were only slightly better. The plight of the people of Vieques became so bad that the Navy conceived a plan in 1947 to remove all the island's inhabitants permanently to St. Croix. That drastic measure, however, was never taken.

As the first arrivals worked their way up the ladder, others followed behind them, increasing their numbers until they came to constitute a significant percentage of the local population. While they adapted readily to their new homes, they tended at the same time to retain ties of family, friendship and cultural identity in Vieques, Culebra and Puerto Rico. These ties have served as a source of renewal for the immigrants and lent strength to the strong sense of Puerto Rican identity that has remained prominent among them down to the present day.

So in summary, it may be noted that the connection between Puerto Rico and its off-shore islands on the one hand and St. Croix on the other has been long and varied. Throughout several thousand years of Indian prehistory, the flow of people has generally been reciprocal, with an emphasis no doubt on those at the periphery being attracted to the center. Under the subsequent Spanish domination, from 1492 to about 1650, there was a long period of stasis and at times conflict. But with the advent of sugar and slavery under the French and Danes, from about 1734 to 1848, a significant change occurred, one in which individuals from the enslaved population of St. Croix escaped regularly to freedom in Puerto Rico, establishing a steady flow in that direction for a century or so. And finally, just after World War I, from 1920 to the 1950s, a steady flow of Puerto Ricans issued from their native islands to the promise of the Virgin Islands, especially St. Croix.

Along with them they have brought us their language, their music, their dances, their food, their love of the land, their sense of family values and, not least, their vibrant embrace of life. They remain strongly Puerto Rican, largely due to the proximity of the original homeland, and they therefore continue to provide a conduit of influence into local society from the heart of the Hispanic Caribbean world. And yet, at the same time, their embrace of elements of the local order has, in the process, resulted in economic stimulation, bilingualism, intermarriage and a strong, enduring new Puerto Rican element in our already multicultural Crucian society.

Today, as the beneficiaries of a long view of history, we are in a position to recognize that the commingling of our peoples—Crucian and Puerto Rican—is not recent and certainly not one-sided but rather the product of long years, indeed centuries, of people coming and going in accordance with needs and motives that are still only partially understood today. But this much can be said about it. These demographic exchanges over so many centuries have been the result of natural forces at work in natural contexts. And few can be heard to complain about the benefits that have accrued on both sides of the ledger. Just as freedom abounded for the enslaved who set foot on Puerto Rican soil two centuries ago, so opportunity has been the bounty enjoyed by Puerto Ricans who landed on these shores in more recent times. In both giving and receiving such gifts, both sides have been the better for it.

Buck Island and its fringing reef located off the
northeast coast of St. Croix

CHAPTER 22

BUCK ISLAND:
A JEWEL IN THE SEA

UNLIKE ST. THOMAS with its dozens of off-lying islets, cays and rocks, St. Croix has but few marine curiosities. Among them, however, is our Buck Island, not to be confused with the Buck Island that lies to the south of St. Thomas and yet another Buck Island at the entrance of Coral Bay harbor in St. John. Need we be reminded that what we lack in quantity, we make up for in quality. For Crucians the sun rises every day over our Buck island, reminding us that it is a prized, natural gift, set delightfully for us in the sea.

Buck Island is some 2,000 yards in length and about 750 yards wide, comprising 17.6 square acres in surface area, with 2.6 miles of shoreline and lying on an east–west axis. It is located about 1⅜ miles off the northeast quadrant of St. Croix and 5 miles to the northeast of Christiansted town. Its slopes rise to 360 feet above sea level at its highest point, providing a panoramic view of its bigger brother to the south, St. Croix. Along the shoreline extend white sand beaches in every direction, sloping off into the clearest of blue water imaginable. On every side the eye meets with incomparable delights.

But that is only half the story. The other half lies below the surface of the surrounding waters. A near perfect fringing reef encircles the eastern end of the island, creating a calm lagoon of glistening seawater suspended over a bottom of unblemished white sand and coral outcroppings. Everywhere white sand bottoms abound providing light and clarity. To the east, beyond that reef, extends an entire forest of coral growth—elkhorn, stinging, and brain coral—far out into the ocean, perched on the same underwater shelf as Buck Island itself. And to the north and west lie extensive patches of reef, over which the sea breaks in pleasant white surf in calm weather. The only open approach to the island is from the southwestern lee side, onto a marvelous gleaming beach.

Buck Island is a dry isle and the consequent lack of heavy run-off accounts for the clarity of the surrounding sea water. It also explains the nature of the vegetation, which is similar to that of the dry east end of St. Croix. Palms line some of the beaches while gennip, turpentine, manchineel and frangipangi trees and other drought-resistant species stand among and above the bramble and cacti of the interior. Omnipresent bromeliads smugly perched in the branches of these trees oversee from above the passage of visitors who undertake the trek along the trail that leads up to the Coast Guard maintained lighthouse.

Land fauna is even sparser than flora species. The St. Croix anole and the Cotton ginner gecko both exist there, but their numbers have in recent decades been threatened, in part due, perhaps, to the numbers of daily visitors and the inadvertent introduction of predators, such as rats, mongooses and cats from time to time. Marine bird-life has likewise thinned out. Frigate birds roost there and brown pelicans have a rookery or two. But least terns, boobies and other species that were in presence in large numbers in the 1950s appear to have gradually abandoned the island as nesting places due to the relative degree of human activity in such a limited area. Goats and perhaps a few donkeys were introduced in the 18th century, but they have all disappeared along with the decline of local agriculture.

When one thinks of Buck Island, however, it is undersea marine life that immediately comes to mind. Though some degradation has inevitably taken place, there remains a great deal to see and enjoy. In the waters inside the reef there are snappers, angelfish, squirrel fish, multicolored parrot-fish, jacks, rays, squid and an array of other species. Cruising along the interior of the reef can be seen several large but well-fed and docile barracudas. From within the reef a moray eel might poke out his head to check out the traffic for lunch. Early in the morning, green turtles are very much in evidence; they still nest on island. And occasionally a lobster pokes out a gundy from his hole in a curious kind of salute. But the calm so apparent in this underwater neighborhood is deceiving, for a fierce Darwinian struggle for food, procreation and life still rages on beneath the illusory tranquility.

What's in a name? Most likely it was the Dutch in the early 17th century who first named the island, "Pocken Island" for the stands of pockwood (*Lignum vitae* and *Guayaco*) that grew there. These woods were considered essential in Europe for the treatment of the various pox-producing diseases, especially smallpox, and were therefore highly prized.

When the French took over in 1651, they called the island *Isle Verte* (Green Island, cf. Green Cay). Later, under the Danes from 1734 onward, the name was settled more or less as "Buck Island," owing, more than likely, to a misunderstanding of the term "Pock," plus confusion due to the goats (Dan. *Gedebukker*) that were then grazed by settlers on the isolated island. From 1770 until the 1840s, the island also bore the name *Frederiks Gav* (Frederik's Gift, perhaps after the Danish King Frederik V, who reigned from 1746 to 1766). That name, however, never became popular and the island has been known since then as "Buck Island" though under a number of diverse pronunciations and curious spellings (Pocken, Boiken, Booken, Bocken, Bokken and Bukken).

Buck Island is uninhabited today because it has been a part of the National Park Service since 1961. But that was not always the case. Although there are only a few archaeological remains that point to Indian activity, it is a certain bet that, what with its teeming sea-life, the island provided wonderful camp-sites for food foraging expeditions by means of canoe trips.

Later, once most of the arable land on St. Croix had been purchased by colonial settlers and put into cultivation under Danish rule (1734), some hopeful souls cast covetous eyes at Buck Island. The first known settlement was undertaken in 1754 by Johann Hendrich Diedrich, well known as the Christiansted town clerk as well as the local champion of debauchery and lechery. Although he constructed the first buildings on Buck Island—a dwelling, a kitchen, a well and some retaining walls—and settled 14 people there, 12 of them slaves, he nevertheless preferred life in Christiansted, perhaps for all the wrong reasons. For a time the island was called "Diedrich's Plantation" and "Diedrich's Cay."

The little plantation perched near the top of the island's one hill subsequently passed through several hands, first to Nicholay Salamons in 1773, then to Joseph Coakley in 1775. In 1781, it was purchased by John Heyliger Abrahamsen, who, except for a brief period, retained ownership until 1821. In 1823, the *St. Croix Landkasse* took control and leased it for a number of years, its tenants including two Free-Colored couples in 1844. All of the owners raised some goats, fished a bit, collected scarce water in make-shift cisterns and grew provisions. One can only imagine that those hardy souls lived there by choice as a consequence of their love for solitude and the unmatched beauty of the place.

During the United States period, Cornelius Penthany leased the island in 1917 and simply raised goats there, once again legitimizing the name "Buck Island." In 1948, the V.I. government created the Buck Island Park and opened the island for public use. In 1961, President John Kennedy proclaimed the island as part of the National Park system under the Department of Interior. And finally, in 2001, President Bill Clinton added considerable acreage to the park and gave it greater ecological protection. It must be said that the island has fared well under the aegis of the National Park Service.

As an important recreational and ecological destination for tens of thousands of tourists each year, Buck Island has made a significant contribution to our local economy. As early as the 1950s, boatmen such as Bill Miller with his little fleet of long-boom Tortola sloops and Dick Newick with his trim, locally designed trimarans daily carried hundreds of delighted visitors to Buck Island's white sand beaches and crystal clear lagoons for an unforgettable outing. This brought money into local coffers and a solid reputation concerning the charms of Santa Cruz.

Buck Island, however, has always offered much more than simple economic advantages. Anyone who has ever sat on the deck of one of those returning Buck Island boats as they raced one another back to Christiansted harbor, what with sails edges stuttering in the light afternoon airs, with conch shells booming from every deck and with seaman such as the mighty Bomba with his steady hand on the tiller and his broad smile gracing the proceedings is the fortunate owner of a memory that easily matches anything in his experience.

At festival time, some of the barriers of race and class came down

CHAPTER 23

THE CRUCIAN CHRISTMAS FESTIVAL

CHRISTMAS CELEBRATIONS on St. Croix have been around, in one form or another, for the better part of the past two hundred and fifty years, dating back to the mid-18th century. As such they are the product of African and European traditional festival arts that coalesced in our Islands during colonial times, around the twin axes of plantation life and the quest of the enslaved for momentary escape from their condition during the Christmas holidays.

Our Festival has known a long history, extending from simple beginnings in celebrations by the laboring populations on individual estates to road marches, street tramps and beyond, through the introduction of elaborate costumes, the appearance of celebration themes, troupes and floats, and the introduction of Queens and Kings, along with the evolution of a local music down to the present. Today we are the heirs of that long and evolving tradition, to be played out once again this year between Christmas and Three King's Day.

The early European celebrations of Carnival date back to the 13th century. They were festivities that took place in Catholic countries as a witness to the onset of the forty-day fasting period preceding Easter, hence the name "carnival," derived most likely from "carne + vale," or "goodbye to meat." Then, as now, a central feature of the celebration was the temporary relaxation of control over the social order, or sometimes even an inversion of that order itself. Music, dancing, feasting, role reversal, costuming, masking and the loosening of social constraints that govern otherwise normative behavior were stressed. In this manner the church and society were able to maintain their dominance over

· 267 ·

the masses at the small cost of allowing its members a short period of almost total freedom from the system, albeit in preparation for a complete return to its rigors by participation in the strictures of Lent. This paradigm is strikingly similar to that which still occurs in many parts of the present-day Caribbean.

Carnival accompanied the transplantation of Roman Catholicism across the Atlantic into the Spanish, French and Portuguese colonies in the Caribbean basin area, as well as elsewhere. There it was embraced by a predominantly African population and was transformed by strong cultural currents from the Motherland. It might be said that Carnival became infused with and transformed by African spirit, which included specifically African masking, musical forms, dance, and body decoration. And in turn, this powerful combination has continued to evolve over the past many years, drawing on its own inner resources, cultural creativity and regional influences, becoming in the process something uniquely Caribbean.

In the present day Virgin Islands we see clearly these forces at work. Though festival celebrations had been an established feature of the three Virgin Islands (i.e., the Danish West Indies) for many years previously, they were not completely formalized until the 20th century. Tradition has it that the first carnival was held on St. Thomas in 1912 and then discontinued, at least in the formal sense, until its revival in 1952 through the efforts of Ron De Lugo. Though that initial celebration was held in September, it was subsequently changed to the month of April, being not only post-Lenten but also post-Paschal. Neighboring St. John's celebration begins in June and peaks on July third and fourth, with an emphasis on freedom and Emancipation. St. Croix has always danced to a different drummer. Here our Festival begins on Christmas Second Day and continues through to Three King's Day. Originally it was a three-day affair that marked the temporary lull in the regime of sugar cultivation, a short respite between the hard work of cultivating the crop during the late months of the year and the subsequent harvest of the crop in the early part of the new year.

But what were the distinctive characteristics of the festival arts in our islands in those early years? In the first place, since Denmark was an exclusively Protestant country with the Lutheran Church as its national ecclesia, Catholic practices were universally eschewed, along with the accompanying Carnival practices. Moreover, Moravian Pietism, the dominant religion through the colonial period among the enslaved population not only decried any Catholic influence but additionally condemned music, dancing and the like as corrupting influences in themselves. In the beginning then, the prospects for a circumsolstice celebration were not good.

So it is that we must look to the plantations as the most likely cradle of the spontaneous origins of our festival arts tradition. Indeed, it began on the Crucian estates where there occurred a brief relaxation at Christmas time of the otherwise harsh estate regimen. The Whites themselves were noted for thinking of little more than "having a good time," being fond of going out to "shoot white-headed pigeons," as one source baldly puts it. In addition to good humor, food was more abundant than usual, as one source notes: "Upon Christmas-day, every full-grown negro receives six quarts of wheat flour, and six pounds of salt pork, and the lesser ones as above." And masters showed a measure of generosity in the distribution of presents, which consisted of food, sugar, rum, cloth, other scarce commodities and sometimes even money.

What followed the food distribution was something resembling a rather curious party. "It is customary at this time, for slaves on the different plantations, attired in their choicest dress to go in a body to the house of their master, and to receive admission to his best apartments; where they set up the music of the banjo and commence dancing. The family makes it a point to be present, and not infrequently join in the dance. This is the occasion, when presents of provisions, clothing, or money are distributed among them. The feelings of the slaves towards their master, through the year, depend very much on the treatment they receive at these times," writes Sylvester Hovey, a visitor to St. Croix in 1835.

The fluidity of role shifting involving masters and slaves could be as striking as it was rare. One visitor to the island reports the following incident: "A day or two before one of these holidays, a gentleman told me that he was obtaining small Danish coins in exchange for two doubloons, for distribution among the slaves who would be at his house; and on a visit which I made that day to his house I found him alternatively serving his guests with cakes and wine; and although he was seventy-three years of age, joining with them in their dances." That rare moment of equality was fleeting, as the same writer noted: "The queen of one of the bands at that house was the slave of a mulatto woman. The noise of the music which was drums and kettle drums made it quite impossible for the voice to be heard. But their liberty expired with the day. They slept, and were again slaves."

The momentary good cheer could sometimes spill over onto the island's streets and roads. Johan Carstens, a St. Thomian planter, notes that as early as the 1740s, planters would often partake in heavy drinking with their slaves and then join with them in a kind of drunken road march whose ostensible purpose was a visit to nearby plantations, accompanied by drumming, fireworks and gunshots, much to the prejudice of life and limb of both planter and slave alike.

The passion of these roving groups was driven by African drums, primarily the notorious bamboula and the goumbay. This is not to say that the enslaved had neither the access to European instruments nor the capacity to play them. A passing aside by the same Carstens tells us exactly how this cultural transfer took place, by noting the curious practice of a certain government official of the Danish Company who "kept on hand a group of slaves who play musical instruments. They are divided into 2 groups and are placed on both sides of his house just outside his bedroom where they must play on violas, oboes, trumpets, French horns and several other wind instruments, first in the morning for one hour before he arises and again in the evening for one hour at bedtime. At noon, they have to play their instruments both as he makes his way to the table and all during the meal. Then they play as everyone withdraws from the table." It is at times through the unlikely that the ordinary makes a place for itself.

In time—we know not exactly when or under what circumstances—other elements of the festival fell into place. Queens, accompanied by Kings and a court, all handsomely decked out, became fashionable. By the mid-19th century Mokko Jumbies appear. There is the first mention of a float of sorts, in the form of a ship pulled through the streets by ponies. And of course sometime in that same period the Quelbé band came together and provided—and continues to provide—the one indispensable element in it all—the sweet music and the strong beat.

Though the authorities tried to prevent it, the festivities spread to the towns and became well established there. From yards all around Christiansted, the sounds of goumbay drums dominated the nights, calling hundreds to sing, dance, drink, and fete. Thurlow Weed, another visitor to the island, noted in 1866 that "in town the Free Colored People and the House Slaves form their parties, elect their Kings, Queens, etc., and dance in like manner. We went the rounds, among them, and were generally received by some complimentary lines thrown, impromptu, into their songs."

Approximately a hundred years after Emancipation and seventy years after Fireburn, some of the more gracious souls in Crucian society began considering the revival of "old time festival," after what appeared to them to have been a hiatus. Thanks to their efforts the event was formally organized and planned for 1952. Since that time, an organized, official Festival has taken place every year on St. Croix down to the present—and nearly every year adding new elements to the mix by means of internal creativity, cultural borrowing and influxes of new participants from a variety of sources.

From Trinidad, for example, came the steel pan, magnificent costuming and jouvert. From the United States came generators and massive audio amplification. And from here at home came the Festival Village and the food booth, the latter perhaps an instinctive recollection of earlier times when private dwellings opened up evenings and served food and drink to all comers by candlelight. And is it perhaps due to the Puerto Rican presence among us, at least in part, that the Festival has been expanded beyond New Years Day to January 6th, Three King's Day.

If imitation is truly the sincerest form of flattery, then our Crucian Festival has been definitely honored by all the recent attention given it. It's been many years now that the Irish in spirit among us have celebrated a Crucian St. Patrick's Day with a parade and other events that bear the unmistakable imprint of our Christmas Festival. And more recently, New Orleans aficionados have created their own version of Mardi Gras in St. Croix with the establishment of Mardi Croix. And not least, the Jump Up and Harbor Nights festivities echo ringingly the spirit of Festival, what with their local bands, Mokko Jumbies, dancing in the street, ubiquitous food vendors and the general Festival Village feeling of good times and good cheer.

As Christmas on St. Croix draws near, it would be timely to recall that our Festival traces its roots far back into our past to valiant people doing their utmost to make the most out of very little. In that effort they have succeeded admirably. And once again, we have the opportunity to celebrate the best that our culture has to offer, and in so doing we also celebrate the lives of those who have gone before us, not in silence but in song.

A Baobab tree set against a striking sunset

CHAPTER 24

FROM BAOBAB TO KAPOK: THE SPIRIT TREES OF THE VIRGINS

SOME YEARS BACK, I experienced a striking encounter with a tree. That day, quite by chance, I happened to walk under the expansive canopy of an ancient ficus tree at mid-island. Sunlight filtered down through the foliage, dazzling my eyes and dappling the leaf-littered floor with patches of brilliance. As the air there was cool and the silence complete, I had the feeling that I had by accident strolled into a cathedral that had simply sprung out of the earth.

As I moved around the great trunk, I came upon something that struck my eye. There at the base of the trunk was piled a little mound of stones, on which someone had recently placed a mango and some nuts. There, I thought, was human nature at its most spiritual, most reverential, demonstrating humility of self before a grand wonder of nature in a simple act of offering.

Nothing that I had recently witnessed took me back so suddenly and dramatically through our long human past. From the beginning of human time, our species has nurtured a special relationship with trees. And rightly so. They have served us as places of refuge, sources of shade, givers of nourishment, providers of weapons and building materials, and, not least, creators of enduring symbols of the narrow relationship between our mother earth and the world that lies above and beyond us. In some very fundamental ways great trees have nurtured not only life in our bodies but also the higher consciousness that occasionally visits our primitive brains.

It is for this reason that they are viewed with respect and admiration in every part of the world. One thinks immediately of the otherworldly looking baobabs of Africa, the coco palms of the Saharan oases, the silk trees of the Orient, the date palms of the Middle East, the great oaks of Europe, the ancient Sequoias of the American west, the sugar-giving maples of the Northeast and, not least, the mighty spirit trees of the Caribbean.

Among our many Caribbean spirit trees here on St. Croix there are several that stand over and above the others, namely the kapok, the baobab, the mahogany, the ficus, the tamarind and the saman. But what is it exactly that qualifies a specific tree species to carry the title "spirit tree?" Quite simply that people believe that spirits, jumbies and the souls of departed ancestors have special connections with those trees and that they may in fact reside among the branches or in their extensive root systems. And through the correct approach to such trees and to their resident spirits, the living may enter into contact with the world beyond the present one.

The kapok, that is, the silk cotton tree or "jumbie tree" (*Ceiba pentandra*), is the prince of all spirit trees. It exudes the presence of mystery and otherworldliness, what with its numerous buttress-like roots that sweep down high up on the tree-trunk to make an altogether dramatic, indeed somewhat foreboding, entry into the earth. It is here, it is believed, that the living can make contact with deceased ancestors. To that end, there were once tree shrines at the bases of these trees; the remnants of one such still stands alongside a kapok trunk at Estate Mt. Victory. It requires little imagination to see how this mighty tree came to be directly associated with the spirit world!

The baobab (*Adansonia digitata*) is without a doubt the most curious of all our local spirit tress. Sometimes called the "Upside Down" tree, this specimen has an enormous trunk and a disproportionately small canopy. It is extremely slow-growing but has a long life-span. As it came from Africa to the Caribbean in the course of the slave trade, it was sensed by the enslaved population to be intimately connected to Mother Africa and thought by many to allow passage back home through the great holes in its trunk and among its cavernous roots. It enjoys great reverence and spiritual significance to this day.

The saman (*Albizia saman*), or rain tree, is everything that the baobab is not—tall, stately, well-proportioned and elegant. Its sheltering boughs literally invite people to come and take refuges underneath them. One such majestic saman tree graces the grounds of the Lawaetz museum on he west end.

The tamarind (*Tamarindus indica*) or taman tree is one of the world's most successful traveling trees, making its way from India, across the Mediterranean and Africa, and finally across the Atlantic to Latin America and the Caribbean. Here in St. Croix it has found a secure home, providing a well shaped tree, abundant shade, a delightful fruit, and a convenient meeting place. One such tree stands to the west of Christiansvaern on the wharf in silent witness to the thousands of Africans who passed that way on their journey into slavery. If there are no spirits in that tree, they are unlikely to be anywhere hereabouts.

Though a relative newcomer to our island, the mahogany tree (*Swietenia mahagoni*) has become firmly established in a short period of time. Perhaps the stateliest of all our trees, it imbues our roadways and lanes with grace and provides our dwellings with fine wood for furnishings. But more than that, it is simply a pure pleasure to sit in the shade of one of these trees on a day when a light breeze is ruffling through its luxurious, green foliage and experience life in its fullest. In such moments the world is at peace.

The ficus tree comes in many sub-species, shapes and sizes, including the native ficus (*Ficus obtusifolia*). It is unmistakable due to the many vine-roots that drop down from its branches and attach to the earth. It can attain enormous sizes and a thick density of foliage. Like the tamarind and the mahogany, its canopy provides a remarkable refuge for the human spirit. Sadly a number of these trees went down in Hurricane Hugo, bringing real grief to many.

Most of these wonderful plants were immigrants, who accompanied living folks on the journeys and took up residence on the same land where those folk settled. They attained remarkable size and rare beauty, both of which revealed the presence of a powerful life-force. Among the endless, monotonous cane fields, they stood out as markers of difference, of potential, of life-personality. But most of all, they signaled the maintenance of contacts with ancestors and with the past, as well as the prospect of passage into an even better future, in their service as palaver trees, meeting points, and places of talk and planning.

So it was that on many a moonlit night Crucian folk gathered under the protective cover of these leafy canopies and, around a small fire, together made music, dance and talk far into the night, marking their own place in the world in the presence of the spirits of family members, departed friends, and other visitors from the other side.

Governor Melvin Evans, M.D., one of the leading
political figures in the Virgin Islands at the onset
of the Constitutional period

CHAPTER 25

A CONSTITUTION FOR
THE VIRGIN ISLANDS?

WHEN THE UNITED STATES acquired the Danish West Indian Islands of St. Croix, St. Thomas and St. John in March of 1917, expectations for the islands' political future were limited indeed. After all, they were purchased in the first place as a strategic measure against possible aggression by Germany in Danish colonial affairs. When the war ended in the following year with the defeat of Germany, concern for that threat quickly waned. Consequently, the new "Virgin Islands of the United States" were all but forgotten, as an unincorporated Territory under Naval rule and management. So the Territory would remain until 1931.

The problems of Naval rule became quickly apparent. Naval governors ruled the islands with largely Naval objectives in mind. The local population was considered a decidedly low priority. And in that regard, racial tension grew as American prejudices replaced the relatively more restrained Danish ones. But above all, two overarching questions remained poorly answered through the period—the question of equitable governance and that of citizenship.

The United States was content for the time being to retain the Danish Colonial Law of 1906, allowing the white minority to dominate the Colonial Councils and continue the state of affairs that had existed under the latter years of Denmark's rule. In spite of the protests of men such as Casper Holstein, in spite of the investigations of the newly founded American Civil Liberties Union and in spite of a spate of Congressional hearings, the imposing imprint of blatant colonialism remained in place. Although the Jones Act of 1927 addressed a part of the question, extending U.S. citizenship to most Virgin Islanders, the matter of government would have to wait.

In 1931, civilian government finally came to the VI when the islands were placed under the Bureau of Territories and Insular Affairs in the Department of the Interior. But it was not until 1936 that real change occurred. In that year, the islands received the Organic Act, which, among many other things, expanded the franchise, ended legislative appointments, and gave natives a real say in government for the first time. The Municipal Councils replaced the Colonial Councils and the minority rule of the merchant and planter class was finally broken after 264 years of slavery, servitude, peonage, and political inequality.

In addition to greater autonomy than ever before, the Act also brought about other substantial changes, including the stimulation of the local political process, the formation of political parties, and eventually the appointment of locally born persons to government and administration. Yet there remained obstacles with which Virgin Islands were destined to struggle for the rest of the century, namely the absence of full autonomy; continued domination from Washington; lack of local control over immigration; and the twin thorns of no representation in the Congress and no vote in U.S. presidential elections.

Wartime always brings rapid changes, and World War Two was no exception. This conflict produced stress lines throughout the Caribbean, not least in the Virgin Islands. One by one some of the obstacles began to give way. First, came the appointment of the first African-American, William Hastie, as Governor in 1946, followed shortly thereafter by the appointment of the first native governor, Morris de Castro, in 1950. During that period there also came a call from Virgin Islanders for amendment of the Organic Act of 1936 to provide for greater local participation in government and for more autonomy.

The response came in 1954 with the passage of the Revised Organic Act, the document that still serves today as the basis of government in these islands. While the act brought more efficient, centralized government for the islands as well as a more practical arrangement for U.S.

administrators, it did not please everyone. In fact, it is seen by many today as the source of numerous chronic problems, perhaps the most pressing being the loss of local government in the form of the Municipal Councils.

The Act created one legislature for all the islands and a capital in St. Thomas. It also underscored the power of the U.S. President in island affairs instead of moving toward greater political autonomy. On the other hand, the advantages of matching funds paid into the Virgin Islands treasury acted to balance out the disappointment. In the short-run, Virgin Islanders found a way to live with the new organic law though objections to it remained persistent, resulting in a number of calls for reform over the fifty years that followed. The effort to write four constitutions over that span has been a direct consequence of deficiencies in the Revised Organic Act and discontent with them.

By the mid-1960s the world was beginning to change rapidly, and those changes were not without consequences for the Virgin Islands. Around the globe, colonialism was discredited and in decline. Modern nations began to emerge in Africa and in other colonial areas around the world. Equally prominent among these transformations were changes in political status of numerous islands in the West Indies, in particular the West Indies Federation and the autonomous states that emerged from it after its dissolution in the early 1960s.

On the American mainland there emerged the Black Power movement, which demanded greater political rights for African Americans. In that struggle, the Voting Rights Act held particular significance for Virgin Islanders in that it mirrored something of their own plight. Moreover, all these events took place against the tension and anxiety of the Cold War, making it a period of instability and change.

At the same time, the economy of the Virgin Islands developed apace in the 1960s. And of course, economic change always entails political accommodation. Higher income resulted in the strengthening of a viable middle class that placed emphasis on better housing, health care and education. These, in turn, necessitated concern for the political process and hence greater political awareness. The flaws of the Revised Organic Act came to be regarded increasingly as needing attention, even change. Economic development, however, proved to be a double-edged sword. While it created greater power for Virgin Islanders, it also promoted the growth of a non-native population of immigrants who soon arrived from other parts of the Caribbean for a share in the new prosperity. This issue posed a quandary that has bedeviled every attempt to write and pass a constitution for our islands since that time.

So by the early 1960s, Virgin Islanders found themselves facing a number of political concerns, the most important of which were the questions of: 1. Status; 2. Immigration; 3. Virgin Islands nativism; 4. An independent judiciary; 5. Participation in the U.S. Congress; and 6. Vote in the U.S. Presidential elections. All of these concerns found voice in the call in the early 1960s for a constitution to amend the Revised Organic Act of 1954. This initial attempt in 1964–65 failed, however, in large measure because it lacked the proper authorization from the U.S. Congress.

In the years that followed, Virgin Islanders turned to the piecemeal approach, which in effect amended the Revised Organic Act relative to certain political questions of pressing importance. In 1968, the Elective Governor Act, resulted in the election of Dr. Melvin Evans, in the election of 1970. And in 1970, the Elective Delegate Act led to the election of the first delegate to Congress, Ron de Lugo, in 1972. These historic events were followed by the second Constitutional Convention in 1971, which, like its predecessor failed because it too lacked Congressional authority.

A remedy was sought for that defect in 1976 when Delegate De Lugo saw the Constitutional Authorization Act through the Congress. This legislation paved the way for an optimistic Constitutional Convention in 1977. The third time, however, did not prove to be the charm inasmuch as the electorate rejected the document.

A fourth attempt to write an acceptable constitution for Virgin Islanders in 1980 failed in a referendum in the following year. Most observers feel that it was the native issue that proved to be the major obstacle to the voters on this occasion. The effort to define a native Virgin Islander proved difficult indeed; to get it past the voters, many of whom were not native Virgin Islanders, proved impossible. In addition, a low voter turn-out at the polls signaled that the electorate had grown pessimistic as a result of the previous failures.

It became apparent to many at that time that the questions of a constitution and of political status for the Virgin Islands were closely linked issues. Some argued effectively that we had been all the while putting the cart before the donkey and that a proper constitution could not be arrived at until we had solved the dilemma of political status and relationship to the United States. Legislation was passed to that end and a status commission was put in place, which worked toward a status referendum throughout the 1980s, with modest success.

In 1993, the status referendum was rejected by the voters, failing to entice the necessary percentage of voters to the polls. It appeared to many that Virgin Islanders could neither select a workable political status option nor write an acceptable constitution. One need not look far and wide for an answer; the polity had become static and resistant to change in large part because the community had grown multi-ethnic and divided over the past fifty years. The Virgin Islands became therefore trapped in the political doldrums.

The 1990s passed in relative quiescence, politically speaking. Yes, there were hurricanes and their costly damaging ways to deal with. Restoration and rebuilding had to come first; politics and constitutions had to wait.

Interest in the constitution reawakened at the turn of the millennium, with some of the loudest noises coming from St. Croix. On that island it was felt that St. Croix continued to muddle through a real depression while St. Thomas forged ahead into prosperity, not an unfamiliar scenario in Virgin Islands history. Those who felt that legislative districting and some form of municipal government might be suitable solutions to the problems that St. Croix faced were quick to speak of the need for another constitutional convention and another go at it. And so the issue worked its way slowly back onto the political agenda.

That idea took substance in the Omnibus Bill of 2004. After several delays and postponements, a date of June 12, 2007, was set for the election of delegates to the fifth convention, whose goal is to create a viable constitution by 2008. In the pre-election debate, the matter of nativism has already emerged as perhaps the most prominent and potentially the most divisive issue to emerge this far.

From a Virgin Islands perspective, the desire to recognize native status simply makes common sense. It should be remembered that after the purchase in 1917, locals were not even recognized as U.S. citizens. They were not politically enfranchised until 1936, and political parties were not actually viable until the early 1940s. In that initial 25-year period under American rule, Virgin Islanders were subject to the effective control of a colonial power, and remained impotent to decide their own political destiny.

Among the critical areas in which they were powerless was immigration, and, in practice, that remains the case until this day. As a result of catering to the labor needs of the tourist, commercial and industrial business interests, the vast majority of which were non-Virgin Islands in their ownership, the U.S. government allowed a flood of immigrant laborers to pour into the Territory. This, many Virgin Islanders argue, upset the political balance of power within the electorate, thereby making it impossible to write a constitution today that would reflect the political will of Virgin Islanders. Hence, conventions dominated by native Virgin Islanders have optimistically proposed and the general electorate has flatly disposed.

The other side of the coin is equally compelling. Those who came here many years ago from numerous other Caribbean islands struggled for green card status and then became citizens have generally worked hard, established families, paid taxes, practiced the art of good citizenship and contributed to the Virgin Islands community in one way or another. It therefore follows, the newcomers contend, that they should have full political rights in accordance with democratic principles. Second-class status as inscribed in a constitution holds very little appeal for them and understandably so.

Here is the crux of the matter, a standoff of sorts that has muddied the waters of present attempts at dialog and discussion. Certainly there are other issues that demand answers. Will, for example, the issue of local government to provide some equity between the islands be possible? And in the broader sense, will our framers be aware of the dangers to a fledgling small state democracy when perched on the perceived necessity of a burgeoning bureaucracy and the inevitable threat of corruption? While it is admittedly possible to envision some sort of compromise on these and other issues, the nativist issue is an entirely different matter, as outlined above. Both sides believe that they are completely right.

Will statesmen and stateswomen emerge from among the delegates in the coming weeks to lead the way to a viable, workable compromise that will prove acceptable not only on the floor of the convention but also in the polling booth? And will their work be inspiring enough to cause voters to show up at the polls in numbers adequate to side-step yet another voided referendum? We should have the answers to these questions within a matter of weeks.

Anna Heegaard, a leading Creole figure
and mistress of Governor-general
Peter von Scholten

CHAPTER 26

THE CREOLE SOCIETY OF THE DANISH WEST INDIES

TODAY THE TERM CREOLE evokes things exotic, sensuous, erotic, things spicy, tasty, mysterious. But most of all the term looks back to a past that is perceived to be colorful, romantic and distant. Yet it is increasingly difficult to find anyone today who calls himself a Creole, to encounter someone who speaks a real Creole language, to hear real authentic Creole music and so forth. In a word, the reality behind the word Creole is fading rapidly into our past.

The word Creole traces its origins to Iberian history in the New World in the late 15th century. It comes from the Spanish verb *criar*, meaning to "raise," as in someone or something being raised or grown in a new environment. Most likely, it was first applied to the offspring of animals—cattle, sheep, goats—brought from the Old World to the New by the early immigrants. Those that survived the experience developed adaptations to the new conditions—the climate, the food sources, the diseases, the parasites and the new environment in general. Thus, these creatures were "raised" in a new ambience and showed certain differences with their antecedents. And so they came to be called *criollo*.

In a short time, the range of this term was expanded to people. Spaniards born in the new colonies were called *Criollos* as opposed to those who came out from the motherland, or *Peninsulares*. Those individuals who were produced by mixing between the two races—Indian and Spaniard—were termed *Mestizos* and they, by definition, were Creoles, though seldom called such. Ultimately, the origin of the term as it applied to humans had as its goal the need to distinguish between people of Spanish descent who were native to the colonies on the one hand and Spaniards from Spain on the other. Though now in full decline, the need for such birth-based social distinctions has endured from the late 16th century to well into the 20th century.

Words seldom stay put for long, however. In a short time, Creole came to designate also an African-born in the New World as opposed to an African-born person, the latter generally called a *Bozal*, or *Bussal*. The Creoles among the slave population quickly adapted themselves to the new lifestyle and to the Europeans as well, to their languages and their ways. Creoles were therefore considered more desirable as workers. These two designations were therefore always present on the plantations' demographic records.

In time, the other European colonizers of the region underwent similar experiences and borrowed the term and its usage from Spanish. First, it appeared in French as *Creole* and from there filtered into the other European tongues in a similar form. In Danish, for example, it often appeared as *Criol* or *Kriol*. By the middle of the 18th century, it was in widespread use all over the Caribbean and had already spread to Europe. The expression "rich as a Creole" became common in Europe in the 18th century.

By 1700, the Danish West Indian islands—our Virgin Islands of today—had begun to generate its own variety of Creole culture, but with a curious idiosyncrasy relative to the Creole societies of the other islands. In the latter, the process of creolization was realized in large part as a result of the encounter between the European newcomers and the native Indians. From the Tainos and Kalinago (Caribs), the Spaniard and French Creoles in the Greater Antilles and the larger islands of the lesser Antilles learned to cultivate and eat yams and cassava, to prepare cassava bread as a staple, to sleep in hammocks, to use local spices and herbs, to make effective use of the seas and littorals, to turn turtle, to travel by canoes, to *boucanier* (barbeque) their meats and the like. These material culture practices came to mark Creole society, as a result of contacts with the Indians whom they encountered there.

That contact, however, was lacking in the Danish islands for there were no Indians in residence by the time Danish settlement began. By

1530 or thereabouts, the so-called Indian folk had all fled our islands for refuge in St. Christopher, Guadeloupe, Dominica and other islands temporarily beyond European reach at that time. So then, how did creolization and Creole culture come to the Danes and other Europeans in the Danish West Indies?

Creole ways were first introduced into St. Croix by the French who held the island from 1650 to 1733, so that the distinction was made between Frenchman from France and French Creoles born in the islands. Even though there were few if any Indians on St. Croix at that time, there was heavy traffic with St. Christophe, Guadeloupe and other French colonies in the eastern Caribbean, islands where Indians still lived and where creolization had existed for nearly a century. In this manner, all the elements of Creole culture flowed into St. Croix from the French islands of the Carib-populated eastern Caribbean, and not from the larger, Taíno-populated islands of the western Caribbean, then under domination of the Spanish enemy.

It was under these circumstances that Denmark took possession of the island in 1734. From the start there appeared Creoles of various national backgrounds from St. Thomas, which had been a Danish colony since 1672. And in addition, Creole planters arrived from a number of other islands in the eastern Caribbean—St. Kitts, Nevis, Antigua and so forth. Within a short time, Creoles of a Danish background were being born on St. Croix. And under these circumstances, marking the distinction between Creoles who inhabited the island and the European-born Danes who administered and governed it was significant.

C. G. A. Oldendorp, the ever-attentive Moravian Mission inspector, is only one commentator who remarks on the nature, the behavior and attitudes of these Creole folk, at times in a none-too-complimentary manner. J. L. Carstens, the St. Thomian planter, was far kinder, making interesting observations about Creoles on St. Thomas. It is observed in general that the Creoles deviated significantly from European norms of behavior. They were nursed and raised as infants by black women, they spoke the Dutch Creole fluently, they preferred Creole foods to all others, they were sometimes given to casual sexual liaisons, and they easily fell into an array of self-indulgences, at least as perceived by their critics. It was even said by some that they provided an unsavory model for their slaves. Clearly, the view of Creoles in the Danish islands, from the purely European perspective, left much to be desired.

Creoles and Creole families endured through the decline of the 19th century and into the 20th. Their numbers included Alexander Hamilton, who was born in Nevis and who spent part of his youth in St. Croix. Anna Heegaards, the well known mistress of Peter von Scholten, was born in St. Croix, the daughter of a "mulatto" woman and a European man. Anna Murphy Mudie was the Creole wife of planter John Mudie, who bore him 13 children and managed his estates after his death. And Thomas de Malleville in 1795 became the first native-born, or Creole, Governor of the Danish islands. Marriages between European men and Creole women were not at all uncommon.

But the Creoles' days were numbered. Economic decline in the 19th century undercut their financial resources, and political evolution in the 20th removed them from effective power as a group. Gradually, they disposed of their land holdings. Some went into business and some emigrated. Others intermarried into the local population. As a distinct group they all but disappeared by the end of the 20th century.

In time, the term Creole ceased to have any real linguistic function, at least in its application to people, being replaced by new designations such as Native, Crucian, Virgin Islander, Down-islander, Continental and Statesider, all of which tended to regard the population of our islands from different angles, for different purposes. And most of all, the need to make a distinction between Whites born in the islands and Whites from a distant colonial country had all but vanished.

What had originated as a term to cover a broad set of West India cultural phenomena in counter-distinction to things European in time has fallen out of usage because those original features became completely naturalized and common. Distinctions no longer needed to be made with things Danish, for Denmark had simply disappeared from that context.

PEOPLE

The indefatigable Moravian Inspector C. G. A. Oldendorp (1721–1788)
visited the Danish islands in 1768, after which he wrote a
comprehensive report on the Moravian
missionary effort there

CHAPTER 27

THE WITNESS OF
C. G. A. OLDENDORP

T HE WORLD IS just full of curious coincidences. Who ever
could have guessed that a young German lad in the 18th century
would travel to the island of St. Croix in the distant Danish West Indies
and undertake the first really serious scholarly study of the islands and
their people? How did such an unlikely destiny ever play itself out and
what have been its consequences?

Christian Georg Andreas Oldendorp was born on March 8, 1721, in
the village of Grosserlafferte in Germany, the son of a Lutheran minister.
His parents died while he was still young, and he grew up in the household of his brother, receiving a rather typical education in the Grammar School at Hildesheim. At the age of 20, he joined another brother
at the University of Jena, where he imbibed the prevailing rationalist
philosophy and Weltanschauung of the day, namely that it was through
reason that a man could best fully understand the temper and destiny of
his age. Oldendorp's initial training was therefore set against the ideals
of the Enlightenment.

In a short time, however, he became involved with university students who were focused on the Moravian faith, and he gave himself
over entirely to that group's religious beliefs. Under the influence of the
teachings of Count Nicholas von Zinzendorf, he was soon accepted
into the Moravian community at the university. From there, he travelled
about considerably in Western Europe from one Moravian community
to another—Herrnhaag, Marienborn, Herrnhut and Barby—serving the
movement in a variety of ways as preacher, tutor, teacher and the like.

In 1759, he underwent an experience that convinced him that God had a special task for him. He was traveling from Orellen in Liefland where he had been serving as a house preacher, to Riga, where he was to board a ship for Germany. But en route he took a bad fall from a wagon and severely injured an arm, which forced him to remain behind and miss his ship. As it turned out, however, the ship met with grave misfortune after it sailed and Oldendorp's life was spared. He took the accident as a sign of the intervention of Divine Providence on his behalf and so redirected his life.

In 1762, he made his way to Niesky where he served the school there as a lecturer and also labored as an assistant preacher in the congregation. To that point in his life, he had shown himself to be such a dedicated servant in a number of Moravian congregations that he was chosen in February of 1767 to travel to the Caribbean and compile a report on the progress of the first 33 years of the Moravian mission in the Danish West Indies. He landed on St. Croix on March 22, 1767, and took up his new assignment, which occupied him completely over the next 18 months, before departing for the home mission in Europe on October 23, 1768. From the time of his return, he worked assiduously on his massive handwritten manuscript, bringing it to press in 1766. It was published as a very large book in 1777, which was entitled *Geschichte der Mission der evangelischen Brüder auf den caraibischen Inseln S. Thomas, S. Croix und S. Jan* (Barby:1777. 1,113 pp.)

The finished volume that Oldendorp produced during the year and a half of his sojourn turned out to be nothing short of phenomenal, even though a significant amount of the original manuscript was edited out by Johan Jakob Bossart, the editor. Not only did he write an exemplary history of the mission beginning in 1732 but moreover he produced a general description of the islands, including accounts of the African background to slavery, the Slave Trade, the captive Africans and their culture, the Europeans, the Creoles, the local flora and fauna, agriculture, language and much more. This he accomplished in astonishing detail and surprising accuracy. He also produced a number of excellent drawings to accompany the text, some of which are elaborately detailed

drawings of plants. Modern scholars have universally expressed astonishment at the sophisticated level of Oldendorp's writing and analysis.
In addition, he found time to write a dictionary of the Dutch Creole language of the islands (*Criolisches Wörterbuch*: 1767–68). In these
works, he has bequeathed to present-day Virgin Islanders, remarkable
gifts in the form of these "databases" for the study of their early history
and language, gifts that are simply lacking in the other islands of the
Caribbean.

Several years after his return from the Danish islands to Europe, he
married Sister Anna Cornelio Labelingh in 1770. Their union produced
two sons, who also served the Moravian Church. From that time until
his death, he labored in various capacities in Moravian congregations
around Europe, including Marienborn, Neuwind, Amsterdam, Gnadau,
Barby, and Ebersdorf, whereby he reinforced his reputation for piety,
dedication to goals, timeliness and disciplined work. But time took its
toll on him. In 1786, his energy was slowed by illness, and on his 67th
birthday on March 8, 1788, he passed from this life. He left behind him
a testimony to his energy in his work and dedication to his faith.

But what a life it had been! In addition to his groundbreaking mission history, he also maintained a lifelong journal, produced excellent,
detailed drawings, wrote poetry, composed songs for religious services,
lectured widely, taught in a number of Moravian educational institutions, preached effectively and competently, and travelled to nearly all
of the Moravian congregations in Europe. It was moreover said of him
by the many who knew him that he was an inspiring fellow worker and
a gentle man of great piety.

Shortly after Oldendorp's death, several translations of his book in
abridged form in Danish and Swedish made the Danish West Indies
and their slave societies well known in the Germanic world. The likes of
Ernst Schimmelmann, as one example, had access to this source available to him when, in 1792, he created legislation to abolish the slave
trade. In more recent times, in non-German-speaking Europe and the
rest of the world, Oldendorp's legacy has been all but neglected outside

the Moravian circle. It was, after all, a tome of some one thousand pages, written primarily about a relatively obscure 18th century religious movement in archaic German and in a difficult script.

That situation changed considerably in the latter part of the 20th century when the man and his work were rediscovered by historians and anthropologists who had developed an interest in the study of ethnic groups, in particular Africans and their history in the New World. An English translation appeared in 1987, with the result that a number of English speaking students and scholars found in the thick volume a base for renewed interest and study of the Moravian period, slavery included. Moreover, that translation rekindled interest in Oldendorp in general, culminating in an edited German edition of the entire manuscript by a team of German scholars. (*Historie der caribischen Inseln Sanct Thomas, Sanct Croix und Sanct Jan, insbesondere der dasigen Neger und der Mission der evangelischen Brüder unter denselben.* Berlin: Verlag für Wissenschaft und Bildung, 2000)

Some of the leading anthropologists and historians of the 20th century have shown great appreciation for Oldendorp and his work. Both Sir Edmund Leach, author of *Social Anthropology* (Oxford University Press: 1982) and Melville Heskovits in his celebrated books *The Myth of the Negro Past* and *The New World Negro: Selected Papers in Afroamerican Studies* have remarked that he was a man far in advance of his time, a man who offers us unique gifts from the past. If the comments of men such as these have any validity, then the Virgin Islands and their people find themselves in a privileged position indeed in regarding the potential for the study of their past.

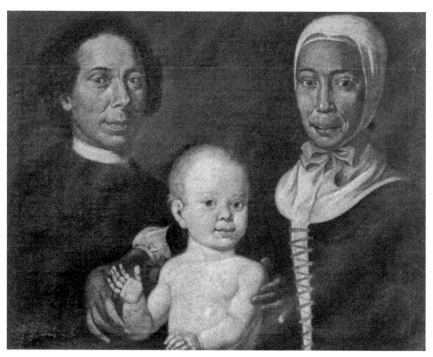

Rebekka Freundlich Protten, with her husband Christian Protten and their son in the painting "First Fruits"

CHAPTER 28

REBEKKA FREUNDLICH PROTTEN: A WOMAN OF FAITH

SHE WAS BORN IN ANTIGUA sometime around 1718 as a woman of mixed race. She came to the Danish West Indies at an early age. There she became involved in the Moravian Missionary movement. That involvement carried her to other islands in the Caribbean, to Europe and finally to Africa. She was Rebekka Freundlich Protten, a woman of great faith.

At the beginning of her life, she was known simply as "Rebekka," or the "mulatto Rebekka." She was kidnapped from her home in Antigua sometime around 1724 and taken to St. Thomas where she was sold as a slave. The young girl was purchased by Lucas van Beverhoudt, a prominent planter of St. Thomas and raised as a part of his family, evidently as a house servant or attendant. As a consequence of that close relationship, the most important event in her life occurred at an early age—she learned to read. Once the world of books had opened to her, she read the Bible and other works, thereby taking her first halting steps into the world of the Europeans. Equally important, she received her freedom from Adrian van Beverhoudt, Lucas's son, around 1730.

Early in life, she developed an intense interest in religion. Her attempts to become a Christian, however, were thwarted by the prevailing social circumstances, for neither the official Lutheran Church nor the Dutch Reformed Church allowed non-whites to be baptized at that time. Occasionally, itinerant Catholic priests would visit the Danish islands and sometimes they baptized a few Blacks. Rebekka appealed to one such priest and he baptized her.

Some time later, in 1732, missionaries from the Moravian Church arrived in St. Thomas for the express purpose of proselytizing among the slaves. The young Rebekka heard of the work of a Moravian named Friedrich Martin and went to see him. When she expressed a concern about the validity of her earlier baptism by the Catholic priest, Martin, as well as his visiting colleague, the noted Bishop Spangenberg, reassured her. Thereafter, she began to visit the Mission of the Brethren regularly, with the consent of her employer. Martin immediately saw in Rebekka a genuine spirituality as well as a potential worker for the mission. And Rebekka sensed in Martin and in the Brethren, acceptance and a sincerity on a level lacking in the other Europeans she had known to that point in her life.

In several month's time, she became a dedicated worker for the Mission, attending to the spiritual needs of slave women, both black and colored. Her literacy and ability with languages, as well as her spiritual commitment, made her the ideal person for the task. By 1737, the Moravian mission on St. Thomas was still struggling for its survival. Understaffed, overworked and threatened by hostile forces in the European community, the Mission did not appear to have favorable prospects at all at that time. And there were but four missionaries.

In addition to the Mission leader Friedrich Martin, who was himself ailing, the mission consisted of Matthäus Freundlich, a young shoemaker, and Johann Schöneweck and his wife. When both the Schönewecks died in November of 1737, the considerable burden of mission work fell squarely on the shoulders of Martin, Freundlich and young Rebekka. It was at this critical point that Martin proposed that Freundlich and Rebekka marry. She was, after all, a dedicated Christian, a free person, and an effective missionary worker among the slave women though only twenty years of age. Moreover, Martin felt that her close association with both himself and Freundlich might lead to rumors, even accusations, of improper conduct.

On the negative side of the ledger, marriage between Europeans and people of color, though not specifically illegal, was rare, in spite of the fact that concubinage was relatively common. Although Rebekka herself harbored some hesitations about the propriety of the action, Matthäus

Freundlich readily agreed. Martin joined the couple in matrimony on May 4, 1738. Rebekka Freundlich's married life was an extremely busy one. She not only continued her work among the female slaves, but she also ran the Mission household. Additionally, she acted as a surrogate mother to the wayward children that Friedrich Martin was constantly bringing to the Mission home in Tappus, the only town on St. Thomas. In a short time, he opened an informal day school aimed at promoting literacy and Christian belief. Rebekka soon found herself in the middle of that undertaking.

Throughout 1738, hostility toward the Mission grew in the St. Thomas community. Most planters felt that their slaves were picking up dangerous ideas from the Missionaries. The marriage of the Freundlichs only served to increase the opposition. At the best, the three missionaries endured daily insults from nearly everyone; at the worst, their meetings were interrupted and they were threatened with physical violence. In the summer months of 1738, the mounting opposition found a voice in the person of Pastor Borm of the Reformed Church.

Teaching slaves the fundamentals of reading and Christianity was one thing; interracial marriage was quite another. So it was that the Freundlich marriage became the event that sparked serious opposition to the Moravians. On August 27, 1738, Pastor Borm filed charges with the government, challenging the validity of the marriage. He argued that since Friedrich Martin himself had not been properly ordained for his Missionary post, then he lacked real authority to perform the sacraments, including marriage. This tactic attacked not only the Freundlichs personally but also the foundation of the Moravian Mission itself. If these allegations were true, Borm argued, then all three of the offenders should be punished to the full extent of the law.

Before Borm's petition could be heard by the court, the three Moravians became embroiled in another court action, this one raising another issue. Timotheus Fiedler, the last active Moravian on St. Croix at that time, abandoned his post in 1738 and took a job as manager of a plantation on St. Thomas. He was accused shortly thereafter of theft and hauled into court. The authorities made the most of the opportunity in order to pull Martin and the Freundlichs into the case, on October 11, 1738. Upon their refusal to take an oath in court—an important tenet of their religious beliefs—they were fined a large sum and then thrown into jail when they could not pay it. For several days Rebekka, along with Martin and Freundlich, endured harsh solitary confinement in the small fort at Tappus. Subsequently, the fine was doubled, then tripled to ninety imperial thalers, an impossible sum.

In early November, Pastor Borm mounted an initiative that put the Freundlichs in an even more precarious position. To their astonishment, he agreed to marry them legally in the Reformed Church. To accept his offer, however, would be tantamount to an admission of Martin's invalid ordination and, as well, to the illegality of the entire Moravian enterprise. To refuse, on the other hand, would constitute a clear admission of guilt on their part (i.e., living in the married state without legal authority), for which there was a severe punishment—for Freundlich, life imprisonment, for Rebekka, sale into slavery.

Pastor Borm had laid a clever trap. Whatever the Freundlichs' decision, Borm would win. On December 22, they appeared in court but refused to recant the validity of their marriage. The judge fined Matthäus Freundlich 100 imperial thalers and committed him to life imprisonment at the notorious Danish prison at Bremerholm, not far from Copenhagen. He further ordered that Rebekka be excommunicated and then sold into slavery, the proceeds of which would go to the public hospital. Such was the reaction of the Danish colonial government to the Moravian experiment with interracial marriage. Friedrich Martin was likewise found guilty and summarily thrown into prison after a short illness. Rebekka and her husband languished in jail through the month of January, 1739. At the end of the month, when all seemed hopeless, help arrived from an unexpected quarter.

On January 29, 1739, Count Ludwig von Zinzendorf, leader of the Moravian movement in Europe and a well known nobleman, arrived at St. Thomas with four reinforcements for the Moravian Mission. He immediately contacted the governor and requested that Martin and the Freundlichs be released from prison. The count's prestige and influence were such that the governor immediately complied. The three Moravians were freed and an enormous obstacle to progress had been removed.

The illness that had been plaguing Friedrich Martin forced him to undertake a trip to Europe in November of 1741 for treatment and rest. The Freundlichs received permission to accompany him. The group also included Hanne, a Black woman from Posaunenberg estate and a slave boy Koffee, who had been given to Martin as a present in 1736. On November 14, 1741, they sailed to St. Eustatius where they were to catch a Dutch vessel for Europe, the usual pattern of travel at that time. While waiting on that island, Martin received word that his replacement on St. Thomas had just died; he was forced to return, on short notice, leaving the Freundlichs at the head of the small party. They finally set sail on February 23, 1742. After this short period of relative peace, ill fortune would shortly befall Rebekka Freundlich once again.

After five weeks crossing the Atlantic, the Moravian party arrived at Amsterdam on April 29. On May 23, at Marienbaum en route to Herrnhut, Matthäus Freundlich suffered a stroke and died instantly. After a two-day pause to bury her husband, Rebekka rejoined the group and journeyed on to another Moravian community, at Wetteravia, arriving there on June 3, 1742. At that point in her life Rebekka might have simply given up and returned to the West Indies. Life had not been kind to her—kidnapped, sold into slavery, imprisoned and finally widowed at the age of twenty-two in a totally alien world, many thousand miles from home. But her energy was far from spent. She made her way on to Herrnhut, headquarters of the Moravians in Europe to see what fate might have in store for her there.

Herrnhut was rapidly becoming the center for a worldwide missionary network, with Brethren constantly traveling to and from such distant places as Africa, the West Indies, Pennsylvania, and Greenland. There the next chapter in Rebekka's life unfolded quite unexpectedly when she met a certain Christian Protten. This young man was the son of a Danish soldier and an African mother of noble birth, a so-called mulatto like Rebekka. Because of this background he had been baptized as a Christian, taken to Denmark and given access to an education with an eye for enabling him to do Missionary work. He traveled to Copenhagen where in 1735 he met Count Zinzendorf. The Count took him to Herrnhut where he remained until 1737, being groomed as a missionary to carry the word of God back to the Africans along the Gold Coast. In that latter year, he finally returned to the coast where he attempted to establish and operate a school for mulatto children, whose numbers were growing due to the slave trade.

In a short time, however, Protten ran afoul of the nearby Dutch authorities and was thrown into prison. When he was set free about a year and a half later, he made his way back to Herrnhut. It was there that he met the recently widowed Rebekka Freundlich. In a short time, in 1746, they were married. Rebekka soon became a partner in Protten's plan to educate mulatto children in his African homeland. Perhaps her eagerness to help was because she shared with her new husband a sense of alienation, being totally accepted in neither the white nor the black world. Whatever the reason, they traveled to the Danish Fort Christianborg on the Gold Coast where they established their school, with the support of the Danish authorities.

But tragedy continued to follow Rebekka. While cleaning a gun, her husband accidentally killed one of his students, and this unfortunate event led to the closing of the school. Protten found himself once again forced to return to Herrnhut. The tremendous promise that Zinzendorf had seen in him now seemed to be fading. Christian's failures were offset, at least in part, when Rebekka bore her husband a son, an extremely light-skinned child who became the object of much curiosity. But apparently, the couple enjoyed a brief period of peace and perhaps even happiness.

As Christian Protten continued in his attempts to acquit himself on his native soil, Rebekka assisted him in his work. He certainly possessed certain abilities. He translated Luther's Little Catechism into the

Ga-Fante language. And he made one last attempt to return to Africa, traveling to Zeist in Holland to board a Dutch vessel. But before he could begin, he fell victim to strong drink. It was some time later that he returned to the Gold Coast to make another effort at opening a school. As for Rebekka, she traveled along with her husband to Africa for the final time in 1763. And then, Christian Protten died at the relatively young age of fifty-five. Rebekka remained in Africa where she died in 1780. Their marital partnership lasted some twenty-three years, most of them under difficult circumstances.

But her poignant story remains as a legacy to us all. Rebekka Freundlich Protten began life as a slave but ended it as a free person. She became a Christian at a time when it was no easy achievement for a person of color to do so. In time, she became an effective teacher, in part because she parlayed a liability into skill, namely that of spanning the considerable gap between two worlds, Africa and Europe. These qualities, coupled with her natural abilities and her strong motivation, enabled her to assume a significant role, one that even now is not fully appreciated, in the work of the Moravian Mission on St. Thomas in the Danish West Indies.

In her first marital union, she challenged the contemporary society's prevailing beliefs and practices relative to race and marriage. And during the punishment that she received for that challenge, along with her husband, she comported herself with courage and stoic dignity. In a time when the overwhelming majority of people remained in the village of their birth, Rebekka traveled broadly, visiting in due course the continents of both her African and her European ancestors. She made the very most of the limited opportunities that life afforded her. And her adversities—her life was full of them—she bore without apparent complaint and continued along the path that she had chosen. Her life was the focus of many of the constraints, stresses and anxieties generated spontaneously in a society mesmerized by race, color and domination. As a woman of extraordinary faith, she was able to elevate herself by the noble manner in which she handled those obstacles.

Qvou Orsu, depicted in full battle garb

CHAPTER 29

THE INCREDIBLE ADVENTURE
OF QVOU ORSU

I MET POUL OLSEN some thirty years ago when he visited St. Croix as a student with a group of other young Danes who were pursuing the study of the Danish West Indies. If I had any doubts concerning the usefulness of such study trips, I would soon be enlightened. Some years afterward, Poul secured a position in the Rigsarkiv (Danish Royal Archives) and quickly moved up the ladder to his present position as Senior Archivist. And along the way, he, along with his friend and fellow archivist, Erik Gøbel, became an expert on the records and the history of these islands, producing valuable research and writings over the intervening years. From the immense resources of the Danish archives, he has rescued more than one lost soul from the jaws of the past and restored to us voices to speak of other lives and other times. One such person was Qvou Orsu.

In the early 1750s a young African on the Gold Coast found himself ensnared by fate in a curious adventure. Qvou Orsu was from a good family, the son of the sister of a certain Soya, who was the assistant cabuceer, that is, an African who dealt with the Danes in the slave trade. The affair started when young Qvou entered the Danish fort Christiansborg as a "pawn slave," that is, someone who was held temporarily as a guarantee against a short-term obligation or debt.

For reasons that are not altogether clear, Qvou was treated as a "trade slave" in spite of his protected pawn slave status and transported on the vessel of Captain Jens Rasmussen Knie to the West Indies. The former were sold readily as slaves at the Danish fort whereas the latter were considered free men with traditionally protected rights. Qvou's sale to a Danish slave vessel therefore caused a great deal of commotion among Africans in the area around the Danish Fort Christiansborg, especially among members of Qvou's family.

The young people of Accra were so angered that a free man with a wife and children had been so badly treated that they attacked and nearly killed Wilhelm Heiberg, the Danish assistant factor in the fort. Soya was forced to flee the area and seek refuge inland for a time. But these events had little immediate impact on the fate of Qvou, who soon found himself with a new name, "Christian," and a new job as a field slave on the Royal plantation La Grange near Frederiksted on St. Croix.

Having his roots in a family of some substance in Africa and having never experienced the lowly status of a slave, Qvou found it quite difficult to adjust to his new lot in life. He complained bitterly about his misfortune and repeatedly demanded his freedom. And on occasion he went maroon and ran away from the plantation. He told his story to anyone who would listen, but the language barrier made that difficult. And no one would believe him anyway.

Qvou's one piece of luck in all this was his good fortune to have been sold to a royal plantation, where a certain Schmidt was employed as a merchant and slave trader. At that very same time, Schmidt happened to find himself at Fort Christiansborg on the Gold Coast where he heard the story of Qvou's bad fortune. As he was well known on the coast, Schmidt was contacted by Qvou's family who requested his assistance in restoring their kinsman to his homeland and promised to deliver two prime slaves upon his return to Accra.

Why should Schmidt lend his influence to save a single African who had fallen into slavery? In the first place, he was aware that the Danes had made a serious mistake by enslaving a free man, by mistreatment of a pawn slave, by breaking long-established customs and by insulting a well-established African family. Certainly, all these offences would damage trade relations between Danes and African merchants if left unaddressed. Schmidt therefore promised to investigate the matter upon his arrival in St. Croix.

Herein lies an important but usually overlooked insight into the dealings of the Danes on the West African coast. The assumption has for a long time been that the Danes sailed to the coast, marched ashore and simply did as they pleased. Few events in our history have been so grossly overstated. The fact is that they were constrained to activities for the most part in and immediately around their forts and trading lodges along the coast. Disease, the political disposition of neighboring rulers and the threat of war against Danish interests all conspired to force them to deal with the Africans in accordance with certain mutually agreed upon conventions. In general, African rulers and merchants provided the captives from points inland, and the Danes converted them into slaves and shipped them across the Atlantic.

In any event, when Schmidt arrived on St. Croix, he looked for Qvou and found him on the La Grange plantation. As a trader on the Gold Coast, Schmidt was well acquainted with the Ga language and was consequently able to communicate at length with Qvou. In addition, his knowledge of local African customs enabled him to understand the impact that this affair would most likely have on Danish trade, not only in slaves but in other products as well, such as gold and ivory.

One can imagine the young African's relief when he finally encountered someone who could understand his story and who had connections to his homeland. As a result of the meeting, Schmidt immediately made the case to Governor General von Pröck and to the St. Croix Privy Council that Qvou should be freed and returned to Africa at the earliest, in return for the delivery of two prime slaves to be supplied by Qvou's family on a subsequent ship from Africa.

Von Pröck responded without delay, ordering that Qvou be allowed to depart with Schmidt on the next vessel bound for Copenhagen. Upon his arrival there, he found that the Danish King readily validated the Governor's ruling and went on to grant Qvou his freedom. In the short time that Qvou spent in Copenhagen, he was treated well and soon became a minor celebrity of sorts. The King granted him a weekly allowance of one rigsdale, a considerable sum at that time. Moreover, the artist Bauenfiend painted a rather impressive portrait of Qvou in full battle garb.

In September of 1761, Qvou departed from Copenhagen for the Gold Coast on the vessel "Cronprintzens Ønske" in the company of his benefactor Schmidt. However, his story ends abruptly at that point, because the voice of the archival records here goes mute. We assume that Qvou made his way home and hopefully led a good life. We are therefore tempted to see the best of human nature in the outcome of this adventure—the Danes acting with magnanimity by returning a wronged individual to his homeland and the Africans standing up for basic human rights.

Would that such were true. In reality, the Danes acted in narrow self-interest to protect their trading rights on the Gold Coast, and the Africans, for their part, were quite willing to send two innocent fellow Africans into slavery to redeem a single free man, to say nothing of the thousands who continued to be sold to the Danish agents at the fort. The actions on both sides were, sadly, aimed at insuring that the base commerce in human beings would continue. In spite of the revelation of this less than noble behavior, we are nevertheless fortunate to have these exceptional insights into 18th century life in the Danish West Indies, thanks to a visit by a Danish student to St. Croix some forty years ago and his inspiration to become an archivist.

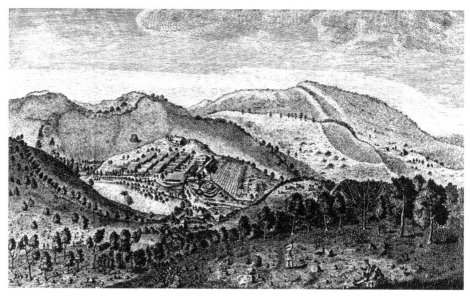

New Hernnhut, the Moravian Mission Station on St. Thomas where Mingo served

CHAPTER 30

DOMINGO "MINGO" GESOE:
AN IMPROBABLE LIFE

INTRODUCTION

IF HISTORY TEACHES anything, it's that the unexpected and the improbable sometimes emerge as the ordinary. What we are not able to foresee does not necessarily render the unforeseen improbable. Let the following case in point bear witness. By the middle of the 17th century, a plan had been put into place concerning how the Danish West Indies were to function as colonies of Denmark. Capital was invested from Danish sources, slaves were purchased along the West African coast, plantations were constructed in several Caribbean islands, sugar cane and a few other crops were cultivated there, and that commodity was exported for sale at a profit on the European markets. What this simple paradigm sometimes produced, however, was at times at variance with the intended design. How shocked and perhaps even horrified would those Danish investors be who drew up the Charter of the Danish West India and Guinea in 1671 by many of the events that marked the subsequent years of their colonial adventure. War, harsh times, brutality, piracy, corruption, miscegenation, the genesis of a new culture, new languages, and eventually alienation and conflict all figured into that tally. Even though a straight path to the simple accumulation of wealth had been laid out with all circumspect intentions, it was trodden by errant feet. This paper proposes to look at such improbable outcomes in the intertwined lives of two very unlikely men in early 18th century St. Thomas.

What were the prospects of a slave in early 18th century St. Thomas, Danish West Indies, rising to the position of assistant plantation manager while still a slave, in the absence of European supervision? If, to that scenario, were to be added that the same slave might assume the prominent roles of missionary and preacher in the newly established Moravian community on the island, the possibility becomes even more implausible. If it were moreover to be proposed that the same slave might enter into a close personal and familial relationship with his master and in time travel to Denmark completely on his own to attend to the plantation's business affairs, the supposition then becomes absurd in terms of what is presently known of the plantation system and the slave society in which it flourished in the colonial Danish West Indies. But such improbable events did occur and such a slave did exist. His name was Domingo Gesoe, better known simply as Mingo.[1]

Domingo's curious trajectory through life would not have been possible without Johan Lorentz Carstens (1705–1747).[2] And likewise, the life of Carstens would have been vastly different without Domingo Gesoe. Carstens himself was a native, white Creole born in St. Thomas and well connected in that small society. His paternal uncle Johan Lorentz had on two occasions served as governor of St. Thomas (1689–92 & 1694–1702).[3] Through hard work his own father, Jørgen Carstens, acquired a plantation in the country and a dwelling in the town of Charlotte Amalia.[4] These possessions the father left to his son upon his death in 1720. In time, Johan Lorentz Carstens became connected to several of the leading Creole families on this island through marriage, namely the Holtens and the Magens. By those means, he acquired several other plantations on both St. Thomas and St. John. Through careful management and circumspect business practices, young Carstens, by the mid-1730s, became one of the leading planters and traders in the Danish West Indies. He exported sugar, cotton and pockwood directly to Denmark, and in turn, imported Danish trade goods from Europe and slaves from West Africa.[5] He was, by any measure, a successful Creole.

EARLY LIFE OF MINGO

Domingo "Mingo" Gesoe was the offspring of two of those many Africans brought across the Atlantic to St. Thomas in the slave trade. He was most likely born on a sugar plantation on that same island. His name Mingo, a reduction of "Domingo," is apparently an Hispanic rendering of a West African day name; it was not an uncommon one in the Danish islands at that time. In fact, Domingo "Mingo" Gesoe is not to be confused with the better known Mingo Tamarin of St. Thomas and Mingo the Mulatto of St. Croix, both of whom also lived during the 18th century. The name Gesoe (Jesus) was most likely adopted sometime later in life when he became involved in religious activities. Since this name is not at all common in the Protestant traditions of western Europe, it is likely that it belies again an Hispanic influence early in his life. His was to have been the life of a field slave, a station that should have restricted him to pass his days as a lowly laborer in the cultivation of sugar cane and in the production of muscovado sugar. That, however, was not the way things turned out.

In spite of such humble beginnings, it was his connections to Carstens that conspired to shape Mingo's destiny. Carstens was, in many ways, an exceptional individual. As a Creole, he understood the ways of the islands and their people, white and black alike. But there was also a European side to him. He knew several languages, including Danish, Dutch, Dutch Creole and English. He knew men—planters, sea captains, merchants, slaves. His judgment was quick and decisive, and he possessed a determined will. These qualities paid dividends in the form of business success and prosperity throughout his life.[6]

At some point while still a young man, he became aware of Mingo and must have recognized in him some talent, some spark of energy and ambition. Intelligence certainly must have been apparent in the young man as witnessed by his subsequent achievements. Almost immediately Carstens saw the rudiments of an education develop in him—reading, writing and perhaps the Bible as a moral compass. A lifetime partnership formed in that manner.

Somewhere along the way, however, the young Mingo fell into difficulties that jeopardized his relationship with Carstens and even threatened his own life. Sometime around 1730, he was accused of getting a
young white woman, one Magdalena Kambeck, with child, or at least he
was blamed for it. While sexual relations at that time between a white
man and a black woman were illegal but relatively common, they were
illegal and punishable by death, in particular if those acts involved the
engenderment of a child.[7] The appearance of a mixed-race child from
the womb of a white woman confronted that society with an all but
irreconcilable problem. Mingo most likely would have been executed
for this offense had he remained on St. Thomas. Instead, he managed
to escape to eastern Puerto Rico where he lived in exile for a time.
On April 21, 1732, Carstens intervened on his behalf by writing to the
Directors of the Danish West India and Guinea Company, claiming
that Mingo was completely innocent of the charge and had only fled to
Puerto Rico to avoid the threat to his life.[8] Moreover, Carstens argued,
he needed Mingo for the running of his plantation on St. Thomas; the
entire operation, Carstens implied, was dependent on him. He continued that Mingo was the most valuable of his possessions, having
paid some 1,300 rigsdalers for him, a princely sum indeed. Carstens
therefore requested safe conduct for Mingo to St. Thomas and a par-
don for him, and it was granted by the Directors. It would appear that
Carstens called upon his significant influence in St. Thomian society to facilitate Mingo's return to St. Thomas though little is known
concerning what happened to the mother and her child. Nor are the
details of this episode ever likely to be completely known. What is
known is that the bond between the two men survived this grave threat
and emerged even strengthened with Mingo's return to St. Thomas.

Mingo must have demonstrated his potential early in his life because
by the time he reached maturity, he had learned to read and write.[9]
In addition to those key abilities, he acquired a trade, he developed
managerial skills and he demonstrated an ability to deal effectively
with various kinds of people. Sometime during this period Carstens

accepted Domingo Gesoe as assistant manager of his plantations, Moskito Bay and Pearl. Such an action was unheard of at that time; in fact, it established a precedent for the Danish West Indies. Although Mingo remained a slave, he worked closely with his owner, received orders from him, carried them out and directed the work of the slaves under his charge. Using his own talents, he navigated his way through these difficult straits, giving his fellow slaves orders that were none-too-gentle, while at the same time remaining a slave himself. This speaks of a man of extraordinary will and determination.

THE MORAVIANS

In 1732, an unexpected arrival at St. Thomas had a great impact on the future course of the island and its people.[10] It greatly transformed Mingo's life. Two Moravian brethren arrived on St. Thomas from the German states with a plan that was as curious as it was unexpected, namely to evangelize among the slaves of the colony. Who were these Moravians and why were they interested in proselytizing among the slaves of the Danish islands?[11] In a few words, they were the awakened "hidden seed" of the Hussite movement in Bohemia in the 15th century. Unable to practice their sectarian faith openly there in their native land in the face of the hostile Catholic establishment, they traveled from their homeland to Bertelsdorf in what is today Germany to the lands of Count Nicholas von Zinzendorf, then a dedicated Lutheran Pietist.[12] The central Moravian belief was that piety, not reason and understanding, was the key to attaining God's grace for the cleansing of human sin and the attainment of salvation. The story of Anton Ulrich, a slave from St. Thomas, and his visit to Copenhagen in 1731 where he met Count Zinzendorf is now a familiar one to Virgin Islanders.[13] Ulrich's appeal to the pietistic Moravians to bring Christianity to the enslaved of St. Thomas and his subsequent visit to their center at Ebersdorf produced a keen response. The Moravians saw quickly that the enslaved population was in dire need of spiritual help. Moreover, if their pietistic formula for salvation was to be tested, what better subjects than the enslaved of the Danish islands for they were completely without any means to make an appeal through "reason and understanding?" Thus in 1732 were sent the first two missionaries to St. Thomas, where they made contact with Johan Lorentz Carstens.

Carstens, who was a member of the Dutch Reformed Church and widely known for his humanitarian spirit and moral disposition, was among the first on St. Thomas to make contact with the newcomers. The two strangers, David Nitschmann and Martin Dober, made a strong impression on him, and he forthrightly extended to them his support and encouragement in the form of food, lodging and friendship. His two plantations, Moskito Bay and Pearl, as well as his house in town, in a short time came to serve as the first mission stations for their initial missionary work on the island.

It is a fair supposition to say that if the original missionaries had not found an able and willing friend in Carstens, the mission might well have foundered in a short time. Indeed, he extended them a helping hand at a time when things were most difficult. Moravian missionaries, however, did not expect their efforts to bear fruit as a result of the charity of others. Indeed, it was a principle of their faith that they themselves were to work at their calling full-time in order to satisfy their own needs and at the same time support their missionary activities. In this regard, they faced an enormous challenge in St. Thomas where there was little remunerative need for such talents as they possessed.

Through his relationship with Carstens, Mingo came to meet these curious white men from Europe. It was moreover Mingo's ability to interact with the Moravian Mission, with its leading missionary workers and some of the principal supporters of the Mission that allowed him to demonstrate skills and energies that ordinarily would have gone unnoticed under the ordinary regimen of slavery. Indeed, the mission brought numerous changes to the small island. Quickly, Mingo understood these men and their goal of implementing one of the modern world's first missionary programs, in this case among the slave population of the Danish West Indies. Consequently, he became one of the first persons to be evangelized. He responded quickly and rose through the ranks of the Moravian program, first with study and learning, and then baptism, which permitted him to become one of the first "National Helpers" on the island, a position created by the Mission to bring natives themselves into the work of the missionary enterprise.

As a result of that early contact, Carstens' two plantations served as mission centers for the slaves employed on those and neighboring plantations until after the deaths of both Carstens and Mingo. In addition, Mingo was put in charge of the "awakened Negroes" in the town of Charlotte Amalia or Tappus, that is, those who were accepted into the Moravian Church.[14] In the absence of permanent European missionaries, Mingo acted as their leader until 1739, praised by no less a figure than Count von Zinzendorf as the "blessed and accomplished teacher of the heathen" who had administered to them with "faithful care."[15] In time, he was completely integrated into the Mission hierarchy. He became a National Helper and then Elder, as well being recognized as an effective preacher and a trusted leader of the black congregation. In the years that followed, the very highest-ranking members of the Missionary Church, Spangenberg and Zinzendorf himself, consulted with Mingo when they visited the island.

In the late 1730s, Carstens grew restive and began making plans to leave St. Thomas, an action of his that would once again impact on Mingo's life. He visited New York in the North American colonies and finally decided on Denmark, where he ultimately traveled with his family and household.[16] It seems that Carstens sought to make the transition from West Indian planter to Danish trader and businessman. However that may be, Mingo benefited by being put in charge of Carstens' plantations and business operations on the island. Right away Mingo became occupied with the activities in his new post. He proposed to missionary Johann Böhner that he build a new mill on the Carstens estate and with permission received, the missionary proceeded to build it.[17] He proposed the acquisition of new slaves for the plantation and oversaw their labor once they arrived.

At that same time, Mingo became more deeply involved through the 1740s and into the 1750s in the activities of the Moravian Mission congregation. First, he provided assistance to the new Moravian Helpers who were constantly arriving from Europe, dedicated men such as Johann Böhner and his wife Veronica. At one point, this particular missionary was so impecunious that Mingo had to loan him money for his subsistence. A rather curious situation—a St. Thomian slave lending money to a European in order to underwrite his missionary work among his own enslaved people.[18] He donated the land in town needed for a meeting house from which to evangelize among the slaves who lived there. His broad linguistic background enabled him to act as a translator for the congregation in the multilingual community that was St. Thomas, on one particularly auspicious occasion translating a sermon by Count Zinzendorf from Dutch into Dutch Creole for the congregation. And his ability to read and write several languages made him the natural candidate to handle the correspondence between the various congregations and mission stations. In one such instance, he composed a letter from the congregation in St. Thomas to the Moravians in Bethlehem, Pennsylvania.

But his most important role was that of preacher. By most every account he was both effective and moving in the pulpit.[19] As an extension of his preaching, he came to be known as a caring, sensitive man of God, as witnessed by his care of the aged and the dying, in particular the Moravian sisters Adriana and Magdalena. When Maria Magdalena, a dedicated Moravian and respected woman among the Moravians, grew old and feeble, she fell ill, only to have her Free Black master put her off his plantation to face death, abandoned and alone. Without hesitation, Mingo took her into his own household and attended to her with great compassion as she lay dying.[20]

His rewards for his religious service were simple. He was loved and respected across the island by Moravians and non-Moravians alike and that seemed to satisfy him. In 1741, he was invited to take communion with the leaders of the Congregation. In taking these final steps, Mingo advanced as far and as high in the Moravian hierarchy as was possible for a member of the enslaved community. That he took some pride in this first-ever achievement is evidenced by his polite refusal of an offer of freedom from servitude by Carstens, for the Moravian Mission served only the enslaved. He could not bring himself to surrender that affiliation; it had come to reside at the core of his identity.

THE DEATH OF CARSTENS

In 1746, Mingo received word that his master and his friend Carstens had passed away in Denmark. In May of that same year, he undertook a voyage to Copenhagen to perform the task of settling Carstens' St. Thomas affairs, to report on his estates and to look after the interests of his widow, tasks which he managed ably.[21] There is no other known instance in which a person with the status of slave in the Danish islands ever carried out such a commission. Unfortunately, not a great deal is known of his activities during these two years in Denmark. It is known, however, that he desired to make a visit to the Moravian center at Herrnhut, but, for whatever reasons, was unable to do so. In 1750, he made the return voyage to St. Thomas, where he was warmly welcomed home by the Brethren as the mission's "devoted elder servant."[22]

The last eight years of his life were spent largely engaged in Moravian activities. He continued to promote the mission's work of catechizing and proselytizing both in the town and on the two Carstens plantations, Pearl and Miskito Bay as well as on other estates where the slaves showed an interest in conversion. In this period he became essentially the respected head of the "Awakened Negroes" in St. Thomas. He showed a special concern for the material, as well as the spiritual, welfare of the many who were sick, infirm and abandoned. It was a dreaded horror of many slaves that their masters would put them off their estates when they became aged and no longer able to work, a status termed "manqueroon" in the estate registers. Many did so. Mingo showed a special compassion for those unfortunates, rescuing them and providing them with refuge in their last days.

When Mingo himself fell ill in late 1758, hundreds flocked to his sick-bed, as was then the common demonstration of respect shown for the highly esteemed and admired person at the end of life.[23] On October 27, he passed from this life. His funeral was presided over by the Moravian Missionary Brother Weber, the leader of the Mission congregation; it was attended in the Moravian church at New Herrnhut by some 1,500 mourners, white and black alike. These were unprecedented events for that time. Never had so many ever turned out in such numbers for the funeral of anyone, least of all a slave. Even more striking was the fact that Mingo was buried among the white Brethren, paving the way for integration of the graveyard, the much respected Brother Abraham soon finding a place right beside him. It may presently seem like a very petty matter, but at that time it represented a major step forward for a people who only a few short years previously had been universally regarded as hopeless "heathens." Mingo's example was major in establishing new-found respect for slaves, both as Christians and as human beings.

AN ASSESSMENT

Any assessment of Mingo Gesoe's life must take into account that he was, first of all, a talented, resourceful man by nature. At the same time, his fortunate association with a man such as J. L. Carstens contributed greatly to his opportunity for the success that he achieved and for the precedent that it set for many years to come. His rise through the ranks to assistant manager of the plantation bore the marks of the relationship and association between the two men. In addition, Mingo played an important role in the founding of the Moravian Missionary congregation in the Danish West Indies; he similarly rose up through its ranks to the highest position possible for a slave in the Mission at that time. If his advancement in the service of Carstens marked his material success, his entry into Moravianism marked his spiritual and personal development. That development was twofold: first, he himself certainly benefited from the unexpected opportunity that the Moravians presented to become Christian; and second, he demonstrated to the missionaries that people whom they originally considered ignorant and uncivilized could in fact teach them certain things about their mutual humanity.

Finally, it might be argued by some that Mingo practiced accommodation rather than resistance in regard to the very Europeans and to the economic and religious culture that oppressed his own people. There is some truth in that assertion. However that may be, Mingo was among the first to enter into open conversation and dialog with the dominant classes in St. Thomian society. By his example, he proved that unprecedented exchanges were possible and that they could produce positive results. As such, he was therefore among the first to contribute to the coalescence of African and European cultural elements in these islands, which helped form, for better or worse, depending on one's perspective, a nascent Creole society, in which those on the very bottom had an active part to play beyond that of mere faceless, meaningless slaves. Consequently, it turned out that Mingo's life was an unexpected element that occurred in the course of the Danish colonial project, which, at its inception, had no understanding about what their enterprise had set in motion, nor of what it would lead to in time. It is because of the influence of that unexpected element that the community which has evolved here to this day, however we may chose to value it, clearly bears Mingo's signature, in its own right, just as clearly and forcefully as that of the most important among the colonizers.

NOTES

1. Although his name appears in the documentation under several different forms (Gesu, etc.), the form Gesoe is used here inasmuch as Domingo used it when he signed his name. Although the names "Domingo" and "Mingo" appear for the first time in 1725 on the slave lists of Carstens' plantations, valued at very low amounts, it is not likely that either of the two references refers to Gesoe inasmusch as Carstens himself later states that he paid 1,300 rigsdalers for Mingo.

2. For an overview of the life of Carstens, see Arnold R. Highfield, "Johan Lorentz Carstens: Planter and Merchant on early 18th Century St. Thomas," *Caribbean Historical & Genealogical Journal* 5:2 (April 1997):18–27.

3. On the political life of J. L.Carstens' uncle, John Lorentz, see Kay Larsen, *Dansk Vestindien 1666–1917* (Copenhagen: C.A. Reitzel, 1928), pp. 45–46.

4.On the relationship between father and son, see Fr. Krarup, "Jørgen Carstensen og Joh. Lorentz Castenschiold, Fader og Søn." *Personalhistorisk Tidsskrift* (1888): 129–34.

5. Cartens papers provide valuable insights into his business activities, his personal life and affairs. See: *Samling af Dokumenter vedr. Personer og Forhold paa de vestindiske Øer 1703–50: De Castenskjoldske Papirer.* (Ny kongelig Samling 3642–4°: typewritten documents, 1940), 118 pp. For a detailed description of St. Thomas at that time, including plantation life and the position of the slave population, see the manuscript attributed to Carstens, see: Arnold R. Highfield [ed.], *J. L. Carstens' St. Thomas in Early Danish Times: A General Description of all the Danish, American or West Indian Islands* (English edition and translation by Arnold R. Highfield. St. Croix: Virgin Islands Humanities Council, 1997), 44+148 pp. [Original Danish edition: J. L. Carstens, *Dansk Vestindien for 250 År Siden: En Almindelig Beskivelse om alle Danske, Americanske eller Vest-Jiniske Ey-Lande.* (Copenhagen: Dansk Vestindisk Forlag, 1981), 164 pp. Ill.

6. For an overview of Danish law as it related to slaves in the Danish West Indies, see Poul Olsen in this same volume "Slavery and the Law in the Danish West Indies."

7.Cartsens' letter of April 21, 1732 to the Directors of the West India and Guinea Co., contains information concerning Mingo's flight to Puerto Rico and his efforts to secure his slave's return to St. Thomas. See: "Letter from J. L. Carstens to the Directors of the West Indina Guinean Company 21 April 1732" in *Danske Kancelli* D 37-2: Koncepter og indlæg til vestindiske sager 1730–1746: No. 2/1733. Also see: "Petition of 25 July 1732 from the Directors of the West India and Guinea Company in West India and Guinea Company," vol 38: *Copybook of petitions* 1732–1740.

8. Mingo's writing skills can be seen in a series of letters written in Dutch to J. L. Cartens, as well as to Anna Maria, the wife of Carstens, 1740–42. *Landsarkiv: Johan Lorentz Carstenschiold Privat Arkiv II.*

9. J. Taylor Hamilton and Kenneth G. Hamilton, *History of the Moravian Church: The Renewed Unitas Fratrum, 1722–1957,* (Bethlehem, PA: Interprovincial Board of Christian Education, Moravian Church in America, 1967), 723 pp.

10. C. G. A. Oldendorp, provides the most comprehensive view of the Moravian Missions in the Danish islands available in his *A Caribbean Mission: Oldendorp's History of the Mission of the Evangelical Brethren on the Caribbean Islands of St. Thomas, St. Croix, and St. John.* Translated and edited by Arnold R. Highfield and Vladimir Barac. (Ann Arbor, MI: Karoma Publishers, 1987), 35+737 pp. [Original edition: *Geschichte der Mission der evangelischen Brüder auf den caraibischen Inseln S.*

Thomas, S. Croix und S. Jan. Barby: Johann Jakob Bossart, 1777. 2 v. (450+663 pp.) Ill., maps] A good deal concerning the life of Mingo is recorded in the second volume of Oldendorp's account.

11. August Gottlieb Spangeberg, *The Life of Nicholas Lewis Count Zinzendorf, Bishop and Ordinary of the Church of the United (Or Moravian) Brethren.* Translated by Samuel Jackson with an Introductory Preface by Rev. P. LaTrobe. (London: Samuel Holdsworth, Amen-Corner, 1838), 511 pp.

12. Oldendorp, pp. 270–71.

13. Tappus was the name used among the slaves for the town in St. Thomas. Other names were the Brandenburgeri and Sucasa.

14. Oldendorp, p. 365.

15. Highfield, "Johan Lorentz Carstens: Planter and Merchant . . ." p. 2.

16. Oldendorp, pp. 405–406.

17. *Ibid.,* p. 402.

18. *Ibid.,* p. 500. Oldendorp provides a short excerpt from one of Mingo's sermons. pp. 419–420.

19. *Ibid.,* p. 435.

20. *Ibid.,* p. 470.

21. *Ibid.,* 546–47.

22. *Ibid.*

23. *Ibid.*

Carstens, though born in St. Thomas, returned to Denmark in 1741 with many of his slaves, was ennobled in 1743 and given Knabstrup Hovedgård by the King in 1745, where he died in 1747

CHAPTER 31

JOHAN LORENTZ CARSTENS: PLANTER AND MERCHANT ON EARLY 18TH CENTURY ST. THOMAS

JOHAN LORENTZ CARSTENS (1705–1747) was born on St. Thomas on May 18, 1705.[1] As a person of European extraction born in the Danish colonies, he was a Creole. His father was Jørgen Carstens (1678–1720) of Flensborg, and his mother was Margrethe Volkersen (??–1728), a Creole born in St. Thomas to Lucas Volkers and Maria Selwain, who were both of Dutch background and among the earliest settlers on the island. Jørgen Carstens had originally ventured out to the West Indies in quest of his fortune because certain of his relatives from his native city had preceded him there and done rather well for themselves, most prominently his mother's brother and his uncle, Johan Lorentz, among others. Soon after his arrival on St. Thomas, Jørgen Carstens found employment in the service of the Danish West India and Guinea Company in the capacity of "boutteler," that is to say, the official in charge of the Company's beverage provisions and stores. He held that position from 1694 to 1696, fulfilling the customary three-year contract while working out of the Company's warehouse located near the newly-constructed Danish fort at the harbor's edge. It was a low-paying job, yielding a salary of three rixdalers per month, about the same as the wages of a common soldier, very near the bottom of the social order. But Jørgen Carstens had other sources of potential income and opportunities for personal advancement in the colony after the completion of his stint with the Company. His uncle Johan Lorentz, who had served as Company official since the 1680s, became interim governor of St.

Thomas from 1689 to 1692 and governor from 1694 until his death in 1702.[2] By all accounts, Lorentz was a talented, responsible administrator, who played a significant part in the development and growth of the island through the 1690s.

In 1699, Jørgen Carstens married a young creole girl, Dorothea Barents, daughter of Thomas Barentsen.[3] In the same year he undertook the cultivation of a plot of land on the north side of the island, thereby making the transition from petty Company official to planter. After bearing her husband a daughter in 1700, Dorothea passed away in 1702, and, later in that same year, Jørgen married Margrethe Volkersen, who was the young widow of Johan Lorentz's stepson, Zent van der Lindenhoff. It was apparently Johan Lorentz, looking out for family interests, who made the match between his nephew and the recently widowed young woman. Margrethe was not without means, for soon after they were married, Jørgen Carstens found himself in possession of a dwelling in town and a plantation called "Kabritteberg" in the Mosquito Bay area, located several miles to the west of the town in St. Thomas. And in addition, when Governor Johan Lorentz died on June 6, 1702, he left a part of his estate to his nephew.[4] In this manner, Jørgen was able to become a planter and a man of some means and respectability in the St. Thomas community over a rather short period of time.[5]

The marriage of Jørgen and Margrethe Carstens produced three children, namely Carsten Carstens (1703–1709), Johan Lorentz Carstens (1705–1747) and Anna Carstens (1707–1709). The only child to survive childhood, Johan Lorentz Carstens, was baptized on July 4 of his birth year and named in honor of his recently deceased great-uncle. After becoming well established in the colony as a property owner, the head of his own family with important connections and a man of affairs of some consequence, Jørgen Carstens aspired to prominence in the small island society. When he died in 1720, his only surviving son, Johan Lorentz Carstens, 15 years of age and still a minor at that time, became the sole heir to his property—the house in the town and the plantation at Kabritteberg.[6] But in a curious turn of events, his widowed mother

Margrethe remarried in the following year, to Jacob Magens, head of another of the established Creole families on St. Thomas, giving young Carstens another important connection within the island's plantocracy. As a result of his mother's marriage to Magens and her predecease of him, Magens eventually became the legal guardian for young Carstens until he attained majority in his 25th year.

Little is known of Johan Lorentz Carstens' life in his early years. Although he must have spent at least a part of his youth on his father's estate learning plantation management, his name is missing from estate records for a part of that period, indicating that he may have been sent off-island to receive an education, not an uncommon practice among the wealthier planter families at that time. On May 23, 1728, at the age of 23, he married Jacoba von Holten (1705–1751), daughter of Joachim Melchior von Holten (1671–1708) and Maria van Beverhoudt (†1728). Joachim von Holten had entered the service of the Danish West India and Guinea Company in 1690 and served as governor from 1706 until his death in 1708.[7] For young Carstens, the marriage alliance with a daughter of one of the most prominent and wealthy families on the island was a good one. On the day following the marriage ceremony, however, his mother, Margrethe Carstens Magens, suddenly passed away, creating a rather curious legal relationship involving Carstens, his new wife and his stepfather, Jacob Magens. Not only did Magens become Carstens' official guardian, but he had also been serving as the guardian for Carstens' betrothed as a result of his previous marriage to the widow of von Holten, that is, Maria Beverhoudt von Holten, some time after Joachim von Holten died in 1708. The Carstens-Magens-von Holten legal relationship provides a passing glimpse of the complex interrelationships that might occur on the island at that time as a consequence of several converging social phenomena, namely the small size of the European-Creole community, the prevailing high mortality rate and the propensity of widows and widowers to remarry readily after the demise of a spouse as suitable opportunities presented themselves. But in spite of the legal complications, the marriage to Jacoba was a fortunate one for Johan Lorentz Carstens in several respects. Not only did he ally himself with one of the island's better families, but he also acquired another plantation through his new bride, this one on St. John. Several years later, in 1731, he disposed of that plantation to Adrian Beverhoudt, scion of a leading creole Dutch family and his brother-in-law by marriage to his wife's sister, Anna Maria von Holten. Moreover, it would appear that Jacoba was a good wife, fulfilling her part of the nuptial contract nobly; in return, she was loved and respected by her husband during their 19 years together.

In the years that followed, the young Carstens continued to acquire property and to prosper. In 1734, he received plantation Pearl at Little Northside Quarter, St. Thomas through the offices of Jacob Magens. In 1738, he bought the widow Dorothea Saloman's plantation at auction, along with 8 slaves for 920 rixdalers, a property which he later transferred to the Moravians. Carstens became a central figure in plantation and business affairs on the island throughout the 1730s. At the same time, he and his wife started a family. Of the four children that Jacoba brought into the world in St. Thomas, only one, a daughter named after her sister Anna Maria, lived past her second year. Later, in Denmark, she bore her husband three sons, namely; Carl Adolph Carstens (1740–1820), who was the godchild and namesake of high-ranking Carl Adolph von Plessens and who eventually inherited the Carstens estate in Denmark; Joachim Carstens (1743–1817), who became an officer in the Danish military; and Johannes, who died only several months after his birth in 1747. Carl Adolph and Joachim later became well-known in Denmark for their own accomplishments in government service and military affairs.[8]

Although Carstens was himself technically a Creole, that is, an individual of European parentage born and raised on the island, his writings portray a man who apparently did not consider himself altogether as such. His own direct antecedents had all been relatively recent arrivals of exclusive European extraction, his father, Danish-born and his mother, St. Thomas-born of Dutch parents. In his own writing and from his own perspective, he characterizes Creoles as persons of pre-dominantly European, but nevertheless mixed, blood, however lightly, a quality that would have excluded both him and his wife from that group by his own definition. In the *Beskrivelse* he opines that unions between such Creoles and noble persons were "unfortunate."[9] He recounts several stories of Europeans marrying Creoles with less than happy results. These ostensibly contradictory attitudes remain puzzling. But if actions count for anything, Carstens himself chose to "return" to Denmark in his mature adulthood, rather than spend the remainder of his life in the Creole society of the island of his birth.

Carstens appears to have had a naturally religious disposition, coupled with a personal inclination toward humanitarianism. Although he was a member of the Reformed Church congregation, he was nevertheless tolerant, even supportive, of other views and interests. When the Moravian Brethren arrived on the island for the first time in 1732 to begin their work of evangelizing among the slaves, Carstens was one of the very first to lend them assistance.[10] This gesture was especially remarkable in light of the fact that the Reformed minister strenuously opposed the Herrnhutters at that time. In a short time, Carstens became the leading Creole proponent of the Moravian program of proselytizing among the slaves in the Danish islands. When David Nitschmann and Leonhard Dober arrived on St. Thomas in 1732, earnest but naive in the pursuit of their missionary calling, it was Carstens who gave them work and lodging. True, Carstens did show himself resistant to the eager attempts of the two young men and their successors to convert him, but that disposition did not prevent him from becoming their friend and benefactor. His status as a leading planter, an official of the Danish West India and Guinea Company and a prominent Creole allowed him to play a significant role in assisting the missionaries both materially and morally as they struggled to gain a toe-hold in an environment where the slaves were often as indifferent to them and their message as the Whites were outright hostile to their presence.

Over the first several years of the mission's work, Carstens' material support was absolutely crucial to the development and success of the mission. His two estates, Moskito Bay[11] and Pearl, along with his house in town, became centers for Moravian religious meetings and proselytizing. Moreover, on July 10, 1738, he purchased at auction the estate of Mrs. Saloman and then immediately ceded the property to the Brethren, who renamed it "Posaunenberg" (later New Herrnhut) and made that plantation the focus of their operation on St. Thomas over the next two centuries. All in all, the Carstens properties remained central to the Moravian effort on St. Thomas until well after his death. It was not until 1758 that the missionaries withdrew from estates Mosquito Bay and Pearl to concentrate their work on their own recently acquired properties.

It is not a mere coincidence that, in 1736, the first baptisms of slaves by the Moravians occurred on the Carstens estates and that, in time, prominent "national helpers" drawn from the slave community—that is, baptized slaves who became teachers and preachers in the proselytizing activities among their fellow slaves—came from among those living on the Carstens plantations. Prominent among these "first fruits," as the Moravians called them, were Andreas and Mingo Gesoe, the latter a slave who, in time, became not only an assistant overseer with authority over both Mosquito Bay and Pearl plantations but also the outstanding black Moravian in the Danish Islands in his lifetime.[12]

Johan Carstens befriended the most dynamic and productive of all the Moravian missionaries, Friedrich Martin, when he arrived on St. Thomas in 1736.[13] He allowed Martin to use part of his dwelling in the island's only town as a meeting place for his missionary work among the town slaves. And when Martin and his assistant Mattäus Freundlich ran afoul of The Reformed Church minister Borm and the Danish government as the result of Freundlich's interracial marriage with a "mulatto" woman, a certain Rebekka, it was Carstens who supported the three of them during their trial and later during their imprisonment.[14] He cared for Martin when he fell seriously ill and later did not hesitate to testify in favor of the three accused missionaries at their trial, putting his own reputation and standing in the community at some risk in the process. And subsequently, when certain inhabitants of the island sued Martin on trumped up charges of slander in an obvious attempt to be rid of him, Carstens once again came to the missionary's rescue by using his personal influence in the small community to have the parties drop the charges.

Carstens was generous in his concern for the missionaries, often extending material aid and hospitality to them in moments of duress. When Friedrich Martin and his assistant fell seriously ill in 1736 and were unable to look after themselves, Jacoba Carstens sent a black woman to care for them, perhaps saving their lives in so doing. Whenever ranking Moravian missionaries visited the island in the course of their well-known "inspections," they invariably conferred with Carstens at length. Such was the case with Bishop August Gottlieb Spangenberg in September of 1736 and Count Ludwig von Zinzendorf later in January of 1739. The latter, in fact, resided with the Carstens family during his important visitation to the island and took counsel from him. In return, Carstens became an unconditional supporter of the Moravian religious program among his slaves. In fact, he expressed the concern that those slaves who had the greatest access to the Christian message were the very ones who made least use of it. Perplexed, he asked Zinzendorf, a tireless teacher, to instruct his slaves on a daily basis during his stay on St. Thomas. The latter preached to them every day and then directed the missionary Georg Weber to do likewise after his departure. This initiative marked an important turning point in the progress of the mission, beginning the practice of Christian instruction on the Carstens estates for not only Carstens' slaves but also for other slaves from nearby estates as well. Carstens' plantations, therefore, became the earliest points of systematic dissemination of Christianity among the African population. All these matters considered, it would be difficult to exaggerate the role played by Carstens in the establishment of the Moravian missionary movement in the Danish West Indies.

As long as he lived in St. Thomas, Carstens oversaw the operation of his own plantations, which produced sugar, cotton and some pock-wood.[15] The labor force on his estates came from the slaves he owned; they may have numbered as many as several hundred in all. In 1730, he expanded his operation when he acquired an interest in a five-ton brigantine that had been built in New England, the *Vrou Jacoba*. In that vessel he shipped his produce to Denmark, where he offered it for sale, first, to the Danish West India Company and, then, to other merchant firms, whenever the former was unable or unwilling to acquire it all. He travelled extensively, but, in particular, he made trips to Denmark, during which he looked after business concerns and cultivated contacts within the Company. In the company of his brother-in-law Adrian Beverhoudt, whom he generally referred to as his "brother," he made one such trip to Denmark in 1733–1734; during that voyage he kept a journal, which reveals something of the character of the man, in particular his strong concern for order and detail.[16] While he was in Denmark, he made contacts with merchants, whose cooperation was essential to him in doing business from distant St. Thomas. It was Carstens' practice to consign his cargoes to a Copenhagen merchant, whom he directed to dispose of their contents in accordance with his written instructions. Fairly typical of Carstens' manner of doing business can be seen in a cargo that he shipped to Denmark in June of 1735. Under the command of Capt. Pieter Swann, the *Vrou Jacoba* was loaded with sugar, cotton and pockwood and sent to Carstens' present agent in Copenhagen, one Johan Wilhelm Engelbreght. The latter he instructed by means of accompanying correspondence to offer the Danish West India and Guinea Company the usual right of first refusal, and, that failing, he was then to send the ship and its cargo on to Baltic city of Lübeck.[17] And so it proceeded.

In addition to his plantations and shipping concerns, Carstens was also a shareholder and leading figure in the Danish West India and Guinea Company, holding five shares. During his trip to Denmark of 1733–1734, he purchased shares in the Company and made the acquaintance of its directors and leaders. Those leading figures, powerful men in government and commerce such as Carl Adolph von Plessens and Frederik Holmsted, regarded Carstens as one of the more knowledgeable and trustworthy planters in the colony, and they therefore valued his opinions. Through connections such as these, Carstens became rather well-known and trusted in high circles. In 1739, King Christian VI sought him out and expressly requested his opinions about the present state and future potential of the new royal plantations on St. Croix; Carstens responded directly and candidly to the royal request with a number of concrete recommendations.[18] It was no doubt service of this kind and the resulting recognition that led to his subsequent ennoblement.

On April 5, 1735, Carstens received a letter from the Company that may well have played a crucial role in helping him decide the future course of his life. In that correspondence the Company Directors explained that each shareholder was being assessed a payment of 150 rixdalers per share at a rate of 6 percent per annum in order to raise capital for the development of St. Croix, which had been recently purchased from the French in 1733.[19] Carstens made his payment of 750 rixdalers and then watched the center of gravity begin to shift rather suddenly from St. Thomas to St. Croix, owing to the latter island's extensive tracts of heavy forests and fertile, flat land. Some St. Thomas planters hastened to move there with their families and with their slaves in order to take advantage of the new opportunity. The future of sugar production on St. Thomas must have appeared dim to Carstens and other St. Thomians at that time. In Carstens' case it apparently influenced his plans for the future.

Carstens did not commit his thoughts on these changes to paper, but his actions speak rather clearly. Sometime shortly after the acquisition of St. Croix and the onset of its settlement, he applied for naturalization in the North American English colony of New York. In October of 1737, he travelled to the city of New York to receive his documentation; one of its conditions stipulated that within a year he and his family should remove to New York and then reside there permanently. At the same time, he petitioned to have his Brigantine, *Vrou Jacoba*, registered in that colony under his ownership, apparently in order to continue doing business in the West India sugar trade. These actions make it clear that Carstens had every intention of relocating in New York and becoming a merchant there.[20]

By the following year, those plans appear to have been changed entirely for reasons that are not altogether clear. On May 7, 1739, he departed from St. Thomas with his wife Jacoba, his daughter Anna Maria and four personal servants, destined, not for New York, but for Europe. After stopping briefly in Amsterdam in midsummer to allow his ailing wife to rest and to give himself an opportunity to attend to business matters, Carstens proceeded on to Copenhagen, arriving there in October of that same year.[21] In that same month, he wasted no time in acquiring another vessel, revealing his intention to remain in the maritime trade where he had already enjoyed such success.[22] His plan appears to have been something as follows. With trusty men overseeing his estates in St. Thomas, including his one-time slave, Domingo Gesoe, he would remain in the sugar and cotton business. In Copenhagen, on the other hand, he could look after his investment interests in the Danish West India and Guinea Company. Thirdly, knowing the West India trade as he did, it was quite possible that he planned to act as merchant broker in the metropole for planters on both St. Thomas and the new settlement of St. Croix, many of whom he knew personally. He was, after all, well-connected, related directly and by marriage to the most powerful and influential families in the Danish islands at the time, including the Beverhoudts, the Magens and others. Fourthly, in the years that followed, his correspondence reveals that he entertained an interest in entering the slave trade as well as in establishing himself in the sugar refining business in Denmark. His death at an early age, however, prevented the realization of these latter plans.

Lastly, Johan Lorentz Carstens had always fancied himself as something of a writer. He had composed an unpublished literary dialog between "Venus and Mars" just after his trip to Copenhagen in 1733.

And from time to time he had jotted down a poem or two here and there, nothing serious but betraying just enough talent to inspire him to consider himself a writer of sorts and provide him with the impetus to write about his experiences as a planter in the West Indies. To this inspiration we are indebted for the writing of the *Beskrivelse.* Moreover, the presence of Creoles such as Carstens, along with the exotic members of their households from distant tropical colonies, must have excited a good deal of curiosity among the inhabitants of that northern land. It was perhaps the questions that Carstens faced regularly about life in the tropical colonies, along with, no doubt, a sense of nostalgia, that may have moved him to commit his thoughts and recollections to writing. Whatever his motives, some time in the early 1740s, perhaps 1742, he apparently did just that.

Whatever the exact nature and extent of his business and commercial activities in Denmark, Carstens continued to prosper. In 1745 or thereabouts, he was ennobled by King Christian VI, taking the name "Castenschiold." Until that time, he and his still growing family had lived in Copenhagen. Some time around 1745, doubtlessly to mark his growing status in Danish society, he acquired the landed estate at Knabstrup, which was located not far from Holbæk in Sjælland; after his death two years later, his widow added the estate at Hørbygaard on the Holbæk Fiord.[23]

Johan Lorentz Carstens died at the age of 42 on June 19, 1747, and was followed in death by his wife Jacoba on December 4, 1751; they were buried side by side in the cemetery at the Mariakirk at Helsingør, not far from the narrow strait where ships in passage between Denmark and the West Indies would sail for the next 200 years. The Carstens name continued to thrive in Denmark through the persons of the two sons whom Johan Lorentz left behind.

NOTES

1. Fr. Krarup, "Jørgen Carstensen og Joh. Lorentz Castenschiold, Fader og Søn," *Personalhistorisk Tidsskrift* (1888): 129–34 and "Rettelser og Tillæg til Artiklen om Jørgen Carstensen og J. L. Castenschiold," *PHT* (1889): 101–03. See also Aug. Fjelstrup, "General Joachim Melchior Holten von Castenschiolds Ridderbiografi," *Personalhistorisk Tidsskrift* (1908): 151–52 and various articles in the *Dansk Biografisk Lexikon*.

2. See Kay Larsen, *Guvernører, Residenter, Kommandanter og Chefer samt enkelte andre fremtrændender Personer i de tidligere danske tropekolonier* (Copenhagen: Arthur Jensens Forlag, 1940), p. 88.

3. See David Knight, "A Brief Look into the Heritage of Johan Lorentz Carstens," (unpublished report, December, 1996), p. 1.

4. See Fr. Krarup, "Jørgen Carstensen og Joh. Lorentz Castenschiold, Fader og Søn," pp. 130–31.

5. *Ibid.*

6. C. G. A. Oldendorp, the Moravian missions inspector, and other later sources refer to the Carstens plantation as "Mosquito Bay." A plantation by that name, however, does not appear in the records until 1759 (personal communication, David Knight, Feb. 9, 1997). More than likely, Carstens or his heirs merged the Kabritteberg plantation with Mosquito Bay some time before that date.

7. Governor Joachim Melchior von Holten (1671–1708) served in the Danish West Indies from 1690, rising to the position of governor from 1706 to 1708. In 1692, he married Maria van Beverhoudt, a daughter in one of the island's leading Creole families. Their daughter, Jacoba, was born on St. Thomas and was, like Johan Lorentz Carstens, also a Creole. See Kay Larsen, p. 78.

8. Most of the information for Carstens' life as a planter in St. Thomas is taken from *De Castenskioldske Papirer* (Copenhagen: Royal Library), 118 pp.

9. See pp. 10–11 below.

10. The Oldendorp history contains numerous references to Carstens and his relationship to the early Moravian mission and its missionaries.

11. The use of the name "Mosquito Bay" rather than "Kabritteberg" follows the cited sources, principally Oldendorp.

12. *Ibid.*

13. E. Grunewald, *Friedrich Martin der treue Zeuge.* Kleine Traktate aus der Brüdermission No. 22 (Herrnhut: Missions-Expedition, [n.d.]).

14. Arnold R. Highfield, "Rebekka Freundlich: A Moravian Life," *Conference Proceedings of the Society of Virgin Islands Historians*, edited by Robert V. Vaughn (St. Croix: The Society, 1992), pp. 51–61.

15. The major events in Carstens' life in this period can be reconstructed from his short journal. See "Blad af Dagbog, der er ført af J. L. Carstens, 23 Maj 1728 til 23 Maj 1740," *De Castenskioldske Papirer*, pp. 81–83.

16. "Rejesedagbog, ført af J. L. Carstens paa Rejse fra St. Thomas til København, 1733," *De Castenskioldske Papirer*, pp. 19–30.

17. "Brev fra J. L. Carstens, St. Thomas, til Johan Wilhelm Engelbreght & Soon [sic], København, 16 Juni 1735," *De Castenskioldske Papirer*, pp. 44–46.

18. "Kopibogsomslag fra November 1739, København, inbeholdende: Kopi af Brev fra Christian VI til J. L. Carstens [og] Kopi af Brev fra J. L. Carstens til Christian VI," *De Castenskioldske Papirer*, pp. 56–60.

19. "Brev fra det Westindiske og Guineiske Compagnie, København, til J. L. Carstens, St. Thomas, 5 April 1735," *De Castenskioldske Papirer*, pp. 42–43.

20. See the following documents: "Naturaliseringsbevilling for Johannes Lorentz Carstens ved Borgmesterkontoret i New York, 10 Oktober 1737"; "Naturalisering-spatent for J. L. Carstens, udstedt af Borgmester i New York Gerardus Stuyvesant, 18 Oktober 1737"; and "Beediget Erklæring fra J. L. Carstens vedrørende Skibet 'Jacoba' New York, 19 Oktober 1737," *De Castenskioldske Papirer*, pp. 48–52.

21. "Rejsejournal, ført af J. L. Carstens paa Rejse til Europa, 7 Maj 1739 til 22 Maj 1739," *De Castenskioldske Papirer*, pp. 69–72.

22. "Notariel Bekræftelse af J. L. Carstens Køb af Skibet 'De Straet Davids' ved befuldmægtigede Abraham Scherenber, Amsterdam, 2 Oktober 1739," *De Casten-skioldske Papirer*, pp. 76–77.

23. Krarup, "Jørgen Carstensen og Joh. Lorentz Castenschiold, Fader og Søn."

Brother Cornelius who was a leading National Helper,
master mason, builder and preacher in
the Moravian congregation

CHAPTER 32

WHAT BROTHER CORNELIUS CAN TELL US

O NE DAY SOME YEARS AGO as I was leading a group of students on a tour at Whim Museum, we came to the wonderfully-preserved estate windmill and I began to talk about it and the other well-preserved structures on the estate. There was a young man in the group who was standing near the edge of the circle, obviously uncomfortable with the proceedings. After the visit I approached him, and he blurted out: "if these windmills and old buildings were about nothing more than sugar and slavery and that kind of stuff, then why do we bother coming here to look at them? Why don't we just tear them all down and be done with it?" On that particular day I didn't have a good response for the young man and I regretted it. But since then I have had a lot of time to think about his perceptive question.

Over that long interval, I stumbled upon the life of a man who gave me cause to reflect on the entire matter. His name was Cornelius (c.1717–1801) and he was born into slavery on a sugar plantation on the Danish Island of St. Thomas sometime around 1717. His mother was one Benigna, a Moravian Mission Helper who gave her son a good start in life. In the early 1740s, Cornelius met the tenacious Moravian missionary Friedrich Martin, and that encounter transformed his entire life. Martin brought Cornelius into the Moravian congregation at New Herrnhut where he was baptized on July 1, 1749, by Brother Johann de Watteville, Bishop of the Brethren's Church, who happened at that time to be visiting the Mission in the islands. Brother Cornelius became known almost immediately for his humility and simple piety. Soon he began to preach and in 1754 he became an Assistant in the Church. His course in life was set.

Cornelius married a fellow Moravian named Barbara, also a helper in the congregation. Their union produced five children, all of whom became deeply involved in the Moravian faith. Together they endured slavery but found a way to lighten its load in the service of their fellows in the Moravian congregation.

By trade Cornelius was trained as a mason, and with time he rose to the top of his profession though still enslaved. His experience earned him the position of Master Mason of the Royal Buildings, and his work soon became admired and respected across the three Danish islands. The reputation of his labors and the demand for his services allowed him to travel from estate to estate and island to island, thereby meeting numerous people and expanding his knowledge. By the time he had reached mature manhood, he was not only a gifted master mason but also fluent in several languages—Dutch, Dutch Creole, German, and English.

In 1764, Cornelius was sent to St. Croix to construct buildings and mills and was forced to part company with his wife and children for a time. The separation weighed heavily on him, but he was then a slave and had no say in the matter. And so he turned his attention to preaching among the slave population of St. Croix, where he made many converts to his faith. In the meantime, Barbara was sent to the fort in St. Thomas where she worked as a baker. In a short time, she was able to acquire her freedom, with help from her husband. In 1765, she joined him on St. Croix to their mutual joy. From that point in time, only death had the power to separate them.

In 1767, Cornelius overcame one of the great ironies that lay at the heart of slavery. Slaves were often permitted to buy their freedom in a process termed manumission. In this process they simply paid their owner the price that had been set upon their heads for purposes of taxation, determined by the nature of their skills and the value of their labor. So it was that a field slave would ordinarily have a low manumission value but at the same time enjoyed little prospect for earning any money at all.

As a mason, Cornelius had numerous opportunities to acquire earnings but his manumission price, set in relation to his highly skilled talents, was correspondingly high, in fact, very high. For many of the enslaved, this system held the danger of inspiring reverse motivation—the more one might advance in life, the higher the price for his freedom, which could result in apathetic resignation. It was this considerable obstacle that Cornelius overcame in 1767 when he manumitted himself and became a free man, at no little expense.

It is a little known fact that it was Cornelius who laid each of the foundation stones for all six of the Moravian chapels constructed at that time in the Danish Islands, from which rose the Moravian Churches of today. Likewise he had a hand in the construction of the various Moravian buildings—houses, dwellings, church-related structures—that went up in the same period, as well as structures on private estates. It is no exaggeration then to say that without the talents and imagination of Cornelius and his fellow black workers, the Moravian establishment in these islands as we know it today would not have been. The same is true of numerous plantation structures on all three islands.

But here is the important point. Though enslaved, neither Cornelius nor his fellows were driven to do this work under the lash of the whip. They undertook it willingly and with pride, because, from this and other labors, he was able to set aside earnings, with which he first bought the freedom of his wife and then his sons and daughters. Through these efforts he saw his grandchildren and great grandchildren all born free, a grand achievement for a man who himself had been born a slave. Herein lies the true measure of the man—putting his family first through the resources of his own hard labor, a gift he willingly gave in the service of those closest to him.

Moreover, his struggle illustrates that the buildings that we see still standing in our islands today, ironically enough, provided, over the long run, the force that liberated the very same enslaved men who built them. Those structures therefore stand as curious monuments to a system of oppression and at the same time as emblems of the forces that eventually weakened and then destroyed that system. Gradually, over time, free men arose from slave labor and it is Cornelius who provides us with perhaps our clearest model of this process. In that way the buildings, churches and mills all stand as silent witnesses to a long, complex process that has brought us, for better or for worse, to where we are today.

There was another side to this man, and it needs to be equally known. Brother Cornelius became a Preacher and Elder in the Moravian congregation, where he taught others and led by his own exemplary life. He was respected for his charity and sensitivity toward his fellows, especially those who enjoyed less than he. In the final analysis, the real measure of this man lay in his inner moral stature. When his wife Barbara died in 1796, he retired from active labor at the age of 79 and dedicated his remaining years to the service of the Church and to his fellow man. He moved among the people of the community, performed many good works and preached powerful Christian sermons. So famed was he for the latter that he often attracted white listeners into the otherwise all-black Moravian Church to hear his words, not the least of whom was Governor Thomas de Malville, whom Cornelius converted, making him the first white member of the Moravian Church in the Danish Islands. Thus began in a modest way, the breaking down of the walls that separated the races and classes.

In November of the year 1801, in his 84th year, Brother Cornelius fell ill. White-haired, bent and enfeebled, this faithful servant of Christ nevertheless remained strong in his faith. He called for his children to be summoned to his bedside and they all came to pay their final respects to their beloved father. That meeting reveals what he held most dear. Here is what he had to say to them.

"I rejoice exceedingly, my dearly beloved children, to see you once more together…Sometimes I have dealt strictly with you in matters which I believe would bring harm to your souls and grieve the spirit of God and I have exerted my parental authority to prevent mischief but it was all done out of love for you. However, it may have happened, that I have sometimes been too severe—if this has been the case, I beg you, my dear children, to forgive me."

And his final words were these: "Attend to my last wish and dying request. Love one another! Do not suffer any quarrels or disputes to arise among you after my decease. . . . Let each strive to show proofs of love to his brother and sister." In the early morning hours of November 30, 1801, Brother Cornelius passed from this life, with his children gathered in mourning around his bedside. They heeded his words as they all became Mission Assistants in the Church he loved so dearly. Herein lies the greatest achievement of this pious man—the setting of all his children on the straight path.

And that brings me back around to the beginning. Tear down the works of Brother Cornelius and others that have stood for these several hundred years? I think not. Rather we might take a new look at them as the labors of a man who lived in a far harder time than our own but who achieved far greater results than have most of us in this present age in spite of the deck being heavily stacked against him. And in so doing, we might also humbly ask ourselves if there is any way that we might learn from this man's life, especially in regard to the manner in which we relate to our fellow men, to our families and to our children, especially in regard to their upbringing and training. In this regard, Brother Cornelius, I believe, has a great deal to tell us. We have but to listen.

Born of a Black Crucian mother and a German
father, Leidesdorff (1810–1848) was a leading
figure in the early history of California as
well as the founder of San Francisco

CHAPTER 33

WILLIAM LEIDESDORFF: A CRUCIAN WHO DARED

IN THE QUIET Cemetery Gardens of the Mission Delores Church in the city of San Francisco lie the earthly remains of a long forgotten son of St. Croix. Just how he ended up so far from home and all that he did along his journey to that place make for a truly remarkable story.

William Alexander Leidesdorff was born on the island of St. Croix in the then Danish West Indies in 1810, the son of Wilhelm Leidesdorff and Anna Maria Spark. The father, said to be of a Jewish background, was a merchant and sugar factor from the Danish city of Altona near the Free City of Hamburg, who had business connections on St. Croix. And the mother has been variously described as a "mulatto" and a half-Carib Indian from the island of Dominica. Whatever her origins, she presented Wilhelm with a handsome baby boy.

Young William spent his first 16 years—1810 to 1826—on St. Croix. As a member of the Free-Colored class, his social position was far better than that of the slaves but remained, nevertheless, far below that of the Whites. Members of this Free-Colored class met with social and economic discrimination at every turn. William would remember these early circumstances all the days of his life.

If his later successes are any indication, he received a solid education though we know little about the particulars. He received some education at Flensburg in Denmark. Certainly, he knew enough of mathematics and the communication arts to become a real success in business and civic affairs in the larger world. In addition, he was multilingual, knowing English and Crucian Creole as his maternal languages, and most likely as well some Danish, German, Spanish and French.

Leidesdorff shares some interesting parallels with another, earlier Crucian emigrant, Alexander Hamilton. Both came from divided families. Both emigrated at around the age of 16 to the North American mainland and enjoyed great success in their respective undertakings. Both suffered from social discrimination. And both died tragic, premature deaths, never returning to their roots on St. Croix.

As the story goes, young Leidesdorff was adopted by an English planter on St. Croix at a young age. We can only surmise that the foster father wanted a better life for his son than contemporary St. Croix could offer a man of color, however brilliant he might be. So he arranged an apprenticeship position for William with a business firm in New Orleans, where he migrated in c.1826. The city was at that time a bustling, vibrant commercial entrepôt that connected the Mississippi basin with the Caribbean, South America and the great world beyond. In that city, energy, hard work and imagination might be rewarded for their own merit. To that end, in 1834, Leidesdorff became a naturalized American citizen.

The young man Leidesdorff soon became involved in business, shipping, and international trade. He made numerous trips to various points abroad, including New York, the Caribbean, and South America. With experience, his reputation grew and he prospered, eventually going into business on his own with a small fleet of ships funded in part by an inheritance from his foster father.

Thus launched in his career, he sought what most men seek—a wife, children, a family. His physical looks were such that he was able to "pass for White," perhaps as a Spaniard or of Latin American background. It is said that he fell in love with the daughter of an established Creole New Orleans family and was completely accepted; plans were soon being laid for the wedding. Though New Orleans was comparatively liberal and open in comparison with the rest of the South at that time, there were limits. Interracial marriage was one of them. As the story goes, word from St. Croix reached the parents of the bride-to-be that the prospective groom was the offspring of a "black woman." Upon learning that, the fiancée's father returned William's engagement ring along with the notification that he would no longer be welcome at their home.

Leidesdorff was crushed by this unexpected turn of events. In a short time, he closed his business, disposed of his dozen or so ships and took to the sea that had long nurtured him. The coming months found him in his 105-ton schooner "The Julie Ann" sailing up the coast in the Pacific Ocean. In 1841, he came upon a beautiful, spacious bay along the coast of California and was attracted to its small Spanish settlement, Yerba Buena. He dropped anchor and decided to stay. There he traded with both Russians to the north and Mexicans to the south in commodities such as wheat, tallow and hides until he had amassed enough money by 1844 to purchase several lots in the heart of the town; there he built a warehouse.

The real payoff came a short time later. California was part of Mexico from 1821 until 1846. In order to obtain more land, Leidesdorff declared Mexican citizenship in 1843. He was rewarded by the Mexican government with a grant of 35,000 acres of land, known as the Rancho Rio de los Americanos, which today constitutes a large section of the city of San Francisco. Leidesdorff set immediately to developing his holdings and quickly established himself as one of the wealthiest and most influential men on the coast.

After July 1846, when California was annexed from Mexico by the United States, Leidesdorff's star blazed across the western sky. In that same year he was named Vice-Consul to Mexico. In 1847, he was elected to the Town Council. He also held the position of Town Treasurer in 1848 and was a prominent member of the School Council that established the city's first school. In addition, he built the town's first hotel and owned and operated the first steamship to service the Bay area. But more important than his titles was his growing reputation as a man of honesty, integrity and compassion. A brilliant future lay before the 38-year-old pioneer.

In January of 1848, when gold was discovered at Sutter's Mill, the nation and the world focused their attention on the Bear Flag Republic. As gold-seekers poured in, the population soared to nearly a half million. The economy prospered and land values rocketed. Leidesdorff stood on the threshold of incomparable wealth. But that door did not open and let him pass. That same spring on May 18, 1848, he fell ill and died of either pneumonia or typhus at the age of 38, with his entire life beckoning before him.

Another adventurer was waiting in the wings, Joseph Folsom, recently arrived in California from Ohio. After investigating Leidesdorff's background, Folsom made two trips to St. Croix where he purchased rights to Leidesdorff's massive California landholdings from his mother Anna Spark for the unheard of sum of $75,000.00, a veritable fortune in today's dollars. Not surprisingly, Leidesdorff's European relatives contested the Folsom purchase and kept it in court for the next fifty years or so. Folsom, for his part, soon followed Leidesdorff to the grave, in 1855, also a man in the prime of his life. But it was Folsom who was largely remembered in California in the years that followed. By the turn of the 20th century, the name William Alexander Leidesdorff had been, sadly, all but forgotten.

In recent years, Leidesdorff's memory has been revived. A plaza and a highway now bear his name. A recent book and a spate of articles have restored to him some of the recognition he so richly deserves. In the flurry of attention that presently swirls about his name, many are quick to claim and label him—American, African-American, California pioneer, and Mexican—in accordance with their own agendas. We must make certain that the world does not forget that he began his illustrious journey as a Crucian, a son of St. Croix, in the former Danish West Indies.

Memorable 61-round prize fight between
Gentleman Jim Corbett and St. Croix-born and
Australia-based Peter "The Black Prince" Jackson
that ended in a draw

CHAPTER 34

PETER JACKSON: "THE BLACK PRINCE" OF ST. CROIX

THE VIRGIN ISLANDS has produced its fair share of out-standing athletes. Tim Duncan, Elmo Plaskett, Joe Christopher, Valmy Thomas and Horace Clarke are just a few names that come immediately to mind. Among boxers the list is equally impressive—Julian Jackson, Emile Griffith and Livingston Bramble, each one a great fighter and a champion. But one name is and has long been missing from this list, Peter Jackson, a master of the sweet science who in his own day toward the end of the 19th century was known as "Peter the Great" and "The Black Prince" of the ring.

Though detailed facts about Jackson's early life are few, this much is clear. He was born on the island of St. Croix on July 3, 1861. His father was a warehouseman, who had more than likely received his freedom in the Emancipation of 1848. Peter attended school long enough to learn the basics and was then apprenticed as a young seaman sailing the great oceans. He was already at sea as little more than a boy of ten. It was a hard life but it made him resilient and strong.

The year 1878 found Peter in Sydney, Australia, at the tender age of 17. More than likely, he had arrived there completely by chance. During that stay, a brawl broke out on board ship. The young Crucian intervened with his fists and brought the situation under control. That incident and his near perfect physique attracted a good deal of attention which con-vinced the young Peter to settle down in Sydney. He held a number of odd jobs over the next several years but his real passion soon became boxing. He pooled his money and bought a set of boxing gloves.

In 1882 at the age of 21, young Peter was spotted by Larry Foley, a one-time bare-knuckle champion and trainer of a number of great Aussie fighters, including Bob Fitzsimmonds. Foley recognized the young man's raw talent and began to train him. Soon Foley scheduled fights for him. His protégé progressed rapidly and showed great promise. Two years later, Jackson entered the ring in Melbourne against the Australian champion, hard-hitting Bill Farnan. Peter was knocked out in the fourth round. This inauspicious beginning taught him lessons he would never forget; he did not lose again until the very end of his career.

In 1886, he fought again for the Australian heavyweight title, this time beating Tommie Lees in a hard-fought 30-round decision. For the next couple of years, Jackson fought and beat every available contender "down-under" and was recognized as the undisputed Australian Heavyweight Champion. But with no one left to fight, he packed his bags and headed for the United States where John L. Sullivan reigned as the World Heavyweight Champion.

In 1889, Jackson took every available fight. From California, to Chicago, through Buffalo and on to New Jersey, he convincingly defeated every top American heavyweight boxer. Now in his physical prime, standing 6' 1" in height and weighing about 195 pounds, the Crucian challenged the unbeaten John L. Sullivan, only to be turned down because the champion refused to enter the ring with him because of his race. "I will not fight a Negro," said Sullivan. "I never have and never shall."

Peter Jackson immediately departed for England where he fought several exhibition fights in London. Soon he was matched against Jem Smith, whom he wasted no time in dispatching in two rounds. At 28-years of age, he had beaten the best that England had to offer and the sky seemed to be the limit. He once again went looking for John L. Sullivan, whom he met face-to-face in Australia in 1890. But once again the American champion declined to fight him.

Jackson returned to the United States, and on May 21, 1891, he took part in one of the legendary matches in boxing history. At the California Boxing Club, the "Black Prince" entered the ring with "Gentleman

Jim Corbett," one of boxing's rapidly rising new stars. For four grueling hours and over 61-rounds, the two men went at each other full force. With both men finally exhausted and unable to continue, the fight was called a draw, instantly becoming a classic in the early history of the sport. On September 7, 1892, Corbett fought Sullivan and knocked out the battered champion in the 21st round. In retrospect, it might just as well have been Jackson who stepped into the ring that night had it not been for the racial issue. Corbett in fact later remarked that Jackson could have beaten any heavyweight that he, Corbett, had ever fought.

Jackson returned to London, and after a number of bouts and exhibitions, fought another classic battle, this time winning a 10-round knock-out over a very tough Paddy Slavin, to gain the title of "Heavyweight Champion of the British Empire." After an attempt to arrange a rematch with Champion Jim Corbett fell through, Jackson continued to tour America, Canada, Australia, France and Great Britain widely recognized as perhaps the greatest fighter of his time. He was received everywhere with enthusiasm. He also found time to perform in Vaudeville shows, to open a boxing school in London and do some acting in America, submitting in the latter, unfortunately, to the prevailing racial attitudes of the day by taking on a humbling role in *Uncle Tom's Cabin*.

By that point in his life, Peter Jackson was universally admired not only as a boxer but equally as a man and a gentleman. But there was also a negative side to his character. He led a fast lifestyle, marked by an overindulgence in strong drink. The late 1890s witnessed a deterioration in his superb physical condition and in his health. In spite of his condition and advancing age, he fought the World Champion James Jeffries in California on March 23, 1898, and was badly beaten in three rounds and knocked out. In the following year, he was knocked out in Vancouver, Canada, by Jim Jeffords in four rounds. Suffering from serious rib injuries, his health had spiraled downward in a rapid decline. He soon fell victim to tuberculosis.

Peter Jackson found himself broke, beaten, and seriously ill in a hospital in Canada, conditions all too familiar among many of boxing's even brightest stars. With assistance from a wealthy admirer, however, he made his way back to Australia in September of 1899 and sought out the dry climate of the desert, where he hoped to recuperate from his debilitating disease. But such luck was not in the cards. On July 13, 1901, at the premature age of 40, Peter Jackson died in Roma, Queensland, Australia. The world lost perhaps the finest fighter who ever stepped into a ring to that point in history.

In his book *The Legendary Champions*, Lardner noted that Jackson "is considered by many experts to have been the greatest heavyweight who ever lived." And Gentleman Jim Corbett himself remarked that Jackson was along with Jeffries "one of the two greatest heavyweights of all time."

Known far and wide as a fine gentleman as well as a strong, highly skilled boxer, Peter Jackson, widely mourned by his adopted Australians, was buried in Toowong Cemetery and a monument was constructed over his grave, on which the following words have been inscribed: "Here is a man." It is regrettable that The Black Prince has received little to no such recognition in the land of his birth.

Hubert H. Harrison, Crucian-born
writer and political activist in
New York in the early
20th century

CHAPTER 35

HUBERT H. HARRISON:
A FORGOTTEN CRUCIAN

ONE IS ALMOST STARTLED when one considers the numbers of individuals from the Virgin Islands who have mi-- grated far beyond our shores—most notably to the United States—and succeeded admirably in those distant parts. Far back in our history there were the likes of Alexander Hamilton, William Leidesdorff, Denmark Vesey, Judah Benjamin, Edwin Blyden, Peter Markoe and Camille Picasso. More recently the names Raymond Jones, Terrence Todman and Roy Innis come to mind. And then, of course, there are the dozens of athletes—basketball and baseball players—whose names crowd major team rosters. Truth be known, there are probably few areas in the U.S. of comparable size and population that have contributed so many talented people to the American mainstream. But sometimes a name gets lost in the shuffle. One such is Hubert H. Harrison.

Hubert H. Harrison was born on April 27, 1883, on the island of St. Croix in the then Danish West Indies. He was the son of Cecilia Elizabeth Haines and Adolphus Harrison who resided on Estate Concordia on the west end of the island. It was a sugar-producing area and its focus was on the town of Frederiksted. Hubert's parents lived in the wake of slavery. The Great Fireburn occurred just five years before his birth and was still fresh in memory.

The 1890s were years of economic decline in the Danish islands. Sugar cultivation was waning. Wages were depressed. Whoever could escape from the rural estates to the towns did so in order to better his lot in life. And long before the islands were purchased from Denmark in 1917, some Virgin Islanders were already making their way from the islands' towns to New York City, principally to Harlem. For most of those émigrés it was a sobering experience. For some, it was soul-shaking. For young Harrison it was the latter.

In 1900, this seventeen-year-old Crucian made the long voyage to New York City. His arrival was a dazzling experience. Massive concrete buildings clawed skyward at almost the same pace as immigrants passed frenetically through the city's port. They came from every part of Europe in a frantic attempt of the Old World to catch up with the New. The city was alive and dynamic with people and growth, moving ever upward and outward at a dizzying pace.

From the southern states came another stream of migrants, African-Americans, just one or two generations removed from slavery. Like the Europeans they were attracted by the lure of opportunity and the chance for a new life. And just as the Europeans encountered discrimination based on ethnicity, the African-Americans found discrimination based on race and color. Ethnicity can change, albeit slowly, but the reality of race and color is another matter. So here we see the situation faced by American Blacks and the newly arriving Virgin Islanders, including Harrison—the promise of opportunity on the one hand and the limitations imposed by society on the other. That predicament radically transformed the young Crucian's life.

Harrison drank from the bitter cup of racism and class discrimination and reacted to it almost immediately. He wrote his first letter of protest to a New York newspaper in 1903. He read widely and discussed matters with a broad array of individuals—history, politics, literature, theatre, and criticism all fell within his purview. He quickly learned that he had a natural talent for analysis and philosophy. Equally important, he could communicate his ideas in a reasonable, even forceful manner. He began to speak out in public places in Harlem, and people gathered and listened to him. In a short time, he became known as the "Black Socrates" for his street-corner oratory, and he collected a following. That was just the beginning.

At the same time, he was building his life. He married Irene Louise

Horton in 1909, and their union produced four daughters and a son. He worked for the Socialist Party for a time and later found a position in the Post Office, a job that he lost two years later due to his outspoken politics. For a while he taught and served as editor of *The Negro World*. If his material life was one of modest means, his intellectual life was certainly not.

As a dedicated bibliophile and autodidactique, he continued to read, analyze, write and speak out. He drew enthusiastic crowds to the street corners along Lennox Avenue in Harlem. Henry Miller, the novelist, remembered hearing him and commented that he was "electrifying... able to demolish any opponent." Joel Rodgers called him "the foremost Negro intellect of his time."

Though his learning was broad, his politics was focused. His organizing activity was essentially aimed at the promotion of class consciousness among workers, race consciousness among Blacks in general and a higher level of liberating consciousness among all people, all framed in a program of cogent radicalism. As the foremost member of the Socialist Party in New York before World War One, he was of course strongly anti-capitalist. After the U.S. purchased the Danish West Indies from Denmark in 1917, he took great interest in local politics and worked with local leaders such as Rothschild Francis, Casper Holstein and others.

Harrison's wide-ranging influence has been neither appropriately credited nor adequately appreciated until recently. He was, first, a dominant figure in the "New Negro" movement of the last century. And as such, his influence has extended over a broad range of race-conscious leaders from Marcus Garvey to Malcolm X. At the same time, class-conscious African-American leaders from A. Phillip Randolph to Rev. Martin Luther King have been affected by Harrison's ideas and teachings in the advancement of their own movements. In both these African-American political traditions, Harrison's influence has been central and powerful.

Harrison's writings were published largely in journals, newspapers and magazines, and for that reason they have not been widely read over the years. Today, however, that situation has been remedied by the labors of the American scholar Jeffery B. Perry, who has collected and published in 2001 *A Hubert Harrison Reader*. At present Perry is at work on a two-volume biography of Harrison, which should go a long way toward securing Harrison's position as one of the foremost African-American leaders of the early twentieth century.

On December 17, 1927, Hubert Harrison died rather suddenly from complications related to appendicitis at the premature age of forty-four. Had he lived a full life, he might well have attained even greater recognition for his role in that turbulent period of American history between the great wars. All the same, there remains much to be learned, especially by the people of the Virgin Islands, about and from this remarkable man who began his life-journey at Estate Concordia, St. Croix.

Terence A. Todman was United States
Ambassador to a number of countries
during his long career, including
Denmark, Spain and Argentina

CHAPTER 36

TERENCE A. TODMAN:
AMBASSADOR EXTRAORDINAIRE

I AM ALWAYS a bit perplexed when I hear it said that our kids in the Virgin Islands are lacking in role models. I have compiled a list of outstanding individuals who hail from these shores, and I daresay that it would compare favorably with any area of comparable size in the entire country. And right at the top of that list is the name Terence A. Todman.

Terence Todman was born on St. Thomas on March 13, 1926, the son of Alphonso Todman and Rachael Callwood. He was educated in the islands, receiving his diploma in 1944. Just after graduation, he entered college at Inter-American University in Puerto Rico, but interrupted his studies when he was drafted into the Army in the final year of World War Two. He was commissioned a Second Lieutenant at the Army Officers School at Fort Benning, Georgia. During his service in Japan from 1945 to 1949, he learned Japanese and was effectively involved in the organization of the first elections in Japan in 1947 in the crucial, early post-war period. Already he was beginning to mark himself as a person of distinction; after he left Army service, he was inducted into the Hall of Fame of the Infantry School at Fort Benning in 1952.

Upon completion of his military service, Todman returned to the Caribbean, where he resumed his studies at Inter-American University and received a B.S. in Political Science in 1951, graduating summa cum laude. He went on to receive an M.P.A. in 1952 from Syracuse University in New York and then went on to American University in Washington, D.C.

Having completed his education, he married Doris Weston, also of

St. Thomas, and together they began their family, which ultimately produced four children—Terence, Jr., Patricia, Kathryn, and Michael.

Terence Todman was never willing to relegate education completely to his past, having received a number of honorary doctorates from various universities over the years, among them Colgate, Syracuse, Morgan State and Boston Universities. In addition, he served as a Member of the Board of Trustees at the University of the Virgin Islands for many years. He has also made contributions to various advisory boards at several prestigious universities, including Syracuse, Duke, and Georgetown.

During his early years, he developed a strong interest in international affairs while at the same time demonstrating an extraordinary ability in languages. This combination turned his attention toward the United States Foreign Service. In 1952, during the Truman presidency, he assumed a position in the Foreign Service in the State Department, where he remained for the duration of his career, distinguishing himself in the eyes of diplomatic leaders. It was at that time that he pushed an agenda at the United Nations for encouraging colonial nations to set timetables for independence, a program that paid rich rewards in the 1960s.

In 1969, Terence Todman received from President Richard Nixon his first appointment as a U.S. Ambassador, in this instance to Chad in North Africa, where he remained until 1972. It was there that his skills in diplomacy, international understanding and language abilities stood out markedly. In that regard he worked with France to assist against Libyan sponsored aggression toward Chad, giving that latter nation a period of relative calm in which to develop. His fluency in both French and Arabic made him ideally suited for that task.

At the end of that term he took over the top post at the U.S. Embassy in Guinea in West Africa, where he served from 1972 until 1974. At that time, Sekou Touré was in charge, promoting a strongly anti-America agenda. Todman's diplomacy went far in turning Touré around and reducing his hostility toward the U.S.

Under President Gerald Ford, he was named Ambassador to Costa

Rica in Central America from 1974–1977. His fluency in Spanish and his close familiarity with the Caribbean and South American regions, made his stay there another strong success, resulting in his appointment by President Jimmy Carter as U.S. Assistant Secretary of State for Western Hemisphere Affairs from 1977 to 1978. His name was being mentioned increasingly by national leaders for broader responsibilities.

While Assistant Secretary, he led a delegation to Cuba to negotiate a maritime boundary between Cuba and the U.S. In addition, he opened resident diplomatic channels with Castro and negotiated the return of U.S. property that had been seized during the Cuban Revolution. Finally, Todman was instrumental in the creation of an information program for the ratification of the Panama Canal Treaty. These major achievements qualified him for a major career advance.

In 1978 under President Jimmy Carter, he made the jump to a major European country as ambassador. Some regard this appointment as the high point of his diplomatic career. During this sojourn, he negotiated the U.S. use of crucial naval and air bases in Spain. Moreover, he oversaw the entrance of Spain into NATO. Both of these achievements boosted U.S. military strength in Europe during the crucial years of the Cold War. When the Socialists came to power in Spain in the early 1980s, President Reagan asked Todman to remain on as ambassador. He did so and responded by getting the Socialists to develop trust in the conservative Republican administration and to work with the United States effectively.

When Ronald Reagan was elected president in 1981, his later appointment of Todman as Ambassador to Denmark in 1983 had special significance. The Danes had held the Virgin Islands as a colony from 1671 to 1917, leaving behind certain cultural marks and traditions in the islands, to which Todman and other Virgin Islanders were the heirs. Todman quickly attained fluency in Danish and became an extremely popular and effective Ambassador until his term ended in 1988. During that term, Todman convinced the Danes to play more fully their security role in NATO, while working for better treatment of Greenland, where the

U.S. had bases. Not least he promoted his native land in his work for the return of colonial records to the Virgin Islands, as well as highlighting the virtues of the islands as a tourist destination.

In 1987, Todman received the crowning honor of his career when he was named Career Ambassador. He was the first African-American to ever receive that distinction and one of the very few of any ethnic group to be so honored. He holds this position with distinction to this day.

Terence Todman undertook his final ambassadorial appointment in 1989, this one from President George H. W. Bush, when he took up residence in the American Embassy in Buenos Aires, Argentina. His work there was of major importance. He succeeded, first, in blocking a German missile company from building missiles there for shipment to Middle Eastern countries. He also promoted privatization and helped move the Argentines away from non-aligned politics toward greater cooperation with the U.S. He served in that post with distinction until 1993, at which point he retired from active diplomatic life after 41 years of service to his country.

The U.S. Congress honored Ambassador Terence Todman in November of 1993 for his contributions to U.S. foreign affairs at a ceremony in Statuary Hall. He was recognized as having served the nation "with dignity, honor, and true professionalism." Though all of his awards and honors would be far too numerous to cite, here are a few of the more prestigious among them: the Department of State, Superior Service Award, 1966; Virgin Islands Medal of Honor, 1977; The Department of State's Distinguished Service Award, 1985; and The Presidential Meritorious Service Award, 1988. In addition, he has been decorated with the National Orders of the governments of Chad, Spain, Denmark and Argentina. To the end of his professional journey, he carried the coveted title of "Career Ambassador," an honor bestowed only on the very select few.

All of these things Todman accomplished at a time when less than two percent of the Foreign Service was minority. In that sense he was a trailblazer, a gate-opener, a point man. As America's first African-

American Ambassador, it would be no exaggeration to say that what Jackie Robinson did for Baseball, Terence Todman did for the Foreign Service though he would more than likely and quite characteristically make very little of that accomplishment.

Since the end of his ambassadorial service, he has remained extremely active. "I don't want to stand still," he has remarked. "Keep moving onward and upward," has been his advice to himself and to others. He continues to follow that advice, serving as a Board Member of the National Endowment for Democracy, which lends support and encouragement to various world organizations in the development of democracy on the level of the individual. As a member of the American Academy of Diplomacy, he has worked for the training for young people in the field of diplomatic service. For a time he worked with the Organization of American States in the attempt to develop sound government and human rights in Haiti, working in particular with former President Aristide. He remains an active member of the National Academy of Public Administration. His interest and participation in the issues of the world in 2009 are nothing short of astounding. When asked about the possibility of writing his memoirs, he responds that he is quite simply "too busy."

During his career Terence Todman served his country for more than four decades years, in six United States embassies, under six presidents. He mastered more than a half dozen languages (Arabic, Japanese, Spanish, French and Danish, in addition to his own native English and Virgin Islands English), became conversant with scores of different cultures, left his imprint on hundreds of important negotiations and was influential among countless leaders around the world. He remains active, energetic and vocal to this day, offering his expertise both here at home and abroad. Here is a man who effortlessly combines overwhelming achievement with understated graciousness; every Virgin Islander can be rightly proud of him.

Ansetta Muckle de Chabert was businesswoman, political activist
and beloved Crucian mother, known and loved far and wide
simply as "Miss Annie"

CHAPTER 37

MISS ANNIE DE CHABERT: A TRULY REMARKABLE WOMAN

OVER THE YEARS, these islands have produced a number of remarkable women—Rebekka Freundlich, Anna Heegaard, Mary "Queen Mary" Thomas, Evelyn Richardson, Marie Richards and Emma Francis—to mention only a few. Each of these women in her own way nourished and strengthened her people and her homeland. It is appropriate to add to this list the name of Ansetta Muckle de Chabert, better known to several generations of Crucians as "Miss Annie."

Ansetta Muckle was born on February 11, 1908 in Christiansted, St. Croix, Danish West Indies. Her parents were Ernest Muckle and Sarah Jeffers. Her father Ernest, who was a successful local business-man, seems to have exerted the stronger influence in her early development. The family lived in a modest dwelling on Smith Street around the corner from Alexander's office and warehouse. The family business, called *The Little Red Shop*, was located in Water Gut just to the west of the present Antilles Airboats.

According to reliable witnesses, Ernest Muckle was engaged in both fishing and business. In the morning he would go out in his boat with several other men to bring in the catch and then return to sell it, spending the rest of the day in his dry goods store. Young Ansetta spent many of her youthful days in that shop. Being both intelligent and energetic, she quickly learned the rudiments of business. While she was still a teenager, her father began to put her in charge of *The Little Red Shop* whenever he went out in his boat to fish. This arrangement taught her many valuable lessons—responsibility, initiative, hard work, and perhaps the most important of all, the importance of cooperation within the family framework. Mr. Muckle came to rely heavily on his young daughter and she in turn learned from him with each passing day.

It was in *The Little Red Shop* that Ansetta earned the name which she carried throughout her life. Mr. Muckle respected his daughter, not only for the love and affection which she showed him, but also for her dedication to his enterprise. For that reason, he insisted that his customers show her a similar respect by addressing her in the shop as "Miss Annie," even though she was still only a young girl. The name seemed so fitting that Mr. Muckle himself took to calling her that, and so the name stuck for life.

In the 1920s Mr. Muckle purchased a Model-T Ford, which he used to transport and sell merchandise in the country areas. Miss Annie often accompanied him on those trips, learning all the while of the vagaries of business and coming to know more and more of her people and her native island. These early experiences cannot be overestimated as an influence in the development of the remarkable business and political acumen that she displayed later in her life.

During these same years, she became acquainted with Ralph de Chabert, a well-educated native of St. Croix who had been a leader in the labor union fight for higher wages along with D. Hamilton Jackson and others from 1916 to 1922. Although some years her senior, Ralph saw in Miss Annie the dynamic partner whom he needed to realize his own life ambitions. And so they were married in 1929, beginning a partnership which was to lead them both to remarkable accomplishments in their community.

During the 1930s Ralph's stature as a community leader continued to grow. He edited his own newspaper, *The Tribune*, from 1922 until 1936 and then won a seat in the Municipal Council where he introduced the Homestead Act. Later he served a number of years as Tax Assessor. Miss Annie was equally active. She opened a general store called *De Chabert's Fashions* on King Street in Christiansted, where she worked long hours as both the manager and seamstress. Her boundless energy and dedication made the venture successful and thereby supplemented the family income. During this same period she bore her husband five children and created a happy, healthy home for them.

In the early 1940s the family's hard work and thrift began to pay dividends. The couple purchased Estate Rosegate and Olive, a thirty-five acre farm, and went into the dairy business. Several years later in 1945, they purchased Estates Jerusalem, Hope, and Blessing from their friend Joseph Alexander. On these southside estates they expanded their dairy operation, unmindful that someday those holdings would become the location of one of the world's largest oil refineries.

In February of 1955, the family fortunes took a turn for the worse. Ralph de Chabert departed this life at the age of 65. The burden of all the family's responsibilities—business, educating the children, politics and the like—fell squarely on the shoulders of Miss Annie. And she rose magnificently to the task.

Miss Annie continued to acquire and renovate property. In 1965, she met Mr. Leon Hess and sold him a large tract of land that became the location of the giant Hess Oil Refinery. That transaction led to the immediate development of the Virgin Islands economy, bringing prosperity to many. Wisely, she invested the capital from that sale in the development of St. Croix and the Virgin Islands. A large shopping center and other land developments, both of which provide numerous jobs for the people and revenue for the government, were among the last of her undertakings. It was those actions that provided the spark for the most important economic advance of the Virgin Islands economy of the 20th century.

In politics, Miss Annie was a dedicated Democrat, serving her party for many years in innumerable ways. She was its treasurer from 1956–64. During that same time she was perennially the Head Fund Raiser, a true dynamo of energy and ideas. Her party in turn paid her the highest tribute by naming her *National Committee Woman* for the period 1960–72, during which time she attended national conventions and became known to such prominent national figures as Hubert H. Humphrey and

Lyndon B. Johnson. It was a giant leap forward from her childhood working as her father's assistant in the *Little Red Shop*.

Miss Annie was a great believer in the power of education, having been denied access to it in her youth. She served from 1964 to 1967 as Vice Chairman of the V.I. Board of Education. Her interest in that field, however, went far beyond the administrative level. Above all, she inspired the idea of education in her own children, producing a lawyer, a doctor, and three educators. In her later years, she busied herself carrying the same message of inspiration to her grandchildren. Her belief in education was, in fact, so profound that she was willing to help almost anyone who showed a sincere interest. Time and time again she would help pay a poor child's tuition or slip money into the hand of a college student who lacked sufficient financial means to continue in his or her studies.

Health care was another of her primary interests, and her participation here is indeed impressive. She was a long time member of the American Red Cross and a charter member of the St. Croix Community Blood Bank Center. In addition, she served on the Charles Harwood Memorial Hospital Auxiliary for many years. She also dedicated a great deal of energy to the Caribbean Mental Health Association, whose regional meetings she often attended. Beyond these solid accomplishments, however, Miss Annie was herself a healer, as anyone who ever benefitted from her care can attest. Her bush teas and other traditional remedies, as well as her strong dedication to and reverence for life, brought strength and health back to more than one sufferer. Likewise, her activities in the area of community service are too numerous to name because she usually acted informally and unofficially with no desire for recognition or reward.

Finally, Miss Annie was always active in church affairs. A dedicated Episcopalian, she brought to religious life the same unconquerable spirit that characterized other facets of her life. Decorating the church, landscaping the rectory grounds, acting as godmother in baptismal ceremonies, arranging weddings and consoling the bereaved were but a few of the endeavors into which she threw herself with an energy and dedication that few could equal. In November, 1970, she married Father Seymour Clarke and moved into St. John's rectory, withdrawing somewhat from business and politics in order to dedicate herself more fully to family and religious life.

Miss Annie was a people person. She cultivated friendships among people from the island's diverse groups—Hispanics, Eastern Caribbean people, Whites; her friends knew no limits because color, race, ethnicity, class and wealth made no difference to her. She accepted people for who they were, as they were. On a trip through Europe near the end of her life, she passed through a half dozen countries and made numerous friends, speaking only English. In truth, she spoke from the heart and she was always understood.

Miss Annie was thought of by some as a rich lady. The truth is that in the last years of her life she literally gave everything away. She made loans to locals to pay off mortgages, to begin businesses, to address family crises and the like, usually never seeing a return on her kindness. To her children she gave everything before she passed from this life, to facilitate their entry into business in the form of a large shopping center and land development, which, by the way, turned out to be the largest locally owned business on the island. This became not only a means of employment for thousands of her people and source of significant revenues for the government but also an object of pride for many who were at the time witnessing their economy being flooded by outside capital and development and Crucians sometimes being pushed into the background.

In January of 1976, Miss Annie suffered a sudden, massive stroke, and several days later she passed from this life in the Charles Harwood Hospital. A stunned Crucian population turned out in unprecedented numbers to pay last respects to this grand lady at her funeral and interment at the St. John's Episcopal Church in Christiansted. It was a sad, solemn day in an atmosphere of disbelief.

Such were the external facts of this grand lady's life. But it is more important to know that to the very last day of her conscious life, Miss Annie remained what she had always been—a truly unique, remarkable person, who was totally dedicated to her children, to her people and to the principle that right conduct will always prevail in the final analysis. Anyone who ever met Miss Annie must know that death did not still her indomitable spirit.

Ole Vinding was born Danish but became a Crucian at heart, admired by many

CHAPTER 38

OLE VINDING:
A DANE WHO CAME TO STAY

SOME EVENING in the next couple of weeks, Ole Vinding will close the door to Ole's Deli in Sunny Isle Shopping Center for the last time. He is retiring after thirty-five years in the restaurant business. "I'm tired," he said recently, "and I need a little rest."

Ole first set foot on St. Croix in 1967 as a young pastry chef fresh out of Denmark. Born in Copenhagen, he was apprenticed at a young age to a baker. That job accustomed him to early hours, long days and hard work. The years 1964–65 he spent in New York where he worked in the Danish pavilion at the World Fair. After completing an apprenticeship as a pastry chef in Sweden, he traveled to California where he helped open a restaurant and a bakery. Along the way, he met Mr. Armstrong of the Buccaneer Hotel of St. Croix, who, impressed by the young Dane, hired him as a pastry chef for the Buccaneer Hotel on St. Croix. His destiny was forged in that moment.

After a short stint at the Buccaneer and the former Top Hat Restaurant in Christiansted, he started Ole's Deli in 1970 in the newly opened Sunny Isle Shopping Center. It is a testament to his hard work and tenacity that his is the only business that has survived from that time until now. "I've seen them come and go over the years," he said, "and now it's my turn."

Ole's Deli has been unique in St. Croix in many ways. It has been one place where you could expect to meet the entire spectrum of St. Croix's rich multicultural population every day—Crucians, Hispanics, Continentals, Texans from Hovensa, folks from every island in the Caribbean and sailors of a dozen nationalities off the oil tankers. Dozens of languages and dialects filled the open-air deli on a daily basis. It was no one's home turf and everyone's home turf at the same time. People of all kinds rubbed shoulders there easily, comfortably. And that was Ole's own creation, his own unique style, his contribution to our island.

Over the years, Ole's became something of a local institution. It was a place to see and be seen, to pick up on the latest "mellay" over a cup of coffee with a friend, to have a hot paté or Johnny cake on the run or simply enjoy a cold beer with the guys in the evening after work. In that role, Ole has now served three generations of loyal customers. "Mothers bring in their kids to say hello and get a chicken leg," he says with no little pride. "I get them all at one time or another."

In his service to the people of St. Croix, Ole has become a familiar figure, a regular part of the landscape in the lives of many, all decked out in his checkered Danish baker's pants and double-breasted white vest, all topped off by a red handkerchief around his neck. For many years, locals got a real kick out of his wooden shoes. But those "clogs" never prevented him from moving about the Deli with speed and dedication, stopping only momentarily to take a draw on his famous corn-cob pipe or chat with a customer. Many's the Crucian who remembers their fascination when, as a child, they saw for the first time this curious "Dane man" flip burgers and roll Johnny cake dough with the best of them.

But what really set Ole apart from the crowd was his polite manner and his humble demeanor. He treated everyone who came into his establishment—young and old, black and white, local and off-islander, rich and poor—with respect and courtesy, and he invariably got that back in return. "Ole watches his pennies," said a longtime customer, "but he's a good man." A good man indeed.

"I have loved this job," he reminisced a few weeks ago. "It's a small place but it's been mine and I have been able to make it into what I always wanted—a place where people can get good food in a friendly setting. And I have met some great people here over the years." One of them was lovely Gallowsbarian Carmelita Larsen, now his wife of 27 years.

Along the way, Ole became an American citizen and perhaps more importantly, an adopted Crucian, in spite of his reluctant Danish accent. "It seems like only yesterday that I was starting out in business here. How the time has flown past, especially these past few weeks! But the years have been good to me here. It has been a good life I have had here, among good people. I want to thank each and every one of them for their business and for their kindness over the years."

And Ole has been good for St. Croix. For many folks, Sunny Isle Shopping Center will be a little less like home away from home with Ole no longer standing behind the counter in the open-air Deli looking out onto the Plaza. What is certain is that it will be a good long time before another like Ole Vinding comes this way.

LANGUAGE

Die ben noc al Sommig Jaar geleeden, dat ons
a Ka Leveer jender een Creol Psalm-Bocki, dat
Jender a Sal Kan help vor Sing wanneer ons
hab ons verSamlingen, Sooveel as van jender
Ka leer vor lees, en vor mak gebruk van die
ookal, wanneer jender Sett na bin jender Hoes
Sonder, ~~Sonder~~ vor wees na Werk, vor Kom be
Kent met die Psalmen (of Liederen.)

Handwitten sample of a Negerlollands (Dutch Creole) text
from an 18th century manuscript

CHAPTER 39

TOWARD A LANGUAGE HISTORY OF THE VIRGIN ISLANDS

INTRODUCTION

THE PRESENT PAPER will attempt to present an introduction to a language history of these islands. As such it will be primarily descriptive and not analytical, diachronic and not synchronic, and general in scope, not specific. It will attempt to pull together what little is known on the subject at this point in hopes of indicating the direction in which research might be focused.[1]

The natural language abilities of Virgin Islanders have been remarked upon by more than one observer. "Virgin Islanders are very imitative, adaptable and self-possessed, and a St. Thomian or a Crucian has the ability to lose himself in a London crowd, or on a San Francisco waterfront, and to become for the moment one of the people of that section. His background has made it easy for him to learn languages and he avails himself of every opportunity to acquire some alien tongue, much to the wonderment of foreigners who are often astonished at meeting natives spouting fragments of German, French, Spanish, Russian, Dutch and Danish."[2] And while a certain amount of that can be laid to hyperbole, there remains a nugget of truth. A perusal of the historical sources immediately adds support to this claim. In the middle of the 19th century, for example, the well known British novelist Anthony Trollope visited St. Thomas and commented on the linguistic abilities of the people of that island: "In the first place, all languages seem alike to them. One hears English, French, German, and Spanish spoken all around one, and apparently it is indifferent which. The waiters seem to speak them all."[3] The Moravian missionary C. G. A. Oldendorp observed a similar linguistic situation during his visit to the same islands earlier, in the 1760s.[4] In truth, then, the existence of multilingualism as a hallmark of Virgin Islands culture extends further back into the past than is commonly recognized.

But what were the major languages that have been spoken here? How long were they spoken? How did they interrelate during their periods of parallel existence? To what extent have they survived into present times and what are their individual and collective influences in these islands today? These are the most important of the questions to which this introductory essay will address itself.

It is curious that we know least about those languages that were spoken here the longest. By conservative estimate, Amerindian languages were in use in these islands for no less than five thousand years, beginning with the so-called Paleo-Indians (i.e., also called the Aceramic or Archaic Indians) and extending through the periods of the Island Arawaks (Taino or Sub-Taino according to some) and Island Caribs, well into the 16th century. The sad fact of the matter is that we have no direct documentation, written or otherwise, for those languages in the Virgin Islands. What we know has been gleaned from other sources from other areas.[5]

Paleo-Indians

It appears that these so-called Paleo-Indians were the first humans to inhabit these islands; the present level of archaeological knowledge would place them here as early as the 3rd millennium B.C. Theirs was a gathering-foraging culture. They lived near the sea, used fire but had no known ceramic tradition. Furthermore, they have left no evidence that they possessed writing. We can only assume that, like other known peoples at that level of cultural development, they must have employed symbolic communication—most certainly spoken language and perhaps sign language. We might further infer that their language was related to that of the peoples in the areas whence they originally sprang. And finally, it would appear that this language, or languages, would have been in use for a period of perhaps 3,000 years, from the third millennium B.C. to the first. Further than this we cannot venture with any surety at all.[6]

Island Arawaks

Sometime toward the end of the first millennium B.C., a massive migration into the Antillean islands by peoples from South America took place. In a few centuries the newcomers had colonized all of the major islands of the Greater and Lesser Antilles. Though they came over many years, with representatives perhaps of several ethnic groups and certainly different cultures, they spoke a language of the Arawakan family.[7] As a consequence of that identification, they have inherited the popular name "Arawak," though some specialists refer to them as Tainos.

Over the next thousand years or so, these Island Arawaks gradually displaced, through both conflict and assimilation, to one degree or another, their less advanced Archaic predecessors. Based on primitive agriculture, hunting, fishing, foraging and limited trade, the centers of their culture took root and thrived, particularly in the larger islands and in the Greater Antilles. And of course, their language developed parallel to these events.

The archaeological evidence indicates that St. Croix was for many centuries a thriving Island Arawak center, communicating culturally and economically with the larger Taino centers to the west, especially Puerto Rico, Hispaniola and possibly even Cuba.[8] Although there is no evidence that they possessed a system of writing, they did leave carvings in stone (petroglyphs) at Salt River on St. Croix and at Reef Bay on St. John. These glyphs show a close correspondence with similar carvings in other Arawak-settled islands, Puerto Rico being one example. Even though we have no direct material evidence for their language in the Virgin Islands, we can safely infer from other evidence that a variety of Island Arawak was spoken here for perhaps as long as 1,500 years.

What then is the evidence for a statement such as the foregoing? Toward the end of the 15th century, the first Europeans arrived in the West Indies. Within three decades, this original migration, at first a mere trickle, became a flood. Contact between Mediterranean and Antillean cultures occurred at all points of habitation in the islands. Enjoying a long written tradition first in Latin, and more recently in the national vernaculars, the Iberians recorded a great deal of information, including linguistic information, about the latter, especially in the islands of the Greater Antilles. Writers such as Bartolomé de las Casas, Gonzalo Fernández de Oviedo, Antonio de Herrera y Tordesillas, Dr. Diego Alvárez Chanca, Bernal Diaz, Ferdinand Columbus, Ramón Pané and others experienced the language and culture of the various Arawak peoples firsthand and recorded various aspects of them.[9] And though they did not record all that they might have, they did in effect, leave us a considerable body of knowledge of that language in the Caribbean.

Unfortunately, we have no material of this type taken directly from the Virgin Islands Islands at that same time. Nevertheless, this corpus of the other islands can be viewed as valid, though indirectly so, for the cultures and peoples of St. Croix since the archaeological record shows that a very close cultural relationship existed between the Island Arawaks of these islands and those of the Greater Antilles, for which the Spanish sources are abundant.[10]

Island-Caribs

The people whom Columbus encountered on November 13, 1493, at Salt River, St. Croix, were Island Caribs. It is a reasonable estimate that they had migrated out of South America some time after the Arawaks, arriving in St. Croix perhaps in the late 14th/early 15th century; this dating is established on one part loose inference, one part guesswork. However that may be, the residents of St. Croix continued their incursions into the Taino centers of the Greater Antilles for the rest of that century.[11]

The linguistic situation of the Island Caribs was more complex than that of the Arawaks. Again we are heirs to no direct linguistic evidence for the Virgin Islands. Like the Arawaks, they had no known system of writing and, again, what we do know about them has been gleaned from European sources. But in this case it was the French—for the most part priests such as Breton, DuTertre, Labat and Pelleprat—who lived and worked among the Caribs, leaving a substantial record of their culture and language.[12] However, there is no reason not to rely on these sources if we are to create a linguistic history of the Virgin Islands. To put it another way, we might justifiably assume that the Carib population of St. Croix possessed a linguistic inventory similar in essential respects to that of the Caribs in Dominica and Martinique.

The languages of the Island-Caribs were spoken on St. Croix for perhaps as long as a century and a half, that is from the early 15th century until around 1515, at which time the Caribs were driven from that island by Spanish military pressure, principally from nearby Puerto Rico. The Island Caribs left no known specific linguistic evidence on St Croix; what we know of their linguistic situation is derived from records created in the Windward Islands, principally Martinique, Dominica and Guadeloupe.[13]

Douglas Taylor is of the opinion that Island-Caribs was essentially not Carib at all but rather a form of the Island Arawak language which the invading Caribs acquired through the many Taino women whom they had captured over the years and taken as wives. Children of these unions spoke their "mother tongue" with, of course, influences from Karina.[14] This linguistic situation must have evolved in much the same manner as the German-speaking Franks adopted the Gallo-Romance of their Gallic wives, the latter tongue evolving over time into what came to be called the French language. A variety of Karina itself, or at least its lexicon, was kept alive by the men, that is, the warrior caste, as a secret, specialized "war language" in pidgin form. Locally, this linguistic state of affairs prevailed primarily on St. Croix, as St. Thomas, St. John and the other islands in the Virgin archipelago to the north remained largely uninhabited until European settlement began in earnest in the mid-17th century.

The Island Caribs abandoned St. Croix sometime around 1515, retreating to the safety of the more rugged mountainous islands of Dominica and Martinique, where they would remain an independent, if culturally penetrated and declining, force until into the early 18th century. St. Croix and the Virgin Islands for the next century, until 1635, remained essentially devoid of permanent indigenous voices, save for those of flibustiers, pirates, Spanish fishermen, Caribs in passing war parties and the occasional "stranded" outcast.

EUROPEAN LANGUAGES

The age of European expansion and the rise of the sea-borne empires carried the languages of that continent to all parts of the world. For the next four to five hundred years, several of those European languages—Spanish, French, English, Danish and Dutch, for the most part—dominated the linguistic landscape of these islands.

Spanish

The Spanish language has played a major role in the modern history of these islands. Although early Spanish explorers gave many of them their names, the islands remained little more than loosely controlled frontier outposts in that early colonial period. In 1650, the surging French finally drove a small Spanish garrison out of Santa Cruz, established a permanent colony and renamed the place "Ste. Croix." And in 1672, the Danes established a settlement in St. Thomas, effectively ending Spanish hegemony in the Virgin archipelago.

In spite of this loss of territory, the geographical proximity of Puerto Rico and its economic importance dictated that the Spanish language would continue to be an important force in local culture. Trade and shipping between the islands, for instance, remained dynamic and vital throughout colonial times. Additionally, human migrations moved in both directions between the jurisdictions: slaves from time to time escaped from bondage to the safety of free colored settlements in Catholic Puerto Rico to the west and revolutions and wars periodically sent waves of Spanish-speaking immigrants into these islands, principally to commercially minded St. Thomas.

In the late 19th century, well after Emancipation, Spanish-speaking laborers from Vieques and Culebra began to appear in St. Croix.[15] In the 1920s, the trickle became a wave, breaking first over the western part of the island. Subsequent spurts occurred during World War II and during the industrialization phase of the late 1960s. After the Puerto Ricans came Santo Domingans, Cubans and Colombians. It has been estimated, conservatively perhaps, that by the 1970s, Spanish-speakers made up some 35% of the population of St. Croix, considerably less in the other two islands. With them came Hispanic culture in the form of the language itself, musical traditions, print matter, television, and radio, all principally from Puerto Rico. Bilingualism, especially among the Hispanic immigrants, thereafter became widespread.

French

French has undergone an equally checkered and interesting development here. First, it was the primary language of the several thousand inhabitants who struggled to develop St. Croix when it was officially French, from 1650 to 1734.[16] Most of them departed the island for St. Domingue (later Haiti) in 1696, leaving behind little more than a handful of place names (e.g., *Bassin*, Christiansted; *Pointe du Sable*, Sandy Point; *Rivière Salée*, Salt River, etc.) But the French tradition did not end there. The Haitian Revolution, as well as subsequent political turmoil in that country, regularly sent thousands of Francophones fleeing to all parts of the Caribbean, not least to St. Thomas, in the late 18th century and throughout the 19th century. By the mid-1800s, a considerable number of the 7,000 Catholics on St. Thomas were French in background. In 1859, a visiting Italian priest noted that "on St. Thomas, almost everyone speaks three or four languages, including English, French, Spanish and Creole. . . ."[17]

The French community on St. Thomas received unexpected reinforcements in the persons of resourceful fishermen and farmers from the island of St. Barts in the 1860s and 1870s. These fisher-folk settled in the area that was originally known as Carenage, today as Frenchtown; they spoke a variety of archaic French, apparently of northwestern, maritime Gallo-Romance background.[18] The farmers, on the other hand, settled on the northside of the island in the Hull Bay area; coming from another section of St. Barts, they spoke a French Creole, closely related to the Antillean (ka) variety spoken in Guadeloupe.

Curiously enough, the members of the two communities, though from the same island of origin and of the same ethnic background, considered themselves to be two separate, distinct groups for many years. Moreover, both communities remained relatively isolated within the larger St. Thomas society, both culturally and linguistically, until the last several decades. Emigration and acculturation in recent years have both served to diminish the number of French speakers on St. Thomas, as well as their cultural presence.

English

Although English is the official language of the U. S. Virgin Islands today, its origins here were modest indeed. English-speakers from St. Kitts and Barbados attempted to plant settlements in St. Croix, first in the 1630s and later in the period 1642–1650; on both occasions they were driven out by Spaniards.[19] Once again, after the last Frenchmen departed in 1696, English settlers drifted back into St. Croix from Anguilla and the Northern Virgins. In fact, when the Danes took possession of the island in 1734, they encountered several hundred impoverished English farmers already established on the island.[20] From that time down to the present, St. Croix has maintained a significant English-speaking tradition.

During the colonial period, that tradition continued to flourish and grow, first and foremost because the economy of the then Danish West Indies developed and maintained strong ties with English and North American markets. Consequently, English speaking planters, merchants and seamen were ever increasingly in evidence in both St. Thomas and

St. Croix.[21] Moreover, in the first two decades of the 19th century, the Danish West Indies was twice occupied by Great Britain (1801–1802 and 1807–1815), leading inevitably to an enhanced English influence.

As Great Britain became the major international power of the 19th century, its language grew in prestige, attracting numerous erstwhile Danish, Dutch, and Creole speakers into its service. By the middle of the century, English had everywhere in the Danish West Indies become the language of choice—by dint of English commerce, shipping, military power, educational and religious institutions, and general culture, forcing the Danish language and Dutch Creole increasingly into the background.

The final triumph of English came in 1917 when the Danish West Indies passed into the hands of the United States, becoming the Virgin Islands of the United States. Swarms of northern Naval administrators, government officials, educators, missionaries, and, eventually, business people channeled the linguistic traditions of the islands in the direction of an emerging American standard. At the same time, Danish rapidly disappeared; St. Thomas French became increasingly isolated; the moribundity of Dutch Creole was quickened; and a full-scale assault was mounted against Virgin Islands English Creole. At the same time, the simultaneous American possession of both Puerto Rico and the U.S. Virgin Islands provided the immediate cause, along with subsequent Naval and New Deal rehabilitation and development programs, for the massive immigration of Spanish speakers from Eastern Puerto Rico, Vieques and Culebra into the Virgin Islands, principally St. Croix.

Danish

Danish was introduced permanently into the Caribbean area in 1672 when Denmark colonized St. Thomas. That small but energetic Scandinavian colonial power extended its dominion over St. John in 1718 by simple possession and over St. Croix in 1734 by purchase.[22] The immigration of Danes to the tropics, however, was never linguistically significant. True, they held onto the reins of government and military power tightly. And a few merchants and planters carved out places for themselves. But the fact remains that these few Danes remained ever a minority in their own small dominions.

These demographic circumstances, along with Danish inclination to remain content within the long cultural shadows cast by the two dominant Northern European Germanic languages—German and English—accounts for the failure of the language of Denmark to send down any permanent roots into the willing West Indian soil. Under Danish sovereignty in these islands, Dutch on St. Thomas and English in St. Croix flourished among the planters and merchants throughout colonial times, while their respective Creole progeny—Virgin Islands Dutch Creole and Virgin Islands English Creole—thrived even more so, among the laboring classes. To this order of things, the Danish authorities accommodated themselves without apparent discomfort or complaint.

Dutch

The Dutch had been active in colonial America for well over a century before the appearance of the latecomer Danes, first in Pernambuco in Brazil and later in the Caribbean Sea. The aggressiveness of collective Dutch commerce and the resourcefulness of individual Dutch merchants provided the model and the impetus for the first Danish colonial efforts in the early 17th century. It is therefore not surprising that Dutchmen would be present in significant numbers in the first Danish colonies.

In matters of language, these Dutch reveal themselves sharing a linguistic trait with the Danes, namely a willingness to embrace one or several dominant foreign languages—primarily English and German—in order to satisfy the requirement of expediency in matters of trade. So it was in the Danish West Indies. The Dutch language was always present but never forcefully or aggressively so, in sharp contrast to English. Consequently, the significance of the Dutch heritage in the Danish West Indies is to be found not in the survival of the Dutch language itself, but in the parallel development of a powerful, vital Dutch-based Creole, spoken widely among the African population of the islands, originating in St. Thomas and St. John, and subsequently being introduced into St. Croix. Long after the Dutch language ceased to be heard in the Danish islands, its prodigious offspring, Dutch Creole, continued to thrive as the first language for the vast majority of the islands' Black population as well as for many of the Whites.

AFRICAN LANGUAGES

The original African populations of the Danish West Indies during the colonial period owed their origins to that broad swath of tropical West Africa known as Guinea, stretching between the Senegal River in the north to the Bight of Biafra to the south and east. Over a hundred thousand Africans of various nations in this region were introduced into the Danish West Indies between c. 1673 and 1807 by the incalculable evil of the Atlantic slave trade. In spite of the severity of that experience, many of those resourceful people survived the experience, bringing with them an impressive measure of their cultures, including, of course, their languages.

Wherever African place names and ethnic designations survive in Danish shipping, missionary, and government documents, it is possible to trace the origins of certain individuals and groups to specific areas in Africa. From our limited experience and data, it can be tentatively stated that many of the enslaved Africans in the Danish West Indies might trace their cultural and linguistic roots to the Niger-Congo group of the Congo-Kordofanian family of languages (e.g., Twi, Ga-Adagme and Ewe among others).[23] As only one example, the documentation left by the Moravian missionary C. G. A. Oldendorp shows a positive correlation between the African languages which that missionary identified through interviews with Africans in the Danish islands and those of the Kwa category within the Niger-Congo group.[24] Oldendorp and other Moravian sources have had a good deal to say about the Amina people and others who belong in general to the Akan group (Twi) within the larger Kwa grouping. Using information of this kind it is altogether possible to reconstruct a profile of the linguistic background of the African peoples of the Virgin Islands.

Members of the Amina nation, as well as the Akwambo, played a central role in the St. John Revolt of 1733–34.[25] In the coordinated military action taken by the leaders, it is nearly certain that the African languages in question remained very much alive and in use, figuring prominently in the degree to which the African insurgents succeeded. There are numerous similar suggestions in the historical record that these same languages and perhaps others may have remained alive, if only marginally, in the small but persistent Maroon communities on St. John and St. Croix.[26]

The prospects for the long-term survival of these African languages were, however, not good, as various societal forces were aligned against them. First, and ironically enough, the official termination of the Danish slave trade (1803) effectively ended the arrival of native speakers of the African languages in question. Second, the plantation system itself was inimical to heterogeneity among the African labor force, that is, the diverse languages of the various ethnic groups remained under strong pressure to give way to a single plantation lingua franca. Third, the origin and growth of that lingua franca—one or the other of the Creole languages—militated against the retention and use of multiple languages among the laborers, resulting, in the eyes of the authorities, in a more pragmatic, stable linguistic homogeneity. And last, the lifestyle that lent itself most effectively to the retention of African languages and Africanisms—the Maroon lifestyle—was indeed a marginal and difficult one, rendered all the more so by the limited geographical size of our islands.

CREOLE LANGUAGES

So it is that we catch only faint traces of the survival of African languages through colonial times. Nevertheless, these systems manifested their influence in a manner perhaps not readily apparent to the casual observer. Pidgin and Creole languages have sprung into being in many diverse parts of the world when members of differing ethnic and linguistic communities have come into contact and established the need to communicate, most usually for purposes of trade of one sort or another. Without belaboring the point, it should be added that the languages of the communities of those encounters become the "parents," so to speak, of the new linguistic system, the "offspring."

This latter is most usually termed a "pidgin," a language system with a minimal, highly utilitarian stock of words and a reduced, compact set of grammatical rules. It exists for a specific purpose and it ordinarily is *not* identified as the first language of any speech community. Pidgins endure as long as they serve a communication function for those who ordinarily speak other languages. A Creole language may form very quickly from a pidgin environment. As it does so, it becomes identified with a specific speech community, and therefore its scope broadens considerably. Its vocabulary grows significantly, usually rapidly, and new morpho-syntactic forms emerge to meet the communication needs of a larger, more complex, socially evolving group of speakers.[27]

Creole languages have appeared in various parts of the world but circumstances in the Caribbean region in the early colonial period were particularly favorable to their genesis and rapid growth. The long history of the Virgin Islands has, in fact, produced three Creole languages—a French, a Dutch, and an English Creole.

French Creole

Our native French Creole originated in St. Croix in the early 1650s. During that decade several hundred, relatively poor Frenchmen arrived from the French islands in order to try their hand at tobacco farming. Over the next twenty years the economy shifted its focus to sugar, resulting in the rapid introduction of Africans, primarily from the area of the Senegal River basin, as enslaved laborers. Thereafter, a French-based Creole developed rather rapidly. Although we do not have a great deal of firsthand information on this language, it is safe to assume that it closely resembled the much commented upon French Creoles of the larger islands of Guadeloupe, Martinique, Dominica, St. Lucia, etc.[28] It is from these sources that we draw most of our present information.

This Crucian French Creole vanished almost as abruptly as it had appeared. In 1696, the French Crucians loaded their goods and slaves on vessels and sailed to St. Domingue, taking with them an emerging Creole culture and language, leaving behind a few structures, some stray cattle and the name "Ste. Croix."

Dutch Creole

The destiny of Dutch Creole has been strikingly different from the French. In the first place, it was born in St. Thomas in the 1670s on the bases of the linguistic interactions between the numerically superior Dutch planters (among the Europeans) and the newly arrived Africans. Over the next several decades, the emerging "Dutch Creole" became the "lingua franca" of St. Thomas, spoken by anyone and everyone with permanent ties to the island, slave and free, Black and White alike. When St. John was settled, the creole quickly spread there. And later, after 1734, it extended its territory to St. Croix, but there it met with competition in the form of the English Creole spoken by the enslaved laborers of the small English population already settled there, as well as by the groups of enslaved laborers subsequently brought in during the years that followed by immigrating English planters from other islands, in particular Antigua, St. Kitts, Nevis, and Barbados.

Virgin Islands Dutch Creole stands unique as the first Creole language—depending of course on just how one defines Creole languages!—to have been fully committed to writing as early as the mid-18th century. This was largely the work of German-speaking, Pietistic, Moravian Missionaries, and to a lesser extent Danish Lutheran, missionaries. The fact that the language, Dutch-based Creole, spoken by their intended charges was partially intelligible to them must have been crucial to their decision to undertake such an ambitious enterprise in the first place. It should also be noted that many native speakers used it as a medium of written, as well as spoken, communication.[29]

Over the next century, the German missionaries all learned to speak the Creole as a prerequisite for evangelizing among the Blacks and for making a living in the Danish islands. So important was the Creole to their work that they translated the Bible and numerous other religious works into their written version of the Dutch Creole.[30] Danish Lutheran missionaries later undertook a similar project. Just as Dutch Creole was a *sine qua non* for the prospective missionary, so it became the same for the proselytized as they entered the faith. As the mission grew in importance then, so did the language. This dynamic symbiosis remained vital and productive for as long as religion remained the exclusive local institution that recognized the humanity of the enslaved.

It would appear that the Dutch Creole attained its fullest power and vitality in the first two decades of the 19th century. Thereafter it began a slow, steady decline, under the influence of competition from a rapidly emerging English Creole, strong currents of immigration, and economic decline and eventual stagnation. But perhaps most deleterious was the perceived association of the language with slavery, especially in light of British Emancipation in 1834, some 14 years *before* Emancipation in the Danish islands. Additionally, the immigration of English Creole-speaking immigrants from the Eastern Caribbean from the post-apprenticeship period in the early 1840s down to the present time contributed mightily to the ultimate domination of English Creole over Dutch Creole.

The decline of Dutch Creole was very much in evidence in the mid-19th century.[31] That decline continued apace through the end of the century, with its use being increasingly restricted to countryside and recess areas, and particularly to St. John. The transfer of the islands to the United States in 1917 and the general enthusiasm for Americanization drove the final nail in the coffin; moribund and lacking a new generation of native speakers, the language gradually expired, its last native speaker, according to the best informed sources, passing away in the 1980s.

ENGLISH CREOLE

As has already been mentioned, the origins of Virgin Islands English Creole can be traced to St. Croix in the early 18th century (c. 1715–1730s), when English squatters and a few of their slaves drifted into the island while it was still officially French though abandoned and not yet Danish.[32] The western section of the island has in fact always been associated with this tradition, perhaps giving rise to the particularism and "distinctiveness" of the "Westend" that survives down to this day.

During the first century of Danish hegemony over these islands, the English Creole maintained a stable presence and a slow, if not spectacular, growth. The Creole's development depended in large measure on uninterrupted ownership of plantations by English speaking planters, as well as the general use of the English language, in some form or the other (i.e., Irish, Scots and English), by estate functionaries. The historical record shows that these conditions did exist in a number of areas on St. Croix through the 18th and into the 19th century. Additionally, Africans in involuntary servitude continued to arrive from "Guinea" well into the first decade of the 19th century, providing the other linguistic ingredient, the African element. By the middle of the 19th century, perhaps even somewhat before, this rapidly growing English Creole was well on its way to replacing the older Dutch Creole, for reasons already commented upon above. It might be surmised that this period of transition was one of widespread bilingualism involving the two Creoles. However that may be, the English Creole was definitely in the ascendancy.[33]

The effect of Americanization on Virgin Islands English Creole (VIEC) was similar to the effect on Dutch Creole, though with less extreme and immediate results. Afforded low social status, VIEC fell under attack by educators, missionaries, and bureaucrats in the various departments of the new military and later civilian authority. Rather than attempting to reach Virgin Islanders through the medium of the Creole, as the Moravians had done over two centuries previously, the North American mandarins sought to replace "defective local speech" with "good English."

But that was not all. With the growth of travel and tourism and the North American discovery of tropical real estate, VIEC speakers found themselves rather abruptly face to face with hundreds and then thousands of English speaking Americans. The earliest American administrative authorities had made American English the language of the government and the schools; soon it became the standard of the market place as well. Not far behind came the same media revolution that swept the United States in the 1950s and 1960s, bringing a flood of the latest American cultural and linguistic practices.

The invasion was not all one way. Virgin Islanders themselves traveled to the United States mainland to study, to serve in the military, to seek temporary or permanent employment. Many eventually returned home. With them they carried the inevitable linguistic influences. The sum total of all this was linguistic change that was both rapid and far-reaching. In time—it is difficult to say exactly when—Virgin Islands English Creole all but vanished. In the short span of just several generations, most native born Virgin Islanders have come to speak what might be best termed Virgin Islands English (VIE), that is, a characteristically local form of speech that retains some connections with its Creole past but which at the same time has lost its most significant Creole features and its coherency as a distinctly Creole system.

Immigration of English Creole and Caribbean English speakers from the Eastern Caribbean, especially since the 1960s, has acted as something of a brake against a complete destabilization of the Caribbean cultural and linguistic paradigm here. However, it must be borne in mind that they too, as well their children, have been subject to the same forces of change that affect Virgin Islanders in general.

PRESENT DAY CIRCUMSTANCES

A linguistic description of present day Virgin Island society would be a most complex and difficult undertaking, one that goes far beyond this modest essay. But a few words should be added to bring the story down to the present. At the present time American English certainly has become the dominant language in the Virgin Islands, being the official language of government, administration, education, the economy, and most other "formal" situations.

Virgin Islands English Creole, the true Creole, has become rare, limited to intimate social use (i.e., among family and friends) by members of the older generation. The decline of agriculture in general and the small family rural holding in particular has hastened its demise. Among most Virgin Island natives today, its place has been taken by Virgin Islands English, which is used in many environments alongside the so-called American standard, though generally on the informal as opposed to the formal level, in the personal as opposed to the institutional mode. Moreover, it serves the important function of identifying and marking the complex boundaries between native Virgin Islanders and the hosts of newcomers and outsiders who have swept ashore in recent years.

The importance of Spanish has surged in the past two decades, especially on the island of St. Croix. Given the presence of large Hispanic islands nearby, suffering from chronic underemployment and persistent overpopulation, it is likely that the relative prosperity of the Virgin Islands will continue to attract significant numbers of Hispanophones in the immediate future. As it has been in the past, Spanish will remain one of the important languages in our society, enriching our experience and giving rise perhaps to a continuing tradition of real bilingualism. St. Thomas French, on the other hand, appears to be in rapid decline, its speech community being drawn ever increasingly into the mainstream of St. Thomas.

Caribbean immigration continues to add diversity to our society and its overall linguistic repertoire. From the Eastern Caribbean have come tens of thousands of immigrants over the years, bringing with them their cultures and languages. Varieties of Caribbean English, as well as English Creoles, from Antigua, Montserrat, St. Kitts, Nevis, Barbados, Grenada, Trinidad-Tobago, and others, with all their richness and distinctiveness, have added diversity and have enhanced our multicultural society. Dominica and St. Lucia have sent us thousands of French Creole, or Patois, speakers, just as Aruba, Bonaire and Curaçao have sent us Papiamento with its resonances of Spanish, Portuguese, Dutch and Yoruban. In fact, it would by no means be extravagant to say that native speakers from nearly every country of the Caribbean, including the South and Central American littoral areas (e.g., Guyana and Belize), are represented in Virgin Islands society to one degree or another.

International immigration of the past thirty years has added an entirely new dimension as well. Our watch industry brought in small numbers of Germans and Swiss, some of whom have stayed on. In greater numbers came Palestinians, bringing with them their business acumen, their tremendous energies and, not least, their Levantine Arabic. On St. Croix, the latter is heard now every day as one moves from grocery store to clothing store to gasoline station. Similarly, some Indian merchants (i.e., from India) have made a strong impact on the business life of St. Thomas. In all of these cases, the languages of these people remain by and large connected with their personal and family lives, not, as yet at least, entering the mainstream.

NOTES

1. For a comprehensive bibliographic treatment of the subject to that time, see John E. Reinecke, *A Bibliography of Pidgin and Creole Languages*, Oceanic Linguistics Special Publication No. 14 (Honolulu: University of Hawaii Press, 1975). This comprehensive work contains short bibliographic sections on Virgin Islands English Creole (pp. 413–14), Dutch Creole (pp. 318–21) and the French Creole of St. Thomas (p. 274). For references to materials specific to language in the Virgin Islands, see Robin Sabino, *A Selected Bibliography of Materials on Language Varieties Spoken in the Virgin Islands*. Occasional Paper No. 6 (St. Thomas: VIDCCA, Bureau of Libraries, Museums and Archaeological Services, 1980). It presents short, annotated entries, arranged by author, on Virgin Islands language varieties, namely VI English Creole, Dutch Creole and Virgin Islands French Dialect. The most general scholarly treatment of the subject to date is Gilbert A. Sprauve's

"Pre- and Post-Emancipation Language Development in the Virgin Islands," In *Freedom's Flame: A Publication of Project Emancipation—A Second Look* (St. Croix: VIDCCA, Bureau of Libraries, Museums and Archaeological Services, 1981), pp. 89–95.

2. J. Antonio Jarvis, *The Virgin Islands and Their People* (Philadelphia: Dorrence & Co., n.d.), pp. 33–34.

3. Anthony Trollope, *The West Indies and the Spanish Main* (New York: Harper and Bros., 1860), p. 235.

4. [C.G.A. Oldendorp], *C. G. A. Oldendorp's History of the Mission of the Evangelical Brethren on the Caribbean Islands of St. Thomas, St. Croix, and St. John.* Translated and edited by Arnold R. Highfield and Vladimir Barac. (Ann Arbor, MI: Karoma Publishers, 1987), pp. 137–138. [Original title *Geschichte der Mission der evangelischen Brüder auf den caraibischen Inseln S. Thomas, S. Croix und S. Jan.* Barby: Johann Jakob Bossart, 1777. 2 v.]

5. Douglas Taylor, *Languages of the West Indies* (Baltimore and London: The Johns Hopkins University Press, 1977), pp. 13–148. The first half of this book, entitled "Amerindian Languages of the West Indies," is the best general summary of the question presently available. See also Julian Granberry's review of Taylor's book, "*West Indian Languages*: A Review and Commentary," *Journal of the Virgin Islands Archaeological Society* no. 10 (1980): 51–56.

6. A recent summary of the archaeological, linguistic, and historical knowledge on these early migrations is found in two works by Irving Rouse, *Migrations in Prehistory: Inferring Population Movement from Cultural Remains* (New Haven and London: Yale University Press, 1986), pp. 106–56 and, more recently, his *The Tainos* (New Haven/London: Yale University Press, 1992). A more general work is Gordon R. Willey, *An Introduction to American Archaeology: Volume Two, South America* (Englewood Cliffs, NJ: Prentice-Hall, 1971). See also José M. Cruxent and Irving Rouse, "Early Man in the West Indies," *Scientific Monthly* 221 (Nov. 1969): 44–52. Finally, there is a new review of the field by Ricardo Alegría in his "Tainos," *The Christopher Columbus Encyclopedia* v. 1. Edited by Silvio A. Bedini (New York: Simon & Schuster, 1992), pp. 354–49.

7. Fred Olsen, *On the Trail of the Arawaks* (Norman, OK: University of Oklahoma Press, 1974).

8. Sven Lovén, *Origins of the Tainan Culture, West Indies* (Göteborg: Elanders Boktryckeri, 1935). This is the revised, English edition of the author's *Uber die Wurzeln der tainischen Kultur* (Göteborg, 1924). Much of the contents of this book (e.g., agriculture, economics, religion, and social mores) assumes the close relationship of archaeological remains in the Virgin Islands and in Puerto Rico. In addition, there are specific references to the Island Arawaks (Tainos) of the Virgin Islands,

on various areas of material culture, namely: axes (p. 195); celts (pp. 149–50); earthenware stamps (p. 647); grooved celts (p. 170); pottery (pp. 271–78); and religious figurines (p. 608). It would seem clear, then, that the Arawak inhabitants of these islands were closely related culturally to the larger populations in Puerto Rico and the other islands of the Greater Antilles. See also Jesse Walter Fewkes, *The Aborigines of Porto Rico and Neighboring Islands*. Twenty-Fifth Annual Report of the U.S. Bureau of Ethnology to the Secretary of the Smithsonian Institution, 1903–04 (Washinton, D.C.: The Bureau, 1907).

9. Two of the more prolific writers of this group were Spaniards. See Bartolomé de Las Casas, *Historia de las Indias* (Mexico/Buenos Aires: Fondo de Cultura Economica, 1951), 3 v. This early history of the West Indies contains abundant information on the Tainos of the Greater Antilles as well as brief references to St. Croix, including Columbus's first visit and encounter with the Indians (I, p. 355), a subsequent brief visit (II, p. 33) and the landing of Nicuessa to capture and enslave some of the Indians (II, p. 427). See also Gonzalo Fernández de Oviedo y Valdés, *Historia general y natural de las Indias* (Madrid: Real Academia Española, Ediciones Atlas, 1959), 5 v.

10. J[esse] Walter Fewkes, "Prehistoric Cultural Centers in the West Indies," *Journal of the Washington Academy of Science* 5 (1915): 443. Notes that the artifacts of the Danish West Indies are related—along with those of Puerto Rico, Santo Domingo, and Haiti—to Eastern Cuba and the Bahamas.

11. For the context of these incursions, see Carl Ortwin Sauer, *The Early Spanish Main* (Berkeley/ Los Angeles, CA: University of California Press, 1966), p. 158. See also Arie Boomert, "Arawaks and Caribs." *The Christopher Columbus Encyclopedia* v. 1. Edited by Silvio A. Bedini (New York: Simon & Schuster, 1992), pp. 351–53.

12. The most important French sources for the Island Caribs are: Raymond Breton, *Relations de l'Isle de la Guadeloupe* (Basse Terre: Société d'Histoire de la Guadeloupe, 1978); Jean-Baptiste DuTertre, *Histoire générale des Antilles* (Paris: Th. Jolly 1667–1671), 4 v. ; Jean-Baptiste Labat, *Nouveau Voyage aux Isles de l'Amérique* (Paris, 1722), 6 v.; Pierre Pelleprat, *Relation des Missions des Pères de la Compagnie de Jésus dans les iles et dans la Terres Ferme de l'Amérique Méridionale (1655)* . In *Voyages et Travaux des Missionaires de la Compagnie de Jésus, Mission de Cayenne et de la Guyane Française* (Paris: Julien, Lanier, Cosnard et Ce, Editeurs, 1857); Charles-César de Rochefort, *Histoire naturelle et morale des Isles de l'Amérique* (Rotterdam, 1658), 2 v.

13. Evidence such as contained in Raymond Breton's *Dictionnaire Caraibe-François*. (Auxerre: Gilles Bouquet, 1665).

14. Douglas R. Taylor and Berend J. Hoff, "The Linguistic Repertory of the Island-Carib in the Seventeenth Century: The Men's Language—A Carib

Pidgin?" *International Journal of Anthropological Linguistics* 46:4 (1980): 301–12. See also Simone Dreyfuss, "Island Caribs," *The Christopher Columbus Encyclopedia* v. 1. Edited by Silvio A.Bedini (New York: Simon & Schuster, 1992), pp. 349–51.

15. Clarence Senior, *The Puerto Rican Migrant in St. Croix* (Rio Piedras, Puerto Rico: University of Puerto Rico, Social Science Research Center, 1947).

16. Aimery Caron and Arnold Highfield, "Unsuccessful Colonists: The French on St. Croix in the Seventeeth Century," *Daily News 50th Anniversary Edition*, (Aug.1,1980). Also see Caron and Highfield, *St. Croix Under French Dominion* (Forthcoming).

17. "... benchè a dir vero, a S. Tommaso quasi tutti parlono tre o quattro linque, cioè l'inglese, il francese, lo spagnuolo ed il creolo che è un miscuglio di tutte le lingue delle Antille ..." [Monsignor GeorgeTalbot], "Un Viaggio alle Antille," *Civilta Cattolica* s. 3 (1856): 503.

18. Arnold R. Highfield, *The French Dialect of St. Thomas, United States Virgin Islands: A Descriptive Grammar with Texts and Glossary* (Ann Arbor, MI: Karoma Press, 1979).

19. Alfredo E.Figueredo, "The Early European Colonization of St. Croix (1621–1642)," *Journal of the Virgin Islands Archaeological Society* no. 6 (1978): 59–64.

20. An early map notes in the legend that the island of St. Croix had been purchased by the King of Denmark from France but that "the inhabitants are chiefly English from Nevis and Anguilla." See "An Hydrographical Chart of the Virgin Islands," By C. Mortimer (London: 1739).

21. Jean Louise Willis, *The Trade Between North America and the Danish West Indies (1756–1807) with Special Reference to St. Croix* (Ph.D. dissertation, Columbia University, 1963).

22. By far the most comprehensive account of this period is that of Waldemar Westergaard, *The Danish West Indies Under Company Rule (1671–1754), with a Supplementary Chapter (1755–1917)* (New York: Macmillan Co., 1917). This study contains an excellent bibliograghy of the primary sources for that period.

23. The system of classification used here is based on the work of Joseph H. Greenberg in his *The Languages of Africa* (Bloomington Indiana: Indiana University, 1970), pp. 6–41. It should be noted that the leading authorities are by no means in agreement on this matter. For a discussion of these differences, see Merritt Ruhlen, *A Guide to the World's Languages,* (Stanford, CA: Stanford University Press, 1987), pp. 76–124. For more on the role of Denmark on the Gold Coast of Guinea during the colonial period, see the following: Ole Feldbæk and Ole Justesen, *Danmarks Historie: Kolonierne i Asien og Afrika* (Copenhagen: Politikens Forlag, 1908). The second part of this book (pp. 289–468) is written by Justesen

and deals specifically with Danish colonialism in West Africa. It is useful in the identification and location of the various ethnic groups. The standard has long been Georg Nørregaard's *Guldkysten, de danske establissementer i Guinea*, which is volume eight of the series *Vore gamle tropekolonier*, second edition, edited by Johannes Brøndsted (Copenhagen: Fremad, 1968). There is an English translation of this important work: *Settlements in West Africa 1658–1850* (Boston, MA: Boston University Press, 1966). The work of Kay Larsen, though dated, contains useful information. See his: *De danske i Guinea* (1918); *Krønniker fra Guinea* (1927); and *Dansk Vestindien 1666–1917* (Copenhagen: C.A. Reitzel, 1928). A more popular work is Thorkild Hansen's *Slavernes Kyst* (Copenhagen: Gyldendal, 1967).

24. Oldendorp, pp. 207–65.

25. [Pierre Joseph Pannet], *Relation de l'Excerable Conspiration, mise en Oeuvre par les Negres Minois en l'Isle Danoise St. Jan en Amérique 1733* (Copenhagen: Ms, Werlauffs Manuskriptsamling 22 fol., Royal library, Copenhagen., 1733. 11 pp. (Translated and edited by Aimery Caron and Arnold R. Highfield as *Execrable Conspiracy Carried Out by the Amina Negroes on the Danish Island of St. Jan in America 1733*, St. Croix: Antilles Press, 1984. 23 pp.); see also Aimery P. Caron and Arnold R. Highfield, "St. John Slave Revolt, Nov. 23, 1733—A Look 250 years later," *Virgin Islands Education Review* 1:8 (Nov. 1983): 9–17, 19–20.

26. Polly Pope, "Maroon Settlement on St. Croix," *Negro History Bulletin* 35: 7 (1972): 153–54. See also Oldendorp, pp. 233–38.

27. There exists a great deal of literature, both theoretical and descriptive, on Pidgin and Creole languages. Note the following which contain extensive bibliographies: John Reinecke, *A Bibliography of Pidgin and Creole Languages*; Dell Hymes, ed. *Pidginization and Creolization of Languages* (Cambridge: Cambridge University Press, 1971); Albert Valdman and Arnold Highfield, eds., *Theoretical Orientations in Creole Studies*, (New York: Academic Press, 1980); Albert Valdman, *Le Créole: Structure, Statut et Origine*, (Paris: Editions Klincksieck, 1978); and more recently Suzanne Romaine, *Pidgin and Creole Lannguages* (London: Longman, 1988).

28. Morris F. Goodman, *A Comparative Study of Creole French Dialects*. Series IV in *Janua Linguarum* (The Hague: Mouton and Co., 1964).

29. The sources for Dutch Creole are many and varied. For a review of the literature, see Reinecke, pp. 318–21 and Anne Graves, *The Present State of the Dutch Creole of the Virgin Islands* (Ph.D. dissertation, University of Michigan, 1977), pp. 1–35. See also Gilbert A. Sprauve, "Chronological Implications of Discontinuity in Spoken and Written Dutch Creole," *Journal of the College of the Virgin Islands* No. 5 (1979): 40–57.

30. Jens Larsen, *Virgin Islands Story: A History of the Lutheran Church, Other*

Churches, Slavery, Education, and Culture in the Danish West Indies, now the Virgin Islands (Philadelphia: Muhlenberg Press, 1950), pp. 112–28.

31. In 1881, Dr. Erik Pontoppidan visited the Danish islands and noted: "Jetzt ist Kreolisch auf St. Croix fast ganz verschwunden, auch in St. Thomas werden in der Stadt nur noch sporadisch einige alte Weiber gefunden, denen die Sprache noch geläufig ist. Nur auf mehr entlegenen Plätzen auf dem Lande, wie in den Missionen der mährischen Brüder zu 'Neu-Herrnhut' und 'Niesky', und auf der kleinen, verkommenen und halb verwilderten Insel St. Jan hat sie sich besser erhalten." Pontoppidan also recognized at the same time that the Creole was fast approaching its end: "Sie ist da Muttersprache und Umgangssprache der älteren Generation, welche schlect und mit Schwierigkeit Englisch, aber Platt–Kreolisch mit Geläufigkeit spricht; die Jüngeren dagegen haben Englisch adoptirt, und man kann sicher sagen, dass die Kreolensprache sehr bald eine todte Sprache sein wird; in einem Menschenalter wird man schwerlich noch Jemand finden, der es sprechen kann." See his "Einige Notizen über die Kreolensprache der dänisch-westindischen Inseln," *Zeitschrift für Ethnologie* 13 (1881): 131.

32. As early as 1716, English settlers on Anguilla were petitioning their government for permission to remove to St. Croix. See Abraham Howell's "Petition to Governor Hamilton for the Inhabitants of Anguilla to Settle St. Croix," *Calendar of State Papers,* (Anguilla) v. 29 (April 10, 1716), 1 p. The English presence on St. Croix is well attested in the years that followed.

33. The most important work to date on Virgin Islands English Creole has been done by Gilbert A. Sprauve. See the following by him: *Towards a Reconstruction of Virgin Islands English Creole Phonology* (Ph.D. dissertation, Princeton University, 1974); "Bilingualism and Phonological Filtration in the Dutch and English Creoles of the Virgin Islands," *Journal of the College of the Virgin Islands* No. 2. (1976): 5–19; and "Virgin Islands Creoles: Some Chronological Considerations," *Microstate Studies* No. 1 (1977): 8–28. See also Lezmore E. Emanuel, *Surviving Africanisms in Virgin Islands English Creole* (Ph.D. dissertation, Howard University, 1970).

Taíno culture was prevalent in the
Greater Antilles until the onset
of the 16th century

CHAPTER 40

SOME OBSERVATIONS ON
THE TAINO LANGUAGE

ABSTRACT

THIS PAPER PRESENTS a general, non-analytical description of the Taíno language in the Caribbean. It draws on both
primary and secondary sources, which are reviewed in the bibliography.
Taíno is an extinct language of the Arawakan family of languages of
South America. According to Noble (1965), it belongs to the Proto-
Arawakan sub-group that separated from the main stem of Arawakan
languages before the development of Proto-Maipuran. It was spoken
in the Caribbean from perhaps as early as 300 BC when the first Taíno
people migrated into that region from South America. While it flourished, it had several distinct dialects, probably corresponding in large
measure to the cultural divisions proposed by Rouse, namely Classic
Taíno (Haitian, or Bohian, with a number of sub-dialects); Western
Taíno (Lucayan, Cuban and Jamaican); and Eastern Taíno (the various
islands of the eastern Caribbean). Given the extensive cultural relations
between *Ayay* and *Boriquen* during the Taíno period, the Taínos of St.
Croix doubtlessly spoke a form very closely related to that of the inhabitants of Puerto Rico. Taíno was also related to Island-Carib, which over
time became an Arawakan language due to the Carib practice of bride
capture among Arawakan-speaking people. Taíno was spoken in the
major islands of the Greater Antilles until the mid-16th century, when
it disappeared, due to the strong pressure from Castilian Spanish during
a period of widespread bilingualism and eventual destruction of all the
major Taíno communities by Spanish expansion. Since Taíno had no
script or written language, its remains are relatively limited, consisting

of a few sentences and several hundred words as recorded by peninsular writers (Las Casas, Oviedo, Pané, et al.) during the early contact period. These survivals, however, have been sufficient to establish the identity of Taíno as a member of the Arawakan family. Although the Taíno people were exterminated and their language was driven into extinction, the latter contributed a high percentage of the New World Amerindian words that entered into Spanish and eventually into other languages of Europe and other parts of the world.

The coming of the first Europeans to the New World was followed not only by a clash of peoples but by a conflict of cultures and languages as well. The invading Spaniards superimposed their Castilian language over those of the indigenous populations whom they encountered, first, in the West Indies, and, later, in Mesoamerica and in South America. In a number of those areas, however, native languages, such as Nahuatl, Quechua and Guarani, managed to survive, albeit in a subordinate position to Castilian, in most instances as a result of pure demographics, that is, their massive numbers serving as an effective contrepoids to the military superiority of the invaders. In other cases, some indigenous languages survived due to the influence of geography and relative inaccessibility. The language of the Yanomami, for example, endured simply because its speakers did not at that time inhabit those areas coveted by the invaders.[1] However, Taíno, the very first language encountered by the Spaniards in the islands of the Caribbean and the one that made the initial and, in many ways, strongest impression on Castilian, became effectively extinct within about a century of the initial contact with the Iberians. The life-cycle and curious fate of that language constitute the focus of this paper.

LINGUISTIC OVERVIEW OF THE CARIBBEAN AT THE TIME OF THE ENCOUNTER

Since our most important sources for the indigenous languages of the Caribbean are the ethnohistorical accounts which were written at the time of the initial encounter between peoples of the Old World and the New, as well as in the years immediately thereafter, our story then begins in the late 15th century with the arrival of the first Spanish ships in the West Indies. What exactly was the linguistic situation as encountered by Columbus during his early voyages? [2]

In the Greater Antilles, Taíno was the predominant language, forms of which were spoken in the *Lucayos* (The Bahamas), Eastern *Cuba*, *Jamaica*, *Haití* (Española) and *Boriquen* (Puerto Rico). The archaeological record as interpreted by Irving Rouse and others points to the division of these islands into major cultural zones, namely the following: Classic Taíno (*Haití* and *Boriquen*, with nearby *Ayay* [St. Croix] included before the Carib intrusion); Western Taíno (*Cuba*, *Jamaica* and the *Lucayos*); and Eastern Taíno (the islands of the northern Lesser Antilles, to the east of *Boriquen* and the Virgins).[3] The ethnohistorical data generated by European observers who were present at the earliest contact, supported by the later archaeological evidence, argue that the people of those zones, with the exception of certain recess populations, spoke closely related forms of one and the same language—Arawakan-based Taíno.[4]

Scattered through the islands of the Greater Antilles, adjacent to and among these Taíno-speakers, were small pockets of non-Taíno speakers, about whom very little is known. It is assumed, for example, that the Guanahatabey of western *Cuba*, the remnant of a preceramic, paleolithic people who may have migrated there much earlier from Central America, evidently spoke a language other than Taíno; nothing, however, is known directly of those people and their speech beyond a few vague references and these general suppositions.[5]

The Spaniards also encountered pockets of other non-Taínos in northeastern *Haití* (Española). They were known as the Ciguayo, and they inhabited the cacicazgo of Macorix. They are mentioned in the early literature by Las Casas, Martyr and Oviedo.[6] However, very little is known about their language, beyond a couple of words. Were they also the remnants of a paleolithic people who inhabited the Greater Antilles before the arrival of Arawakan-speaking populations or were they communities who migrated to the island, perhaps from the north, at a later date? A paucity of both ethnohistorical and archaeological information may leave this question forever unanswered. It is a telling commentary that one of the two words preserved from their language during the initial contact with the Spaniards was *tuob*, or "gold."[7]

Further to the east lived the Igneri, an Arawakan-speaking people who settled in the smaller islands of the eastern Caribbean as the main thrust of the Pre-Taíno, or Saladoid, migration proceeded over several centuries toward the west, into the Greater Antilles. Apparently, they were forced into the recess areas of various of the islands of the Lesser Antilles upon the arrival of Carib-speaking migrants from South America sometime in the second half of the first millennium. According to some, the first of the Arawakan-speaking women taken by the Caribs came from this group.[8] However that may be, very little is known directly of their language, beyond the supposition that it was Arawakan and that it played a significant role in the formation of the Island-Carib language.

Further to the south, on the island today called Trinidad, several Arawakan languages were spoken into historical times, that is, Lokono, Jaoi, and Shebayo.[9] Although all that is known of their speech is several short word lists, the data which they offer are sufficient to establish their relation to the Arawakan family of languages, as well as to Taíno.

Many centuries after the migration of Arawakan speakers into the Caribbean area, there occurred another migration from South America. These were the Kalina (or Karina), later the self-styled Kallinagos and better known today as the Island-Caribs. Originally, they spoke Galibi, a language which was related to the larger family of Cariban languages in South America.[10] The expansion of that warrior society into the Caribbean archipelago and their practice of bride capture, particularly from the ranks of Arawakan-speaking peoples, led in time to their adoption of a form of speech which soon came to be essentially Arawakan, though embedded with numerous Cariban lexical survivals. That linguistic transition occurred as captive Arawakan-speaking mothers, taken from Igneri, Taíno and other Arawakan-speaking communities, communicated in their native languages to their sons and daughters engendered by Carib men. That language—paradoxically enough called Island-Carib— was the one spoken in *Caloucaéra* (Guadeloupe), *Cayre* (Dominica) and *Ayay* (St. Croix) at the time of the second voyage of Columbus in 1493. According to Taylor and others, the remnants of the original Cariban language, Galibi, came to be used exclusively as a ritual men's language in that warrior society.[11] Under those circumstances, that mixed form of Arawakan, but principally Igneri, laced heavily with Cariban words, became the everyday language of Island-Carib societies.

In very broad strokes, such was the linguistic state of affairs in the Caribbean region at the time of the encounter and subsequent pro-longed contact, first, with Spaniards and later with other western Euro-peans. It can be summarized in the following manner. First, Arawakan, in one form or another, was, by a wide margin, the dominant indigenous language of the Caribbean area at the time of the initial contact with people from Europe at the end of the 15th century. Moreover, it had already occupied that position for a considerable period of time, and its speakers most probably numbered in the hundreds of thousands. Second, even though the language was intelligible over wide areas, it neverthe-less had dialectal divisions, not only among the various islands but also within some of the larger islands as well. Third, the language, perhaps by dint of its numerous, well-established population of speakers and its relatively advanced culture had expanded, by one means or another, into areas where other languages had previously been established. In the Greater Antilles, for example, it became established in areas where the languages of the preceramic peoples had been previously spoken. In the Lesser Antilles, it became the basis of Island-Carib. And fourth, only a few other, recess languages were in evidence at the time, and either they were much older languages that had been forced into marginality by the growth of the Taíno domain or they had only recently been established in the region and were therefore of only minor status in their presence and influence. The former seems to be the more likely scenario. What emerges, in the final analysis, is a picture of the dominance of one linguistic group, Arawakan-based, in one form or another, covering the area from Trinidad in the south to central Cuba on the west.

Given such an advantageous position at the onset of the 15th century, Taíno, one would likely conjecture, might well have had at least an even chance of surviving the coming Spanish onslaught just as did other languages on the mainland in the years that followed. But such was not to be the case. In the short span of just several generations, the Taíno language was all but extirpated. Several questions arise in the context of any attempt to explain that abrupt and unforeseeable fate. Who were the Taíno people and where did they come from? What was the essential nature of their culture? What is known about their language and its correspondence to that culture? What were the circumstances that resulted in the disappearance of the Taíno language? And finally, how, if at all, did that language leave traces of its existence on the peoples and cultures with which it came into contact?

GENERAL OVERVIEW OF THE TAÍNO PEOPLE

The Taíno people owe the name by which they are known to history to the very first contact with the Spaniards. When the invaders inquired of the inhabitants of the islands of the Greater Antilles just who they were, the latter responded in their own language with the words *"Nitaino, Nitaino,"* that is, "the good [people]." That initial communication, along with the persistent belief on the part of most Spaniards that the natives were indeed "good people," guaranteed that the misnomer would stick. But the newly christened "Taínos" and their forerunners had, in fact, already been present in the Caribbean region for perhaps more than 1,500 years before the coming of Europeans and had gotten along quite well without an official name. That long history merits some comment as an introduction to a consideration of their language.

The Taíno people and their culture trace their origins ultimately back to the Amazon basin in South America. Over long periods of time, groups of Indian people roamed along the continental river systems,

SOME OBSERVATIONS ON THE TAINO LANGUAGE

some eventually finding their way to the delta of the Orinoco River and along the Caribbean littoral of the continent. Although the exact date remains uncertain, their earliest forerunners migrated to the Caribbean area from that continent sometime just before the beginning of the common era. The original causes behind the movement are not clearly understood, but pressures from other migrating peoples may offer one explanation. Or it is possible to suppose that technological advances led to enhanced food production and hence increased population, which in turn spawned population pressures of one kind or another, culminating in migration. Whatever the causes may have been, the resulting move-ment of people is generally known as the Saladoid migration, and its initial energy carried Arawakan-speaking people from the Guianas as far north and west as Puerto Rico, the eastern threshold of the Greater Antilles. The bearers of that culture and tradition we might call, for want of a better, more precise term, Pre-Taínos.[12]

Such a migration could not have been undertaken without the exis-tence of a well-developed technology. The people of that migration took along with them the tools needed to enter into, adapt to, and survive in their new insular habitats. First and foremost among those tools was their *canoa* (canoe) technology which enabled them to navigate, not only the rivers of the continent, but also the open waters of the Carib-bean that lay beyond their riverine homeland. In addition, they carried with them a knowledge of the cultivation of *yuca* (i.e., manioc, *manihot esculenta*) as their staple crop, along with the use of other plant foods, notably *mais*, *aje* and others, which they cultivated in worked mounds, called *conucos*. Closely interfaced with this *conuco* agriculture was the production of refined stone implements and of ceramics. Thus equipped with the necessary tools and encountering little human resistance, few serious diseases and neither threatening predators nor prohibitive envi-ronmental obstacles along the path of their migration, the migrating people moved rapidly from island to island in a northerly direction, making a swift and effective adaptation to the new, island environment of the Caribbean.

· 419 ·

Irving Rouse has suggested that the migration out of South America may have begun as early as the middle of the first millennium BC; it carried those people as far as the island of Puerto Rico.[13] The culture that established in the islands where the migrating peoples passed during that period has been termed the Saladoid. Archaeologists identify the associated cultural evolution primarily in terms of the development of material artifacts, that is, ceramic remains. That initial Saladoid period came to an end around 600 AD, when new ceramic styles began to appear. The cultural period that followed is known as the Ostionoid series, and it extended from that time until 600 to 1493 AD Archaeologists divide the Ostionoid series into four subseries, namely the Elenan, Ostionan, Meillacan and Chican.

By 900 AD, the movement of the people who had settled Puerto Rico, The Virgin Islands, and various of the islands of the Lesser Antilles, which had slowed at the Mona Passage at around 600 AD, penetrated through the archipelago as far to the west as the eastern regions of Cuba and southern Jamaica. As it did so, the migrating peoples not only continued to deploy the elements of the culture with which their ancestors had begun the migration, but they also made adaptations to conditions which they encountered en route, including interaction with the more ancient peoples and cultures that had been previously established there by an earlier migration from Mesoamerica. This contact is evidenced in the appearance of two new subseries, namely the Meillacan and the Ostionan. During the last of these subseries, sometime during the 13th century, the culture of the Taíno people reached its florescence on the large island of *Haití* (Española) and from that focus began to radiate out in the direction of the immediately surrounding islands. It is with this Chican sub-series of the Ostionoid, 1200 to 1492, that the Taíno people have been most closely identified.[14]

The Taíno people produced the most complex and advanced material culture to flourish in the Caribbean islands before the coming of the Europeans. Its economic underpinnings were founded on *conuco* agriculture and manioc cultivation, while the development of *canoa* marine technology enabled them to travel widely in order to exploit the surrounding seas for marine resources and trade. Central to the Taíno economy was the production of finely wrought stone tools and implements, including adzes, celts, and ceremonial collars. In addition, they enjoyed ceramic technology whereby they created a remarkable variety of ceramic griddles, containers, and vessels. Based on this solid economic foundation, their political organization evolved to the chieftain level (*cacicazgo*), in which rulers called *caciques* exercised considerable power over their people, their domains, and communal projects. Both kingship and the societies which it directed were hierarchical. The aristocratic element, the *nitainos*, controlled and directed the other members of the group, called the *naborias*. The effects of this hierarchy are reflected in the larger islands, in particular, where public works of considerable size were undertaken, including irrigation projects, dance plazas, and ceremonial ball courts, which were lined with large, incised stones. The Taíno economy, society, and polity were conjoined by a religious system that featured shamanism, strong animistic belief, ancestor worship, and a pantheon of nature-based deities. Zemi veneration was central to the system. Religion, in turn, gave impetus to artistic expression and to the diffusion of essential beliefs, through the media of sculpture and symbolic representation on ceramic vessels, in both painted and incised form. Deities and forces of nature were artistically represented in and on the ubiquitous three-pointed stones, closely associated with zemi worship. Similarly, petroglyphs were carved on rocky outcroppings and large ceremonial stones. In a very few words, this was a fully functioning, well-articulated society that the Spaniards happened upon at the end of the 15th century.[15]

The culture of a people expresses and articulates itself in and through its language. Language, in fact, may be viewed as the medium through which a culture reaches its ultimate expression and manifestation, accounting, paradoxically enough, for both the conservative forces which constrain and stabilize it as well as the transcendental impulses which engender innovation and change. Travel and trade between the

Taíno-settled islands, rendered possible by *canoa* technology, sustained the need to communicate and thereby kept the distant Taíno communities in direct contact with one another over the period of their habitation there without any apparent interruption. As members of the various islands visited communities in the other islands, language contacts were maintained, checking the linguistic drift that often occurs when speech groups become totally isolated or separated by insurmountable obstacles. Even though some inevitable linguistic drift must have taken place and the speech of the most distant spheres of the Taíno realm doubtlessly became differentiated to varying degrees, the regular visits, accompanied by trade and communication, enabled insular Taíno communities to remain in unbroken linguistic and cultural contact and thereby maintain central commonalities. The Taíno language then was essential to the unity of Taíno culture.

The nature and organization of the core economic, political and religious institutions of the Taínos did not as yet require, it seems, symbolic communication beyond the glyphs incised on stone, shell, bone, and pottery. Therefore they did not develop a written language, having no written script, created or imported. Taíno remained, as a result, an essentially spoken language in a preliterate culture. It is for that reason that our linguistic record of the Caribbean region begins only with the arrival of Europeans at the end of the 15th century. What extends back in time before then must necessarily be based on inference. However that may be, it seems clear that the Taíno language of the Arawakan family was dominant in the region at the time of the encounter and had been so previously for a considerable time.

THE TAÍNO LANGUAGE

Having reviewed the Caribbean as Columbus found it and surveyed the linguistic situation at that same time, it now remains to have a closer look at the Taíno language itself. The sources for our present knowledge of the Taíno language are threefold. First, there are the early documents of the encounter written by various Europeans. As the Taínos are said to have been pre-literate, our present information on their language has been derived principally from the writings of early observers who visited the Spanish Indies in the late 15th century and well into the 16th, men such as Christopher Columbus himself, Bartolomé de Las Casas, Gonzalo Fernández de Oviedo, Dr. Alvarez de Chanca, Michele de Cuneo, Fernando Colón and others. Ramón Pané, a Catalan cleric, visited the Taínos of *Haití* and attempted to write a short description of their religion. Peter Martyr, on the other hand, never visited the Indies at all, but he did speak with numerous men who had gone there and who had extensive contacts with the *Indios*. Though no single one of these writers focused specifically on the languages of the region, all of them did, each in his own manner, record numerous Taíno words for salient phenomena, especially those for which the Spanish language had no exact equivalent. Those items cover a broad spectrum, including elements of the flora and the fauna, along with place names, personal names, names of caciques, toponyms (mountains, rivers, bays etc), cultigens, and various aspects of the culture of the people, both material and non-material. [16]

Secondly, there is the great volume of administrative and legal documentation and official correspondence that passed between the Spanish Indies and Spain. Early in the colonization period, many of those documents touched upon "Indian matters." In particular, place names and individual names occur frequently in those sources.[17]

Elsewhere a good number of Taíno and other Indian words passed into Spanish by less formal means, that is, into the contemporary colloquial tongue. Many of those words have survived in the everyday speech of the generations of people who have lived in the Spanish Indies from the 15th century down to this very day. Some of those Taíno words were, moreover, dispersed from the Spanish Indies into other Indian languages elsewhere in the newly conquered Spanish domains; some passed into languages in other parts of the world. In the larger islands of the Indies—Cuba, Española and Puerto Rico—numerous place names and toponyms have survived in the day-to-day speech of the people, especially in the country areas.[18]

What the early Spanish writers did not do, unlike later French writers and chroniclers in the 17th and 18th centuries living among the Island-Caribs of the Lesser Antilles, was fashion a grammar, create a dictionary, or record the direct speech of the Taínos.[19] That oversight has placed certain limitations on how well the language might be known from a modern perspective. Since, however, Island-Carib itself is essentially an Arawakan language—indeed perhaps a fusion of Igneri, Taíno and Arawakan elements from the mainland—then it may well turn out that, after careful study, the documentation relating to Island-Carib will, in due time, provide a rich linguistic harvest on the matters under discussion here. For the moment, those three sources discussed above—the early writers, the administrative and legal documents, and the colloquial sources—must suffice in providing the bulk of our information on the long since vanished language of the Taínos.

Origins and History

Taíno is an extinct language of the Arawakan family of languages which arose in South America.[20] Evidently, it separated from the other languages in that family at a relatively early date. There is no complete agreement among scholars, however, as to how early that separation took place. According to Noble, Taíno belongs to the Proto-Arawakan sub-group that had separated from the main stem of Arawakan languages before the development of Proto-Maipuran.[21] Others maintain that Taíno is more closely related to the main body of Arawakan languages that formed at a later date along the northern coast of South America. It follows, according to this reasoning, that Taíno must therefore have diverged from the main body of that linguistic group at a much later date than Noble has proposed. Douglas Taylor, for example, sees Taíno deriving from the Proto-Maipuran group, if not in fact later. José Arrom and Irving Rouse believe that, insofar as Taíno appears to be closely related to the languages of the Northern Arawakan group (i.e., Lokono, etc.), then it must have emerged from the Proto-Maipuran Arawakan family, not Proto-Maipuran as Noble maintains.[22] Given our present archaeological knowledge of the pre-Taíno migration from South America into the Caribbean, the later date would appear the more likely.

Whenever the separation of Taíno did in fact occur, it is certain that an early form of Taíno was spoken in the Caribbean from perhaps as early as 300 BCE, when the earliest pre-Taíno peoples had migrated well into the Caribbean archipelago from South America. Along with their material culture they, of course, brought their spoken language with them. Encountering unfamiliar peoples, new ecosystems, and varying circumstances from island to island, their language adapted and diversified itself in response to the needs of the new environment.

Variation

With the exceptions of the Guanajatabey tongue in Western *Cuba* and the language of the Ciguayo in Macorix in northwestern Española, Taíno was spoken throughout the Greater Antilles. From the time he arrived in the *Lucayos* (Bahamas), Columbus observed that the inhabitants understood each other, that they were "friends," and that "their language was one."[23] Arriving in *Cuba*, after having already passed through a number of other islands, he fretted that he did not yet know the language, but he conceived a strategy to learn it because he saw that "the language was all one up to that time."[24] Several days later at the island of *Bohio* (i.e, *Haití* or Española), his ship was visited by a beautiful Indian woman of the place and Columbus noted that "she spoke with those Indians with me since they all have the same language."[25] It was only further along the coast while visiting the territory of the great cacique Guacanagarí that Columbus observed some linguistic variation for the first time, remarking that a good deal of time was spent trying to communicate with the *cacique*'s emissaries "because the Indians with me had difficulty understanding these Indians. There is some difference in the names of things."[26]

There is substantial evidence to support these initial observations by Columbus. Concerning these same people, Bartolomé de Las Casas wrote that "They speak only one language in all these islands."[27] Concerning the languages of *Haití* and the people of the *Lucayos*, Las Casas further noted that "almost everywhere there is one language and one manner of speaking." In a similar vein, Peter Martyr observed that the peoples of *Cuba* and *Bohio*, or *Haití*, were of the same culture, origin and language.

Finally, it should be remembered that those same interpreters whom Columbus picked up in the *Lucayos* in 1492, travelled all the way to Spain with him, returning to the West Indies on the second voyage in the Fall of 1493. When the ships made their first landfalls in the Lesser Antilles, those "Indios" from the *Lucayos* were able to communicate effectively with the Taíno women from *Boriquen* (Puerto Rico), who were being held as captives on *Caloucaéra* (Guadeloupe) by Island-Caribs. They duplicated the feat in *Ayay* (St. Croix). All in all, the interpreters from the Lucayan islands communicated effectively on separate occasions with Taínos from *Cuba*, *Haití* and *Boriquen*. And not many years later, the native Taíno interpreters Juan Gonzáles and Juan de León, who spoke the Taíno language of Española as their mother tongue and who accompanied Ponce de León in the conquest of *Boriquen*, communicated easily with the natives of that latter island. Taken collectively, these facts argue convincingly that one language—Taíno—was spoken across the Greater Antilles at the time of the encounter.

However, not everyone has been in complete agreement on this point. Gonzalo Fernández de Oviedo, for one, has suggested otherwise, writing that "The first language which the Admiral don Christopher Columbus, the discoverer of these parts, initially found was that of the islands of the *Lucayos*, secondly, that of the island of *Cuba*, and thirdly, that of this island of *Haití*, or Española. None of these understands the other."[28] Did Oviedo, in the final analysis, overlook the significance of mutual intelligibility in the expectation of finding complete homogeneity? The truth of the matter, as in most cases, most probably lies somewhere between the two extreme positions of Las Casas and Oviedo. In other words, one principal language was indeed spoken throughout the

Taíno domains, but it most likely consisted of closely-related dialects rather than one totally homogeneous tongue. And those dialects, most probably corresponded in large measure to the cultural divisions subsequently proposed by Rouse, namely Classic Taíno (Haitian, or Bohian, with a number of sub-dialects within each island); Western Taíno (Lucayan, Cuban and Jamaican, with similar dialectal divisions); and Eastern Taíno. Given the extensive cultural relations between *Ayay* and *Borinquen* during the Taíno period, the Taínos of St. Croix doubtlessly spoke a form very closely related to that of the inhabitants of Puerto Rico.[29] Whatever the nature of the variation that existed, it is to be stressed that Taíno peoples could communicate among themselves and readily understand one another across their wide geographical domain.

At the same time, the paucity of data makes it a difficult task indeed to specify exactly the nature of this putative linguistic variation among the Taínos. Scanning the early documentation, the modern observer can detect only fragmentary evidence here and there in support of this thesis. For example, it is known that the Taínos of the *Lucayos* and those of *Cuba* called the island of Española, *Bohio*, while the inhabitants of Española themselves called it *Haití*. Columbus was told by the people of the *Lucayos* that there was much gold (*nucay* or *nozai*) in *Bohio*, but when he arrived there, he found that the inhabitants of that island called it *caona* through most of the island and *tuob* among the Ciguayos. As another example of lexical variation, the word employed in *Cuba* for the warlike people to the east (i.e., the Lesser Antilles) was *caniba* whereas the people of *Haití* referred to them as *caribe*. It has been observed that in modern times certain terms for the same things in the respective islands of Cuba, Puerto Rico and the Dominican Republic vary rather considerably, indicating that lexical variation may have been deeply rooted in the respective linguistic histories of those islands.[30]

Fortunately, there is, in addition to the foregoing bits and pieces, some further evidence for linguistic variation in the early sources. While Las Casas repeatedly notes that Taíno was the language that was "universal throughout the entire land [i.e., *Haití*]," he also indicates that one form of that language—the speech of the cacicazgo of *Xara-guá*—took precedence over the other regions of the island. "In this (i.e., elegance, abundant vocabulary, and softness of sound), the [language] of Xaraguá, as I said above, prevailed in all things and was, by far, the foremost language."[31] Elsewhere Las Casas adds that "all of the people of this kingdom of Behechio [i.e., *Xaraguá*] exceed all others of this island in that their language is the most refined and its words are better, smoother, and more polished."[32] The testimony of Las Casas constitutes clear proof of the existence of linguistic variation within the island, however slight it may have been. But, on the other hand, it would be mistaken to posit a dialect for each and every one of the cacicazgos mentioned by Las Casas and other writers, principally because the lines adumbrating those caciquedoms may well have been more of a reality for the state-conscious Spaniards than they were in fact for the more loosely organized Taínos themselves.[33] In other words, it appears that the Spaniards may have been straining to see political and cultural divisions as they existed in the Iberian peninsula when in fact they were apparently much more fluid in *Haití*. The drawing of conclusions and making inferences relative to the linguistic circumstances at that time based on data of this kind should be approached with due caution.

Grammatical Categories

Very little is known about the phonology, morphology, and syntax of the Taíno language. In regard to the first of these categories, nearly all of the available data were committed to writing by native Spanish speakers. That data, therefore, passed through the collective phonological filter (i.e., Castilian Spanish) of those writers, giving us, in essence, a representation of the language as it sounded to them at that point in time. As a result, all but the most salient features of the language went ignored and unrecorded. Las Casas appears to have been aware of the problem, to a certain extent at least, inasmuch as he repeatedly gives instructions concerning the position of the accent in the Taíno words that he employs in his works. Beyond that, however, he did no more than the other chroniclers of his time in the matter of making phonological notations. The sound system of Taíno can therefore only be imperfectly inferred as a result of the unsystematic manner in which words were recorded by various writers.[34]

We find ourselves in a similar position in regard to Taíno syntax largely because precious few texts were recorded. The extant material consists generally of short, one-sentence fragments, for the most part random renderings of Taíno speech, recorded in an unsystematic, almost casual manner. Since those texts are both brief and few in number, it would be instructive to include them at this point.[35]

- *Ahiscavo Guarrocoel.*—"We know this, our grandfather."
- *Dios naboria daca.*—"I am a servant of god."
- *Guaibbá, Cynato machabuca guamechina.*—"Look. What does it matter to me if God is angry?"
- *Mayanimacaná, Juan Desquivel daca.*—"Don't kill me, I am Juan Desquivel."
- *O cama guaxeri guariguen caona yari.*—"Listen señors, come look for the stone that gives gold."
- *Técheta cynato guamechina.*—"The Lord is very angry."
- *Ita.*—"I don't know."

All of those who have investigated the linguistic history of the Spanish Indies agree that of the various grammatical categories, it was the lexicon of the Amerindian languages that had the greatest impact on the language of the Spaniards. Moreno de Alba has written that "it is clear that the aboriginal languages of America were only able to exert and influence on the Spanish language in general at the level of the lexicon, the most superficial element within the linguistic structure."[36] Of all the so-called aboriginal languages it was moreover the Taíno language that came into contact with Castilian first, exerting, with the passage of time, the greatest and most enduring lexical influence. In testimony of this encounter, Zamora Vicente has noted that "where the marks of the indigenous languages are clearest and strongest is in the area of the lexicon. The oldest source of such influence is Arawak, a language spoken in the Antillean islands in the very first lands with which the conquistadors had contact."[37] It is no way surprising then that our best knowledge of the Taíno tongue is in the domain of words themselves, in the vocabulary.

The Taíno Lexicon

The following is intended as a cursory description of the Taíno lexicon as drawn from the historical sources. It is presented here for strictly non-analytical descriptive purposes, with an eye for showing something of the language itself in the context of the culture that it represented. We must assume that like all other languages Taíno had lexical resources adequate to serve the needs of the Taíno people's material and non-material culture. That is to say that since the Taínos had, as one example, a strong interest in agriculture—indeed their very survival depended on it—then one would expect that their language would be fully formed in that area, altogether capable of describing the concepts, artifacts, practices, etc., fundamental to that pursuit. What is actually known today about those lexical resources, however, is another matter, one limited and defined by the perspectives and limitations of the contemporary mind-set of those Spanish writers who were present at the time of the initial contact with the Taínos. The Spanish chroniclers focused their attention on those things, by and large in the physical world (plant and animal), that were new and unknown to them, as well as on those things that were most immediately apparent. Root crops such as *yuca* and *aje*, animals such as *hutias* and *manatees*, and cultural artifacts such as *canoas* and *zemis*, to mention only a few, were both new to them, that is, beyond their peninsular experience, as well as readily apparent. As a result, they dutifully recorded the names of those categories of creatures and things, namely the terms for not only plants and animals, but also those of geographical regions and locations (toponymy), names of prominent people, caciques in particular, some terms relative to agriculture and mining, and the terminology and lexicon of religion and mythology (e.g., priests, myths, spirits, deities, rituals, etc.).

To understand fully the nature of the remains of the Taíno lexicon, it is equally important to know what the Spaniards did *not* record, that is, what they ignored or omitted for one reason or another. Plants and animals that had apparent counterparts in the Old World were often referred to using the familiar Spanish word. Avifauna, for some reason, seemed to attract scant attention. The same is true for the Taíno terms for the parts of the human face and body, which, obviously enough, could have been referred to by the use of Spanish equivalents. Similarly little attention was paid to Taíno verbals, most probably because their own verbs, especially those signifying common actions, could be effectively employed, along with signs or gestures and thereby effect the minimal necessary understanding. Adjectives too attracted little attention, perhaps for the same reason. In the final analysis, the attention of the Spaniards was attracted primarily by things and the terms for those things. Not surprisingly, it is also that element—substantives—that has persisted in the Spanish of the islands today.

The following is a brief descriptive overview of that part of the Taíno lexicon which has survived by one means or another and come down through the sources outlined above.[38] It should be recalled in perusing it that it is partial and fragmentary as the direct result of the manner in which it was collected. Not only does it render a partial, incomplete perspective of Taíno culture and the words that described that culture, but, moreover, it illustrates a good deal about the manner in which the invading Spaniards viewed the people whom they were in the process of conquering and eventually exterminating.

The Taíno lexicon, as it has survived to the present time, is top-heavy with nouns, which far outnumber adjectives, verbs and other word forms. Nevertheless, some adjectives are in evidence, as in the following examples: *cynato*, "irritated"; *estarei*, "shining"; and *manicato*, "strong," "of great spirit." Verbs are equally sparse in the sources. The few that are attested appear to have been formed by adding the suffix *a* to certain stems, of which the following are examples: *cama*, "listen"; *macaná*, "to kill"; *teitocá*, "to be quiet"; and *serra*, "to exchange." A negative particle *ma-* could be prefixed to verbs as in *mayanimacaná*, "Don't kill me." Even a quick perusal of the numerous substantives that have been preserved in various texts reveals the presence of numerous roots, prefixes and suffixes as the means through which the dynamics of the Taíno language expressed itself. Although even a brief overview of these linguistic resources would extend far beyond the intent and scope of the present study, the following examples give an idea of the nature of those linguistic means.[39]

A great number of roots occurs throughout the Taíno lexicon. As one example, the stem *-caira*, or *-caera*, "island," appears in the names of several islands, such as *Calocaera*, "Guadeloupe," and *Cibuquiera*, "St. Croix?" The root *-heri*, or *-hari*, "man, person," appears in several terms of address, including *matunherí*, "exalted person." The root *-arima*, "end part, anus" is present in the place name, *Guaccaiarima*, "the extreme southwestern part of Haití." And finally, *-aco*, or *-caco*, meaning "eye," occurs in the terms *xeiticaco*, "black eyes," and *hicaco*, "fruit in the shape of an eye."[40]

The language is rich in prefixes, of which the following is a sampling: *ay-*, place names such as *Ayay*, "St. Croix," *Ayaibex*, "place in Santo Domingo"; *Ayqueroa*, "a place in *Guaccaiarima*; *ma-*, a negative particle, meaning, "not," "without," or "lacking," which may be prefixed to a substantive as in *mahite*, "missing a tooth." The prefix *ni-*, an oft-used prefix that may be either an article or perhaps the first person singular pronoun, as in the following examples: *Nibagua*, "a cacique," *Niti*, "a place in *Haití*," *Nizao*, "a river," and *nitaino*, "a Taíno noble."

The language is richly endowed with suffixes, of which only a sampling is offered here, including the following: *-bo* is in some instances a shortened form of *bohio*, meaning "house of" or "place of," as in the example of the name of the cacique *Caonabo*, "Lord of the House of Gold," according to one interpretation.[41] The same underlying meaning may be present in such words as *ceibo*, "the giant silk-cotton or kapok tree," (*Ceiba pentrandra* L) and *cobo*, "conch" (*Strombus gigas*). The suffixes *-abo* and *-coa* both appear to be locatives, the former in particular being present in the names of a number of rivers, as in *Maunabo* and *Bucarabón* both in *Boriquen,* and *Cayabo,* "an ancient province in *Haiti.*" Examples of *-coa* are available in *Cibacoa,* "place of rocks" and *Baracoa,* "near the sea." The suffix *-nacán* carries the meaning "in the middle of," as in the place name, *Cubanacán,* "settlement in the middle of Cuba." Several other suffixes worthy of note are the following: *-el,* added to personal names, means "the son of," as in *Jayael,* "the son of *Jaya*" and *Guavaoconel,* "the son of *Guavaenequín*"; *-ex,* as added to the names of numerous caciques is perhaps an honorific particle, as in *Guarionex, Yamarex* et al; and *-quin* or *-quen* which may mean "numerous, abundant," as in *Boriquen,* "Puerto Rico" and *Duiheyniquen,* "a river."

It now remains to have a look at the general lexical resources of the Taíno language in relation to the principal elements of Taíno culture. The Taínos developed a sharp awareness of the physical world in which they lived. They kept a regular eye on the *turey,* "sky"[42] and on the *bagua,* "sea." They travelled over the latter and had a broad knowledge of the *cayos,* "islands," which they encountered there. They were most certainly aware of the great forces of nature to which they were subject, in particular the tremendous force of the *huracán,* "hurricane" that descended on their islands from the Atlantic. Their islands were covered with *arcabuco,* "forests," *sabana,* "savannah," and *maguá,* "vegas," or "fertile plains." Depending heavily on lithic industries, they were concerned with *cibu,* "stones," and other minerals. It is a result of the Spaniards' quest for gold, however, that we have been left with a disproportionate number of terms for that mineral, namely *nozay* among the *Lucayos, caona* in *Haiti,* and *tuob* among the non-Taíno *Ciguayo.* The *yari,* "ore," that produced the gold and items made from it, such as *guanín,* "low-grade gold jewelry," were also of interest to the Spaniards.

That the Taínos travelled widely and readily in their waters is evident in the names which they assigned to both nearby and distant islands and places. The very first of their lands that Columbus happened upon, *Guanahaní,* was only one of a larger group known as the *Lucayos.* There was a host of others in that group, including *Bahama, Caycos,* and *Ciguateo,* to name only a few. All the larger islands of the Greater Antilles had Taíno names—*Cuba, Jamaica, Haití, Bohio* and *Boriquen,* as did the smaller islands and cays lying off the larger islands, *Camito* off the northern coast of *Haití* being one example. In spite of the efforts by the Spaniards to give these islands Christian names, a surprising number of the original Taíno names have survived to the present day. The island located just off the eastern coast of *Boriquen,* presently called "St. Croix," had two recorded names of apparent Taíno origin—*Ayay* and *Cibuqueira.* To the east of the Taíno domains lay several islands inhabited by the *Caribe or* "*Caribs,*" namely *Caloucaéra* and the fabled *Matinino.* And far across the waters, etched in their ancestral memory, lay a region of unlimited land, which the Taínos called *Caribana* or *Caribata* and which the Spaniards would later call "Tierra Firma," the mainland.

The islands of *Haití, Boriquen* and eastern *Cuba* were especially rich in toponyms. Nearly all the rivers in the Dominican Republic today have retained their Taíno names, the *Agmina* River that empties into the *Yaque* and the *Jaina* river that empties into the sea being only two of many examples. Likewise, names for valleys such as *Hathathiei* and for mountains like *Hybahaino* and *Macaya* abounded in all these islands. Those that attracted the attention of the chroniclers, for whatever specific reason, were duly recorded. The designations for various other geological features have survived in the colloquial Spanish speech of those islands.

The Taínos called their settlements *yucayeque,* and numerous of these have survived including *Guanahibes,* "Gonaives" and *Hincha,* "Hinche," in present-day Haiti, along with provinces such as *Agueybana* and *Baoruco* in *Haití,* regions such as *Cibao* and cacicazgos such as *Xaraguá, Maguana, Higüey, Magua,* and *Marien* in *Haití,* in present-day Hispaniola.

Taíno people depended heavily on plants, both cultivated and uncultivated, for a large portion of their food supply. And since the newly arrived Spaniards were also interested in the plants of the new lands as an important element in their own adaptation and survival, it is not surprising that the words for numerous plants found their way into the written record, especially since many of them were new species with which the newcomers were completely unfamiliar. Among the trees that were important for the construction of dwellings and other elements of material culture were the *caoba*, perhaps mahogany (*Swietenia mahogany* L); *damahagua*, "*hibiscus tiliaceous*"; the *manaka*, "a variety of palm"; the *ceiba*, "the silk-cotton tree" (Bombacaceas) that was considered sacred by the Taínos, as well as by many of the African peoples who arrived later in the West Indies; the *córbana*, "a large hardwood tree," (*Pithecolobiun Beteroanum*); the *guao*, "a caustic tree" (*Rhus metopium*); and the *guayacán*, "lignum vitae" (*Guaiacum officinale* L). This list, like the ones that follow, is by no means exhaustive but is rather intended to present a general overview of the manner in which the Taíno marshalled their ecological resources and represented those resources in their language.

Fruit trees were both plentiful and important in the Taíno economy. Foremost among them were the following: the *bagua*, or *xagua*, "the genip tree" (*Genipa americana* L); the *hobo* and *hikako*, (*Chrysobalanus icaco L*) varieties of West Indian plums; the *mamei*, "the mamey tree" (*Mammea americana* L); the well known *papaya* tree and its fruit; the *guanábana*, "soursop" (*Annona muricata*), "a fruit supposedly eaten by the dead" (i.e, the *opia*); the *guayabo*, "the guava" (*Psidium pomiferum* L.); the *casina*, "edible apples," according to some authors. In addition to these, there were other plants and their fruits, including: the *yayagua*, "pineapple," as well as the terms *boniama* and *yayama* for other varieties of the same fruit. The presence of multiple names, both here and elsewhere in the Taíno lexicon, points to a certain level of sophistication in their approach to horticulture.

Central to Taíno agriculture was the cultivation of several root crops, the most important of which was *yucubia* plant which produced *yuca* (*Manihot esculenta*), "the manioc root," from which *casabi*, "cassava," was produced. There were varieties of this plant, including *diacanan*, *hobos* and *tubaga*, as well as *boniata*, "a sweet variety of the plant." The food provided by *yuca* and its varieties were supplemented by *aje*, or *age*, "a species of sweet potato," the very first food plant encountered by the

Spaniards in the islands.[43] According to Oviedo, *athibuineix, anigua-mar, guaraca, guacarayes,* and *guahanagax* were all names for different varieties of *aje.* Other edible tubers were the *lerén,* or *lirén* (*Calathea allouia*), the *yahutía* or *yautía,* "any one of several species of edible tubers of the genus *Xanthosoma,* such as *Xanthosoma sagittifolium*" and the *maní* (*Arachis hypogeae*), "the name for both a plant and its edible fruit." In addition to these, the Taíno fields were planted with *mahíz,* "corn," *ector,* "tender corn," and *aji,* "a pepper."

Additionally, the Taíno economy made use of several important "industrial plants," from which products were consumed by the local communities and also used in trade. In addition to the food-producing trees already referred to directly above, the tropical forests produced large hardwood trees from which the Taínos fashioned *canoas.* Other trees provided utensils, such as the *hibuero* tree (*Crescentia cujete*), whose fruit, the *hibuera,* "the calabash," was used as a vessel. Another plant, the *cabuya,* (*Furcraea tuberosa* Ait.) produced cord or thread. The *cohiba* plant provided the leaves from which tobacco was made. *Cohoba* was the name given to the religious ceremony in which the plant was used as a hallucinatory agent. The term *tabaco* was the pipe in which the pulverized leaf was consumed. The Spaniards' confusion relative to these items resulted in the loss of one term and the misuse of another, the latter surviving and spreading rather widely in other languages. *Bixa* (*Bixa orellana*) was an important dye-plant. Finally, *digo* was a plant used in washing. Cotton was in general use among the Taínos, but, curiously enough, the Spaniards did not record the indigenous name, most probably because they were well-acquainted with the plant in the Old World, as well as with the fiber that it produced. This omission is instructive relative to the manner in which the Spaniards viewed the Taíno culture and language.

Animal life received less attention from the early writers than did plant life because it did not exist in great abundance or variety to begin with; but, perhaps equally important, the role of native fauna in Taíno life itself was less important than was agriculture. The most important of all the animal groups were the mammals, particularly several varieties of small quadrupeds which resembled rabbits or large rodents and which were hunted as a source of food. Among these were the *curics*, or *corí*, the *hutía*, the *guaminiquinajes*, the *mohics*, and the *quemí*. The *aon*, "a small, barkless dog," was perhaps a semi-domesticate. And the *manati* "a large marine mammal," (*Manatus americanus*) was hunted in the estuaries and in the shallows around the larger islands.

Several reptiles were prized as a food source, namely the *iguana* (*Cyclura carinata*) and some turtles, particularly the *carei*, which was valued, in particular, for its shell and the *hicotea*, "a small turtle," (*pseudemys palustris*). The *caiman*, or Caribbean crocodile, inhabited streams and waterways near the sea.

Among the avifauna are the *giahuba-bagiael*, a bird that "sings like the ruiseñor"; the *guaraguao*, "a species of raptor"; and the *higuaca*, "a parrot valued for its feathers," (*Chrysotis vittatus*).

From the sea, the Taínos took the *cohobo*, or *cobo*, "a large conch," (*Strombus gigas*) that provided meat and a prized shell. The Taínos were expert fishermen, taking a selection of fish, including the *biajaiba*, "a sea fish." They also utilized the *xayba*, "an edible crab" and the *guabina*, "a river fish." Although limited mention is made of insects and other lower life-forms, there were the *cocuyo*, "a flying insect" and the *xixén*, "a small stinging insect," perhaps the sand-fly.

The Taínos had names for the various other peoples that lived around them, including the *Ciguayo*, the *Caribe*, the *Caniba*, and the *Guanahatabey*. The names of their highest leaders, the *caciques* and *cacicas*, were well known throughout the islands over which they ruled. *Amanex, Behechio, Cotubanamá* and *Guacanagarí* are but a few examples of these personal names. *Anacoana, Cabomba* and *Higuanamá* were all female chiefs, *cacicas*. Though the names of non-rulers are less abundant in the records and sources, we nevertheless know of a certain *Ganauvariu*, one of the first persons encountered by Pané, as well as *Guaticavá*, the first Indian who died baptized, and *Nabeca*, an Indian in Haití. A rather extensive collection of Indian names has survived in the legal documentation of Puerto Rico.[44]

The remnants of the vocabulary of the human body and person are curiously lacking. This may be attributable to the fact that Spanish, like all languages, naturally had a complete set of terms for these items and therefore few inquiries were made about them. The term for "man" was *eri* or *ari*, as embedded in certain honorific titles such as *guaoxerí*, etc.[45] Some words, did, however, attract the direct attention of the Spaniards. The term *goeiz* referred to "a living person," who at death (i.e., *operito*), was transformed into a *hupia*, or *opia*, that is, "a dead person's soul or spirit." The term *aco*, or *caco*, designated "the human eye" and was present in several expressions such a *peiticaco*, "a man with black eyes," or *buticaco*, "man with light-blue eyes." Among the scant number of other words in this category are *yarima*, "anus or end part" and *ahi*, which probably meant "tooth." *Caracaracol*, "an infirmity of the skin, a rash," was one of the few recorded diseases.

The Taíno social and political order attracted greater attention, especially those elements that reflected hierarchy and power. The *cacique* was the chief or leader of the tribal unit. There were numerous of these *caciques* as well as under *caciques* or sub-*caciques*, who ruled over provinces and smaller areas in a universally recognized hierarchy. In general, Taíno society was sharply stratified between the privileged aristocratic *nitainos* and the *naborías*, who were commoners and who obeyed the former and did their bidding. The title *guamiquina*, meaning "great lord, or person," was the term used by the Taínos when referring to the greatest of men; it was the title the Taínos used, for example, in referring to Columbus. The aristocratic order was also organized in an internal hierarchy with appropriate terms of address for individuals in accordance with their rank and position in society. The term of highest respect and honor among the *nitainos* was *matunherí*, which translates as "Most noble" and was reserved for the very highest *caciques*. The title *guaoxerí* referred to the intermediate category and *baharí* to the least of them. Social bonding and great friendship were expressed by the use of *guatiao*, or *daihao/datihao*, that is, "the exchange of names between two persons, as a sign of great friendship."

Of all their economic activities, agriculture was the most important in that it provided the basis of all daily life as well as the rest of their material culture and the basis of much of religious belief. The principal food plants—*yuca, aje, yahutía, maní, lerén, mahiz,* and *aji*—have already been mentioned above. These were cultivated through swidden agriculture and, in many instances, in *conucos,* small mounds of loose earth in which the tuber crops grew rapidly and well. The existence of a variety of names for different kinds of *yuca, aje* and *yayagua* point to an intensive concern with and understanding of agriculture.

The fields were cultivated by the simplest of means. A dibble stick, called a *coa,* was employed to make holes in the worked mounds loose earth, *conucos,* into which seeds and stalks were manually inserted. In several months, a crop of tubers, small ears of corn and small peppers was harvested. The crops from the fields were converted into several simple foods, the most important of which was *casabi,* "a bread, or biscuit," made from a coarse flour derived from the *yuca* root. After the *hyen,* "poisonous juices," had been extracted from the crushed tubers by means of a long, flexible sieve, the dough was then cooked on a *burén,* a flat ceramic griddle. *Xabxao* was a kind of fine *casabi.*

The village, or *yucayeque,* a collection of thatched structures situated around a central plaza, was the center of Taíno life. The *bohios* were the common dwellings of the *naborias,* while the *caney* were larger structures reserved for the *caciques* and the higher-ranking *nitainos.* We are told by Oviedo that there was also a type of *bohio* called an *eracra.* In the interior of the dwellings, *hamacas,* "hammocks," were strung between the structural posts of the dwellings by means of *hicos,* "cords," which allowed the inhabitants to sleep well above the ground and the annoyance of insects and other pests. *Duhos,* or "ceremonial stools made of wood and sometimes inset with carvings" were used by ranking members of the society. The *barbacoa* was a platform on poles used for storage and perhaps smoking and drying of foods. The Taínos wore scant clothing, principally the *nagua,* "a short loincloth."

The *batey* was the central plaza in the village, where a ceremonial ball-game of the same name, it is believed, was played and where other cultural activities, including, most prominently, the *areitos*, took place. In warfare and battles, known as *guazábara*, the Taíno warrior fought with a *macana*, "a simple wooden club." Otherwise the *coa*, "a sharpened and fire-hardened all-purpose stick," was used for a variety of purposes.

The Taínos were able to exploit the rich marine resources of the surrounding seas as a result of their manufacture and adept use of *canoas*, "large canoes made from the hollowing out of large tree trunks." The *cayuco* was a "small canoe," perhaps of Carib origin, suited for one or several persons. Both were propelled by a *nahe*, "a paddle of simple design."

Taíno cultural activities were all closely associated with their religious practices. The *cohoba* rite was enacted by the *cacique* or the *behique*, "shaman." It involved, first, the inducement of vomiting for purposes of purification, followed by the inhalation of the powder or smoke of *cohiba* "powdered tobacco" (*Nicotiana tabacum*) through a instrument designed for that purpose called a *tabaco*. The *cacique* thereupon fell into a trance, during which he communicated with *zemis*, or "spirit forces in the other world." He returned to consciousness with a message and instructions from the spirits. Positive responses from the deities were followed by the convocation of *areitos*, which consisted of singing, dancing, and chanting on the part of the people, activities that communicated among the members of the group the central cultural and religious repertory of the tribe. These events were accompanied by the playing of drums, *maiohauay* or *baiohabao*, as attested by Pané and *maguey*, by Martyr. The ceremonial culture also included the employment of *guaizas*, or "masks."

Taíno religion was marked by polytheism, animism, shamanism, and fetishism. The *cacique* acted as a kind of "pontifex maximus," while the *behique* performed healing and other ritual duties. The Taínos believed in an all-powerful god, *Yocuhu Vagua Maorocoti*, whose name meant "The giver of Yuca, the Sea, the one without a grandfather," according to Las Casas. His mother, *Atabey*, or *Atabeira*, had five names in all, which, according to Pané, were *Apito, Guacar, Yermao*, and *Zuimaco*.

Beneath the mother and son in importance were other deities, all represented by idols called *zemis*, or *cemis*, many of which were seen to reside in incised, three-pointed stones of the same name. In general, those *zemis* originated and dwelled in the primal forces of nature. For example, *Guabancex* and *Guatauba* were *zemis* who were associated with hurricanes, whereas *Boiniael* and *Maroho* were related to rain. And there were numerous others. The principal rites of the Taínos were the *cahoba* rite and the *areito*, both already mentioned above, which were aimed at interpreting the will of the deities and then venerating them. Ritual purification by vomitting and fasting were a means of ritual sacrifice through which the *caciques* and *behiques* approached the *zemis*. Additionally, they maintained certain beliefs, such as the notion that humanity, that is, the Indian peoples, originated in a cave called *Cacibagiagua*. A certain mythological figure *Machochael* was the guardian of the cave whence issued those first humans. *Jouanaboina*, was another cave which was believed to have been the source for the sun and the moon. Another legend had it that there was an island in the sea, *Matinino*, where only women lived. As rich as the Taíno religion appears to have been as witnessed by the short sample of the foregoing, it is certain that the early writers, especially Pané, Las Casas, and Martyr, collected only a part of the Taíno lore and, at that, imperfectly. Christian writers, after all, had no real interest in promoting "pagan" belief and ritual.

Not a great deal of the Taínos' knowledge of the physical world and its workings was recorded by the early observers. Since such information would have been viewed as non-productive and not usable toward any specific end by the chroniclers, it was neither solicited nor recorded. Certainly it must have existed. It is difficult to imagine, for example, that such intrepid seafarers had no knowledge of the secrets of the seas and the heavens so important in navigating them. But, in general, we know little of the intellectual content of their culture beyond the fact that they had a system of counting that did not extend beyond twenty, the first four numbers of which are supplied by Las Casas, namely *hequetí, yamocá, canocúm,* and *yamoncobre,* etc.[46]

Taíno During the Early Spanish Period

Las Casas was of the opinion that the Taínos in the Greater Antilles had been extinguished by the middle of the 16th c. It presently seems clear that Taíno was spoken in the major islands of the Greater Antilles, especially Puerto Rico and Cuba, until the middle of the 16th century and perhaps even into the late 16th century by small, isolated pockets. Some scholars have posited that the language remained alive and was spoken until indeed much later. What is certain is that no viable, effective Taíno speech communities survived the 16th century, due to the swift destruction and collapse of the Taíno people and their culture and due to the strong pressure from Castilian Spanish during a period of widespread bilingualism.

The destruction of the Taíno peoples in their own lands has been well documented, beginning with the writings of Las Casas.[47] Taíno communities were first defeated militarily and then subjugated under the harsh labor systems known as *repartimiento* and then the *encomienda*. Wherever they rebelled or resisted in any way they were either massacred or reduced to outright slavery. Under this oppressive system of forced labor, groups of Taíno people were simply assigned to certain Spaniards who had fought in the conquest, and, who, therefore in theory, were entitled to receive a grant of labor as a recompense from the crown and as tribute from the vanquished. For their part, the Indians were expected to produce gold in the mines and food from their *conucos* for the newcomers. The excessive demands for labor in gold mining, however, made it impossible for the Taínos to maintain the *conuco* system, and to feed themselves, not to mention the Spaniards. Their failure to keep pace led to harsh reprisals, which only served to weaken them further. They were further weakened by newly introduced European diseases, and, equally, in a psychological manner, by the rapid deterioration of their culture, way of life and belief system. These latter were ruthlessly replaced by an uncompromising Christianity, the Spanish colonial state, and, to accompany them, a new language, Castilian. Under these unrelenting pressures, the population of the major islands dropped precipitously, from perhaps 550,000 individuals just before the encounter to negligible numbers by the mid-16th century.[48] The Taínos in the Greater Antilles had, in effect, been annihilated, as a culture and as a people.

Since Spanish women were present in the Indies in only limited numbers during the early decades of the conquest, Spanish men competed within Taíno communities for Taíno women. The early chroniclers tell of Spaniards living with Taíno wives from the first decades of the settlement of the larger islands, enthralled by their natural beauty and innocent ways. This practice produced several noteworthy results. First, it meant that the birthrate of pure Taíno infants was drastically diminished from the start of the colonial period, thereby reducing at the very same time the numbers of persons who would have been raised and enculturated in a purely Taíno environment under normal circumstances. And second, those Spanish-Taíno unions produced significant numbers of so-called *mestizos*, who, in the course of their lifetimes, engaged in widespread bilingualism, of a variety featuring increasingly more Spanish and increasingly less Taíno. In an amazingly short time, perhaps less than three generations, the indigenous people were no longer capable of being authentically Taíno; nor were they permitted to become fully Spanish. Under such stresses as these, the remnants of the Taíno communities were unable to function effectively and competitively within the newly imposed Iberian colonial system.

Other ethnic groups and their concomitant cultural and linguistic influences were introduced into the Spanish islands at the very time that the Taínos were being decimated. Indians from other parts of the Caribbean, as well as from the South American continent, were captured and introduced into the mines of the Spanish Indies as slave laborers. And enslaved Africans were brought from West Africa in even larger numbers in the course of the 16th c. to provide the labor that the Indians had been expected to provide, particularly in Santo Domingo and to a lesser extent in Puerto Rico and Cuba. The overall effects of these forced migrations were deleterious for the demographic stability of the remaining Taíno population. In both cases, the introduced laborers were largely male, and they sought women in the Taíno community, producing *mestizos* from yet another quarter.

The hierarchy imposed on the Taíno communities in general placed them in a subordinate position to the Spanish conquerors, bureaucrats, and settlers; it followed that their culture and, correspondingly, their language and their way of life were systematically devalued. With the exception of certain members of the clergy, the majority of Spaniards had little motive to learn and use the Taíno language. Las Casas has noted rather poignantly that "...no clergy, neither regular nor secular, knew anything perfectly of the indigenous languages...not because it was difficult to learn but rather because no one, either ecclesiastical or secular, cared in the slightest way at that time to present the doctrine or knowledge of God to those people but rather used them without learning any more words in their languages than 'daca pan' and 'va a las minas saca oro.' and those things that were essential to serve and fulfill the wishes of the Spaniards."[49] For these reasons the period in which bilingualism existed in Española was brief and rather lopsided. In practice, the Taíno remnant accepted Spanish by default, but few Spaniards learned Taíno. Moreover, Christian evangelization insisted on the domination of its own official language, Latin, in tandem with the imposition of the official language of the state, Spanish. The very nature of Christianization required immediate and direct Hispanization. With no official place within the colonial system, no status, no specific function nor having the power of resiliency inherent in overwhelming numbers of speakers, as would subsequently be the case for Nahuatl and other mainland Amerindian languages, Taíno declined rapidly and, perhaps, inevitably.

The Nature of Taíno Lexical Survivals

The Spanish scholar Rafael Lapesa has observed that "the oldest and principal nucleus of Americanisms [in Spanish] proceeds from Arawakan [i.e., Taíno]. Since the Antillean islands were the first lands to be discovered, it was there that the conquistadors became acquainted with the nature and life in the New World. Such words as *canoa, cacique, bohío, maíz, batata, carey, caníbal, naguas,* or *enaguas, sabana, nigua, guacamayo, tabaco, tiburón,* and *yuca* are Arawakan."[50] It is curious indeed that even though the Taínos and their societies were annihilated in very short time by the onslaught of the Spaniards, more words have survived from their language than from any other Amerindian language that came into contact with Castilian. What explains this anomaly?

First, it should be noted that Taíno was the very first language that the Spaniards encountered in the New World and as such, it left a deep imprint on the invaders. In the period from 1492 to the year 1519 when the conquest of Mesoamerica began, the Spaniards in the Greater Antilles gained their fundamental knowledge of life in the islands of the New World and among the native peoples and institutions there. When they launched into new adventures in the other realms of America, they carried that Antillean knowledge and lore with them and employed it in dealing with other Indian peoples whom they encountered elsewhere. Second, it is to be noted that even when the Indians had disappeared as a distinct ethnic group, they left behind them both their blood and the elements of their culture in the persons of the numerous *mestizos* engendered through contacts with both Europeans and Africans. Something of the Indian experience survived the trauma of genocide and found its way into the cultural mix that was already being called *criollo,* that is, "creole," as something distinct from that which was *peninsular* or European. It is doubtlessly by this route that most of the linguistic elements survived and gained an extended life in Spanish and, eventually, in other world languages as well. That phenomenon merits a few comments here.

In the most general terms, elements of the Taíno language may be said to have survived in the following cultural and linguistic strata: survivals in the islands of the Taíno homeland; survivals in other areas of Latin America, in the colloquial forms of other Amerindian languages and in colloquial Spanish; survivals in both spoken and written

Spanish; and, by extension, survival in other European languages and in other languages in the world.

1. Taíno Homeland   Taíno had no script or written language, but, nevertheless, a significant number of Taíno words has survived, principally in the directly descended colloquial Spanish of the three islands of Hispaniola, Cuba, and Puerto Rico. In particular, all three islands are rich in toponyms and terms for cultural practices derived from the vanished Taínos. The works of Tejera and Hernández Aquino testify eloquently to that tradition.

2. New World   The conquistadores who landed in central America and then surged inland, turning both north and south in the process, took with them the experience that they had acquired from the encounter with the native peoples of the Caribbean, especially the Greater Antilles. "Those Arawakan words which they had learned in Santo Domingo and Haití," notes Lapesa, "they extended to other regions of America."[51] As a result they carried such terms as *cacique, canoa, maiz, huracán, hamaca, casabi* and others to new lands where they quickly joined *cacahuete, cacao* and *chocolate* from Nahuatl, *alpaca, vicuña, condor* and *papa* from Quecha and *tapir* and *gaucho* from Guarani. Some of these terms which were acquired in the Taíno islands became indispensable to the Spaniards as they invaded other Indian lands and therefore become embedded in the other Indian languages as well as in the Spanish of both the New World and the Old.

3. Spain and the Spanish Language   Several New World Indian languages—*Nahuatl, Chibcha, Tupinamba, Guarani* and others—had a major impact on Spanish. But of all these languages it was Taíno with which the men of Spain had their very first contact for the period of approximately a generation, the period 1492 to 1519. And it was from Taíno that the rest of America and the Old World received some of its most powerful and enduring linguistic pictures of the encounter. Just as Taíno words were carried on the tide of conquest through the New World so they were also conveyed back the Old World by soldiers, priests, merchants and bureaucrats, in the various forms of letters, such as the one written by Columbus, of verbal testimony, such as that received by Peter Martyr, who spoke with witnesses returning from the New World and of the written reports and histories of the early chroniclers.

4. European and Other Languages in the World   Rather quickly numbers of Taíno words passed into Spanish, just as had Visigothic and Arab words centuries beforehand. And since Spain's was a world culture at the time and since her language was one that was widely admired and respected, it followed that other nations would be disposed to readily adopt the new terms. In the first place, the people of Europe were interested in the news of the curious new things and novel practices flowing into the continent from other parts of the world on the first ebb tide of colonialism. Since Spain was the country initially in closest contact with people of the New World, it was natural that other Europeans would be subject to linguistic innovations from that country and its language. It was for that reason that France, England, The Netherlands, Germany, and other nations received words from the Taíno language and later from other Indian languages through the intermediary of the Spanish language, rendered primarily, of course, from the perspective of the conquistadores.

A cursory examination of the survivals reveals that certain conditions favored the survival of some words beyond the Taíno homeland but not others. If, for example, a particular word represented an essentially new thing or phenomenon, then it stood a greater probability of survival and transmission, especially if the invaders considered the knowledge and the use of the objects in question to be of some practical value. There is no clearer example of this condition than the relationship between the word *tabaco*, which the Spaniards took, mistakenly, to mean the plant represented by the Taíno term *cohiba* (i.e., of the genus *Nicotiana*) on the one hand and the cotton plant on the other. The newcomers had no previous experience at all with the tobacco plant or its uses and it therefore passed immediately into Spanish. The acceptance of the new word was also conditioned by a parallel acceptance by Europeans of the uses which could be made of the plant as well as the desire for the potential profits derived therefrom. Even though they confused the name of the device (i.e., *tabaco*) in which the plant was consumed for the plant (*cohiba*) itself, they nevertheless accepted the new term into their language readily. The contrast of this experience with that of cotton, on the other hand, is instructive. Even though the Taínos made use of the cotton plant and produced quality cotton cloth, the Spaniards took no notice of the Taíno word for the plant insofar as they had long since been acquainted with it (*algodón*) and its products, having been introduced to the plant and its name much earlier from Arabic. An analogous relationship is to be seen between the Taíno words *huracán* and *caona*. The Taíno term for the hitherto not experienced tropical storms, *huracán*, found an immediate and permanent place in Spanish and, from there, spread into many other languages of the world, while the various Indian expressions for gold, *caona* and *nozay*, did not. Gold had been known to the people of the Iberian peninsula from earliest times; its name derives from Latin (Sp. *oro* < Latin *aurum*). Hurricanes of the kind generated in the Caribbean were altogether new experience for Europeans whereas gold was not. For that reason the term *huracán* passed quickly into Spanish while *caona* did not.

Second, the potential utility of the phenomena in question similarly enhanced such chances of linguistic acceptance. Without delay Europeans found that various Taíno devices and products, such as *tabaco* already commented upon, along with the *bohío*, the *barbacoa*, the *hamaca*, the *canoa* and *casabi* were important, indeed in some cases absolutely essential, to their survival and success in their imperial undertaking in the larger world; their names therefore passed readily into Spanish. On the other hand, such was not the case for the greater number of spiritual phenomena, such as the terminology of numerous Taínos religious practices and concepts, which were considered repugnant to Christian belief and counter-productive to the missionary enterprise. The latter have only survived therefore as curiosities in the texts of the chroniclers.

Likewise transportability played a less obvious but nonetheless significant role in the selection process. Those things that could be trans-

SOME OBSERVATIONS ON THE TAINO LANGUAGE

ported beyond the limits of the Taíno cultural domain and put to effective use elsewhere enjoyed a greater possibility of survival. *Mahíz*, as one example, could be taken to other geographic regions—Europe and Africa— and easily grown in certain areas there while *aje* could not. Consequently, the former is widespread in other languages, the latter is not. Much in the same manner, a *hamaca* could be taken about anywhere, including on sailing vessels, and effectively employed whereas a *caney* could not and so on and so forth.

The Taíno language had flourished in the Caribbean area for nearly two thousand years before it came into violent contact with Spanish culture at the end of the 15th century. In less than half a century, the Taíno people, their culture and language were effectively destroyed as independent, autonomous entities. Yet in spite of that sudden catastrophe, traces of the original people of those islands and elements of their culture have survived by being ultimately assimilated and absorbed into the colonial establishment of the conquerors. As that was occurring, the process of assimilation of the vanquished effected a partial transformation of the conquerors. In the first place, the Taíno bloodline mixed with European and African elements, giving rise to new physical types, particularly in the larger islands. Running parallel with that biological process, certain salient aspects of the Taíno culture, already commented upon above, were selectively adopted by generations of successors in the Indies, along with those linguistic elements that gave those cultural features expression. In time, new people and new cultures appeared in the West Indies, identified by the Spanish word *criollo* (creole), a term which takes on its full meaning only when it is contrasted to other designations—"peninsular," "Spanish," "European." The Taíno contribution to that creation of a creole identity and lifestyle, not least in the area of language, has been considerable.

NOTES

1. For an overview of the Indian languages of the Americas, see Merritt Ruhlen, *A Guide to the World's Languages. Volume 1: Classification* (Stanford, CA: Stanford University Press, 1987), pp. 200–51.

2. For a brief linguistic overview of the West Indies, see Douglas Taylor's "The Amerindian Languages of the West Indies," in his *The Languages of the West Indies* (Baltimore and London: The Johns Hopkins University Press, 1977), pp. 13–148. Useful also are his "Languages and Ghost-Languages of the West Indies," *International Journal of American Linguistics* 22 (1956): 180–83 and his "Languages and Ghost-Languages of the West Indies: A Postscript," *IJAL* 23 (1957): 114–16. See also C. H. de Goeje, "Nouvel examen des langues des Antilles," *Journal de la Société des Américanistes* 31 (1939): 1–120.

3. Irving Rouse, *The Tainos: Rise & Decline of the People Who Greeted Columbus* (New Haven & London: Yale University Press, 1992), pp. 5–19.

4. Studies restricted solely to Taíno are to this point few in number. See José Juan Arrom's, "La Lengua de Los Taínos: Aportes Lingüísticos al Conocimiento de su Cosmovisión," in *Las Culturas de América en la Época del Descubrimiento*, Coleccíon Encuentros, Serie Seminarios (Spain: Turner S.A., c. 1992), pp. 53–64 and his Estudios de lexicologia Antillana (Havana: Casa de las Américas, 1980) In addition see, Julián Vivanco, *El lenguaje de los indios de Cuba* (Havana: Editorial Ilustración Panamericana, 1946). Also important are the early pioneering works of C.H. de Goeje, *The Arawak Language of Guiana* (Amsterdam: Koninklijke Akadamie van Wetenschappen te Amsterdam, 1928) and Daniel G. Brinton, "The Arawack Language of Guiana in its Linguistic and Ethnological Relations," *Transactions of the American Philological Society* 14 (1871): 427–44.

5. Irving Rouse, *Migrations in Prehistory: Inferring Population Movement from Cultural Remains*, (New Haven & London: Yale University Press, 1986), pp. 20–21. These were the people referred to by Las Casas as the "Ciboney." See Emilio Tejera, *Indigenismos* (Santo Domingo: Editora de Santo Domingo, S.A., 1977), pp. 398–400.

6. For a compilation of all the early texts relative to the Ciguayo, see Tejera, pp. 417–21.

7. Robert H. Fuson, ed., *The Log of Christopher Columbus* (Camden, ME: International Marine Publishing, 1992), p. 172.

8. Père Raymond Breton, *Relations de L'Ile de La Guadeloupe (1647)* (Basse-Terre, Guadeloupe: Société d'Histoire de La Guadeloupe, 1978), pp. 52–53.

9. Taylor, *The Languages of the West Indies*, pp. 14–16. The word lists date from

the early 17th century and were preserved in the work of Johannes de Laet, *Nieuw Wereldt ofte Beschrijvinghe van West-Indien enz* (Leyden: I. Elzevier, 1625).

10. Marshall Durbin, "A Survey of the Carib Language Family," in *South American Indian Languages: Retrospect and Prospect*, edited by Harrtiet E. Manelis Klein and Louisa R. Stark (Austin, TX: University of Texas Press, 1985), pp. 325–70. Contains a discussion of Galibi in South America, as spoken along the coast from the mouth of the Amazon to the Orinoco (see pp. 354–60). For recent ethnohistorical works on the Island-Caribs, see Phillip P. Boucher, *Cannibal Encounters: Europeans and Island Caribs, 1492–1763* (Baltimore: The Johns Hopkins University Press, 1992) and Peter Hulme and Neil L. Whitehead, *Wild Majesty: Encounters with Caribs from Columbus to the Present Day: An Anthology* (Oxford: Clarendon Press, 1992).

11. Douglas R. Taylor and Berend J. Hoff, "The Linguistic Repertory of the Island-Carib in the Seventeenth Century: The Men's Language—A Carib Pidgin?" *International Journal of Anthropological Linguistics* 46:4 (1980): 301–12.

12. Irving Rouse, *Migrations in Prehistory*, pp. 106–56. See also Fred Olsen, *On the Trail of the Arawaks* (Norman, OK: University of Oklahoma Press, 1974).

13. Rouse, *The Tainos.....*, p. 80. See also his "La Frontera Taína: Su Prehistoria y Sus Precursores," in *La Cultura Taína*, in *Las Culturas de América en la Época del Descubrimiento*, Colección Encuentros, Serie Seminarios (Spain: Turner S.A., c. 1992), pp. 27–38.

14. Rouse, *The Tainos...* pp. 109–18.

15. In addition to Rouse's works on the Taínos, see Sven Lovén, *Origins of the Tainan Culture, West Indies* (New York: AMS Press, 1979. Originally published as *Über die Wurzeln der tainischen Kultur* Göteborg; Elanders Boktryckeri, 1935). See also Jesse W. Fewkes, *The Aborigines of Porto Rico and Neighboring Islands* (New York: Johnson Reprint Corporation, 1970) and Thomas A. Joyce, *Central American and West Indian Archaeology: Being an Introduction to the Archaeology of the States of Nicaragua, Costa Rica, Panama and the West Indies by Thomas A. Joyce, with Many Illustrations & Two Maps.* Part II, The West Indies (Freeport, NY: Books for Libraries Press, 1971, [First published 1916]), pp. 163–263. Other more recent ethnohistorical accounts are the two excellent studies by Roberto Cassá, *Los Taínos de La Española* (Santo Domingo: Editora "Alfa y Omega," 1974) and *Los Indios de Las Antillas*, Colección Indios de América (Madrid: Editorial Mapfre, 1992) and Marcio Veloz Maggliolo, *Arqueologia Prehistorica de Santo Domingo* (Singapore: McGraw-Hill Far Eastern Publishers, 1972).

16. The principal works in question are the following: Columbus's log as herein cited in Fuson, *The Log of Christopher Columbus*; Bartolomé La Casas's two works, *Historia de las Indias*, Colección de documentos inéditos para la historia de España (Madrid, 1875–1876), 5 tomos and his *Apologética Historia de las Indias*, tomo 1 of

the series *Historiadores de Indias,* edited by Daniel Serrano y Sanz (Madrid: Bailly, Baillière e Hijos, 1909); Gonzalo Fernández de Oviedo's two works *De la Natural Hystoria de las Indias,* a Facsimile Edition Issued in Honor of Sterling A. Stroudemire (Chapel Hill, NC: University of North Carolina Press, 1969) and his *Historia General y Natural de las Indias (1535),* edited by Juan Pérez de Tudela Bueso (Madrid: Real Academia Española, Ediciones Atlas, 1959), 5 v.; Diego Alvarez Chanca, "La Carta que escribió a la Cuidad de Seville, Febrero a Marzo 1494," in *Colección de los Viages y Descrubrimientos, Que Hicieron por Mar Los Españoles desde Fines del Siglo XV,* v. 1, edited by Martin Fernández de Navarrete (Madrid: Imprenta Real, 1825); Michele de Cuneo, "Lettera," (15 –28 ottobre, 1495 Savona), in *Raccolta di Documenti e Studi pubblicati dalla Reale Commissione Colombiana pel Quarto Centenario dalla Scoperta dell'America* (Roma, 1892–1894), Parte III, v. II; Ramón Pané, *Relación acerca de las antigüedades de los indios,* 8th edition (Mexico City, 1989); and Peter Martyr d'Anghiera, *The Decades of the New Worlde or West India.* Translated from the Latin original by Richard Eden (London: Guilhelmi Powell, 1555, Reprint by Readex Microprint, 1966).

17. *Colección de Documentos Inéditos Relativos al Descubrimiento, Conquista y Organización de las Antiguas Posesiones Españolas de Ultramar, Tomo I, Isla de Cuba* (Madrid: La Real Academia de la Historia, 1885) and Martín Fernández de Navarrete, ed., *Colección de los Viages y Descubrimientos que Hicieron los Españoles por Mar desde Fines del Siglo XV* (Madrid: 1825–37), 5 v.

18. In particular, see the lexicographical works of Emilio Tejera, *Indigenismos* and Luis Hernández Aquino, *Diccionario de Voces Indígenas de Puerto Rico,* Tercera edición (Puerto Rico: editorial cultural, 1993). For the island of Hispaniola, consult Pedro Henriquez Ureña, *El Español en Santo Domingo* (Argentina: Instituto de Filología de la Universidad de Buenos Aires, 1940); for Puerto Rico, see Manuel Álvarez Nazario, *El influjo indígena en el español de Puerto Rico* (Mayagüez, Puerto Rico: 1977) and Cayetano Coll y Toste, "Vocabulario de palabras introducidas en el idioma español procedentes del lenguaje indio-antilliano," *Boletín Histórico de Puerto Rico* 8 (1921): 294–320. Broader studies include Tomás Buesa Oliver, *Indoamericanismos léxicos en español* (Madrid: 1965) and Alfredo Zayas y Alfonso, *Lexicografía antillana* 2nd edition (Habana: 1932), 2 v.

19. In particular, see the writings of Père Raymond Breton, including: *Relations de L'Ile de La Guadeloupe (1647)* (Basse-Terre, Guadeloupe: Société d'Histoire de La Guadeloupe, 1978); *Grammaire Caraïbe* (Paris: Maisonneuve & Cie., 1878); *Dictionnaire Caraïbe-François* (Auxerre: Gilles Bouquet, 1665); and *Dictionaire François-Caraïbe* (Auxerre: Gilles Bouquet, 1666. Réimprimé par Jules Platzmann, fac-simile édition, *Dictionnaire Français-Caraïbe,* Leipzig: B.G. Teubner, 1900). The works of most of the other early French commentators on the Caribs are

included in Spanish translation in Manuel Cárdenas Ruíz, ed., *Cronicas Francesas de los Indios Caribes* (Puerto Rico: Centro de Estudios Avanzados de Puerto Rico y El Caribe, 1981).

20. For linguistic background on the South American homeland of the Arawakan languages and the place of that family relative to the other principle Amerindian families, see Terrence Kaufman, "Language History in South America: What We Know and How We Know it," in *Amazonian Linguistics: Studies in Lowland South American Languages*, edited by Doris L. Payne Austin, TX: University of Texas Press, 1990), pp. 13–73. See also see Ruhlen, pp. 200–51.

21. Kingsley G. Noble, *Proto-Arawakan and its Descendants*, Publication of the Research Center in Anthropology, Folklore and Linguistics (Bloomington: Indiana University, 1965), p. 108.

22. Rouse, *Migrations in Prehistory*, pp. 122–23.

23. Fuson, pp. 96–97 and 100.

24. *Ibid.*, p. 120.

25. *Ibid.*, p. 133.

26. *Ibid.*, p. 147. It is possible that these were non-Taíno speakers, perhaps Ciguayo.

27. Las Casas, *Historia de las Indias*, v.1, p. 326.

28. Gonzalo Fernández de.Oviedo y Valdés, *Historia General y Natural de las Indias (1535)*, v. 1, p. 235.

29. Arnold R. Highfield, "Toward a Language History of the Danish West Indies and the U.S. Virgin Islands," in *The Danish Presence and Legacy in the Virgin Islands*, edited by Svend E. Holsoe and John H. McCollum (Frederiksted, St. Croix: St. Croix Landmarks Society, 1993), pp. 123–39 and *St. Croix 1493: An Encounter of Two Worlds* (St. Thomas: The Virgin Islands Humanities Council, 1995).

30. Tomás Navarro Tomás, *El Español en Puerto Rico* (Rio Pedras, Puerto Rico: Editorial de la Universidad de Puerto Rico, 1948), p. 181.

31. Las Casas, v. 5, p. 486.

32. Las Casas v. 5, p. 495.

33. Las Casas discusses the principal political divisions of *Haití* in his *Apologética Historia de las Indias*, tomo 1 of the series *Historiadores de Indias*, edited by Daniel Serrano y Sanz (Madrid: Bailly, Baillière e Hijos, 1909). Maps depicting reconstuctions of the cacicazgos of Española are presented in Samuel M. Wilson's *Hispaniola: Caribbean Chiefdoms in the Age of Columbus* (Tuscaloosa/London: The University of Alabama Press, 1990), pp. 108–10.

34. Douglas Taylor "A Preliminary View of Arawak Phonology," *International Journal of American Linguistics* 35:3 (1969): 234–38 and "Some Remarks on the

Spelling and Formation of Taíno Words," *International Journal of American Linguistics* 26 (1969): 345–48.

35. Taken from Emilio Tejera's *Indigenismos*, p. 1,321. Tejera's work is valuable in large part because it cites not only specific lexical items but also long passages from the texts of the early chroniclers as context.

36. José G. Moreno de Alba, *El Español de América* (México: Fondo de Cultura Económica, 1988), p. 49.

37. Alonso Zamora Vicente, *Dialectología Española*, segunda edición (Madrid: Editorial Gredos, S.A., 1967), p. 391.

38. The words in the pages that follow have been taken from a number of sources, but most prominently from the following authors whose works have already been cited above: Las Casas, *Historia de las Indias* and his *Apologética Historia de las Indias*; Oviedo, *Historia General y Natural de las Indias* and his *De la Natural Hystoria de las Indias*; Peter Martyr's *The Decades of the New Worlde or West India*; and Ramón Pané's *Relación acerca de las antigüedades de los indios*. In addition, the following secondary resources have also been relied upon: Georg Friederici, *Hilfswörterbuch für den Amerikanisten: Lehnwörter aus Indianer-Sprachen und Erklärungen altertümlicher Ausdrücke, Deutsch—Spanisch—Englisch,*. Studien über Amerika und Spanien, Exra-Serie No. 2, edited by Karl Sapper, Aurthur Franz and Adalbert Hämel (Halle: Max Niemeyer Verlag, 1925); C.H. de Goeje, "Nouvel examen des langues des Antilles"; Luis Hernández Aquino, *Diccionario de Voces Indígenas de Puerto Rico*; Juan Augusto y Salvador Perea, *Glosario Etimologico Taíno-Español: Histórico y Etnográfico* (Mayagüez, Puerto Rico: The authors, 1941); and Emilio Tejera, *Indigenismos*.

39. The following examples draw predominantly on citations in Tejera's *Indigenismos*.

40. This latter interpretation is that of Arrom in "La Lengua de Los Taínos: Aportes Lingüísticos al Conocimiento de su Cosmovisión," p. 61.

41. *Ibid.*, p. 56.

42. Perea argues that, although they do not appear specifically in any of the early sources, the stems *camuy* "sun," and *aru*, "moon" are present in other words (i.e., *Camuy*, "a river in Puerto Rico" and *Maroho*, "a lunar zemi"). See Perea, pp. 18–22.

43. Fuson, p. 137.

44. See Hernández Aquino's *Diccionario de Voces Indígenas de Puerto Rico.*

45. In Island-Carib, the term for man was "eyeri." Raymond Breton, *Dictionaire François-Caraïbe*, p. 204.

46. Las Casas, *Apologética Historia*, p. 538.

47. Las Casas, *Brevísima Relación de la Destruición de las Indias*, Edición de André Saint-Lu, Sexta Edición (Madrid: Ediciónes Catedras, S.A., 1992).

48. For a discussion of the question of the pre-encounter population of the Taíno islands, see Roberto Cassá, *Los Indios de las Antillas* , pp. 207–12.

49. The two phrases in Spanish can be translated as "get bread for me," and "go to the mines and take out the gold."

50. Rafael Lapesa, *Historia de la Lengua Española*, Novena edición (Madrid: Editorial Gredos, 1991), p. 557.

51. *Ibid.*

Die groote Kerken - Litany.

K Kirie,   Eleiſon!
Chriſte,   Eleiſon!
Kirie,   Eleiſon!
Chriſte,   hoor na ons!

Heer God, ons VADER na Hemel!
Gemeente.* *Joe Naam word geheiligd,
joe Koningrik kome, joe Wil geſkied
na Aard lik na die Hemel; ons dagelik
Brood gie ons van Daag; en vergeef ons
onſe Skuld, ſo lik ons vergeef onſe Skul-
denaaren; en lei ons niet na Verſoekin-
ge, maar verlos ons van die Kwaad!*
Koor,** Want van Joe ben die Rik, en
die Kracht, en die Heerlikheid, na
Eewigheid.
Gem. *Amen!*

Copy of the Lord's Prayer written in Dutch Creole
in the 18th century

CHAPTER 41
THE VIRGIN ISLANDS:
A MODERN TOWER OF BABEL?

CULTURES and their languages are always changing however imperceptible that change might appear at first glance. A comparison of the linguistic situation in the Virgin Islands at the beginning the 20th century makes that point rather forcefully.

In 1900, the linguistic situation in our islands was somewhat as follows. Danish was still the official language, used daily by administrators, by government officials, by a small minority of the planters and by an equally small portion of the general population. Although it was still taught in the schools, its use had in fact never been widespread. Already in the latter part of the 19th century, it had gradually given way before the advance of English and English Creole.

In the 18th century Dutch Creole had been the language of the major portion of the population, particularly in St. Thomas and St. John. Through the 19th century, however, that Creole declined steadily, especially after Emancipation. Its narrow association with plantation life and with slavery no doubt contributed to its weakening. By the beginning of the 20th century, its use was restricted to older people and to country areas for the most part, having been replaced by English Creole as used among younger people especially in the towns.

The English Creole of the Virgin Islands traces its lineage back to the early 18th century. As a member of the overall family of Caribbean Creole languages, it was marked by certain typological features, such as zero copula, a distinct verbal system, aspectual marking, and the like. These linguistic features distinguish the early Creole from the Virgin Islands English that has subsequently replaced it and that is more widely spoken today.

Several factors contributed to English Creole's eventual supplanting of Dutch Creole. First, a number of planters, particularly on St. Croix, had immigrated here from the English islands with their enslaved workers throughout the course of the 18th and 19th centuries, bringing their linguistic baggage with them.

Second, Dutch Creole, which had been closely associated with the Moravian Mission movement appears to have fallen out of favor when that movement began to decline, especially after Emancipation. Finally, Dutch Creole seems to have been inevitably linked with past slavery, whereas English was associated with the policies of the most advanced nation of that age.

A dialect of French (St. Thomas French Dialect) flourished at Carenage (Frenchtown) on St. Thomas at the end of the 19th century. It traced it origins to the migration of French-speakers from St. Barts, beginning in the 1860s. The immigrants were, for the most part, fishermen of European extraction who spoke, not standard French, but a dialect from the maritime provinces of France, dating back to the 17th century

In addition, a small population of French Creole speakers, also of European extraction, settled in that same period on the Northside of St. Thomas. The latter group was distinct, however, from the Carenage group in both language and in their means of economic livelihood; they were mostly farmers. In relative isolation these two communities thrived and persisted well into the 20th century, with their languages intact if recessive.

In general, St. Thomas could boast of being a good deal more cosmopolitan at the beginning of the century than her sister islands. The expansive port at Charlotte Amalia, the predominance of international trade, the presence of mail service ships and regional commerce attracted people to St. Thomas from many parts of the Caribbean and the wider world. It was therefore not uncommon to hear a number of languages spoken on the streets of town. It was this image that J. Antonio Jarvis had in mind when he wrote that every Virgin Islander was a natural linguist, based on the daily contacts with a diversity of foreign languages.

Given more to agriculture and country life, both St. Croix and St. John were linguistically conservative at that time. Along with the official Danish language, both English and English Creole were spoken on St. Croix. At the same time, small numbers of Hispanophones from eastern Puerto Rico and its off-lying islands were beginning to appear as seasonal immigrants.

St. John continued to remain the most conservative of the islands linguistically. In that milieu, Dutch Creole was able to hang on longer alongside English and English Creole there than in the sister islands. Limited contacts with the outside world slowed linguistic change and acted as a conservative influence.

With the transfer of the islands to the United States in 1917, English replaced Danish as the official language of the islands. Naval administrators, sailors, educators, and nurses appeared on these shores in ever increasing numbers in the years that followed. Moreover, Virgin Islanders themselves began to travel to the mainland, returning as the bearers of North American linguistic influences that spread readily among the local population. These influences are witnessed by the appearance of a new verb in local speech, "to yank," meaning to affect American speech.

In the mid-1920s, St. Croix's linguistic fortunes were influenced by events in nearby Puerto Rico. The collapse of the sugar centrals in Vieques unleashed a wave of migration aimed primarily, though not exclusively, at St. Croix's west end. Year after year hundreds of Spanish speakers came to work as laborers in the island's declining sugar business. In time, the workers brought their families with them and settled on the island permanently, becoming small farmers, small business owners and the like.

The depression in the 1930s and the U.S. military takeover of much of the island of Vieques in the 1940s ensured that the migration would continue, as it has done down to the present. The proximity and regional importance of Puerto Rico and the Dominican Republic have determined that the Hispanic culture and language would not be lost as the Hispanic immigrants became a part of the local scene.

World War II brought an increased United States military presence to the Virgin Islands, along with more English-speaking Americans. As baseball replaced cricket as a primary sport, so the American form of speech put increasing pressure on indigenous English Creole speech. In every sphere of local life and especially in government and education, U.S. influence continued apace. The war was followed by the growth of tourism in the 1940s and 1950s. The 1960s brought light and heavy industries, especially to St. Croix. This meant new immigration and new linguistic influences.

At the same time, Virgin Islanders ventured in ever greater numbers to the mainland to work, to study, to serve in the military and so on. As people moved about increasingly, the great media revolution left its linguistic imprint as well. First radio, then television, film, cable television and most recently the Internet have all combined to transform what people hear and how they respond.

To no one's surprise, with these exchanges in culture have come corresponding changes in communication and language. Virgin Islands English Creole has all but disappeared in the second half of the 20th century, its place being filled by what might be called Virgin Islands English. This form of speech resembles American English in its general grammatical structures but retains certain Creole features, in particular in regard to intonation, accent and a number of vocabulary items.

But the economic transformation brought more than just a heavy American English influence. Immigrants arrived from every part of the Caribbean region, as well as from areas all around the world. The sum effect has been to create a society that is as diverse and multilingual as any that one is likely to encounter anywhere.

In this scenario, English and English Creole speakers have arrived here from every island in the Caribbean, but in especially large numbers from St. Kitts, Nevis, Antigua and Trinidad. In addition, we have received French Creole, or Patois speakers, principally from Dominica and St. Lucia, but from Guadeloupe, Martinique, and Haiti as well. Papiamento, or Luso-Hispanic Creole, with speakers from Aruba, Bonaire and Curaçao, were attracted initially by our oil-refining industry.

All the while, Hispanophones have continued to arrive, not only from Puerto Rico and its dependencies but more recently from the Dominican Republic, Cuba and Columbia, adding their numbers to the sizable bilingual Hispanic population already established here for several generations.

Since the late 1940s the numbers of Arabic speakers has grown every year. Political events in the state of Israel in 1948 and throughout the 1950s and 1960s have sent a migration of Palestinians and Jordanians to our islands in small but influential numbers. With them they have brought not only their business acumen but also their families, cultures and language—Levantine Arabic. Though they nearly all learn functional English very quickly, Arabic is still heard daily around their service stations, furniture stores, groceries, and other small businesses. Their custom of maintaining close contact with their former homeland in places such as Ramallah, Jericho, and Jerusalem has had the effect of keeping their culture and language alive for each succeeding generation.

And there are others, such as Hindus from India, Guyana and Trinidad; Tagalog speakers from the Philippines; and Africans in increasing numbers from all parts of the continent and so on. These groups are small but constantly growing at the present time. Nearly all of these newcomers have learned English, at least minimally and function adequately in linguistic interchanges.

At the beginning of our new century then we reflect that in the course of the 20th century the Virgin Islands has undergone considerable linguistic transformation. While we have lost a good deal of our earlier linguistic heritage in the withdrawal of Danish, in the language death of Dutch Creole (the last native Dutch Creole speaker died in the 1980s) and in the decline of V.I. English Creole, we have at the same time found ourselves increasingly attached to the mainstream of North American English.

But that is not to say that our islands have headed on the road to exclusive monolingualism. On the contrary, these islands have in this broader process attracted a host of other speakers of Creole languages and world languages which are used in their full vitality in daily island life. There is no reason at the moment to doubt that our evolving diversification will cease any time soon.

What might we look forward to in the next century, the next millennium? Similar influences as in the past century with perhaps a few surprises. Globalization, migration, travel, economic development, wireless media, and juggernaut of cyberspace will all play important roles. The evolution of our political status could certainly exert a significant influence. Political integration with the United States would most likely hasten the processes that are currently underway. Some form of autonomy or independence might, on the other hand, lead us along another path and allow the shrinking indigenous population to control development and the concomitant immigration rules and at the same time set cultural and language policies that would allow native norms to survive. But whether or not Virgin Islands culture will have the resources and disposition to welcome and enculturate newcomers into its own cultural and linguistic realm is a question that for the moment must remain unanswered.

ATTRIBUTIONS

The articles in this volume originally appeared in the following publications:

"Before the Enterprise of the Indies." In Highfield, *St. Croix 1493: An Encounter of Two Worlds*, (St. Thomas: The Virgin Islands Humanities Council, 1995).

"Notes from the Eye of a Storm: Hurricane Hugo, 1989." In Joseph and Rowe, *Hell Under God's Orders: Hurricane Hugo in St. Croix—Disaster and Survival*, (St. Croix, USVI: Winds of Change Press, 1990).

"Notes from Hurricane Marilyn, 1995." (An unpublished paper.)

"The Danish Atlantic and West Indian Slave Trade." In Tyson & Highfield [eds.], *The Danish West Indian Slave Trade: Virgin Islands Perspectives*, (St. Croix: Virgin Islands Humanities Council, 1994).

"Transatlantic Encounters: Traveling African-Crucians in the 18th Century." Adapted from a paper presented at the Conference, *Transatlanticisms: The Fourth Annual Interdisciplinary Nineteenth-Century Studies Conference*, (Ohio State University. Columbus, Ohio, April 9–10, 1999).

"Ernst Schimmelmann and the Curious Demise of the Danish Atlantic Slave Trade." A lecture presented at The Whim Museum, (St. Croix Landmarks Society, c. 1996).

"Conditions of the Working Class in St. Croix, 1848–1878." A chapter in *Freedom's Flame: Emancipation, a Second Look*. (St. Croix, USVI: Bureau of Libraries, Museums and Archaeological Services, 1983.)

"Myths and Realities in Virgin Islands History." The Isaac Dookhan Memorial Lecture, University of the Virgin Islands, November 14 and 15, 1996.

"Patterns of Accommodation and Resistance: The Moravian Witness to Slavery in the Danish West Indies." In *The Journal of Caribbean History* 28:2 (1994): 138–63.

"Johan Lorentz Carstens: Planter and Merchant on Early 18th Century St. Thomas." *Caribbean Historical & Genealogical Journal* 5:2 (April 1997): 18–27.

"Domingo 'Mingo' Gesoe: An Improbable Life." In Highfield and Tyson, *Negotiating Enslavement: Perspectives on Slavery in the Danish West Indies.* (St. Croix: Antilles Press, 2009).

"Toward a Language History of the Virgin Islands," Holsoe and McCollum [eds.], *The Danish Presence and Legacy in the Virgin Islands,* (Frederiksted, St. Croix: St. Croix Landmarks Society and the V.I. Humanities Council, 1993).

"Some Observations on the Taino Language." Originally prepared for *The Aboriginal People of the Caribbean Conference,* (St. Croix, 1993) and was published subsequently in abbreviated form as a chapter in Wilson's *The Indigenous People of the Caribbean,* (Gainesville, FL: University of Florida Press, 1997).

The following articles all appeared in the *Crucian Trader* in the years 2008 and 2009.

"If Stones Could Talk: The Petroglyphs of St. Croix"; "The Nieuwe Zeeland that never was: The Dutch on St. Croix, 1643–1645"; "When St. Croix was French, 1650–1734"; "The Knights of Malta on St. Croix"; "From Galway and Cork to St. Croix: The Irish Migration to St. Croix"; "The Wreck of the Slave Ship *General Abercrombie*"; "Christiansted: Our Tarnished Jewel of a Town"; "Reparations for Virgin Islanders?"; "The Moravian Mission to St. Croix"; "Sugar Mills of St. Croix"; "The Estates of St. Croix"; "St. Croix and Puerto

Rico: A Long-term Connection"; "Buck Island: A Jewel in the Sea"; "The Crucian Christmas Festival"; "From Baobab to Kapok: The Spirit Trees of the Virgins"; "A Constitution for the Virgin Islands?"; "The Creole Society of the Danish West Indies"; "The Witness of C. G. A. Oldendorp"; "Rebekka Freundlich Protten: A Woman of Faith"; "The Incredible Adventure of Qvou Orsu"; "What Brother Cornelius Can Tell Us"; "William Leidesdorff: A Crucian Who Dared"; "Peter Jackson: 'The Black Prince' of St. Croix"; "Henry H. Harrison: A Forgotten Crucian"; "Terence A. Todman: Ambassador Extraordinaire"; "Miss Annie de Chabert: A Truly Remarkable Woman"; "Ole Vinding: A Dane Who Came To Stay"; and "The Virgin Islands: A Modern Tower of Babel?"